OCEAN

West Coast

0 — 100 miles
0 — 100 km

N

NORTH COAST AND THE HIGH NORTH

WINE COUNTRY AND CENTRAL VALLEY

THE BAY AREA

DOWNTOWN SAN FRANCISCO

AROUND SAN FRANCISCO

THE MONTEREY PENINSULA AND BIG SUR COAST

CALIFORNIA

THE CENTRAL COAST

LOS ANGELES AREA

LOS ANGELES

SOUTH BAY AND ORANGE COUNTY

AROUND SAN DIEGO

SAN DIEGO

Utah

City
Utah

Santaquin
Salina
6 50

Parguitch
89
Tropic
Bryce Canyon NP
Kanab
Jacob Lake

Grand Canyon NP
Grand Canyon Village

Arizona
scott

Phoenix

llendale

Why

Organ Pipe Cactus NM

Milford

Cedar City
Zion NP
Hurricane
St George
Mt Trumbull 8028
Grand Canyon-Parashant NM

Great Basin NP

Callente
White

Grand Canyon-Parashant NM

Lake Mead
Hoover Dam
Lake Mead NRA
Boulder City

Colorado

Ely
93

Ruby Dome 11388

Currant Mtn 11512
Mt Jefferson 11949

Warm Springs

Beatty

Las Vegas

Henderson

Mojave National Preserve

Mojave Desert

Needl

Bly

San Lu
Rio Colorado

MEXICO

Mt Tobin 9774

Nevada

Great

Basin

Tonopah

Death Valley NP

NP

Barstow
15

San Bernardino
40
62

Joshua Tree NP
10

Escondido
Oceanside
86

Mexicali
Tijuana
NM
Ensenada

Austin
Reese

Shoshone Mtns

Bishop

Ridgecrest
395

Lancaster
58

Bakersfield
5

Santa Monica
Los Angeles

Santa Barbara
San Nicolas

San Clemen

Fallon

Pyramid Lake
Sparks
Reno
Carson City
Subsurvine
Lake Tahoe

Hawthorne
Mono Lake
395

Devils Postpile NM
Sequoia NP
Kings Canyon NP
Kern

Fresno
41
Visalia

San Luis Obispo
101

Santa Maria
Point Arguell

Santa Barbara Channel

Channel Islands NP
San Miguel

Santa Rosa
Santa Cruz

Channel Islands

Sierra Nevada

California

Chico
99

Yuba City
Sacramento
Stockton
20
Merced
Los Banos
Modesto
Salinas
San Jose
Santa Cruz

Paso Robles

ng e

Santa Rosa
Point Reyes

Mill Valley NP

Point Arena

Cummins

Point Arena

99

Lassen Volcanic NP

Lake Tahoe
80

SIERRA

Vcanic NP

Utah
50

Kanab

Sevier Lake

Shoshone

Mex

INSIGHT◉GUIDES

USA: WEST COAST

PLAN & BOOK
YOUR TAILOR-MADE TRIP

 **BRAZIL**
 **CHILE**
 **ECUADOR**

TAILOR-MADE TRIPS & UNIQUE EXPERIENCES CREATED BY LOCAL TRAVEL EXPERTS AT INSIGHTGUIDES.COM/HOLIDAYS

Insight Guides has been inspiring travellers with high-quality travel content for over 45 years. As well as our popular guidebooks, we now offer the opportunity to book tailor-made private trips completely personalised to your needs and interests. By connecting with one of our local experts, you will directly benefit from their expertise and local know-how, helping you create memories that will last a lifetime.

HOW INSIGHTGUIDES.COM/HOLIDAYS WORKS

STEP 1

Pick your dream destination and submit an enquiry, or modify an existing itinerary if you prefer.

STEP 2

Fill in a short form, sharing details of your travel plans and preferences with a local expert.

STEP 3

Your local expert will create your personalised itinerary, which you can amend until you are completely satisfied.

STEP 4

Book securely online. Pack your bags and enjoy your holiday! Your local expert will be available to answer questions during your trip.

BENEFITS OF PLANNING & BOOKING AT INSIGHTGUIDES.COM/HOLIDAYS

PLANNED BY LOCAL EXPERTS

The Insight Guides local experts are hand-picked, based on their experience in the travel industry and their impeccable standards of customer service.

SAVE TIME & MONEY

When a local expert plans your trip, you save time and money when you book, even during high season. You won't be charged for using a credit card either.

TAILOR-MADE TRIPS

Book with Insight Guides, and you will be in complete control of the planning process, from the initial selections to amending your final itinerary.

BOOK & TRAVEL STRESS-FREE

Enjoy stress-free travel when you use the Insight Guides secure online booking platform. All bookings come with a money-back guarantee.

WHAT OTHER TRAVELLERS THINK ABOUT TRIPS BOOKED AT INSIGHTGUIDES.COM/HOLIDAYS

Trip to Portugal

Every step of the planning process and the trip itself was effortless and exceptional. Our special interests, preferences and requests were accommodated resulting in a trip that exceeded our expectations.

Corinne, USA ★★★★★

Trip to Vietnam

The organization was superb, the drivers professional, and accommodation quite comfortable. I was well taken care of! My thanks to your colleagues who helped make my trip to Vietnam such a great experience. My only regret is that I couldn't spend more time in the country.

Heather ★★★★★

CONTENTS

Travel tips

Maps

LEGEND
🔍 Insight on
📷 Photo story

THE BEST OF WEST COAST USA: TOP ATTRACTIONS

△ **California's Wine Country.** Emerald vineyards, lush red wines, warm sunshine, and fresh California cuisine make Napa and Sonoma counties ideal for a road trip. For the best views, take a hot-air balloon ride. See page 65.

△ **Golden Gate Bridge.** San Francisco's famous bridge opened in 1937, after four years in the making. Painted not gold but "international orange," it is one of the world's favorite icons. See page 216.

▽ **Olympic National Park.** Washington's most amazing park extends from the wildest shoreline on the entire Pacific coast to the extraordinary old-growth rainforest and the snowcapped mountains of the interior. See page 128.

△ **Pacific Coast Scenic Byway.** As it traces the full length of Oregon's ever-astonishing shoreline, US Highway 101 links more than 60 state parks, each with its own incentive to abandon your vehicle and spread your wings. See page 163.

△ **Redwood forests.** Awe-inspiring ancient redwoods tower over visitors in old-growth state parks. These majestic giants, 1,000 years old and reaching 300ft (90 meters), are the largest living things on earth. See page 184.

△ **SoCal beaches.** There's a reason Southern Californians sport tans year-round – from Santa Barbara to Santa Monica, and Huntington Beach to San Diego, the state's southern coast is packed with miles of sunny beaches. See page 239.

△ **California cuisine.** Alice Waters changed the restaurant industry forever when she persuaded local farmers to supply the freshest seasonal ingredients for her daily changing menus. See page 58.

△ **Monterey.** Coastal Monterey offers something for everyone: Steinbeck's Cannery Row, the Monterey Bay Aquarium (arguably the world's finest), plus diving in kelp forests and swimming with sea otters. See page 231.

▽ **Hollywood.** Synonymous with the movie industry, Hollywood pays homage to its cinematic history with attractions like the Hollywood Walk of Fame and opulent old movie houses. See page 79.

△ **Washington ferries.** You can't claim to know Washington until you've taken a scenic ride on its wondrous ferry network, across Puget Sound to the Olympic Peninsula, or out to the San Juan Islands. See page 110.

THE BEST OF WEST COAST USA: EDITOR'S CHOICE

The Getty Museum, LA.

ONLY ON THE WEST COAST

Totem poles. Seattle's Occidental Park is among many Northwest sites holding monuments to the enduring presence of the region's Indigenous peoples. See page 101.

Cable cars. Wonderfully old-fashioned cable cars creakily lumber up and roll down San Francisco's hills, ringing their bells as passengers hang out the sides. See page 222.

Sea Lion Caves. In this extraordinary natural phenomenon, hundreds of stupendous, stinking, Steller sea lions gather in a sea cave which visitors access via an elevator. See page 175.

La Brea Tar Pits. A famous fossil location, these bubbling pools of asphalt have been revealing prehistoric remains since the 1900s. See page 259.

Forks. Thanks to its role as the setting for the *Twilight Saga*, this everyday Washington lumber town swarms with teenage vampire hunters. See page 131.

Oregon Vortex and House of Mystery. In this random spot in the Oregon woods, the laws of physics no longer apply – or do they? See page 157.

Hollywood Walk of Fame. One of Los Angeles' most famous attractions, where over 2,400 star-shaped plaques are emblazoned with celebrities' names. See page 256.

Cannabis Tours. Once a haven for illegal marijuana growers, Humboldt County is now a haven for . . . legal marijuana growers. Join a farm tour to learn about how it's all done. See page 185.

CULTURAL HIGHLIGHTS

Getty Center. This stunning LA clifftop complex combines art, architecture, and delightful gardens, all of which you can explore for free. See page 261.

Museum of Glass. Built in honor of glass artist Dale Chihuly, Tacoma's eye-popping museum incorporates copious quantities of glass into its design, and stages live glass-working demonstrations. See page 119.

LACMA. With a collection of nearly 130,000 objects spanning from antiquity to the present, the Los Angeles County Museum of Art is the largest art museum in the Western United States. See page 258.

Oregon Shakespeare Festival. Staging as many as seven productions at any one time, Ashland's acclaimed festival is an absolute treat for theater-goers from April through December. See page 157.

Hollywood Bowl. Instantly recognizable by its dome shape, this classic performance amphitheater in Los Angeles attracts music lovers who come to hear classical music and jazz concerts. See page 256.

SFMOMA. The distinctive San Francisco Museum of Modern Art, designed by Swiss architect Mario Botta, and expanded by Norwegian architects Snøhetta, houses Northern California's premier modern and contemporary art collection. See page 212.

Museum of Pop Culture. Designed as a tribute to Seattle's very own Jimi Hendrix, Frank Gehry's dazzling edifice now celebrates all popular culture. See page 105.

BEST FOR KIDS

Disneyland. Mickey Mouse isn't the only attraction: families flock here for Space Mountain, the Fantasmic! fireworks show, and the rides at California Adventure. See page 266.

Universal Studios. Attractions based on Harry Potter, Jurassic Park, The Walking Dead and King Kong are winners for kids – and adults too. See page 265.

San Diego Zoo. Looking for giant pandas? Visit lush Balboa Park for one of the world's most impressive zoos, with a more natural setting that uses moats instead of cages. See page 278.

Oaks Amusement Park. While it has many thrill rides, this vintage Portland theme park delights young kids with the charms of a simpler era. See page 149.

Pier 39 Fisherman's Wharf. Pier 39 has an aquarium, street performers, sea lions, an arcade, and the San Francisco Carousel. Ice cream sundaes at Ghirardelli Square aren't far away. See page 207.

Monterey Bay Aquarium. Don't miss feeding time at this spectacular seaside sanctuary with around 350,000 specimens. See page 231.

Knott's Berry Farm. America's first theme park delights with gunfights, Wild West stunt shows, Camp Snoopy musicals, and fried chicken dinners. See page 267.

Seattle Great Wheel. The highlight of Seattle's waterfront has to be dangling out over the open water in a soaring gondola aboard its Great Wheel. See page 99.

BEST BEACHES

Huntington Beach. Ever wonder where "Surf City USA" is? You just found it. See page 271.

Shi-Shi Beach. Accessible only to hardy hikers, and fronted by jagged rocks, this wilderness beach in northern Washington is a favorite with campers. See page 130.

Cabrillo Beach. Cabrillo has windsurfing, scuba diving, whale-watching, a good aquarium, and views of Santa Catalina Island. See page 270.

Malibu's Zuma and Surfrider beaches. Popular with surfers, sunbathers, and bird-watchers, Malibu's beaches have wetlands, flower gardens, tide pools, and terrific bird-watching perches. You can spot celebrities' houses from the sand too. See page 262.

Venice Beach. There's terrific people-watching potential here, from hippie artists to muscle-bound men. See page 263.

Santa Monica Beach. The soft white sand flanking the pier is a wonderful place to enjoy Pacific sunsets. See page 262.

Ruby Beach. One of Washington's few highway-side beaches, a swathe of russet pebbles sandwiched between eerie sea stacks and forests of Sitka spruce. See page 132.

Surf City USA, Huntington Beach, California.

MOST SPECTACULAR SCENERY

Crater Lake National Park. Cradled deep within the hollowed-out core left behind when an ancient volcano blew its top, this deep sheer-blue lake is an utterly otherworldly sight. See page 155.

Hoh Rain Forest. The highlight of Washington's Olympic National Park, this temperate riverbank rainforest is astonishingly lush, festooned with moss and laced with enticing trails. See page 132.

Avenue of the Giants. Surrounded by Humboldt Redwoods State Park, this 31-mile (50km) stretch of highway offers a jaw-dropping display of giant redwoods. See page 185.

Tillamook Head. This stark headland on Oregon's breathtaking Pacific shoreline surveys a superb panorama of glowing sands lashed by mighty ocean waves, and peppered with bizarre sea stacks. See page 167.

Oregon Dunes. Looming above a 50-mile (80km) stretch of the Pacific, these colossal dunes dwarf any in the Sahara. See page 175.

Big Sur. Hugging the rugged coast in a series of switchbacks, Highway 1 south of San Fran through the Monterey Peninsula to Big Sur may be the most spectacular route in America. See page 235.

California's High North. A remote and stunning domain of mountains, valleys, volcanoes, rivers, canyons, and basins. See page 183.

Muir Woods, redwoods walking trail.

Hearst Castle.

ARCHITECTURAL HIGHLIGHTS

OUTDOOR FUN

Kayaking the San Juan Islands. So long as you're happy to share the waters with killer whales, paddling a kayak around Washington's San Juan islands is a wonderful way to experience the wildlife of the Pacific Northwest. See page 72.

Diving in Monterey. Explore thick kelp forests in Monterey Bay, a popular place to get scuba certified in Northern California. See page 69.

Hiking in Muir Woods. San Francisco in the morning; redwoods in the afternoon. Take a stroll under grand trees and stop at the Pelican

Inn at Muir Beach for a spot of tea or a cold mug of mead. See page 221.

Rafting the Rogue. Oregon's celebrated Rogue River offers some of the finest whitewater rafting in the country, especially along its rapids-strewn central portion, known as the Wild Rogue. See page 73.

Hiking the North Olympic Coastal Wilderness. The oceanfront trek from Rialto Beach to Sand Point on Washington's remote northwest coast requires hikers to ford creeks and clamber across driftwood log jams. See page 71.

Space Needle. The focal point of Seattle's 1962 World's Fair, this space-age spindle remains iconic – and the views from its rotating observation floor are truly out of this world. See page 104.

Academy of Sciences. The award-winning Renzo Piano–designed eco-house in San Francisco's Golden Gate Park boasts a living roof. See page 218.

Balboa Park. Originally built for the 1915–16 Panama-California Exhibition, ornate Spanish Colonial Revival–style buildings fill San Diego's museum-filled park. See page 277.

Bridge of Glass. Home to three glass sculptures by Dale Chihuly, and connecting two major museums, Tacoma's breathtaking Bridge of Glass is a free, round-the-clock visitor attraction in its own right. See page 120.

Hearst Castle. This castle in the sky was built by William Randolph Hearst, the media magnate who was

the subject of Orson Welles's Citizen Kane. See page 236.

Mission Dolores. The only mission chapel that's still intact, Mission Dolores is also the oldest building in San Francisco. Immortalized in Hitchcock's Vertigo, a serene cemetery holds the remains of early city leaders. See page 216.

Painted ladies. These tall, stately Victorian homes can be found all over San Francisco, but some of the brightest, most renowned, and most colorful border Alamo Square. See page 218.

Transamerica Pyramid. Likened to an upside-down ice-cream cone, or dunce cap, the 48-floor building built in 1970 by William L. Pereira is one of San Francisco's favorite icons. See page 212.

Terra Cotta District. Harking back a century, the glazed white terra-cotta towers that adorn downtown Portland make it a joy to while away a summer afternoon in Pioneer Courthouse Square. See page 145.

The Painted Ladies, SF.

WINE COUNTRY HIGHLIGHTS

Calistoga spas. With thermal hot springs feeding warm pools, and sumptuous volcanic mud treatments, Calistoga's luxurious spa retreats are world-renowned. See page 192.

Hot-air ballooning. Get a bird's eye view of the Wine Country with a morning hot-air balloon ride, followed by a champagne breakfast. See page 193.

Dining with a view. Dine with panoramic views on Auberge du Soleil's terrace, one of the prettiest outdoor dining spots in the Wine Country. See page 193.

Napa Valley Wine Train. Take a tour of Napa Valley in lavishly restored 1915 Pullman dining and lounge cars, while feasting on seasonal fare and local wines. See page 194.

Oxbow Public Market. Taste everything from oysters to organic ice cream at the colorful stalls, and check out the many varied events like unique happy hours, cooking demos, and music performances. See page 195.

Relaxed wine tasting. Have a park picnic lunch at affordable Louis M. Martini, followed by another tasting or two at wineries such as Paraduxx or Frog's Leap. See page 194.

The Napa Valley wine train.

ICONIC HOTELS

Hotel del Coronado. Built in 1888, the Coronado's red turrets and Victorian style make it unmissable on the San Diego beachfront. It's unforgettable, too. See page 280.

Kalaloch Lodge. If a windswept, waterfront log cabin in the wilderness, with a fresh-salmon supper to round off your day, sounds like your idea of heaven, head to this lodge in Washington's Olympic National Park. See page 133.

The Beverly Hills Hotel. Affectionately known as the "Pink Palace," this old celebrity haunt has recorded John F. Kennedy, Elizabeth Taylor and Richard Burton, Charlie Chaplin, Spencer Tracy, Marilyn Monroe, John Wayne, and the Duke of Windsor among its guests. See page 259.

The Intercontinental Mark Hopkins Hotel. A fine tea or lunch is a lavish reminder of the city's historic roots. See page 211.

Madonna Inn. With imaginative interiors and bizarre themed rooms, this landmark hotel seems pure kitsch to some, and a creative wonder to others. See page 243.

Rosario Resort. Planted deep into rocky Orcas Island, decked out with magnificent mahogany fittings and complete with pipe organ, this century-old waterfront resort makes an opulent getaway. See page 115.

Hotel del Coronado.

MONEY-SAVING TIPS

National Parks and Federal Recreational Lands Pass. Frequent visitors to US national parks should buy an "America the Beautiful" annual pass ($80) which covers entrance fees for the holder, a vehicle, plus any passengers at over 2,000 federal recreation sites. Go to https://store.usgs.gov/pass.

CityPASS. Visitor cards for Seattle, San Francisco, San Diego, or Southern California provide discounts to major attractions, and cut down on waiting in lines. See CityPass.com. Go City passes (https://gocity.com) cover key attractions in San Diego, San Fran or LA; you can customize passes for sites you plan to visit.

Free museums. Many museums in major cities have a free day once a month, or during evening hours. Call or visit individual websites for details. Always-free museums include the Getty Center and Griffith Observatory in LA, and San Francisco's Cable Car Museum.

State parks Each state sells annual passes granting admission to its state parks, which typically otherwise charge $5–10 per day. Passes cost $35 in Washington (www.parks.wa.gov), $30 in Oregon (https://stateparks.oregon.gov), and $50 in California (www.parks.ca.gov).

The Hall of Mosses trail, Hoh
Rain Forest, Washington.

Sunset over San Francisco.

Seattle skyline at dusk.

THE WEST COAST

Shaped by the Pacific, the West Coast holds an incredible range of natural wonders, animal habitats, celebrated cities, and engaging diversions.

Pike Place Market.

Think of the West Coast, and your mind may turn first to its cities, its culture, its history, its music, or its people. Above all else, though, the region is defined by the elemental force, the sheer eternal presence, of the mighty Pacific Ocean. Dwarfing any human impact or achievement, the ocean has been battering against this magnificent shoreline since primeval times, carving out caves and sculpting sea stacks, shaping sand dunes and speeding salmon back upstream to spawn. Whether you're a beachcomber or kayaker, a surfer or a naturalist, the Pacific can only be experienced firsthand. That's what makes the 1400-mile (2250km) road trip down the full length of the West Coast such an essential, and unforgettable, encounter with the raw power of the wilderness. And don't worry, it also offers plenty of human-scale rewards – electrifying cities, wonderful food, vibrant culture, world-class entertainment, to name but a few.

The coast is at its wildest in the far north, along the western flank of Washington's Olympic Peninsula, where bald eagles soar over seals, sea otters, and migrating whales, and much of the shoreline is unreachable by road. In Oregon, by contrast, the Pacific Coast Scenic Byway runs past beach after superb beach, with each headland revealing further stupendous seascapes ahead.

The Walk of Fame.

Northern California is similarly majestic, with jaw-dropping groves of redwood trees located just inland. As you continue south beyond the northernmost major city on the coast itself, San Francisco, the Pacific shoreline starts to soften. Sunshine supplants fog, and surfers and sunbathers hang out on relaxed resort beaches. There's still scenic splendor to be enjoyed, the drive along the coast to Big Sur is arguably the highlight of the entire trip. Beyond that you'll come to Los Angeles, home to Hollywood and Disneyland, and laidback San Diego. Not far inland, Seattle and Portland, Oregon's Crater Lake, and the mellow Wine Country of California await.

⊘ A NOTE TO READERS

At Insight Guides, we always strive to bring you the most up-to-date information. This book was produced during a period of continuing uncertainty caused by the Covid-19 pandemic, so please note that content is more subject to change than usual. We recommend checking the latest restrictions and official guidance.

PEOPLES OF THE WEST COAST

Throughout its history, the West Coast has attracted waves of immigrants, adding new political, social, and artistic elements into its ever-changing mix.

Home to around one-in-six Americans, the three West Coast states can lay claim to a greater ethnic diversity than any other region of the United States. The West remains the true national melting pot, with a significant presence of the continent's Indigenous peoples – Native Americans – still inhabiting the Pacific Northwest in particular, and the vast proportion of its many other citizens descended from migrants who have arrived within the last two centuries.

From the onset of the industrialized era, fortune-seekers have flocked to the West from every direction, and every part of the world. The 19th-century pioneers whose wagon trains slogged westwards on the overland trail are just one part of the story; at much the same time, Chinese laborers were crossing the Pacific to work on the railroads, while Hispanic farmers were already working the rich soils of California. A hundred years after the Gold Rush spurred California's first great boom – and coincided with it achieving statehood – the huge expansion of industry prompted by World War II attracted another massive influx, this time including many African Americans from the South. And there's no sign that things are slowing down; the exponential growth of the likes of Apple and Facebook in Silicon Valley, and Microsoft and Amazon in Seattle, have lured in the cream of the world's information scientists.

The result of all this drive and energy? A cosmopolitan society made up of Mexicans, Europeans, Chinese, Japanese, African Americans, Russians, Armenians, Koreans, Salvadoreans, Iranians, Filipinos, Samoans, Vietnamese, and many more besides.

TIDES OF IMMIGRATION

In the 1840s, at the time when California had just been wrested from the Mexican government, and

Panning for gold in California, 1849 - engraving 1891.

⊘ THE 2020 US CENSUS:

Stats from the 2020 US Census give the following figures: California: population 39.2 million; 39 percent Latino, 35 percent white, 15 percent Asian American, 5 percent Black, 4 percent multiracial, fewer than 1 percent Native American.

Washington: population 7.7 million; 78.5 percent white, 13 percent Latino, 10.4 percent Asian American, 4.9 percent multiracial, 4.4 percent Black, 2 percent Native American.

Oregon: population 4.2 million: 86.7 percent white, 13.4 percent Latino, 5.4 percent Asian American, 4 percent multiracial, 2.2 percent Black, 1.8 percent Native American.

When Los Angeles was founded in 1781, more than half of the settlers were of mixed Black, Native American, and Spanish blood. To this day, a high proportion of California's Latino population resides in the southern part of the state.

the boundary between the Oregon Territory and Canada had finally been agreed with the British, the West was considered to be the final frontier, a land promising spiritual and social riches. As boosters furiously sold that fable to the rest of the Union, pioneers armed with little more than faith set off in search of sunshine, fertile soil, and freedom from oppression. Soon, the discovery of gold in California's Sierra Nevada made further advertising unnecessary, and the steady trickle turned into a flood.

The blending of cultures had begun long before that, of course. Even before the US Declaration of Independence, Spanish Franciscan monks arrived to set up missions throughout California, and spread Catholicism to Indigenous peoples. Farther north, navigators and overland expeditions were soon penetrating the Northwest. Long before the end of the 19th century, California's Native American population had been decimated, though despite war and depredation the Native peoples of the Northwest survived in greater strength, albeit restricted to reservations.

The development and growth of industries throughout the 19th-century West brought new

tides of immigration. The Chinese initially came to America as railroad workers on the Central Pacific construction gangs, then spread out once the railroads were completed to build new lives for their families throughout the region, branching especially into agriculture and fishing. Toward the end of the 19th century, Japanese immigrants arrived in search of opportunities in California's emerging produce industry, which they eventually came to dominate, from packing and shipping the fruit to setting up small stands to sell it.

Chinese immigrants in Newcastle California in 1926.

⊘ JAPANESE AMERICANS IN WORLD WAR II

When the United States entered the Second World War in December 1941, in the immediate wake of the Japanese attack on Hawaii's Pearl Harbor, an estimated 125,000 Japanese Americans were resident on the US mainland. The great majority were concentrated along the West Coast, where they already faced considerable prejudice. Washington had passed laws prohibiting "aliens" from owning land, while Oregon farmers depicted the industrious Japanese as somehow impinging on American business prospects.

In February 1942, President Franklin Roosevelt signed the infamous Executive Order 9066, which

designated 10 "exclusion zones" on the West Coast, from which military authorities could expel whomever they chose. Although the word "Japanese" did not appear, the order was applied almost exclusively against Japanese Americans. Almost all those on the West Coast were duly interned – around 120,000 in total, of whom two thirds, known as *nisei*, had been born and raised in the US. Their homes, possessions, and businesses were confiscated or fell into ruin, and most lost everything they owned. Some but nowhere near all of these families finally received a limited compensation during the 1990s, in the wake of a federal apology.

African Americans also arrived as railroad employees, in small numbers at first and then, during World War II, to fill manufacturing and service jobs. Nothing, however, compared to the twin tidal waves of Anglo-Americans who arrived from the Midwest, first during the 1880s, and then again – fleeing the parched dustbowl farms of the prairies – in the 1930s. Establishing major colonies around San Francisco and Sacramento in particular, they went on to saturate Southern California with their visions of manifest destiny.

Parkside cards in Chinatown.

⊘ LATINO COMMUNITY ACTIVISM

Although Latinos in California are heavily involved in community activism, they are generally under-represented in the political arena. One reason is that the number of Latinos who are citizens – and therefore entitled to vote – has tended to remain significantly smaller than the actual population, while out of those who can, few necessarily register or turn up to vote. For many years the only notable Latino leader was the late Cesar Chavez, president of the United Farm Workers of America. However, more recently Kevin de León and Ricardo Lara have both been active in improving immigrant rights and increasing access to education and economic mobility for all.

The most significant influx of the 20th century occurred in the 1970s and 1980s, with the arrival of hundreds of thousands of refugees from Southeast Asian and Central America.

FAILURES IN MULTICULTURALISM

During the 19th and much of the 20th centuries, the West was no great model of open-mindedness. Both Washington and Oregon saw extensive discrimination against Chinese residents – ranging from restrictive labor laws to the point of forcible expulsion – while Mexicans only seemed to be seen as a necessary component of the Californian economy as and when the need for cheap labor dictated. Thus, during the depression in the 1930s, the county of LA "repatriated" thousands of Mexicans on relief, loading them onto trains like cattle.

Soon afterwards, World War II saw the internment of almost all Japanese residents on the West Coast. During the same decade, African Americans who escaped the repression of the Deep South were barred from living in certain California neighborhoods by restrictive housing covenants.

As a result of such practices, clusters of ethnic communities formed where people could feel protected and cultures preserved. San Francisco's Chinatown is one such example, developing out of necessity as a refuge from abuse: Until the 1960s, when immigration laws changed, the Chinese had been subjected to severe and continual harassment, and discriminatory legislation had deprived them of eligibility for citizenship, ensuring that they had no legal recourse.

Later, as the job market plummeted in recession-hit California in the 1990s, tensions between ethnic groups amplified. The eruption of civil unrest in Los Angeles in 1992 was a wake-up call to the entire US, an indication that the ethnic stew was boiling over.

THE ARTISTIC FACE OF MULTICULTURALISM

It is perhaps the necessity of asserting one's identity amid this sea of cultures that has made California a place in which so many trends and artistic movements take flight. Some trace a connection between rap music, for example, and the malaise that ensued after the Watts Rebellion in 1965. Assembled from the shards of the uprising, the Watts art renaissance delivered up a number of visionaries. Theirs was the poetry of frustration, self-assertion and, unlike some contemporary rap, hope. Bold, bright graffiti art also arrived hard on the heels of disenfranchisement. "Tagging" (initialing) property provided inner-city teens – primarily Latino – with a voice that the larger culture refused to hear. Today, the central role of rap on the media and advertising is beyond dispute.

West Coasters also adopted customs of Asian immigrants. Health-conscious Californians submit to strenuous programs of yoga and meditation, and feed on pad Thai, sushi, and pho. Beat Generation writers, who tumbled around San Francisco in

> *In 2015, for the first time in the modern era, the number of people of Latino or Hispanic descent officially outnumbered non-Hispanic Caucasians in California.*

the 1950s, derived much of their inspiration from Buddhism, and Japanese and Chinese poetry.

Since the 1940s, the experience of facing society as "other" has produced some of America's finest writers and artists, including playwright William Saroyan, who grew up in an Armenian enclave of grape growers and farmers in Fresno; poet and novelist Alice Walker, best known for *The Color Purple*; essayist Richard Rodriguez, who writes about gay and Latino assimilation and the politics of multiculturalism; Filipino-born artist Manuel Ocampo, whose paintings often depict symbols of racism and the brutish imperialism of colonialism; theater artist Anna Deavere Smith, whose performance piece *Twilight: Los Angeles, 1992* addressed the riots that devastated the city, told through the voices of the people who experienced it; and novelist Amy Tan, who found the characters of her widely acclaimed *Joy Luck Club* in the Chinatown (San Francisco) of her childhood.

MULTIETHNIC STYLE

The West Coast states epitomize the tensions and triumphs of developing a truly multi-ethnic society. Some argue that the obsession with tribalism is a leading factor in causing the at-times bitter divisiveness that characterizes so much of modern America. Others say that recognizing the West Coast's many ethnic groups marks the first step towards peaceful coexistence. What has become

more and more evident, though, is that the people are slowly but surely absorbing each other's habits and styles, tastes, and mannerisms.

While many West Coast towns and suburbs remain relatively homogeneous, others are home to diverse pockets of cultures that border one another, highlighting differences in religions and customs. And now, more than any time in the history, multiculturalism is reflected in the offices of elected and appointed officials: mayors and congressional representatives, city council members, and police chiefs.

Cinco De Mayo celebrations in San Diego.

⊘ FESTIVALS

Festivals up and down the West Coast celebrate the region's multiethnic traditions. San Francisco's Chinese New Year festivities are among the biggest in the US, though Seattle, Portland, and LA stage their own events. Vietnamese New Year has devotees in San Jose, Oakland puts on a Greek cultural festival in May, LA a week of Japanese events in August, and San Diego a Pacific Islanders' festival in summer. Cinco de Mayo is celebrated in California and the Northwest, while Brazilians, Scots, Irish, and Germans all have their own street parties. For listings, see the *LA Times* (www.latimes.com), *San Francisco Chronicle* (www.sfchronicle.com), *or Seattle Times* (www.seattletimes.com).

Reconstructing San Francisco after the 1906 earthquake.

DECISIVE DATES

The beginnings of the iconic bridge.

15,000 BC
Nomads from Asia reach the Americas.

4,000 BC
Native peoples fish, hunt, and forage along the western seaboard, enjoying a rich social and material culture.

1542
Spanish galleons reach the California coast.

1579
Sir Francis Drake explores the West Coast, summering at Whale Cove, Oregon.

1741
Russian-sponsored explorer Vitus Bering reaches Alaska; fur traders follow, motivating further Spanish expeditions.

1769
Spanish Franciscan priests found the first of 21 Californian missions, in San Diego.

1792
Captains George Vancouver of Britain and Robert Gray of the US map out the Northwest coast.

1805
Lewis and Clark's overland expedition reaches the Pacific and claims the Northwest.

1843
The first American migrants arrive on the Oregon Trail; half a million follow in the next 25 years.

1846
The US declares war on Mexico and captures California, while the Oregon Treaty divides the US and Canada along the 49th parallel.

1848
Gold discoveries in the Sierra foothills prompt a Gold Rush that transforms California.

1850
California becomes the 31st US state.

1859
Oregon becomes the 33rd US state. Portland is the leading city in the Northwest, while silver from the Comstock Lode turns San Francisco into a prosperous metropolis.

1869
The Transcontinental Railroad is completed, terminating at Oakland.

1873
The world's first cable car runs in San Francisco.

1876
The Southern Pacific Railway reaches Los Angeles.

1886
Harvey H. Wilcox opens a subdivision that his wife names Hollywood.

1889
Washington becomes the 42nd US state.

1892
Oil is struck near what's now Los Angeles' MacArthur Park.

1896
Gold is discovered in the Yukon, Canada; Seattle's role supplying miners in the ensuing Gold Rush enables it to surpass Portland.

Police intervene at the Rodney King Riots, 1989.

1905
Portland hosts the Lewis and Clark Centennial Exposition.

1906
San Francisco earthquake.

1909
Seattle celebrates prodigious growth by hosting the Alaska–Yukon–Pacific Exposition.

1916
Seattle completes locks enabling ships to travel from Puget Sound to Lake Washington.

1930s
During the Great Depression, the Civilian Conservation Corps starts programs in forests and wildlife protection, while the Grand Coulee Dam and Columbia Basin Irrigation project are completed on the Columbia River.

1932
LA's Coliseum, the world's largest stadium, hosts the Olympics.

1937
The Golden Gate Bridge opens.

1939
LA's Union Station, the last great railroad terminal, opens.

1943–46
World War II internment of Japanese-American citizens, in California especially.

1947
California passes a law against smog.

1950s
The "Beats," a bohemian literary group, hang out in San Francisco's North Beach.

1955
Disneyland opens in Anaheim.

1962
Seattle hosts the Century 21 Exposition, starring the futuristic Space Needle.

1965
Rioting in Los Angeles' Watts area kills 34 people.

1967
Hippies congregate in San Francisco's Haight-Ashbury district, celebrating the Summer of Love.

1970s
Hundreds of thousands of Southeast Asian refugees reach the Northwest; environmental movements begin in earnest.

1971
The first Starbucks opens in Seattle.

1974
Oil tycoon J. Paul Getty donates his LA home as a museum. BART (Bay Area Rapid Transit System) starts a regular service in San Francisco.

1978
San Francisco mayor George Moscone and supervisor Harvey Milk are assassinated by a former supervisor.

1980
Mount St Helens erupts, kills 57 people, and spreads ash over the Northwest.

1980s
The phenomenal growth of the computer industry puts California's Silicon Valley on the map; Microsoft establishes itself in Washington.

1992
LA police officers are acquitted of beating black motorist Rodney King, triggering riots in which 50 people die.

1996
The discovery of a 9,300-year-old skeleton in Kennewick, Washington, throws new light on the first Americans.

1999
Riots disrupt WTO in Seattle.

2014
California Governor Jerry Brown declares a drought state of emergency; it remains today.

2020
California endures intense wildfires. Major cities see Black Lives Matter marches.

2021
Trump supporters storm Capitol Hill. President Biden is inaugurated on 20 January.

2022
Verdict on Roe vs Wade case leads to controversial abortion ban in at least 13 states.

The Getty Center.

Greg Red Elk from the Santa Ynez Chumash Inter-Tribal PowWow.

FIRST PEOPLES

Rich in natural resources, the West Coast was home to vibrant and sophisticated Native American societies for millennia before the Europeans arrived.

The first human inhabitants of the Americas are believed to have been Siberian nomads, who migrated across an enormous "land-bridge" from Asia as the ice age waxed and waned, perhaps 17,000 years ago. Successive eras of freezing and thawing opened and closed a passageway to North America that effectively served as an airlock, meaning the peoples who ultimately spread through the continent had lost all immunity to the diseases of the Old World. The principal migratory corridor swept down east of the Rockies into the plains, so the original pioneers of the West Coast must have turned west at some point, and reached California and the Northwest somewhat later. That said, some groups may also have followed the shoreline all the way south to California, but as modern sea levels are much higher, all traces of early human activity along the coast have disappeared.

The sheer natural abundance of the West Coast lent itself perfectly to the hunter-gathering lifestyle. Despite the fact that agriculture never played a significant role before European settlement, complex and prosperous societies were able to develop. By 4000 BC, peoples from the Northwest down to Southern California were deriving their sustenance from ocean fishing and hunting sea mammals, harvesting mussels and clams along the shoreline, and catching salmon and trout in the rivers. All that could be supplemented by wild food resources including roots, berries, and especially acorns.

Soft wood like red cedar, spruce, and redwood could readily be shaped into canoes distinguished by their symmetry, neatness of finish, and ornate decoration. Sophisticated tools were not necessary; the main implements used were chisels, curved knives, abrasive stones, wedges, and sharkskin.

Miwok tribal roundhouses were used for ceremonies.

COASTAL NATIONS OF THE NORTHWEST

Long before the arrival of Europeans, the Northwest Coast was among the most densely populated and culturally rich areas in the American West. Its bounty of natural resources supported a great blossoming of cultures, languages and material wealth among the Northwest tribes of Puget Sound and the Oregon Coast. These included the Makah, Duwamish, Quileute, Suquamish, Chinook, Tillamook, Alsea, Siuslaw, Athapaskan and other nations northward along the Canadian coast. To the south, the tribes of the Columbia Plateau supported themselves on the frenzied salmon runs of the Columbia River.

In western Washington, the predominant tongue was Coast Salish, while the Tillamook of Oregon also belonged to the same language group. Elsewhere in Oregon, Chinookan languages were spoken from the mouth of the Columbia to Tillamook Bay and east to the Cascades. Enclaves of Athapaskan-speaking peoples included the Tlatskanail on the Columbia, the Kwalhioqua on Willapa River, and the Tututni on the Rogue River.

Northwest Coastal nations tended to live in stable villages of extended families, groups that

painted on boards. Large cedar trees, plentiful along the coast, were made not only into excellent canoes and huge longhouses, but also into storage chests and watertight containers for cooking, heated by the addition of hot rocks pulled from the fire. Woven cedar strips were fashioned into rainproof hats, while women wore skirts made from strands of white cedar bark, or, in winter winds, in furs.

Promotion to leadership within a village was usually based on a man's capabilities, rather than his familial heritage or material wealth. A

Chinook burial canoe memorial, Columbia River.

never adopted tribal names but simply spoke of each other as "of our people." And they lived well, residing in huge cedar-plank lodges up to 110ft (35m) long. Industrious and inventive, they also built massive salmon traps, smokehouses, storage cellars and construction facilities. All in all, they developed arguably the most complex social structures in North America, which governed them and gave them leisure time in which to develop distinctive arts as well as a rich cultural life.

Native Americans of northwest Washington shared many customs with tribes as far north as southern Alaska. Their skill as sculptors of wood was best expressed in the representation of family heraldic crests or totems carved on poles or

leader was expected to set an example to others. Historian Gordon B. Dodds explains that "leaders would be followed, not obeyed, as each individual participated in warfare or the hunt on an individual basis, and if a man decided to return home he suffered no stigma for deserting the cause." Societies were typically divided into three broad social groupings. The upper class were accorded privileges of honor and rank while the slave class had no rights and could be murdered at will with no consequence. A middle class of skilled artisans and clever workers could use their abilities to ascend to the upper echelons.

Warfare largely consisted of raiding other villages to procure slaves. Some were then ransomed back for large amounts of goods, while captives without status performed any and all menial tasks for their enslavers.

Throughout the region, Native Americans enjoyed a rich oral tradition, sharing ribald fireside tales of larger-than-life creatures – Coyote, Blue Jay, Beaver, Raven and Wolf. The antics of characters in Northwestern mythology might at first seem slapstick, but these lively tales describe how the world evolved, and emphasize the importance of natural resources.

PEOPLES OF CALIFORNIA

The names of the many diverse peoples who occupied California prior to European contact may not be well remembered today, but it's estimated that the region was home to around 10 percent of the entire population of North America. Skills, traditions and preoccupations varied from group to group, each with its own distinct language and identity. Broadly speaking, igloo-shaped homes of reed provided breezy shelter in summer, while deerskin roofs afforded protection during the rainy season. When it grew cool, open fires were built in the homes, with holes in the roof allowing the smoke to escape. In warmer weather, the men and children remained naked except for ornamental jewelry such as necklaces, earrings, bracelets, and anklets. They kept warm when needed with robes of yellow cedar bark or crudely tanned pelts. Some groups practiced the art of tattooing. The women wore two-piece aprons made of deerskins or reeds.

The land around what is now San Francisco Bay probably supported the largest population.

The nomadic Miwok and Ohlone trekked from coastal shell mounds up to the oak groves on what are now the Berkeley Hills, or to meadowland and its rich harvest of deer and elk.

In the south, around modern Santa Barbara, the Chumash were expert boatbuilders, and adept fishermen who used seashell hooks, basket traps, nets, and vegetable poisons, extremely capable of even catching fish with their bare hands. Their discarded shells, from centuries of feasting, form mounds that reach up to 20ft (7 meters) high.

An archaeologist tracing petroglyphs alongside the riverbank at Parrot's Ferry.

⊘ THE WORLD OF THE POTLATCH

Among the Indigenous peoples of the Northwest, the accumulation of wealth gave rise to the institution known as the *potlatch*. This was a complex ritual, involving the payment of witnesses who arrived for the three-week ceremony during which all the tribes' legal matters such as marriages, divorces, berry-patch allotments, widow's settlements, trials and retributions were decided, witnessed and remembered. Initiations, adoptions and honors were also bestowed. Engagements were announced, and birthrights and fishing territories were defined.

The whole event culminated with spectacular rituals performed by secret societies. The celebrations also served to reinforce the leadership of the strongest and wealthiest patrons, through the copious giving of gifts to those who were then charged to "remember" what had transpired. This "remembering," of course, served as a substitute for a written language to document a complex set of civil transactions. If a dispute were ever to arise over a benefit such as a promotion or allotment granted during one of the ceremonies, the witness, who had been gifted, could be called upon to provide verbal testimony on behalf of the person from whom they had received the gift.

EUROPEANS CONTEND FOR CONTROL

From the 16th to the early 19th centuries, Spanish, British, American, and even Russian explorers, traders, and adventurers arrived to investigate the West Coast.

Within a few decades of Christopher Columbus reaching the Bahamas, and the subsequent Spanish invasion and conquest of Mexico, European navigators were starting to venture along the western coastline. Those first voyages were largely exploratory, in search of safe sailing routes across the Pacific to Asia, or back to Europe via the elusive Northwest Passage. Several centuries were to pass before permanent settlement was attempted.

WEST COAST VOYAGERS

Hernando Cortés, the Spanish conquistador who destroyed the Aztec civilization of central Mexico, was sailing up the coast of North America when on May 1, 1535, he encountered the long peninsula now known as Baja California, stretching down between the sea and a gulf. Believing this to be an Amazon-inhabited island described in a chivalric romance of 1510, he accordingly named it "California."

The first European navigator to reach what's now California, however, was Juan Rodríguez Cabrillo, the Portuguese-born commander of two Spanish vessels that sailed from the Mexican port of Navidad in June 1542. He entered San Diego's "closed and very good" harbor that September; experienced the surf off Big Sur ("so great was the swell of the ocean that it was terrifying to see"); and sailed straight past the Bay of San Francisco without spotting an opening. Although Cabrillo died of a broken arm on the Channel Islands in January 1543, his expedition ventured northwards once more, as far as Klamath, 40 miles (64km) south of what's now the Oregon border. Having failed to find gold or other treasure, however, the voyage was soon forgotten.

For most of the 16th century, the Spanish viewed the Pacific Ocean as their private lake.

Painting of Hernando Cortez by O. Graeff, 1892.

That smugness turned to consternation in 1579, when British sea dog Francis Drake appeared off the west coast of South America aboard the Golden Hind, and in an onslaught of piratical raids accumulated a hoard of Spanish gold, silver, and other bounty. Much to the Spaniards' alarm, Drake kept pressing north, rather than returning home around the toe of South America. Historians still debate whether he was attempting to find the Strait of Anian, the legendary western gate of the long-sought Northwest Passage linking the east coast of North America with the west. Whatever his intentions, Drake first sailed west with two ships into the Pacific, and then swept back to reach the West Coast in what's now Oregon, most likely at

Whale Cove, a couple of hundred miles north of the point previously reached by the Spanish. The climate that far north was not to his taste, so he headed southward and spent five weeks repairing his ships around Point Reyes in California, living in a fortified encampment amid hospitable Coast Miwok peoples. He too remained oblivious to the existence of San Francisco Bay a short distance south; indeed, no ship is known to have found the inconspicuous Golden Gate until 1755.

Dubbing his discoveries "New Albion" in defiance of Spanish claims, and falsifying his

> *Francis Drake considered the rain in the Pacific Northwest to be "an unnatural congealed and frozen substance," and described the atmosphere as consisting of the "most vile, thicke and stinking fogges."*

records lest they fall into Spanish hands, Drake then set off homeward across the Pacific, to complete a three-year circumnavigation of the globe.

The next Spanish expedition to reach California arrived in 1602. Sebastian Vizcaíno was searching for safe ports where treasure-laden Manila galleons could find refuge from Dutch and British pirates, on their annual return voyage from the Philippines to Acapulco. He gave lasting names to such California sites as San Clemente Island, San Diego, and Santa Catalina Island, and reported on the virtues of the California coast in glowing terms.

THE SCRAMBLE FOR THE NORTHWEST

Not until the 18th century did foreigners return to the West Coast in significant numbers. Like their Spanish and British counterparts, early Russian explorers such as Vitus Bering, who reached Alaska and named the Aleutian Islands in 1741, hoped originally to discover the elusive Northwest Passage. Instead, they found the potential for a furry fortune.

Freelance fur hunters, known as promyshlenniki, had long been pushing eastward across the frozen wastes of Siberia in pursuit of sable and sea-otter pelts. They now continued through

Alaska into the Pacific Northwest, trading peacefully with the peoples they encountered.

The Russian arrival swiftly roused Spain from its "imperial lethargy," and Spanish ships were soon venturing far up the West Coast to investigate. Relieved to find no permanent eastern European settlements, their captains set out to secure the region – or at least its coastline – as a buffer zone against further Russian expansion.

Soon the British were back. Cruising the Northwest Coast in 1778, Captain James Cook failed to spot the mouth of the Columbia River thanks

Captain James Cook, 1728-79.

to adverse weather conditions. He and his crew traded metal in exchange for furs, which they used for bedding and clothes. After Cook's death in the Hawaiian Islands in 1779, his crew continued to China, where their furs fetched a pretty penny. Word spread, and soon the British hustled back to the Northwest for more fur trading.

The Spanish expeditions that sailed north from Mexico between 1774 and 1795 came to claim, defend, Christianize and explore the Northwest, but never to do business. Typically, they'd map an area, erect a wooden cross high on a hill, and depart. The British, by contrast, sent 25 vessels between 1785 and 1794, scouting the territory for economic resources and good harbors, and in almost every case engaging in the fur trade.

Americans entered the picture, too. In the spring of 1792, two ships were simultaneously probing the craggy Northwest coastline. One, the British sloop Discovery, commanded by Captain George Vancouver, was intent on exploration. The other, the Columbia, was flying the colors of the United States and captained by Yankee fur trader Robert Gray, whose eyes were set on lucrative furs. Gray and Vancouver met at sea and exchanged news, each withholding key information from the other.

Happy to hear that Gray had found little

Lewis and Clark on the Columbian River, F. Remington.

profit in the waters around what's now Washington's Olympic Peninsula, Vancouver went on to explore the Straits of Juan de Fuca and the Gulf of Georgia, and was the first to circumnavigate Vancouver Island, staking a strong British claim to the entire region. Vancouver and Second Lieutenant Peter Puget directed two separate explorations of today's Puget Sound. While proving that no easily navigable Northwest Passage existed, Vancouver named innumerable Pacific Northwest landmarks, in many cases after himself.

Gray on the other hand continued south to the spot where his fellow captain had reported that the sea changed "from its natural to river coloured water." Sailing through a treacherous bar,

Captain James Cook arrived in the waters of the Northwest after the English government had offered a £20,000 prize for the discovery of the Northwest Passage, even though he saw not the "least probability that ever such a thing existed."

he discovered a spacious harbor at the mouth of a mighty river, which he named Columbia after his vessel.

While Vancouver and Gray had amicably divided their interests in the Pacific Northwest, their respective countries were to prove less willing to share.

COMPETITION FOR THE NORTHWEST

In 1804, President Thomas Jefferson sent captains Meriwether Lewis and William Clark to explore the vast and practically unexplored territory known as the Louisiana Purchase, which the United States had bought from Napoleon for $15 million, and which included all of what is now the Midwest. Jefferson didn't exactly believe the remote Pacific Northwest would ever become part of his United States. He viewed the Rocky Mountains as a natural western boundary for the country, but worried that the British had taken "control" of the Northwest. Following an arduous 4,000-mile (6,000km) trek, aided by Sacagawea, their female Shoshone guide, the explorers finally glimpsed the Pacific Ocean on November 15, 1805, and wintered near the mouth of the Columbia River at Fort Clatsop. Disappointed to find no ship on the river to sail them back to civilization, the group returned overland in 1806, bringing back meticulously plotted maps, observations of animal life and valuable scientific collections.

Although American fur trading vessels far outnumbered their British counterparts – between 1795 and 1804, 50 American vessels came to the Northwest to trade fur, as opposed to just nine British ships – British traders were by now arriving overland. Traveling in the far west in 1797–98, the London-born explorer David Thompson set up trading posts across what became Idaho, Oregon and Washington. The Hudson's Bay Company (HBC), the agent for the British, became the dominant force in the Northwest. By 1810, Thompson had mapped the entire Columbia River system, and established British sovereignty down to the lower Columbia River. When American fur traders moved in, they saw so many Hudson's Bay flags that they joked HBC stood for "Here Before Christ." Thompson was only a little concerned when he found in 1811 that Yankee fur trader John Jacob Astor had established Fort Astoria at the mouth of the Columbia. During the War of 1812, a British sloop-of-war "captured" the hastily abandoned fort, unaware that through Thompson it had already been sold. Only in 1818 did the British and Americans agree upon a formula for joint occupation.

The fur trade had a major impact on Native American culture. After all, it was Indigenous peoples who actually hunted for the pelts so eagerly traded by the foreign intruders. A parallel trade sprang up in which tribes acquired pelts from each other, by purchase or by theft. Those with the most furs then monopolized a new supply of exchange goods, with metal, in the form of pots and tools, being particularly prized. While certain Native Americans may have prospered from embracing these opportunities, however, the introduction of Old-World diseases had an appalling impact. Between 1774 and 1874, the population of Native peoples along the Northwest Coast declined by 80 percent, from roughly 200,000 to around 40,000.

THE COLONIZATION OF CALIFORNIA

Meanwhile, California remained largely ignored by the Spanish for the 150 years before the overland arrival of Gaspar de Portolá from Baja, in 1769. Crossing the Santa Ana river and exchanging gifts with friendly tribes, de Portolá's band passed by the bubbling tar pits of La Brea, through the mountains at Sepulveda Pass to Lake Encino, and headed northwards to open up the route to Monterey.

"The three diarists in the party agree that the practical discovery of most significance was the advantageous site on the Los Angeles river," noted historian John Caughey at the time of Los Angeles' bicentennial. "Equally important were the numerous able-bodied, alert, and amiable Indians because Spanish policy looked towards preserving, Christianizing, Hispanizing, and engrossing the natives as a major element in the Spanish colony now to be established."

Over the centuries, Spain had developed a standard method for settling new territory: using the sword to cut down any opposition from the Indigenous population, and pacifying the area with the introduction of Christianity. This was the approach used in California, where between 1769 and the early years of the following century, a chain of 21 Franciscan missions was established between San Diego and Sonoma. These missions enslaved hundreds of Native Americans into an endless round of work and prayer.

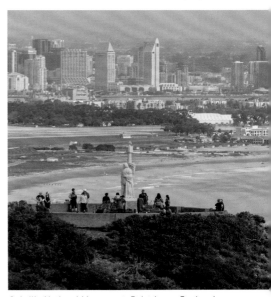

Cabrillo National Monument, Point Loma Peninsula.

Every mission aimed to become self-sufficient, so the men became farmers, blacksmiths, tanners, home builders, vintners, and other types of useful laborers, while the women focused on cooking, sewing, and laundering.

As European-introduced diseases like measles and chicken pox killed thousands, Native Americans developed a mortal fear of mission life. Nevertheless, it was their labor that made the system successful. Not until the Mexican government's secularization decrees of 1834 (following its independence from Spain and acquisition of the province of Alta California in 1821) were they freed – only to exchange their status for that of underpaid peons on the vast ranches.

📷 THE MISSIONS OF OLD CALIFORNIA

The 21 historic Franciscan missions spread along California's coast offer a fascinating insight into the Spanish era.

The chain of Spanish missions that runs from San Diego to Sonoma testifies a significant chapter in California's history. Under pressure during the mid-18th century to establish a presence in its Alta California territories, Spain charged Father Junípero Serra and his Franciscan missionaries with the task of creating a network of missions along the coast, following the example of the successful missions Spain had already built in its colony of Mexico.

Father Serra raised a flag over the first settlement, in San Diego, in 1769. Over the next 54 years, another 20 timber and adobe missions were to be dedicated between San Diego and Sonoma, each roughly a day's journey from the next along the El Camino Real (The Royal Road).

At each mission – all of which feature the thick walls, small windows, and elegant bell towers usually associated with Mexican churches – the Spanish introduced livestock, grains, agriculture, industry, and Roman Catholicism to Native Americans. The missions were also the repository of some of the state's most treasured murals and art.

In the wake of the Secularization Act of 1834, the missions fell into disuse and were abandoned. Interest in them was only sparked once more in the 1880s, when Helen Hunt Jackson's magazine articles brought attention to the plight of former Mission Indians. Now, despite the ravages of time, revolt, and neglect, most of the missions still opxerate as active Catholic parishes.

Further information on missions is contained in the San Francisco (see page 216), Santa Barbara (see page 242), San Juan Capistrano (see page 272), and San Diego (see page 276) chapters.

Pretty altar at the Mission San Francisco Solano.

Basilica San Diego de Alcala, California.

Santa Barbara Mission, one of the most beautiful missions in California.

Mission Dolores is the oldest building in San Francisco.

The Mission of San Juan Capistrano

Several intriguing legends have become associated with Mission San Juan Capistrano in Orange County. The first is very much tied to reality: For at least two centuries, cliff swallows have been visiting the church each spring, building their nests out of mud in the tiled roof. Historically, they arrived each year on or around March 19 – St Joseph's Day – flying north from their winter vacation in Argentina. Legend says the influx began when the original gulp took refuge in the mission's eaves after a local innkeeper destroyed their nests. More recently, the swallows have been finding other places to nest, but the mission continues to try to woo them back.

The second legend – described as "an American Acropolis" – tells of a woman named Magdalena, whose penance was to walk up and down the church aisle with a lighted candle, to atone for disobeying her father by courting a man of whom he disapproved. On occasion, it is said, her candle can still be seen shining amid the ruins of the cruciform Great Stone Church, in which the poor unfortunate perished during an earthquake. One of the oldest sections of the mission still standing, the Great Stone Church, was finally restored to its former glory early in the 21st century.

For more reading on Mission San Juan Capistrano, go to page 272 .

Bells at sunset at San Juan Capistrano, California.

Indian memorial at the Mission Basilica San Diego de Alcala.

Statue at the Mission San Fernando Rey de España, close to the site of the first gold rush in California.

MEMORIAL TO INDIANS
CALIFORNIA'S FIRST
CEMETERY
MISSION SAN DIEGO

Engraving depicting the Gold Rush, 1869.

THE WEST COAST IN THE 19TH CENTURY

As gold and silver discoveries brought migrants flooding in, destiny drew the West to join the United States.

It didn't seem that way at the start of the 19th century, but it's hard now to imagine that the West Coast might not have ended up throwing its hat in with the United States. Only in 1803, after all, did the Louisiana Purchase first extend the nascent nation across the Mississippi. By the 1840s, however, many Americans had come to believe that the US had not only the potential to stretch "from sea to shining sea," it had a quasi-religious duty – a "Manifest Destiny" – to do so.

By then, Mexico had wrested its independence from Spain, leaving California as something of a neglected afterthought. The American government duly attempted to buy the region, and when that failed turned its thoughts to conquest instead. At much the same time, Britain and the United States signed the surprisingly amicable Oregon Treaty (1846), which extended the international border between the US and Canada along the 49th parallel. The Northwest was thus divided between the Americans and the British, and Oregon Country duly acquired official status as a US territory in 1848.

Above all, though, it was sheer force of numbers that determined the future shape of the West Coast states, in the form of the ever-increasing torrent of cross-continental migrants. And for that, there was one great incentive – gold.

THE OREGON TRAIL

When the first wagons rolled along the Oregon Trail, in 1843, barely 150 Americans lived in Oregon Country. By 1845, there were 5,000 or more, while over the next 25 years, until the completion of the transcontinental railroad, up to half a million migrants headed west on the overland trail, an influx that shifted the regional balance

Scotts Bluff National Monument.

of power. Around one-in-ten died en route. Most went to California in search of gold, while others forked north to Oregon's Willamette Valley looking for farmland, and one small group founded New York Alki, marking the beginning of Seattle.

The Oregon Trail – properly, the Oregon–California Trail – generally followed the Platte River to its headwaters, then crossed the mountains. After the California Trail split off in southern Idaho, the Oregon branch followed the Snake River to the Columbia River, which flows into the Pacific Ocean. At first, pioneers had to float their wagons and belongings down the treacherous Columbia River from The Dalles on a hired raft or boat. Pioneer diaries are replete with accounts of boats capsizing and drownings in the icy rapids. In 1845, however, Sam Barlow decided that after six months of bumping across the mountains and plains, it wasn't worth paying the exorbitant $50 fee to float his battered wagon down the Columbia. Hearing rumors of a Native trail that crossed the Cascades just south of snow-covered Mount Hood, he attempted a mountain crossing instead. The next year, he opened the precipitous Barlow Road into the Willamette Valley, which came to be seen as the most grueling part of the entire Oregon Trail.

Lithograph of the Battle of Palo Alto.

CALIFORNIA UNDER MEXICO

On September 27, 1821, Mexico finally broke away from three centuries of Spanish rule, and declared itself a republic. By chance, at much the same time, Spanish-Mexican settlers in California were complaining that the Catholic Church owned too much land, and seeking secularization of the missions. From 1834 onward, eight million acres (3.2 million hectares) of mission land were fragmented into 800 private ranches; some governors handed land to their cronies for only a few pennies per acre. Orange orchards were cleared for firewood, herds given to private hands, and the predominant lifestyle quickly became that of an untamed frontier-style cattle range. Simultaneously, the previously enslaved Mission Indians

were left high and dry. At the height of the mission era, as many as 20,000 Native Americans had been tied to the system as unpaid laborers; they were left ill prepared to cope with freedom.

Author Richard Henry Dana, who passed this way in 1835, called the Californians "an idle thriftless people," an observation lent considerable weight by the lifestyle of the many rancheros who found it a simple matter to maintain and increase their wealth. The influx of prospectors to the north created an immense demand for beef, which the southerners readily supplied.

Yankee trading ships plied the coast, offering mahogany furniture, gleaming copperware, framed mirrors, Irish linen, silver candlesticks, and cashmere shawls. These trading ships were the first opportunity for many native-born Spanish settlers to obtain jewelry, furniture, and other goods from the old world.

Now and again an earthquake rumbled down the San Andreas fault. While the rancheros spent their energy rebuilding damaged haciendas, made from red-tile roofing atop white-painted adobe brick walls, the missions fell into disrepair.

THE MEXICAN–AMERICAN WAR

As the US government grew aware of this land of milk and honey on the Pacific coast, President Andrew Jackson sent an emissary to Mexico City in the 1830s to buy California for $500,000. The plan failed. When James K. Polk took office in 1845, he pledged to acquire California by any means. Pressured by English financial interests that plotted to exchange $26 million of defaulted

⊘ OREGON TRAIL WAGONS

A family of four settlers, traveling west on the Oregon Trail, needed to carry over 1,000lbs (454kg) of food on the perilous, 2,000-mile (3,200km) trek. The only practical way to haul that much weight was by mule- or ox-drawn wagon, on which the box measured just 4ft by 10ft (1.2m by 3m). Most emigrants loaded them to the brim with over a ton of cargo – food, farm implements and furniture – all supported by massive axles. Were an axle to break, the travelers would be in serious trouble. Without a spare, they would either have to abandon the wagon or reconfigure it as a two-wheeled cart, thus reducing their chances of survival.

Mexican bonds for the rich land of California, he declared war on Mexico on May 13, 1846.

News of the war had yet to reach California when a group of settlers stormed General Mariano Vallejo's Sonoma estate. Vallejo soothed the men with brandy and watched as they raised their hastily sewn Bear Flag over Sonoma. The Bear Flag Revolt is sanctified in California history – the flag is now the official state flag – but for all its drama, it was immaterial. Within a few weeks, Commodore John Sloat arrived to usher California into the Union.

Most of the fighting in the Mexican–American War took place in the south. The bloodiest battle on Californian soil was fought in the San Pasqual Valley, north of San Diego, in December 1846. By then the war in the north had effectively ended, when 70 hearty sailors and marines from the *Portsmouth* raised the American flag in the plaza of Yerba Buena village – now San Francisco's Portsmouth Square – on July 9, 1846.

California became a territory of the United States of America on July 4, 1848. It had taken fierce negotiation for the Treaty of Cahuenga to place San Diego on the northern side of the border. On September 9, 1850, when California was rushed into the Union as the 31st state, its constitution guaranteed the right to "enjoying and defending life and liberty, acquiring, possessing and protecting property, and pursuing and obtaining happiness." With hindsight, a typically Californian mix of the sublime and the practical.

THE CALIFORNIA GOLD RUSH

The discovery of gold in 1848 coincided almost exactly with California joining the US. That first major find came when nuggets washed downstream from the Sierra Nevada foothills ended up at a sawmill owned by John Augustus Sutter. By then, Sutter's Fort, in what's now Sacramento, was already a frequent first stop for bedraggled pioneers completing the harrowing Sierra crossing.

Sutter swore his mill hands to secrecy, but nuggets kept popping up in bars and stores all over the region. The news swiftly reached San Francisco, where the population numbered less than 1,000, and soon the madness was in full swing. As word spread throughout California, stores closed, city officials left their offices, soldiers deserted, sailors jumped ship, and the

exasperated editor of the *Californian* suspended his newspaper because the staff had walked out. San Francisco was left nearly deserted, its stores stripped of axes, pans, tents, beans, soda crackers, picks, and whatever else might be of use. Monterey, San Jose, and all Northern California's mission towns and farms joined the scramble.

Gold fever worked its way to Utah and Oregon, where two-thirds of the able-bodied men set off for the diggings. Entire caravans of covered wagons made their way west. Ships in the

President elect James K. Polk, 1844.

Pacific passed the news to Peru, Chile, Hawaii, and Australia. Lieutenant L. Loeser carried a "small chest ... containing $3,000-worth of gold in lumps and scales" back to Washington, DC, where it was exhibited at the War Office. On December 2, 1848, President Polk told Congress the "extraordinary accounts" were true. A few days later, the *New York Herald* summed it up: "The El Dorado of the old Spaniards is discovered at last."

The dreams of the Forty-Niners, as the prospectors became known, centered on the wooded hills and deep valleys of the fabled Mother Lode Country, which ran for 120 miles (192km) from north of Sutter's Mill to Mariposa. That said, mining activities ranged from the streams of the Klamath Mountains in the far north to the deserts of the south.

At first, mining was a simple affair. The Mother Lode was owned by the federal government, and claims were limited to the ground a man and his fellows could work. In 1849, $10 million of gold was mined in California; the next year, four times that amount. In 1852, at the peak of the Gold Rush, $80 million wound up in prospectors' pockets. While there was money in them thar hills, the problem lay in keeping it. Many a fortune was lost to rapacious traders; vanished in gambling halls and bawdy-houses; or was frittered away thanks to the simple foolishness of young men.

SAN FRANCISCO IN THE GOLD RUSH

Nowhere did the Gold Rush exert a greater magic than in San Francisco. In the first English-language book published in the city – *California as It Is and as It May Be, or, A Guide to the Gold Region* (1849) – F.P. Wierzbicki describes San Francisco's abrupt transformation, "it looks ... like one of those cities Only built for a day ...

The Gold Rush, California.

⦾ GOLD TOWNS

Bayard Taylor, then a reporter for the *New York Tribune* and later a poet and diplomat, described the atmosphere of Gold-Rush San Francisco as a "perpetual carnival." Returning from four months at the diggings, he found not the town of "tents and canvas houses with a show of frame buildings" that he had left, but "an actual metropolis, displaying street after street of well-built edifices ... lofty hotels, gaudy with verandas and balconies ... finished with home luxury and aristocratic restaurants presenting daily their long bills of fare, rich with the choicest technicalities of Parisian cuisine."

Four months ago the town hardly counted fifty houses, and now it must have upwards of five hundred, and these are daily increasing."

Real-estate speculation was rife. Each boatload of forty-niners represented another batch of customers. As the city burst beyond the boundaries of Yerba Buena Cove, "water lots" sold for crazy prices on the expectation they could be made habitable with landfill. Indeed, much of today's downtown San Francisco is built on landfill.

Few of California's new tenants had any desire to lay the foundation for the orderly society that lay ahead. In the end, the winners in the great money-scramble were those who took the time to establish businesses and buy land. In 1853, the Gold Rush began to wind down. Real-estate values fell, immigration slowed to a trickle, and merchants were stuck with massive oversupplies.

Whatever chance California had of calming down was swept away by another flood of riches in 1859. This time it was silver rather than gold that was discovered in the bluish clay of the Sierra's dry eastern slopes. Extracting it proved beyond the capabilities of lone prospectors, however. This was a game for capitalists, with the money to dig tunnels, purchase claims, and install the expensive machinery and mills that transformed the "blue stuff" into cash.

The treasures of the Comstock Lode gushed into San Francisco. By 1863, $40 million of silver had been wrestled from the tunnels, with 2,000 mining companies trading shares. In all, the Comstock Lode lasted until the 1880s, and pumped $400 million into the Californian economy.

Meanwhile the Native American population continued to suffer. From 1850 onwards, the Federal government signed treaties (never ratified by the Senate) under which more than 7 million acres (2.8 million hectares) of tribal land dwindled to less than 10 percent of that total.

CHANGE SWEEPS THE NORTHWEST

As the 1840s drew to a close, a surprise awaited newcomers to Oregon's Willamette Valley. Despite good weather, crops were rotting in unattended fields and once-productive farms had surrendered to weeds. By 1849, only 8,779 settlers were living in what's now the state of Oregon.

Blame it on California. With the discovery of gold, two-thirds of Oregon's male population hotfooted it south – a sudden exodus that seemed likely to spell doom for the territory. In the event, some farmers-turned-miners did find easy pickings in California, and returned with $2 million worth of nuggets. Finally, Oregon had a currency beyond wheat, potatoes and rocks. In 1849, the legislature minted standardized coins – so-called "Beaver Money," gold coins stamped in $5 and $10 denominations.

Less successful prospectors at least came home with the knowledge that 100,000 California miners would pay handsomely for Oregon products. In gold-crazed California, Oregon eggs were selling for a dollar apiece. Soon Oregon Territory was booming.

In due course, California prospectors ventured north to the hills of southern Oregon.

Nuggets were found in 1851, and millions of dollars in gold dust were unearthed from ancient streambeds and hilltop ledges in such places as Rich Gulch and Sailors Diggings. Miners even struck it rich along the coast, south of Coos Bay.

Each Oregon pioneer could claim 320 acres (130 hectares), plus the same again for his wife. With most of the rich Willamette Valley lands rapidly taken, the Gold Rush opened the remote yet fertile valleys of southern Oregon to a ravenous market. The wilderness sprouted bustling towns, with Jacksonville as the metropolis

Portsmouth Square San Francisco, 1851.

and Scottsburg as its transportation nexus, and mule trains shared the trails with stagecoaches running between San Francisco and Portland.

As Oregon mulled over its future, many residents were tempted to follow the earlier example of Texas, which had formed the Lone Star Republic. Statehood finally arrived with the realization that only if Oregon were a state could its citizens legislate against slavery. After a seven-to-one pro-statehood vote in 1857, President James Buchanan duly welcomed Oregon as the 33rd state on February 14, 1859.

EXPANSION IN THE NORTHWEST

From the 1850s onward, the economy of the Pacific Northwest became increasingly urban

CHIEF JOSEPH

The heroic and strategic retreat of the Nez Perce, led by Chief Joseph, is the great epic of Northwestern Native history.

Chief Joseph.

Shortly before Tuekakas, leader of the Nez Perce, died in 1871, he counseled his son Chief Joseph: "When I am gone, think of your country. You are the chief of these people. They look to you to guide them. A few more years and the whites will be all around you. They have eyes on this land."

At the start of the 19th century, the Nez Perce formed the largest Native American group in the Columbia River region. Centering on what's now eastern Oregon, their territory included parts of modern Montana, Idaho, and Washington. Although they welcomed Lewis and Clark and befriended the white settlers, friendship was not enough. Americans wanted their land. Tuekakas twice resisted attempts to relocate his people, but after his death, government men once again ordered them onto a reservation. "If ever we owned the land," Chief Joseph responded, "we own it still, for we have never sold it."

His logic fell on deaf ears. The government issued an ultimatum: leave in 30 days or be driven out by force. Some cried for blood, but Joseph knew the odds were against them. "Better to live at peace," he said, "than to begin a war and lie dead."

Joseph's people embarked on a grueling trek, losing much of their livestock to raging rivers and predatory pursuers. Then, one night, a few hot-headed warriors slipped out of camp and killed four whites. "I would have given my own life if I could have undone the killing of the white men," Joseph said later, but before reparations could be made, soldiers were upon them.

THE FLIGHT OF THE NEZ PERCE

For four months, Joseph led 750 people, including chiefs Looking Glass, Toohoolhoolzote, and Ollokot, across 1,300 miles (2,000km) of rugged terrain, first evading then engaging troops far superior in number and firepower. Hoping to join Sitting Bull's band, they headed for Canada, but were halted 30 miles (50km) short. With his camp bogged down by snow at Bear Paws, and surrounded by soldiers, Joseph gave up his rifle, declaring "I am tired of fighting. Our chiefs are killed. Looking Glass is dead. Toohoolhoolzote is dead. The old men are all dead. It is the young men who say yes and no. He who led the young men [Ollokot] is dead. It is cold and we have no blankets. The little children are freezing to death. My people, some of them, have run away to the hills, and have no blankets, no food; no one knows where they are, perhaps freezing to death. I want to have time to look for my children and see how many I can find. Maybe I shall find them among the dead. Hear me, my chiefs. I am tired. My heart is sick and sad. From where the sun now stands, I will fight no more forever."

Despite reassurances, Joseph and his people were sent to an internment camp in Kansas, where nearly 100 died. After exile and a deadly bout of malaria, a few survivors were allowed to return to a reservation in Lapwai, Idaho. Not Joseph, however. Despite his pleas, Joseph was exiled to Washington, where he died in 1904.

Today the eastern Oregon town of Joseph, and a peak in the Wallowa Mountains, retain his name. Of the Wallowa Valley, Joseph said "I buried my father in that beautiful valley of the winding waters. I love that land more than all the rest of the world."

and industrial. Portland, a port for ocean-going vessels at the confluence of the Columbia and Willamette rivers, quickly became its leading city. Farm produce from the Willamette Valley, minerals from Idaho, and wheat from eastern Washington all shipped via Portland.

San Francisco capitalists discovered the vast forests farther north, and by 1884, Puget Sound sawmills consumed a million board feet of wood per day. Only half the native timber in what's now Washington's Thurston County was still standing by 1890. Rafts of logs floated to mills at

Chinese were "escorted" to the waterfront, and were about to be shipped off to San Francisco until a writ of habeas corpus halted proceedings. Believing persecution to be inevitable, most of Seattle's Chinese population left for California aboard the steamer *George W. Edler*.

KLONDIKE FEVER

Seattle has always been something of an upstart. After all, its first town-site was named "New York Alki-," meaning "New York by-and-by." Its rise to become the Northwest's largest

Construction of the Central Pacific railroad.

Port Gamble and Port Ludlow, to be shipped as lumber and wooden products to San Francisco and beyond.

Although the arrival of the railroads in the 1880s boosted Seattle and Vancouver, the Northwest was hit by over-expansion and recession, and the mood turned sour. Many Chinese laborers had come to work on the railroads, while others had arrived during the gold rushes. In both Oregon and Washington, white citizens now pushed for their expulsion, and Washington forbade Chinese to own property. In early 1886, men in Seattle knocked on the doors of Chinese homes, announced the buildings were condemned, and suggested their occupants leave town immediately. Three hundred and fifty

⊘ ALL IN A NAME

In 1852, the US Congress was petitioned to recognize yet another new territorial division, separating off those parts of Oregon Territory that lay north of the Columbia River. Objecting that the proposed name, "Columbia," might be confused with the District of Columbia, Richard Stanton, a representative from Kentucky, suggested that the territory be renamed "Washington," after the first president. Despite the obvious (and continuing) risk of confusion with the nation's capital, President Millard Fillmore signed a bill creating the "Territory of Washington" on March 2, 1853. Another 36 years were to pass before Washington became the 42nd US state.

metropolis owed much to industry and ingenuity, but also to good fortune. Settled in 1851, it was named after the Duwamish chief Sealth, who was befriended by early pioneers. Residents long cherished big dreams for Seattle, while lacking the capital to lend them reality until gold was discovered in Alaska and the Yukon.

On July 17, 1897, a telegram announced "the steamship *Portland* has just arrived in Seattle with a ton of gold on board," and the next gold rush was on. The *Portland* sailed back to Alaska with a full complement of passengers, and

Engraving of a Gold mining camp.

prospectors arrived in droves from California, Oregon, and Colorado.

Although the initial finds were on Canadian soil, neither Vancouver nor Victoria was ready to service the rush, and Seattle became the main loading point for Klondike prospectors or "sourdoughs." Within four years, over $174 million in gold had passed over the scales of its assay office.

THE GROWTH OF CALIFORNIA

During the 1860s, California was still awash with mining wealth. The Comstock's greatest mine owner, Billy Ralston, rebuilt America's largest city hotel in San Francisco, and bought sugar refineries, lumber, and water companies.

As the decade drew to a close, he confidently prepared for what he and his fellow plutocrats thought would be the capstone to the state's rise to greatness – the long-awaited completion of the Transcontinental Railroad.

Although plans for a coast-to-coast railroad had long been in the air, Congress only stirred into action with the outbreak of the Civil War. Intent upon securing California's place in the Union, the Pacific Railroad Act of 1862 granted vast tracts of land out west, low-interest financing, and outright subsidies to two companies – the Central Pacific, building eastwards from Sacramento, and the Union Pacific, heading west from Omaha, Nebraska.

The genius of the Central Pacific, the young engineer Theodore Dehone Judah, had built California's first railroad, the short Sacramento Valley line, in 1856. He spent years crafting the crucial route across the Sierra, only to be forced out by the so-called "Big Four," a group of Sacramento shopkeepers who had invested in his scheme.

The Central Pacific made the Big Four insanely rich, and able to dictate California politics. Between them, the railroad barons raised private investment, earned government subsidies, acquired bargain-priced land, and imported cheap labor from China. As the state's largest landowners and biggest employers, they manipulated freight rates, controled water supplies, kept the most productive land for themselves, and subverted politicians and municipalities. Although Sacramento had been

⊘ THE GREAT SEATTLE FIRE

On June 6, 1889, a handyman in a Seattle paint store noticed a pot of glue had caught fire. He threw on a bucket of water, which mixed with turpentine and wood shavings and caused a fiery explosion. Thus began the Great Seattle Fire. That week had been hot and dry, and Seattle, constructed almost entirely of wood, was a tinder-box. By that night almost the entire business district had burned to the ground. After the fire, merchants replanned and rebuilt downtown using bricks and mortar, effectively raising it by one level. Some original structures survived, and now form part of Seattle's fascinating "Underground" network.

California's capital since 1854, San Francisco ruled a rapidly coalescing state.

The first Central Pacific train breached the Sierra at Donner Pass in April 1868. When the ceremonial Golden Spike was driven at Promontory Point, Utah, a year later, the coasts were finally and irrevocably linked. But the anticipated rush of prosperity failed to materialize. Instead, the railroad brought financial calamity. Severe drought in the winter of 1869–70 crippled California's agriculture, while between 1873 and 1875 over a quarter of a million migrants streamed in. Many were factory workers; few found work.

The 1870s saw the depression at its deepest. On April 26, 1875, a run on the Bank of California forced it to slam its oak doors. Driven into debt, its head, Billy Ralston, drowned during his customary morning swim in the Bay. Most hurt by the great shrinkage of capital were the state's working people, who had enjoyed a rare freedom to move easily from job to job and improve their conditions. California was to suffer recurrent labor strife for another 60 years.

AGRICULTURAL GROWTH

While depression was slow to disappear, California was too rich to suffer forever. Over the ensuing decades, the state's economy grew to the point where it could compete with the East Coast.

Long dependant on mineral wealth, California shifted its attention to agriculture. In the Central Valley, wheat, rice, and cotton became major cash crops; the Napa Valley set about producing fine wines; and the southernmost counties were transformed by the planting of seedless navel oranges.

Until the coming of the railroad, Los Angeles had remained a predominantly Mexican city, infused with a Latino culture and traditions. The subsequent influx of Anglo-American, Asian, and European immigrants eventually outnumbered Mexicans 10 to 1. Doubling its population every decade from 1870 onward, LA prospered, and confronted its perennial problem: the lack of water. To ensure a steady water supply, the city fathers hired Vermont-born shopkeeper Ozro W. Childs to dig a long trench from the river, the Zanja Madre (Mother Ditch). Rather than scarce city funds, Childs was paid a tract

of land bordered by today's 6th and Main streets and Pico Boulevard and Figueroa Street. Meanwhile, at the ocean, frontage at Santa Monica owned by Southern Pacific Railroad magnate Collis P. Huntington almost became the Port of Los Angeles, before intensive lobbying by rival Santa Fe railroad chiefs won out and San Pedro was chosen instead. Already the region was producing almost 5 million barrels of oil per year.

By 1897, LA was sophisticated enough to boast the first orchestra established west of the Rockies. Eight years later, Abbott Kinney's ambitious

Vineyard at Napa Valley.

reconstruction of Venice on coastal marshland added an international touch. Thanks in part to huckstering by railroad salesmen, who went to such lengths as spiking thorny trees with oranges to sell worthless land, real estate was big business. In 1886, Harvey H. Wilcox named his new sub-division Hollywood. After his widow sold a plot of land to French flower painter Paul de Longpré, in 1903, his palatial house and floral gardens became the area's first tourist attraction. That same year, ground was broken for the soon-to-be-famous Hollywood Hotel and the elegant hillside community of Whitley Heights, a favoured home for early movie stars. Hollywood soon found itself obliged, along with its neighbors, to join LA to secure an adequate water supply.

The George Washington Memorial Bridge under construction in 1931.

THE MODERN WEST COAST

Since 1900, the West Coast has transformed almost beyond recognition, embracing future possibilities while preserving the best of the past.

The early years of the 20th century saw the westernmost states thrust into the spotlight where they've remained ever since. Thanks to the Great Earthquake of 1906, San Francisco was forced to change whether it liked it or not, and within a decade its downtown had received a complete makeover, and the city jubilantly hosted a world's fair. Los Angeles meanwhile raced gleefully toward modernity, reveling in its new-found oil wealth, and fame from the growth of the movie industry. Propelled by oil strikes, the acquisition of new water sources, and the development of an extensive network of electric trains, Los Angeles tripled its population to 300,000 in just 10 years. Farther north, first Portland and then, not to be outdone, Seattle, also staged major exhibitions that successfully drew international attention.

By the 1930s, according to The WPA Guide to California: The Golden State by the Federal Writers' Project, California had become "that legendary land of perpetual summer, of orange groves in sight of snowy peaks, of oil wells spouting wealth, of real-estate promising fortunes, of cinema stars and bathing beauties. It seemed to promise a new start, a kinder providence, a rebirth of soul and body."

In both Oregon and Washington, it took a few decades longer for the state economies to pick up speed, though at least the depression of the 1930s prompted a federal-sponsored development of the region's infrastructure.

It was World War II that truly threw the West Coast into overdrive, with a huge expansion of military-oriented industry combined with an influx of the migrants necessary to work in the new factories. Many of the military personnel who passed through on their way to fight in

The making of the Grand Coulee Dam, Washington.

the Pacific returned after the war to build their futures in the West, and the boom continued into the 1950s and 1960s. With the growth of television and the recording industry, California especially became even more of a cultural powerhouse for the nation. More recently, the entire region has spearheaded the rise of the high-tech economy, with the emergence of Silicon Valley outside San Francisco, and the soaring fortunes of Microsoft and Amazon in Seattle.

INTERCITY RIVALRY IN THE NORTHWEST

As the 20th century began, Portlanders were becoming alarmed at how pesky upstart Seattle was draining their business. Something had to be done. In 1905, Portland therefore hosted the widely publicized Lewis and Clark Centennial Exposition. It paid off handsomely: not only did investors realize a 21 percent return, but Portland's population doubled within five years, to reach 270,000 in 1910. What's more, the town planted hundreds of beautiful rose bushes along its streets, prompting its "City of Roses" nickname.

In 1909, Seattle in turn decided to celebrate its prodigious growth and recent refinements by hosting the Alaska-Yukon-Pacific Exposition (A-Y-P). This fair, too, meant many things. Announc-

The Bonneville Dam.

ing that Seattle had passed its "frontier" stage to arrive as a major American city, the A-Y-P proved every bit as successful. Some 3,740,551 visitors turned up over 138 days, and many were convinced to return and settle. In 1910, Seattle's population surpassed Portland's for the first time. With both cities now on the map, the Pacific Northwest had become a saleable item.

The completion of the Seattle Ship Canal, in 1916, enabled ocean-going vessels to navigate easily from Puget Sound through Lake Union into Lake Washington. Such projects had good economic consequences, but major environmental costs; the region's salmon runs were devastated. At the time, however, these were not seen as high priorities.

DEPRESSION AND WAR

Arguably, until the 1930s, the Pacific Northwest played catch-up with the rest of the nation, economically, politically, and culturally. Then things began to change. First came the Great Depression, and the creation of thousands of new jobs in the Columbia Basin Project, between 1933 and 1941. In this massive, federally funded effort to "tame" the Columbia and Snake rivers, armies of men built the mammoth Grand Coulee and Bonneville dams, for hydroelectricity, farm irrigation, and to permit inland navigation by ocean-going vessels. The Civilian Conservation Corps also instigated programs in parks and forests, wildlife protection, public housing, and irrigation projects.

Consequently, by the time the US joined World War II in 1941, the Pacific Northwest had acquired the infrastructure to mobilize for war. Aluminum factories in Spokane and the Portland area, a plutonium plant at Hanford, and aircraft manufacturing at Seattle, all drew power from the Columbia Basin. As the Northwestern economy climbed to new heights, increased job opportunities and high wages for defense work encouraged mass migration that raised the regional population by 30 percent. Between 1940 and 1946, the number of manufacturing companies around Portland doubled. Large war machinery plants around Puget Sound – including Boeing Aircraft and the Puget Sound Navy Yard at Bremerton – were starved for help, and lumber companies, mining concerns, and agricultural industries struggled to keep up with demand.

After the war, inexorable population and military-industrial growth shaped a new profile for Oregon and Washington. While trees and fish remained important, the Northwest shed its backwoods image. The strong military and naval presence, with the importance of space and weapons research during the Cold War, and the re-orientation of Boeing toward commercial aviation, contributed to an era of high prosperity. Washington in particular boomed, with its economy increasingly geared toward technology.

THE WORLD'S FAIR

Echoing the expositions of the early 20th century, Seattle's World's Fair of 1962 introduced the Pacific Northwest to itself and the world as a place of "the future." Standing at the base of the iconic, 605ft (185m) Space Needle, looking up at its white spidery legs and flying-saucer-like top, cannot fail to conjure "jet age" dreams.

The era saw a generational change. During the 1960s and early 1970s, as students were demonstrating against the US presence in Vietnam, the Pacific Northwest came to be seen as clean, enriching, and environmentally conscious, as attractive to disillusioned Americans as its earlier enticements had been to wagon-train pioneers and gold miners. Northwesterners relished this bright, romantic picture of their land, and promoted the region as exclusive – a home fit for the enlightened few. Residents loved it when Oregon governor Tom McCall in the 1970s invited the world to "visit our state of enchantment – but, for heaven's sake, don't stay."

A new environmental sensibility was emerging. Governor McCall gave voice to such perceptions by suggesting that measurements of "success" in the Northwest might be redefined: "Unlimited and unregulated growth leads inexorably to a lowered quality of life." He instituted a state department of environmental quality; protected parts of six streams as "wild and scenic" rivers; expanded the state park system, introducing "greenways" (long narrow parks); and developed a far-reaching land-use planning system. This created urban-growth boundaries and mandated complex state land-use guidelines. Washington was more reluctant, but eventually followed a similar path. With few Northwesterners prepared to renounce growth altogether, however, they spoke of "regulating," "managing," or "limiting" it.

The 1980s and 1990s brought two well-publicized environmental crises, revolving around endangered species: the Northern Spotted Owl and the threatened runs of salmon. Each was held to be an indicator for the health of broader ecosystems, the old-growth forests and riverine watersheds. No solutions found widespread agreement, but the discussions fueled a movement toward environmental awareness.

The numbers and ethnicities of migrants arriving in the Northwest have been steadily changing ever since World War II. Military involvement in Korea and Southeast Asia added Asian migrants to those residents of Chinese, Japanese, and Filipino descent who had already established substantial communities. Whereas previous arrivals had largely been laborers, those who arrived during the 1970s, 1980s, and 1990s brought a range of skills and training. Immigrants from India, the Philippines, China, and Korea ranked among the nationalities with the most professional and managerial workers. Both the Civil Rights Movement and resistance to the Vietnam War accelerated changing attitudes of white Americans to people of Asian descent, and in 1996 Washington State elected Gary Locke as its governor, the first Asian American to hold such office outside Hawaii.

Seattle's Space Needle.

Now, in the Pacific Northwest of the 21st century, relics from the past continue to endure amid the symbols of the present. Native American totems stand by the revitalized docks in Seattle, where tall ships once loaded lumber. The new Northwest strives to meet future challenges more complex than any it's had to face in its richly colored past. As traditional industries faltered – lumber, agriculture and fishing – commerce turned confidently to aerospace, biotech, software, and high technology.

With roughly half the world's population now said to live in the area defined as the Pacific Rim, both Seattle and Portland have reoriented themselves toward these nations as trading partners. Washington's economy was especially boosted by the fast-growing marvel of Bill Gates' Microsoft, which in its early days attracted thousands of young, bright professionals from all over the world, and produced more employee-millionaires than any company in history. That heady high-tech era also brought a boom in silicon chips, attracting yet more talented migrants to serve the likes of Intel and Amazon.

Since 1999, when a series of demonstrations, attracting up to 40,000 participants, disrupted the summit meeting of the World Trade Organization in Seattle, the Northwest has also

shook Northern Californians from their beds. As the deadly San Andreas fault lurched, it sent terrifying jolts through an area 210 miles (338km) long and 30 miles (48km) wide, from San Juan Bautista in the south to Fort Bragg in the north. Church bells jangled, dishes fell, windows shattered, dogs barked, Enrico Caruso (appearing in the opera *Carmen*) was scared voiceless, and San Francisco's new City Hall crumbled. It was all over in just 48 seconds, but the city lay in ruins.

The subsequent fire destroyed 28,000 buildings, across more than 4 sq miles (10 sq km). San

Damage to the Union Street car line after the 1906 earthquake.

acquired a new reputation for political activism. Twenty years on, both Seattle and Portland saw further large demonstrations in 2020 and 2021, after the murder of George Floyd by a police officer in Minneapolis prompted the Black Lives Matter campaign to organize nationwide protests. Each city witnessed a tension between federal intervention urged by the Trump administration, and the more liberal instincts of local citizens and, to some extent, city governments.

CALIFORNIA IN THE EARLY 20TH CENTURY

In California, the 20th century began, literally, with a terrible shock. On April 18, 1906, at 5.12am, an earthquake measuring 8.25 on the Richter scale

Francisco had experienced many earthquakes before, but none on this scale, and the effect was cataclysmic. Coming without warning or preparation, it killed 315 people; the bodies of 352 more were never found, while modern research suggests the toll was much higher still. Only an unearthly low rumble preceded the opening of fissures that spread wavelike across the city.

With its alarm system destroyed, the Fire Department lacked coordination, and the commandant of the Presidio, Brigadier General Frederick Funston, leaped in to fill the gap. When the brigades did arrive, they found the water supply gone, with hundreds dead or trapped in smoking ruins, and 500 city blocks leveled. As Funston's inexperienced militia attempted to keep order, some citizens were even shot or bayoneted. Golden Gate Park became temporary home to as many as 300,000 people. Cooking inside the tents was banned, sanitation was rudimentary, water was in very short supply, and rats (and therefore plague) were a constant menace.

But there was a strong will to recover, and aid poured in from all over the world. A.P. Giannini's tiny Bank of Italy came to the forefront, making loans to small businesses intent on rebuilding, and ultimately grew to become the Bank of America, the nation's largest. Even the much-reviled Southern Pacific Railroad pitched in, freighting in supplies without charge, offering free passage out of the city, and setting heavy equipment and cranes to clear the debris.

Renaissance was inevitable. The new, improved, taller buildings of Montgomery Street, the Wall Street of the west, were needed to process all the money churned out by the state's industries, farms, and banks. The Port of San Francisco remained one of the world's busiest harbors, and San Francisco's historic business of making business proved unstoppable.

In 1911, San Francisco elected a new mayor, James "Sunny Jim" Rolph, a purveyor of goodwill whose reign encompassed some of San Francisco's giddiest times. The 1915 Panama Pacific International Exposition, set on reclaimed land in what's now the Marina, is still ranked among the greatest of the world's fairs. Only one vestige of that flamboyant celebration remains – the Palace of Fine Arts Theatre, saved from decay in the 1960s.

THE GROWTH OF SOUTHERN CALIFORNIA

Spurred by the 1892 discovery of oil in what's now the Westlake area, Southern California mushroomed from an agricultural community to an industrial complex. Realizing it was sitting on a fat reservoir of wealth, Los Angeles developed the "Salt Lake Field," followed by fields in Huntington Beach, Santa Fe Springs, and Signal Hill. Oil derricks sprouted from the hills to the sea.

Southern California's growth spurt owed much to the Owens Valley scandal, and additional water brought in by LA's Water Bureau Superintendent William Mulholland. Even today, these aqueducts still supply 430 million gallons (1.62 billion liters) of water a day.

TRAINS AND TROLLEY CARS

Although downtown LA was linked to Pasadena and Santa Fe by an urban railway, the Southern Pacific's Collis P. Huntington, boasting that LA "can extend in any direction, as far as you like," devised a vast interurban network of electric trains in 1901. Within a decade, his trolley cars, on which passengers could ride 20 miles (32km) for a nickel, impressively connected the entire metropolis. "The whole area within a radius of 70 miles of the city took on a new life," wrote Huntington's biographer, Isaac Marcosson.

Palace of Fine Arts Theater.

☉ WEALTH BY STEALTH

The infamous 1904 plot to steal water from the Owens Valley via a 250-mile (400km) pipeline running to Los Angeles, over the Tehachapi Mountains, made fortunes for a private syndicate, and enabled the city to grow to unprecedented levels.

Syndicate member General Moses H. Sherman acquired his advance knowledge as to which land was about to be enriched from serving on the Los Angeles' Board of Water Commissioners and used this information to set the plan in motion. Recounted in Roman Polanski's 1974 film Chinatown, starring Jack Nicholson and Faye Dunaway, the scandal left the Owens Valley dry.

"Villages became towns; towns blossomed into miniature cities."

Nonetheless, traffic, swiftly became problematic. When Los Angeles held its second annual motor show in 1909, it had more cars on its streets than any other city in the world, and the population was still soaring.

MOVIE MADNESS

It was the film industry that really shot Los Angeles to fame. Rooted in the nickelodeon, the movie industry first emerged back east at

The O.J. Simpson trial gripped the world.

the start of the century. It headed west partly to escape the stranglehold patents of the New York-based Edison company, and also because California's superb climate made outdoor filming cheaper and easier.

Within a dozen years, the sedate boulevards of Hollywood were filled with intruders bearing cameras and megaphones, roping off streets, crashing cars, and staging pretend shoot-outs. Prolific directors were turning out one-reel Westerns or comedies almost daily. The locals didn't like it. "They thought we were tramps," recalled screenwriter Anita Loos. "They saw themselves as being invaded and supplanted as elegant ladies and gentlemen so they ganged up on us."

Comedy became king. Mack Sennett's Keystone Kops and Charlie Chaplin had the whole world laughing. Though studios sprang up in Culver City and Universal City too, by now Hollywood was more or less synonymous with the "movies." As silent movies accompanied by organ music gave way to the "talkies," hundreds of movie houses blossomed. Instant fortunes came to stars, directors, and producers, while novelists earned more from film rights than from their original books. Studios wielded great power, launching instant fads, and shaping tastes and ideas worldwide.

In 1920, the population of Los Angeles reached 576,000. Surpassing San Francisco for the first time, LA was now the 10th most populous city in the country.

MODERN CALIFORNIA

By 1940, the population of Los Angeles had doubled again, to 1.3 million, of whom about 9 percent were Mexican, 3 percent Asian, and 3 percent African American.

World War II plunged California into a frenzy of activity. During 46 months of war, 1.5 million men and women, and 23 million tons of munitions, passed through the Golden Gate. The ports of San Francisco, Sausalito, Oakland, Vallejo, and Alameda were busy around the clock building and repairing ships, and loading supplies for the war machine.

In the Bay Area alone, the federal government spent $3 billion on shipbuilding. A new wave of immigration swept in, as new factories needed new workers – 100,000 at the Kaiser Yards in Richmond, 90,000 more at Sausalito. Even though 750,000 Californians left for military service, the number of wage-earners in San Francisco almost tripled within two years, while the total for the entire state increased by nearly a million in the first half of the 1940s. The federal government doled out $83 million in contracts to the California Institute of Technology (Cal Tech) alone.

Once the conflict was over, and workers and their families settled into postwar prosperity, the great suburban sprawl got under way. The war had also boosted California's aircraft industry, whose employee numbers increased from under 10,000 to more than 300,000. In 1950, the City of Angels' 2 million population made it the fourth largest city in the United States.

THE ANTI-CONFORMISTS

As a new, almost instant society, California has always felt free to experiment. Many of its newcomers, from the "Anglo hordes" of the 1840s, to Gold Rush adventurers, to present-day arrivals, have come precisely to escape the burdens of conformity elsewhere. The great majority of Californians have always been settled and, to one degree or another, God-fearing. But the anti-conformists – the colorful, freethinking minority – have made California a byword for verve and drive.

The beatniks, it seems, mostly wanted America to go away. But it wouldn't; before long, "beat" had become a fashion, and North Beach a tourist attraction.

THE BEAT GENERATION

Beat struck a nerve. Though it was never a coherent movement, it produced juice-stirring literary works like Allen Ginsberg's *Howl* and Jack Kerouac's *On the Road*. Such alienation gave rise to two parallel, dissimilar, but oddly congruent movements: the angry politics of the

Grandstand built for the Hollywood premiere of 'Lloyds of London'.

In the 1950s and 1960s, according to author Mike Davis, Los Angeles became "the capital of youth," but the first stirrings of postwar protest and eccentricity were felt in San Francisco. While the American nation settled into a complacent torpor, the city's historically Italian North Beach area became the haunt of a loosely defined group of poets, writers, declaimers, and sidewalk philosophers – the beatniks.

To the sensibilities of the 1950s, they seemed titillating and somehow significant, a tempting combination for the nation's press who ogled at their rambling poetry readings, sniffed at the light marijuana breezes drifting out of the North Beach coffee houses, and wondered whether civilization could stand such a limpid assault.

New Left and the woozy love fest of the hippies. The first major upsurge of the great, protest-rich 1960s took place in San Francisco in 1961, when the House Un-American Activities Committee held hearings in City Hall. When hundreds of demonstrators met the committee in the rotunda, the police reacted furiously, turning water hoses and billy clubs on the crowds. Dozens were carted off to jail, but their angry shouts were heard around the world.

The locus of dissent was the University of California at Berkeley, where the Free Speech Movement kept up a steady assault on racism, materialism, and the stifling "multiversity" itself. As the horrors of the war in Vietnam grew more apparent, the New Left spread across America and the world, tilting at governments, bombing, marching, and changing the way America looked at itself. The hippies, though, attacked their targets with gentler weapons. While the New Left ranted at the evils of an affluent, smug, hypocritical society, the hippies tried to undermine it with glimmering love and peace, and by wearing farfetched clothes.

THE HIPPIES OF HAIGHT-ASHBURY

In the mid-1960s, San Francisco became the epicenter of the hippie revolution. It was a natu-

Wildfire, August 2019, California.

ral refuge for spacey idealists, having been created by youthful myth-chasers. Former beatniks slid easily into the free-and-easy hippie style centered around the Haight-Ashbury neighborhood, with its funky Victorian houses, and Golden Gate Park handily nearby. By 1967, the Haight was thronged with young, long-haired, men and women, the movement reaching its apogee in the massive Human Be-In assemblage, and the celebrated Summer of Love.

At first, San Francisco was amused by the hippies. But as altogether too many sons and daughters of wealthy, respected citizens took to marijuana-induced meandering, and the LSD hysteria took full flight, public sympathy for the nomads began to evaporate.

TENSIONS AND RIOTING

By the mid-1960s, LA's African American population had multiplied tenfold, and become increasingly unwilling to tolerate discriminatory employment practices and "unwritten" housing restrictions. One hot summer evening in 1965, the palm-shaded ghetto of Watts exploded. For six days, until the National Guard restored order, the inner city boiled.

Almost 30 years later, in 1992, with conditions in the Black and Chicano areas largely unchanged, violence erupted again. The acquittal of four police officers recorded on video beating an African American man, Rodney King, sparked the worst racial violence in California's history. By the time the dawn-to-dusk curfew was lifted, more than 50 people had died and another 2,500 been injured, and 5,200 fires had occurred. South Central LA was devastated. Sparking already existing tension, the Rodney King case set off the intricately connected time bomb of race, poverty, and the state of the inner city. The seemingly never-ending explosion of gang violence in Los Angeles, for example, has focused national attention on urban poverty.

SCANDALS AND CELEBRITY THRILLS

Barely a year goes by without major California events, scandals, and upheavals making world headlines. During the 1990s, TV viewers were riveted by the arrest and trials in Los Angeles of former football hero O.J. Simpson. Next came the 2003 recall of Governor Gray Davis and the subsequent election of mega movie star Arnold Schwarzenegger in his place, followed by the trials and legal woes of Michael Jackson, and starlets like Paris Hilton and Lindsay Lohan. In a precursor of later Black Lives Matter demonstrations, mass protests engulfed Oakland after BART police officer Johannes Mehserle was sentenced to two years in prison for fatally shooting Oscar Grant on New Year's Day in 2009. Further protests followed in 2011 and 2012, as Occupy Wall Street demonstrators filled streets and parks in major cities, from Oakland and San Francisco to Los Angeles. Yet another scandal erupted in 2017, when allegations of sexual harassment and abuse of famous actresses were made against film producer Harvey Weinstein, spurring the global rise of the #MeToo movement.

THE DOT-COM ERA

As the new millennium dawned, the future looked bright in San Francisco. Nearby Silicon Valley invigorated established industries and prompted the mushrooming of thousands of start-up companies. Venture capitalists threw money at shiny ideas, stock prices soared, and the housing market hit new heights. Recent college graduates earned more money than they could count, even if a great deal of the prosperity owed more to innovative bookkeeping than real business acumen. When the bubble burst in 2002, many of these

compounded when the Sierra Nevada snowpack, which when it melts in late spring and summer is relied on to provide 30 percent of the state's water supply, hit its lowest-ever levels in 2015. After a few improved years, as of 2022 it has dropped even lower, and the years of drought seem destined to continue.

Another consequence is the increased susceptibility of the land to wildfires. The seven largest wildfires in Californian history have all raged since 2018, with 2020 as the worst year on record.

Facebook - a Silicon Valley stalwart.

new millionaires were forced to return home to their parents. Since then, and more specifically since Facebook went public in 2012, California's tech fortunes have generally been on the upswing. The ever-increasing concentration of well-paid young professionals in Silicon Valley, the Bay Area, and San Francisco itself has however caused real estate and rental prices to rocket, and forced thousands of young locals to move away from the area.

DROUGHT AND WILDFIRES

Since the ongoing California drought began in 2013, places throughout the state have recorded all-time low precipitation records. Governor Jerry Brown declared a drought state of emergency in January 2014, and the situation was

THE WEST COAST ON THE WORLD STAGE

The West Coast states are clearly destined to remain prominent in the eyes of the world. Home to 50 million, who between them speak almost a hundred languages, it has all the clout of a major nation – it might even end up becoming one, if the current alarming fragmentation of the United States grows any worse. For the last century it's been the epicentre of the global entertainment industry, and even as that role wanes, the region has grown ever more significant as the world's major locus of scientific and technological innovation. Not that it's any way homogenous; its strength lies above all in its diversity, which in turn makes the future seem both endlessly unpredictable, and yet endlessly promising.

WEST COAST FOOD AND DRINK

From salmon to sun-dried tomatoes, tandoori to tacos, the menu of the food-loving West Coast is as varied as its people.

What are you hungry for? One of the most quintessential experiences of touring the West Coast is the food. A multitude of influences and trends have converged here, making this an essential destination for foodies from around the world. Walk just a few blocks in most sizeable cities and you'll face a choice to whet the most cosmopolitan of appetites: noodles and sushi, tacos and burritos, tandoori and curries, pasta and pizza, falafel and bagels, piroshki and baklava, and on through the global menu.

SEASONAL INGREDIENTS

The modern culinary reputation of the West Coast can be traced back to 1971, when chef Alice Waters opened the Chez Panisse restaurant in Berkeley. Inspired by a year spent eating her way around Europe, Waters saw freshness as the cardinal virtue, and cooked foods simply to bring out their natural flavors. Frustrated by an inability to obtain the quality ingredients she'd found in France, she encouraged local purveyors to bring produce to her door. Farmers grew special vegetables to complement specific dishes, and reared livestock and poultry to meticulous specifications. Small-time fishermen sold her their catch, and local oysters were cultivated once more. As Waters-trained chefs branched out on their own, and the Chez Panisse philosophy spread, "California Cuisine" was born, a food movement that emphasizes the use of local, seasonal ingredients.

AN ORGANIC AND SUSTAINABLE APPROACH

Given Westerners' generally eco-friendly leanings, consuming organic foods and promoting sustainable food production has become a badge of honor. Restaurant menus credit their suppliers

Pike Place Market - the oldest farmer's market.

by name – whether by ranch, farm, or cheesemaker. Urbanites buy fresh produce directly from local growers at outdoor farmers markets, where you'll find everything from ripe fruits and seasonal vegetables to sustainably raised beef to cheese, jams, honey, nuts, and herbs.

Seattle's legendary Pike Place Market, the Ferry Building Farmers' Market in San Francisco, and the Original Farmers Market in Los Angeles have become major tourist attractions, while large, popular farmers' markets can also found in Olympia, San Luis Obispo, Santa Monica, and San Diego. Of course, it is easy to shop local in California, whether you're looking for almonds, artichokes, olives, or tomatoes: the state's agricultural industry is the largest in the world, producing more than half of the state's fruits and vegetables. That emphasis on fresh produce ties in with a more general health-focused attitude, so it's no surprise that most restaurants include prominent vegetarian – and often vegan – dishes on their menus.

DIVERSE MENUS

There's much more to West Coast menus that the latest Californian fads, however. You name a world cuisine, and it's here – Peruvian, Korean, Mexican, Vietnamese, Ethiopian, Thai, Japanese, Italian, French, Creole, Chinese. To understand what makes this incredible array possible, it helps to consider the region's geographic and cultural orientation: the influence of Mexican neighbors to the south and Asian neighbors to the west; the vast tracts of rich soil that make this one of the most fertile and productive places on earth; the bounty of fish and seafood to be drawn from the Pacific waters; and, in southern California especially, a climate friendly to growing just about every crop, all year round.

Traditional European fare, especially Italian and French, has long been available, particularly in upscale restaurants. These days, such places are increasingly regionalized, specializing in regional dishes from, for example, Tuscany or Provence.

Above all, it's the citizens of Washington, Oregon, and California who define the local food. The vast majority came from elsewhere in the world – some recently, others a generation or two ago – and brought their native cuisine with them. Sizeable ethnic communities in the larger cities support their own specialty food shops and produce markets, as well as a potentially remarkable number of restaurants (Los Angeles, for example, claims to have around 500 Korean eateries). For the curious diner, the resultant vitality, availability, and diversity makes for a fascinating food experience.

SUCCULENT SEAFOOD

The West Coast is famous for its seafood, and nowhere more so than in Washington and Oregon. The intimate relationship of Northwesterners with salmon, for example, dates back to the various Native American peoples, such as the Chinook, who populated the coast long before the arrival of Europeans. Simply asking for "salmon" hereabouts will get you nowhere – a wider vocabulary is

called for. Thanks to their size and firm, flavorful red flesh, Chinook salmon – also known as king salmon, *tyee* salmon, or Columbia River salmon – are the most highly prized species. coho, or silver salmon, are very common, and yield delicious red meat, while sockeye rank first of all in commercial value even though they aren't the finest tasting. In shops, markets and restaurants, smaller farmed salmon cost less than their "wild" cousins, and tend to taste significantly blander.

Lovers of shellfish are also in for a bonanza. Northwest oysters characteristically have a

Korean grill.

crisp, briny but mild flavor followed by a watermelon-rind-like aftertaste. Southern Puget Sound oysters are noted for their high nutritional content, with meat that is plump with glycogen, yet firm, and very sweet. Most are cultivated on oyster farms, from Washington down into northern California; one Puget Sound hatchery alone, Taylor Shellfish Farms in Shelton, shucks 36 million oysters each year. The only native West Coast oyster, *Ostrea lurida*, also known as the Olympia oyster, is a tiny, slow-growing species that's cherished for its robust, metallic flavor. Driven almost to the point of extinction a century ago, it's now grown alongside imported Japanese varieties including the Pacific, Kumamoto, and Shigako oysters.

Mussels and clams are also widely produced, while the famous Dungeness crab (Cancer magister), has been commercially harvested in the town of Dungeness, Washington, since the mid-1800s. This so-called "cool crab" is regarded as the benchmark for quality, texture and taste. Modem fishermen harvest only the larger males, usually delivering them live to processing plants where they may be prepared for live-air shipment, or cooked and packed ready for market. It is native to Dungeness, see page 127 for more on the area.

Pretty Hood River Valley.

LOCAL SPECIALTIES

Local and regional specialties abound, up and down the West Coast. In California, you can pair tangy sourdough bread with fresh Dungeness crab in San Francisco, while Los Angeles' Koreatown is a hotspot for ethnic authenticity, and East LA is the place for *tacos al pastor* (spicy grilled pork and pineapple). Meanwhile San Diego is famous for fish tacos, and sustainably farmed abalone comes from the North Coast.

Signature Northwestern ingredients include Washington apples, claimed to be "The Best Apples on Earth," and available in such varieties as Fuji, Braeburn, Cameo and the celebrated Pink Lady; pears from Oregon's Hood River and Medford areas; marionberries, boysenberries, and huckleberries; cranberries from the bog fields of western Washington; Oregon's own truffle varieties; and the exquisite Rainier cherry, a creamy yellow-red variety of blushing flavor. Look out especially for Walla Walla onions, originally introduced from Corsica in the 19th century and also known simply as "sweets." So succulent it can be eaten like an apple, the Walla Walla is an onion without "bite." Exceptional and jumbo sized, it's best eaten raw or lightly cooked, and makes a perfect addition to barbecued hamburgers, sandwiches and fresh salads.

DRINKS

There's no separating the manifold eating pleasures of exploring the West Coast from the drinks that go with them. To generalize for a moment, California is especially famous for its wine (see page 63); the Northwest is the spiritual home

⊘ FOOD TRUCKS

One of the most interesting 21st-century food trends has been the unstoppable rise to prominence of high-quality food trucks in cities all over the United States. Effectively small restaurants on wheels, and further boosted during the Covid-19 epidemic for their low overhead expenses and suitability for distanced outdoor dining, food trucks serve everything from burgers and barbecue to donuts or ramen. In entertainment districts especially, many remain open late into the night.

The first food trucks to appear tended to rove at whim from neighborhood to neighborhood, often broadcasting their location for each day's lunch hour on Twitter or their own website. These days, although they're legally required to be capable of motion, they increasingly tend to occupy the same semi-permanent spots, congregating in "pods" so they can share tables, restrooms, and other facilities.

Options for any specific city can easily be found online. In Seattle, look out for Filipino, Native American, Mexican, and Hawaiian trucks; Portland offerings range from Senegalese to soul food, and even Viking flatbreads. San Francisco options include cupcakes, curries and steamed Chinese buns, while Los Angeles is known for south-of-the-border favorites like tacos or ceviche.

of the contemporary international coffee scene; and the entire region is agreed on the virtues of handcrafted beer and ales.

COFFEE

Over the last fifty years, the Pacific Northwest has come to be synonymous with fine coffee. That said, the gospel of coffee has spread so globally that there's little these days to distinguish the undeniably excellent roasters and coffee houses of Washington and Oregon from their counterparts in every international city. Some

HANDCRAFTED ALES

Great beers are part of the fabric of West Coast life. California has more craft breweries than any other state, with Washington and Oregon ranking fifth and eleventh respectively. Oregon in fact surpasses its neighbors in terms of breweries per capita, and played a major role in the renaissance of craft brewing, notably with the opening of Portland's McMenamins brewpub in 1985. Washington and Oregon being responsible for producing around 90 percent of all the hops grown in the US, it's no surprise that the Northwest is known for particularly hoppy beers.

The original Starbucks, Seattle.

of the original credit is of course owing to Starbucks, which opened its first store in Seattle's Pike Place Market in 1971, and now has well over 32,000 locations worldwide, but naturally coffee aficionados eschew chain outlets in favor of the latest independent specialists. Suffice to say, seek and ye shall surely find.

California takes its coffee seriously too. San Francisco's North Beach, for example, is home to much-loved family-run establishments like Caffé Trieste, while Peet's Coffee & Tea (where the founders of Starbucks used to buy beans) originated across the bay in Berkeley. Ritual Coffee Roasters and "artisan micro-roasters" Blue Bottle Coffee Co. approach coffee brewing in much the same way that winemakers approach wine.

With so many beers to choose from, it's impossible to do more than recommend a few current favorites. All the following breweries operate brewpubs in their base cities, many have also opened locations elsewhere, and almost all ship their products for sale in other pubs, statewide and often nationwide too. In Washington, look out for the San Juan Island Brewing Company, Chuckanut Brewery, Cloudburst Brewing, Bellevue Brewing Company, and Twin Sisters Brewing Company. Oregon's top breweries include de Garde Brewing, Cascade Brewing, Migration Brewing and Skyline Brewing Company. And in California, try Modern Times Beer, The Rare Barrel, AleSmith Brewing Company, and Bottle Logic Brewing.

CALIFORNIA WINE

California wines may be world-class, but its winemakers are approachable; from Sonoma to San Luis Obispo, the state's assorted wineries happily welcome 21 million visitors each year.

From the concentrated array of world-class wineries in the breathtaking Napa and Sonoma valleys, to the quiet vineyards of the Santa Barbara region in the south, California wineries are set up to welcome visitors and dazzle with their offerings. Tucked-away wineries in Monterey and Mendocino can give the sense you're the only guest, while at the talked-about vineyards of the Napa Valley you'll feel as though you're in on the latest Wine Country buzz.

CALIFORNIA'S WINE HISTORY

The first winemakers in California were 18th-century Spanish missionaries who need wine to use in religious services. Large-scale vineyards were established around the Los Angeles area in the 1830s by Jean-Louis Vignes, a French vintner. But the true birthplace of California wine is Sonoma County.

Wine grapes were first planted in Sonoma County around 1812 in Fort Ross. Father Jose Altimira, founder of the Mission San Francisco de Solano at Sonoma, and General Vallejo, who colonized Sonoma and Napa counties by granting land to his relatives and friends, were the first northerners to dabble in winemaking. Then Count Agoston Haraszthy, a flamboyant Hungarian political refugee, pushed the Sonoma region into wine stardom. He started out in 1857 at Buena Vista, Northern California's oldest winery, accumulating wine-grape cuttings for California's growers on journeys to Europe. After he died, his protégé Charles Krug, a German political exile, opened Napa Valley's first commercial winery in 1861. By the 1880s, valley wines were winning medals in Europe.

Prohibition almost wiped out California's wine industry, but following its repeal in 1933, Georges

Beringer winery, Napa.

Father Junípero Serra, who founded many of the state's missions, had no taste for California's indigenous wild grapes and instead imported quality vines from his native Spain.

de Latour of Beaulieu Vineyard, the Mondavi family, and others set about resurrecting things. In the 1960s, a wine boom began as large corporations marketed vintage-dated varietal wines at reasonable prices, while small, privately owned wineries produced more expensive, estatebottled wines at higher costs. Old winemaking families were joined by oil barons, engineers, and actors who revitalized old wineries and opened new ones.

California ranks first in wine consumption in the US, followed by Florida, then New York. There are more than 60,000 registered California wine labels.

By 1976, California wines were beating French vintages in European tastings. In the most famous instance, the elite of the French wine industry gathered in Paris for a blind tasting of four white Burgundies against six California Chardonnays. The winner, to the consternation of the French judges, was Chateau Montelena's 1973 Chardonnay.

THE WINE COUNTRY TODAY

In the years since the 1976 grand tasting, California has become the world's fourth-leading wine producer. In the largest international wine competition, the Decanter World Wine Awards, five California wines received platinum medals in 2021, 15 gold, and 76 silver. Some 4,700

Local wines for sale in a wine shop

⊘ WINES OF THE PACIFIC NORTHWEST

Although the wine industry in the Pacific Northwest may be tiny compared to that of California, Washington and Oregon hold around a thousand wineries each, and Washington ranks second only to California in the US in terms of annual production.

The vineyards – and the wines – of the two states are very distinct. Out of more than 60,000 acres (25,000 hectares) of vineyards in Washington, only a hundred or so are in the Puget Sound area. Almost all Washington's grapes are grown instead east of the Cascades, in an arid environment with long, warm, sunny days and cool nights. Once harvested, they're shipped west to wineries concentrated just east of Seattle. The resultant wines are often blends, incorporating grapes from further afield. While reds predominate, using Merlot or Cabernet Sauvignon grapes, the Ste Michelle Winery has become the world's largest producer of Riesling.

Oregon's wine production, on the other hand, centers west of the Cascades, in the fertile and unquestionably damp Willamette Valley, which is the state's agricultural heartland and has been likened to a "cooler, wetter Napa Valley." For over fifty years, it's been especially renowned for its Pinot Noir, but more recently white wines including Pinot Gris and Rieslings have emerged. The warmer and drier parts of southern Oregon, like the Rogue Valley, also produce reds based on Bordeaux and Syrah grapes.

wineries cover the state, from Napa and Sonoma to the Gold Country and Santa Barbara. Indeed, grapes are grown in most of California's counties, and some vintners have discovered pockets of land in Southern California that can match the growing conditions of the great north, especially the south central coast of Santa Barbara and San Luis Obispo counties.

NAPA AND SONOMA VALLEYS

North of San Francisco, the valleys of Napa and Sonoma form the heart of California's

Barrels at Chateau Montelena.

Wine Country. The collection of small towns and villages are set amid miles of vineyards, whose premier grapes are the result of excellent growing conditions: temperate climate and rich, drainable soil. Napa Valley is especially famous for its Cabernet Sauvignon (Merlot and Sangiovese also do well here) and its high-end foodie scene.

Sonoma Valley has a more relaxed, less polished atmosphere than Napa. On the whole it remains less trafficked, especially compared to Napa Valley on weekends. Thanks to the valley's climate and soil variation – Sonoma County can boast more geologically distinct soil types than the whole of France – numerous varietals thrive, including Chardonnay, Cabernet Sauvignon,

Pinot Noir, Merlot, Zinfandel, Syrah, and Sauvignon Blanc.

MENDOCINO COUNTY

Measuring some 35 miles (56km) long by 15 miles (24km) wide, the Mendocino Ridge Wine Country, within Mendocino County, is a non-contiguous trio of burgundy-hued ridges that produce exceptional Zinfandel at high elevations. In 1988, the Kendall-Jackson Winery said the Mendocino Coastal Ridge was one of the world's greatest Zinfandel regions. The area is now achieving recognition for Pinot Noir and more acidic, less oaky, Chardonnay wines.

MONTEREY

An hour south of Silicon Valley, the Monterey Wine Country has around 225 vineyards, concentrated in a 90-mile-long (145km) valley with just eight main viticulture soil types. The northernmost part of Monterey produces Pinot Noir and Chardonnay, while the valley's microclimates help support 42 different varietals. Pick up maps and winery information at Taste of Monterey (700 Cannery Row; www.atasteofmonterey.com), where you can also taste local wines.

SAN JOAQUIN VALLEY AND THE SIERRA FOOTHILLS

The northern wineries produce just a fraction of California's total output. Many of the state's grapes are grown in the hot, arid San Joaquin Valley, several hundred miles south, and are often used to make modestly priced "jug" wines.

⊘ A WINE PRIMER

Winemaking starts at the crusher, which frees juice from grapes. White wines are made from fermented juice; added yeast converts sugar to alcohol and carbon dioxide, with fermentation occurring in stainless steel tanks. Leaving yeast in creates dry wines; stopping yeast action makes sweeter wines. Sparkling wine begins the same way, then undergoes another fermentation. Carbon dioxide is trapped within the bottle, creating bubbles. For red wines, grape skin and pulp are included in the fermenting tank. After adding yeast, grape skins are pressed, then reds are aged in stainless steel or wooden tanks. The wine is clarified, then aged further before bottling.

The Sierra Nevada foothill's 10 counties are now home to more than 250 wineries, including Renwood in Plymouth (Amador Country). Many of these wineries are small and family-owned, and they excel at full-bodied Zinfandel, Syrah, and Petite Syrah. Rhone-style white varietals are also found here.

SANTA YNEZ VALLEY

Just 35 miles (56km) from the beaches of Santa Barbara, the charmingly rustic Santa Inez Valley consists of six distinctive towns: Santa Ynez,

Windmills at Solvang.

Solvang, Los Alamos, Los Olivos, Ballard, and Buellton. Pinot Noir, Chardonnay, and Syrah can be tasted here, along with other varietals. Don't miss the Scandinavian-influenced Solvang either.

SAN LUIS OBISPO

The rocky volcanic soil and marine influence of San Luis Obispo's Edna Valley, Arroyo Grande Valley, and Avila Valley produce grapes with complex flavors and intense varietal character. Small, family-owned wineries in this area pro-

Chardonnay vines.

duce primarily Pinot Noir, Chardonnay, Viognier, Syrah, Grenache, and Zinfandel wines. In Paso Robles, the three-day Paso Robles Wine Festival held annually in May is the state's largest outdoor wine tasting.

TEMECULA VALLEY

The Temecula Valley (32miles/51km north of San Diego) is emerging as California's southernmost wine country. A unique microclimate – with morning mist, cooling ocean air, warm midday sun, and clear nights – and granite-based soil are producing excellent Syrah, Cabernet, and Zinfandel grapes. Popular wineries include Bailey Winery, Maurice Car'rie and Brair Rose, the latter with *Snow White* replica cottages.

FINE WINES OF CALIFORNIA

California's more than 4,000 wineries produce over 80 percent of the country's wine. The quality is just as high as the quantity, with California wines continuing to win awards and worldwide critical acclaim.

In the 18th century, when the Franciscan fathers first started to make wine, the grapes were dumped into troughs, trampled into pulp, and hung in cow skins to ferment before leaking into casks. "In those days the flavor was not described with enthusiasm," wrote the Napa Historical Society's Meredie Porterfield, "but that is what passed for wine in early LA."

California wine has come a long way since then, in terms of both quality and quantity. Today, the state accounts for more than 80 percent of total US wine production, and more than any individual country outside Europe. Reliably warm weather allows wineries to use very ripe fruit, which makes for a fruitier wine, rather than the earthy flavors of Europe. It also means higher alcohol levels – some Californian wines have over 13.5 percent.

Napa and Sonoma get the lion's share of publicity, despite producing less than a quarter of the wine. Many more millions of gallons emanate from the San Joaquin Valley, the so-called "jug wines" that are mass-produced and more moderately priced. Other major wine areas are around Mendocino, Lake County, Paso Robles, Livermore, the Santa Ynez Valley near Santa Barbara, and, in the far south, the emerging vineyards of Temecula.

Despite increasing sophistication in bottling and manufacturing, basic winemaking has changed very little over the centuries. Wine is, after all, just fermented grape juice, not manufactured but generated by living yeast cells that ferment grape sugars into grape alcohol.

For more about wine and the Wine Country, see pages 241 and 191.

SUSTAINABLE WINEGROWING

Sustainable winegrowing and winemaking practices are a constantly evolving trend in California. Many

California wines are now labelled organic, meaning they have no added sulphites to prolong shelf life, that no synthetic pesticides or nonorganic chemicals were used in production, and natural alternatives were used for soil enrichment, pests, weeds, and vine disease management.

Additionally, vintners and growers who represent one-quarter of the state's wine acreage, and 40 percent of the annual wine case production, currently participate in the voluntary Code of Sustainable Wine Growing program. Introduced in 2003, the code aims to establish environmental standards and practices from

Ripe for the picking.

ground to glass, including methods that minimize pesticide use, reduce water and energy use, build healthy soil, protect air and water quality, recycle natural resources, and maintain surrounding habitats.

Examples of such sustainable winemaking practices include using sheep, bats, and beneficial birds to control weeds and pests, using drip irrigation and process ponds to conserve water, and composting and recycling to minimize waste.

In 2012, the California Sustainable Winegrowing Alliance (CCSW) developed a third-party certification program related to the California Sustainable Winegrowing Program (SWP) – essentially like a LEED (Leadership in Energy and Environmental Design) certification scheme for wineries.

Mount Rainier National Park.

THE GREAT OUTDOORS

Like surfers waiting for a wave, West Coast outdoors enthusiasts float on a sea of possibilities: from extreme mountain biking and wilderness backpacking to gentle bike trails and ocean kayaking.

For West Coast residents – and visitors, too – the outdoors is synonymous with activity. And there are endless ways to enjoy the breathtaking landscape of the West, from diving to kayaking, and windsurfing to whale-watching. Whether you're a novice or an expert, the West Coast is filled with outdoor adventure schools, clubs, rental shops, outfitters, and guides to help you get going.

CAMPING

Looking to pitch a tent? Hiking and camping go hand in hand in California, Washington, and Oregon alike, where almost every state park has its own campground. Whether you want to camp with your car nearby and access to showers and bathrooms, or backpack into the wilderness for a few days, you'll find plenty of options to choose from all along the coast. Just be sure to plan ahead; many campsites book up a year in advance.

CYCLING AND MOUNTAIN BIKING

Just north of the Golden Gate Bridge, opposite San Francisco, the Marin Headlands and Mount Tamalpais are considered the birthplace of mountain biking. Miles of scenic trails are perfect for this bouncy recreation, though bikers share many routes with hikers and equestrians. Across the bay, road cyclists take long Wine Country tours on the rolling hills that wind through the vineyards. California's central coast also has many great biking trails.

Prime biking areas in Washington include Tiger Mountain State Forest just east of Seattle; the region around Bellingham north of Seattle, and also nearby Orcas Island; and Dry Hill outside Port Angeles at the northern tip of the Olympic Peninsula. Oregon holds some great

Bike trails in Marin County.

coastal biking opportunities, including the Whiskey Run Mountain trails near Coos Bay, while not far inland the rugged terrain of the Rogue River–Siskiyou National Forest offers memorable challenges.

DIVING

Scuba diving is extremely popular in Monterey – rated by *Scuba Diving* magazine as having the best beach dives in the US – and along the coast to the south. Some 65,000 divers from all over the world explore the waters of the Monterey Bay Sanctuary each year. Safe conditions and good visibility are part of the draw but it's the kelp forest in an underwater canyon that everyone wants to experience. Long and spindly at

Sharks are under far more predatorial pressure from man than surfers and windsurfers are from them; many biologists fear that the prehistoric fish are being hunted to extinction out of misplaced fear and misunderstanding.

the base, stretching up to form thick mats at the surface, the kelp ranges all along the coast, forming fantastic underwater forests through

make cold-water diving gear essential – a 7mm wetsuit, hood, booties, fins, mask, snorkel, along with 20lbs/9kg of lead to sink all that neoprene. Even as far north as Puget Sound, there are still many popular sites, including for example Fort Casey State Park on Whidbey Island.

FISHING

Up and down the West Coast, you can cast from rocks or piers, or head out onto the ocean to probe the depths for salmon, sturgeon, ling cod, rockfish, and other denizens of the deep.

Scuba divers get up close to a great white shark.

which divers swim in search of the Garibaldi, ling cod, and many types of rockfish. Bluefish and Whalers Coves at Point Lobos, Lovers Point in Pacific Grove, and Monterey State Beach, San Carlos Beach and McAbee Beach in Monterey are popular beach dives for all levels of divers. For the more advanced, try Monastery Beach and Carmel River State Beach in Carmel.

Diving is also popular among the kelp beds in the San Luis Obispo region, the Santa Catalina Islands, and Channel Islands National Park, while shark-diving (in cages) can also be arranged out by the Farallon Islands near San Francisco.

Further north in California, and up into the Pacific Northwest, cooler sea temperatures

Whether it's a serious charter vessel you're after, or you're more the "party boat" type, day- or half-day fishing expeditions are easy to arrange in resorts and harbors from Southern California up to Washington. Major fishing destinations in the Northwest include Gold Beach, Newport, and Astoria on Oregon, and Neah Bay and Ilwaco. Freshwater fishing is also widely available, for example on Oregon's Rogue River.

From California right up to Puget Sound, there's unusual and bone-chilling sport to be had pursuing surf smelt: the fisherman uses a big triangular net on a frame, plunging the net into oncoming breaking waves, and tends to get soaked completely. Nets are widely available for rent; the smelt, sometimes caught by the bucketful, are deep fried for dinner then eaten whole.

HIKING

Peppered with state parks, national parks, and wilderness areas, the West Coast provides superlative opportunities for hikers of all levels of energy and experience.

Favored hiking destinations in Washington include, along the coast, the Pacific frontage of Olympic National Park, especially the 17-mile (27km) trail through the North Olympic Coastal

On rainy spring days in the forest slopes above Sonoma, thousands of red-bellied salamanders come out of the woodwork (literally), crawling to the stream beds to spawn.

of the Cascades, and the five-day Rogue River National Recreation Trail.

While many of western California's best hiking trails are to be found in the far north, for

The vast Oregon Dunes offer some great hiking trails.

Wilderness from Rialto Beach to Sand Point, and the hike out to Cape Flattery at the northwest tip of the Olympic Peninsula. There are some spectacular trails up in Mount Rainier National Park, too, while hiking the slopes of Mount Constitution, on Orcas Island in the San Juans, can be utterly exhilarating.

Oregon too offers some dramatic shoreline hikes, for example amid the mighty seafront sand dunes of Oregon Dunes National Recreation Area, or overlooking the ocean from lush Cape Sebastian. For serious adventurers, it also holds some demanding but wonderful long-distance backpacking trails, including the Pacific Crest National Scenic Trail, traversing the remote Sky Lakes Wilderness along the spine

example in Redwood National Park and its various associated state parks, there are also plenty of exciting spots along the coast further south, such as Julia Pfeiffer Burns State Park south of Big Sur. There's wilderness to explore inland, too, as in Pinnacles National Park, 50 miles (80km) east of Monterey, and the enormous Trinity Alps Wilderness Area, up north.

For full lists of state parks and information on their hiking trails and campsites, visit www.parks.ca.gov, https://stateparks.oregon.gov, and www.parks.wa.gov. In general, most parks offer trails with various skill levels, and provide trail maps at visitor centers that help you plan your hikes. Most parks charge a small day-use fee or parking fee.

KAYAKING

A popular pastime in Monterey is to rent simple open-topped kayaks, known as "scuppers," to paddle out to the local kelp beds. There you're likely to encounter one of California's most delightful wild animals, the winsome and intelligent sea otter, once hunted for its fur but now a favorite of animal lovers. The creatures are often seen floating on their backs with an infant sleeping on their belly, lolling about in the water, fastidiously cleaning their fur or crunching on some just-caught shellfish. Other great

Oregon kayakers particularly favor the coast around Tillamook, where the mouth of the Nehalem River makes a good spot from which to emerge onto the open waters of ocean, while around Washington's San Juan Islands, further north, sea kayakers can enjoy some magnificent wildlife-spotting.

SAILING AND WINDSURFING

Sailing is a much-loved activity all along the West Coast. Up in Washington, it's the islands of Puget Sound and the Strait of Juan de Fuca

Surfing competitions are a regular at Moro Bay.

Sailing under the iconic Golden Gate Bridge.

California destinations for beginners include Morro Bay, Sausalito, and Tomales Bay, while more experienced sea kayakers will gravitate towards the Channel Islands, Santa Catalina Island, and La Jolla.

Washington and Oregon may be famous for spectacular beaches and coastal scenery, but their powerful and dangerous waves, replete with riptides and undertows, make it safest to do any actual swimming in the Pacific in Southern California.

that see the most action; the San Juan Islands in particular abound in operators and sailing schools. Further south, sailing is big business in both Northern California – especially around San Francisco Bay, Santa Cruz, and Monterey – and all along the Southern California coast from Malibu down to San Diego in places like Montecito, Encinitas and Oceanside.

Windsurfing is a much bigger deal in California than in Oregon and Washington, though the northern states do offer opportunities around the mouth of the Columbia River, and in Puget Sound. On a spring or summer afternoon, you're likely to encounter hundreds of windsurfers south of San Francisco, braving the cracking swells and blowing sands of Gazos

Creek, Scott Creek, and Waddell Creek. The last is considered one of the best windsurfing spots in the country, where experts are often spotted jumping waves and pulling spectacular aerial maneuvers. Windsurfing is also popular at Jalama Beach County Park on the end of Point Conception, the jutting corner of California where the coast turns east. Wind that whips across the point propels windsurfers up and over the biggest and ugliest of the waves.

SURFING

If you're looking to incorporate a spot of surfing into your West Coast itinerary, then it makes the most sense to do so in California, the state that did so much to popularize the sport worldwide. Recreational and competitive surfers alike take to the waves along the Californian coast. The San Diego and Los Angeles shorelines are particularly popular – the 130-mile (210km) stretch between the two cities stands out for the sharp blue line of the ocean. The water is warm here, pushed north by the Japan current, while the swells are manageable in most places, even for novice surfers. Although surfing has become a rather territorial pastime, and gained a somewhat unfriendly reputation, if you're willing to settle for mushy waves, you can paddle out at almost any non-surfing beach and be assured of a good time.

Other popular waves are found at San Luis Obispo's long beaches, which are interspersed with high cliffs. In the north, competitive surfing is found closer to Santa Cruz. Off the coast of Half Moon Bay, an annual surfing competition is held at Mavericks.

WHITEWATER RAFTING

Whitewater rafting, concentrated in Oregon and northern California, has become hugely popular among thrill-seeking West Coast visitors. The precise dates of rafting season vary from river to river and year to year, but most operators tend to offer excurions from April through September.

The region's finest rafting river has to be the Rogue River in Oregon, which was one of the eight original US rivers that were protected by the Wild and Scenic Rivers Act of 1968. More specifically, it's the 33 miles (53km) of rapids along river's 84-mile (135km) central section,

California's huge Sacramento River is the source of all kinds of water fun: canoeing, swimming, boating, and even floating in the tube of a truck tire for hours.

known as the Wild Rogue, which attracts all the attention. While the Wild Rogue segment ends just a few miles short of Gold Beach on the Pacific, most rafting operators are based way

Inviting waters in Monterey.

upstream, especially in Grants Pass.

In California, the Sacramento area is popular with whitewater rafters of all abilities, while adrenalin junkies seek out the thundering rapids of Burnt Ranch Falls on the Trinity, and the cataracts of Hell's Corner Gorge or the Ikes Falls on the Klamath. The breathtaking forest drops of the California salmon are at once beautiful and thrilling.

If thrill seeking isn't your thing, you can float for many days in inflatable kayaks with nary a ripple on the lower Klamath River and parts of the Trinity. Within sight of fertile vineyards and cottage-style wineries, the Russian River and Cache Creek are popular rafting and canoeing streams.

SAND AND SURF

Rocky shores, sandy beaches and buoyant water make the Pacific Northwest the perfect habitat for sea anemones, plovers, dolphins, and whales.

"Bold shafts of light race across the pinks and purples of the irregular substrate ... twisted bullwhips embrace the tangled masses of bladderwrack and laver ... highlights of red and orange lifeforms ... grinding rocks ... groaning timber." A commentary on Picasso's last canvas? A transmission from the space probe? No, just a page from the notebook of a Northwest tide pooler. Other entries penciled in this weather-beaten volume describe days spent searching for razor clams on a beach in Puget Sound, watching whales from a windswept overlook on the Pacific Ocean, and launching a kite from a rolling sand dune.

Lovers of the outdoors escape to the unrestricted, unchanged splendor of the thousands of miles of wild aquatic habitats along the beaches, preserves, bays, and estuaries that line Puget Sound, the San Juan Islands, and the open coasts of Oregon, Washington, and northern California. Here, an unrivaled abundance of birds, mammals, fish, and invertebrates populate the seaboard.

Northern California's dramatic coastline.

SEASHORE HABITATS

The shores here are fresh and new. As the glaciers receded to reveal virgin stretches of land, seawater moved in, gradually sculpting the volcanic rock and cobbled till into notched fjords, buttresses and spires. Rocky shores, placid sandy strips, and mixed beaches of stones, sand and silt developed between the prominent glacial sculptures. Each type of beach brings with it its own wildlife ecology – plants and animals particular to their own eco-niche. Beach walkers can discover many distinctive habitats and identify hundreds of plants and animals between the tidemarks of the Northwestern seashore.

Rocky habitats are common along northern shores of Washington's Olympic Peninsula and the Strait of Juan de Fuca, while jagged granite boulders, eroded sandstone pillars, blowholes, and arches punctuate the Oregon coast at regular intervals. Crashing waves pound the cliffs in a continuous state of war, regaining the very fortresses that sprang from the ocean during the postglacial epochs. Many of the craggy northern beaches are fringed by forests of evergreen, spruce, cedar, hemlock, and fir. Trees cling perilously to the eroded cliffs, while far below lie casualties of the never-ending struggle – bleached tangles of driftwood heaped at the water's edge.

The interior beaches of the southern Puget Sound are peaceful reminders of passive resistance as sand and mud, slowly deposited by rivers and streams, reclaim the bays and inlets. The characteristic aroma of intertidal life is salty, sandy and a little earthy. Regional aquaculturists have honed the science of shellfish production, yielding the Quilcene oyster and, more recently, a tasty but diminutive Olympic cousin, the Yaquina. When tidal conditions and harvest quotas permit, these calm bays are the best places to search for clams or mussels. Throughout the year, bird-watchers tally a full roster of gulls, sandpipers, plovers, and ducks. The coarse-grained coastal sand beaches of southern Washington and central Oregon may be slim on marine life, but they're rich in rolling dunes and flowering dune grasses.

EXPLORING SEASHORE GARDENS

The Northwest Straits marine ecosystem is naturally interconnected from mountain tops to deep fjord bottoms, from tiny invertebrates to top predators like the killer whale, and from Pacific Ocean tides to fresh waters from rivers and streams. Where the 40–50°F (4–10°C) Japanese current bathes the shore in nutrients from offshore upwelling, the sea blossoms forth strange and beautiful life-forms. This nurturing environment stacks animal upon animal, and color upon texture, in a subtle gradient of life to fill every niche.

The moving waters of the straits bathe kelp beds and reefs close to rocky shores, while kelp and other seaweeds in turn provide food, shelter, and camouflage for prey species. Reefs harbor a distinctive fish community including rockfish and lingcod, as well as the birds and mammals that prey on them. Invertebrates clinging to the rocks draw divers from around the world: sponges, mollusks, crustaceans, sea stars, urchins, sea cucumbers, and, above all, edible shellfish like abalone.

Sea anemones are known as the "flowers of the sea." Strikingly colored relatives of the jellyfish and corals, they use harpoon-like threads on their radial tentacles to ensnare floating prey. Pink and green aggregate anemones resemble faded flowers, like zinnias. Covering the cobbled rocks of mixed beaches, they can divide like an amoeba to form countless clones. A favorite of tide poolers, the green anemone is a true sea farmer. It gets its luminescent body cast from

zoochlorellae, a microscopic green algae cultivated within its tissues. The real flowers in this aquatic garden are the red-headed, and red, and green anemones, the largest and most brilliantly colored deepwater blossoms, glimpsed only during extremely low tides.

Another pigment from nature's palette is in the purple or ochre sea star, a five-rayed, rough-skinned hunter of shellfish. Other stars contribute equally vibrant hues – walkers on the beaches frequently find the bright-red blood star, dusky rose star, and safety-orange

Urticina piscivora on the seabed.

and blue-streaked sun star. A colossus among Pacific sea stars, the twenty-rayed star attains a length of 3ft (1m), and can have as many as 24 arms. The thorns in this rose garden are red, purple and green sea urchins, bristling pincushions related to the sea stars. Urchins thrive in various habitats, from surging surf-swept beaches to the calmer kelp-forested inlets. Huge red urchins prefer deep-water lairs, congregating in prickly mats at the bottom of tidepools.

SNACKTIME FOR SHOREBIRDS

As the tide moves out, shorebirds move in to snack on the litter of live and dead beach animals. The tranquility is shattered by the clamorous squawks of herring, mew, and glaucous winged gulls, squabbling voraciously among themselves for leftovers. In the mud-flats, dunlins, whimbrels, plovers, sandpipers, and killdeers gingerly negotiate the exposed bottom with slender legs and long beaks, in search of shellfish, crabs, and worms. Farther from shore, waterfowl – coots, scaups, and buf-fleheads – tread water, passively feeding on floating plants, or diving to root in the sediment. A large silvery-backed Arctic loon stops fishing to emit a long, yodeling cry. In the fall, yet more

Cormorants can be found around Seattle.

waterfowl arrive from the far north. Their num-bers soar as handsome canvasbacks, widgeons, and harlequin ducks join them in their offshore flotilla.

On the remote outer shores, black oyster-catchers use their chisel-shaped beaks to pry limpets from rocks or chip away mussel shells. Tufted puffins dive through the waves and fill their brilliantly banded beaks with herring and surf smelt, then alight beside stately rhinoceros auklets in their island rookeries. An elegant, great blue heron silently stalks through the grasses that line a salt marsh. Visitors won't forget sighting their first bald eagle, surveying the shoreline panorama from an eyrie atop a sturdy cedar tree.

FISH POPULATIONS

Something like 220 fish species inhabit the waters of Washington and Oregon. Many are less abundant than they were just a few years ago – often alarmingly so. Puget Sound especially has suffered significant losses; stocks of long-lived rockfish are low, and lingcod stocks have col-lapsed. Herring, hake, and pollock stocks are at average levels in the Strait of Georgia, but reduced in Puget Sound, while Pacific cod have become badly depleted. English sole appear to be averagely common in both areas. Only the spiny dogfish is in historically high abundance, while the size of sardine schools seems to fluc-tuate, rising – and thus bringing record num-bers of salmon and other aquatic species – at the end of each El Niño cycle.

MARINE MAMMALS

At the top of the food chain are the marine mammals: the cetaceans (whales, dolphins, and porpoises); sea otters; and the pinnipeds (seals and sea lions). By evolutionary standards, all are recent arrivals to the ocean coast, yet they show a mastery of the aquatic realm, relishing the diversity of marine life along the Northwest's broad expanses of unoccupied coast.

To spy the sleek, 6ft (2m), dorsal fin of a speed-ing orca, see a barnacle-encrusted gray whale, or catch a glimpse of a lone sea lion peering out from between the waves – these are unforget-table high points of a beach stroll or ferry ride. While many such animals were once ruthlessly slaughtered by whalers and fur traders, they now receive rigorous Federal protection. Some North-west species, like the Washington sea otter, sur-vive only in token populations, but several have staged dramatic comebacks.

Commonly known as the killer whale, the 30ft (9m) orca is the largest and most impres-sive member of the dolphin family. These glossy black-and-white predators were formerly har-pooned or shot at by suspicious fishermen, for whom they represent competition as unsur-passed hunters of salmon, cod, sharks, and seals, but there are no records of them assault-ing humans. Orcas travel in family groups called pods. As of 2022, three such groups, consisting of around 75 individuals – identifiable by subtle differences in fin and body markings – are year-round residents of Puget Sound.

PLANNING A BEACH WALK

Beach walkers should always consult a tide table before setting out. These indispensable charts – available online, or from boating or fishing supply stores – detail the time and magnitude of daily high and low tides. As Northwest tides can rise 10ft (3m), an enticing stretch of easy shoreline can be under several feet of seawater six hours later, running the risk of leaving unwary hikers stranded, as tides sneak in to fill the route behind them, or even drowned. Note, too, that long stretches of the Pacific shorelines have dangerous undertows. Many places are not suitable for swimming, and even surf walking can be unsafe.

By checking the tides, beach walkers might also be rewarded by seeing habitats or shore life that are exposed to daylight only a few times each year. Studying a good field identification guide will add enjoyment to any shore walk, while visiting an aquarium or nature center can give you a good preview of fish you may encounter.

WHALE-WATCHING

Every year, something like 20,000 gray whales migrate 5,500 miles (8,900km) between the Arctic and their breeding grounds off Southern California and Mexico. As they pass in each direction, they can be seen off the coasts of Washington, Oregon and California, heading south between December and early February, and back north from March until May. Adult males, immature whales of both genders, and females without calves make the journey "home" first, while the females with their newborn calves arrive in May. Early morning hours, prior to the onset of wind-blown whitecaps, are the best time to see them. Scan the horizon for a "blow" – a whale's exhalation into the air – and stay with it. Other whales should follow.

Whether you want to join a whale-watching cruise out on the ocean, or find a suitable headland in one of the many coastal state parks, would-be whale-spotters can choose between an array of great locations that line the entire West Coast. Washington's San Juan Islands offer cruises galore, while the beaches of the Olympic Peninsula make fabulous vantage points. In Oregon, Depoe Bay is the center of whale-watching activity, with its own resident pod just offshore

in summer, while Coos Bay and Lincoln City also hold plenty of operators. Options along the coast in Northern California include Dana Point, Point Reyes, and Redwood National and State Parks, while Santa Barbara and San Diego (especially Cabrillo National Monument at Point Loma) are good bets in Southern California.

Arguably California's finest whale-watching site is the Farallon Islands, just 27 miles (43km) from San Francisco's Fisherman's Wharf. Once called the "Devil's Teeth," these jagged outcroppings are off-limits to the public, but pro-

The coast offers great whale watching opportunities.

vide a rich sanctuary for 23 species of marine mammals, including 18 types of whales and dolphins, plus seals, seabirds, and great white sharks. San Francisco Whale Tours (https://sanfranciscowhaletours.com) runs full-day expeditions from Fort Mason to the Gulf of the Farallones on weekends from November through June. Get up close to gray, blue, and humpback whales, dolphins, seals, and sea lions as the boat sails from Fisherman's Wharf beneath the Golden Gate Bridge to the roiling waters of the Pacific Ocean. They also offer 2.5-hour whale-watching tours in the Bay. Be sure to dress warmly (the weather is San Francisco changes quickly), and bear in mind that the open ocean waters outside the Golden Gate can be quite choppy.

Early movie set from the 1930s.

MOVIE MAKERS

LA's film industry has enjoyed a century of star-making and style-setting; Hollywood itself may be past its prime, but it's still a must-see for movie fans.

Even though it started out elsewhere, for most people the movie business remains inextricably associated with Hollywood. The early studios grew up on or around Sunset Boulevard, and it was here that the major changes of the 20th century took place, from silence to sound and from black-and-white to color. Sunset Boulevard, the quintessential movie about the early days of cinema, was released in 1950, and if anything, the story of California's movie industry has only grown more interesting since then.

> *William Laurie Dickson is on record at the Library of Congress as producer of the earliest movie: Fred Ott's Sneeze (1890), in which he captured an assistant sneezing.*

THE START OF THE MOVIE INDUSTRY

The moving picture was actually invented as the result of a bet. In 1877, English eccentric Eadweard Muybridge helped California governor Leland Stanford win a $25,000 wager by using 12 cameras to film a galloping horse and printing the individual shots onto a revolving disk, thus proving that a trotting horse has all four hooves off the ground simultaneously. Tripling his battery of cameras, Muybridge devised faster film, mounted his photographs on a wheel combined with light, and called his process Zoopraxiscope.

The Paris inventor Étienne-Jules Marey improved on this by developing a photographic gun, with a long barrel for the lens, and a circular photographic plate that rotated 12 times during the single second the shot was being taken – the first movie camera. By 1888, George

Thomas Edison and George Eastman, 1925.

Eastman had produced celluloid film and the Kodak camera in New York, while in New Jersey Thomas Edison added sprockets to synchronize the sound.

THE MOVE TO HOLLYWOOD

Hollywood's first census, in 1907, showed its population as 3,500, including 103 immigrants from England, 102 from Germany, 86 from Canada, 20 from France, 28 from Ireland, 24 from Scotland, and 158 from New York. Also present was film director Francis Boggs, visiting from Chicago's Selig Polyscope Studios, then battling over patents with Thomas Edison's movie trust.

A year later, filming the Count of Monte Cristo during a severe Illinois winter, Boggs recalled the warmth of Hollywood and moved cast and crew to Laguna Beach to complete the production, thereby becoming the first director to shoot at least part of a film in California.

Four years later, Carl Laemmle's Universal Film Manufacturing Company began operations at Sunset and Gower, absorbing the Nestor Film Company, which had made Hollywood's first studio film, The Law of the Range. Eventually, his company moved through the Cahuenga Pass to found Universal City. Meanwhile, Cecil B. de Mille, Jesse Lasky, Samuel Goldfish (later

THE EARLY YEARS

At first, films were shot casually around Hollywood, using private homes for domestic dramas; banks were taken over during weekends for hold-up scenes, and passersby conscripted for crowd shots. Soon, though, the days when sound pioneer Jack Foley could simulate galloping horses with coconut shells in a sandbox gave way to times when the people required to make a film included visual effects researchers, recording mixers, wranglers, gaffers, dialect coaches, and boom operators, not to mention caterers.

School of Cinematic Arts, USC.

The Partners Statue, Disney Studios.

Goldwyn), and Arthur Friend formed a company under Lasky's name. Finding the scenery in Arizona unsuitable to make The Squaw Man, starring Dustin Farnum, they continued west to Hollywood, completing the film at a rented barn one block north of Sunset.

Charlie Chaplin was not impressed with LA when he first visited in 1910, on tour with Fred Karno's variety troupe. It was, he thought, "an ugly city, hot and oppressive, and the people looked sallow and anemic."

In 1924, Metro and Goldwyn – studios that had moved onto the former lot where the Pickford–Fairbanks studio had begun in 1922 – were merged. Motion Picture Weekly quoted Mayer as saying they aimed to produce 52 films per year, hoping to fill the 250,000 seats owned by the Loews theater chain.

This era saw the birth of the system under which directors virtually ceased to be independent agents and became employees of "a massive, assembly-line organization." So began the great debate about studio versus artist, commercialism versus personal integrity, and "the desecration of great masterpieces and promising careers through the insensitivity of philistine management," as Gary Carey put it in his biography of Mayer.

> *In the early days, Gower Gulch – at Sunset and Gower – became the rendezvous of would-be movie cowboys hoping to work for the small companies operating nearby. The formation of Central Casting eliminated this casual approach.*

THE TALKIES

By 1927, cinema attendances were slumping. The four Warner brothers – Harry, Albert, Sam,

Movie director, Billy Wilder, 1991.

and Jack – had added a musical background to their film Don Juan (John Barrymore and Mary Astor), which was greeted enthusiastically. Then they had Al Jolson say a few words in The Jazz Singer. Despite consisting largely of background music plus a few songs, the picture made millions and forced the other studios into sound.

In July 1928, Warner released The Lights of New York, another instant hit. One month later, MGM's trademark, Leo the lion, roared from the screen showing a semi-documentary called White Shadows in the South Seas. After a scene from the first MGM sound film, Broadway Melody, was re-shot, MGM experimented with leaving the music as it was and having the players mime the number for the cameras – the start

of pre-recording. It cost $280,000, grossed $4 million, and won the best picture Oscar in the Academy's third year of awards.

THE BIG FIVE

By the 1930s, the movie industry was dominated by the "Big Five" majors, all with production studios, large theater chains, and worldwide distribution – Warner Brothers, Loews Theatres (which owned MGM), Paramount Pictures, 20th Century Fox, and RKO – while Universal, Columbia, and United Artists (set up by Chaplin, Pick-

Producer, Lewis J. Selznick.

ford, Fairbanks, and Griffith to distribute their work and that of other independents) played minor roles.

The development of color on celluloid had progressed enough by 1934 for production to start on Walt Disney's first full-length animated feature, Snow White and the Seven Dwarfs, an assemblage

> *Nickelodeons were cheap theaters, usually set up in converted storefronts, that provided entertainment (tickets cost just five cents, or one nickel) that even non-English-speaking immigrants could enjoy.*

> *US Courts ruled in 1947 that as the film studios' method of production and distribution violated anti-trust laws, studios must divest themselves of their theater chains. It took Loews 10 years to finalize this move.*

of 250,000 individually painted frames. Developed by David Selznick, Gone With the Wind was MGM's top-grossing release of 1939 and 1940. After Selznick borrowed money and Clark Gable from Mayer, Loews got to distribute the movie and MGM received 50 percent of the film's profits.

MOVIES AND POLITICS

The world of 1940 held almost 100,000 movie houses. A third were in Russia, twice as many as in the US. Every country's film industry needed foreign sales in order to be viable, which created a touchy situation for the US with the rise of Nazism because Germany was a major market for US films. MGM was cautious; only once

Vitascope was an early motion picture projector, circa 1896.

⊘ CENSORSHIP

From the very start, there were reformers who wanted to censor movies and keep the industry under some restraints. In 1921 and 1922, scandals like the Fatty Arbuckle rape case, actor Wallace Reid's drug death, and the unsolved murder of director William Desmond Taylor lent them ammunition, even as films were appealing to wider audiences. In the words of author Lewis Jacobs, "as the poor became less important as the mainstay of the movies, the ideals and tribulations of the masses lost some of their importance as subject matter."

Hoping to pre-empt would-be censors, the industry invited Will H. Hays, an Indiana crony of President Warren G. Harding, to be its moral watchdog. Just months after taking office, Hays banned Arbuckle from the screen. His authority as head of the otherwise toothless National Association of the Motion Picture Industry was only moral – a smokescreen, charged some critics – but for a while, most producers obeyed at least the letter of the law. Late in the 1920s, however, such daring productions as Raoul Walsh's Sadie Thompson, in which Gloria Swanson portrayed the sad prostitute of W. Somerset Maugham's novel Rain, and the MGM filming of Michael Arlen's banned The Green Hat as a vehicle for Greta Garbo, reduced the Hays office's credibility.

Germany had actually declared war on Poland did it start producing anti-Nazi films.

In 1947, the House Un-American Activities Committee (HUAC) targeted the industry for promoting communist propaganda, and influential columnists urged a boycott of "red" actors. The Hollywood Ten were cited for contempt and denied work, but most top stars escaped attention.

THE ULTIMATE HOLLYWOOD MOVIE

When director Billy Wilder and producer Charles Brackett finished their script for Sunset Boulevard in 1949, they were "acutely conscious of the fact that we lived in a town which had been swept by social change so profound as that brought about in the old South by the Civil War. Overnight the coming of sound brushed gods and goddesses into obscurity. At first, we saw [the heroine] as a kind of horror woman ... an embodiment of vanity and selfishness. But as we went along, our sympathies became deeply involved with the woman who had been given the brush by 30 million fans."

Several former silent stars were approached: Mae West, then 55; Mary Pickford, 57; and Pola Negri, 51. All rejected the role as too close to real life. The final choice, Gloria Swanson, 50, had left Hollywood a decade earlier after a 45-movie career that began as a teenager in Mack Sennett comedies. Swanson embraced a lifestyle that typified its time – extravagant parties at which hundreds of the movie elite were presented with gold cigarette cases as party favors.

Sunset Boulevard, which portrayed the pathos of a former silent superstar in her declining years in a broken-down Hollywood mansion, struck a chord with critics as the ultimate inside-Hollywood movie. It garnered 11 Academy Award nominations and won three Oscars, but not everyone city was pleased with its depiction of the industry. "You bastard," shouted an outraged Louis B. Mayer to Wilder at a screening on the Paramount lot. "You have disgraced the industry that made and fed you. You should be tarred and feathered and run out of Hollywood."

THE MODERN MOVIE INDUSTRY

Today, the movie industry is much more decentralized. Once controlled by a small number of people, it's now a complex network. Instead of a studio-based system, films are produced all over the world.

> "The public wanted us to live like kings and queens," Swanson recalled. "We were making more money than we ever dreamed existed and there was no reason to believe it would ever stop."

To be sure, the movie business is still thriving in LA, where every other person seems somehow connected to "the industry." The largest studios are still here, marketing and distributing

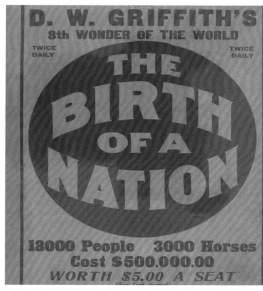

Poster for D.W. Griffiths 1915 fil, The Birth of a Nation.

films made by smaller production companies. Most TV shows are still produced in LA, and the San Fernando Valley is arguably the pornography capital of the world.

As for Hollywood itself, it's now a homage to days of yore, where tourists peruse the Walk of Fame while struggling actors and actresses wait tables and tend bars. Movie stars themselves are a different breed nowadays. Unless it's Oscars night, you're unlikely to see a celebrity in Hollywood; they tend to reside on the coast, in Malibu or Santa Monica, or in exclusive neighborhoods like Bel Air and Beverly Hills. The public may have more access to celebrities than in the past, but some things haven't changed: everyone wants to see one, meet one, or be one.

Crossing the Puget Sound.

Stunning sunset walks.

Cape Disappointment Lighthouse.

Fly fishing at Puget Sound.

INTRODUCTION

A detailed guide to Western Washington, with principal sites clearly cross-referenced by number to the maps.

Adrenalin sports in the alpine peaks.

After a long quiet history of living on the fringes of public awareness, Washington finally burst onto the national stage toward the end of the 20th century. The wartime "Boeing Boom" and the "innovative economy" that spawned Microsoft, Amazon, and a host of others; the retail entrepreneurs who started, and ran with, Nordstrom and Starbucks; the fortunes made by foreign trade with Pacific Rim countries; all created tremendous opportunities and lured in some of world's brightest minds. Similarly, the emergence of bands like Nirvana and Pearl Jam prompted a new sense of cultural identity.

Washington's natural beauty, though, was cherished by its Native peoples long before the arrival of European navigators or Lewis and Clark, with the miles of spectacular Pacific shoreline, ancient forests, and verdant river valleys of its western half as its truest gem. Seattle urbanites in particular pride themselves that there can be few places in the world where you can wake up to a view of snowcapped mountains, ski in the morning, sail in the afternoon and attend a symphony in the evening. You can be a technology engineer during the week and a ski instructor on the weekend; you can hike to alpine lakes one day and bike to vineyards the next.

Taking to the water.

When warm months replace gray clouds, thousands head for their favorite fishing hole, campsite, river, or lake – and there are always enough of those to go around. Washington ranks fourth in the US in the number of visits to state park per person, which is well over three times the national average.

With sandy coastal beaches, crashing surf, and the sheltered islands of Puget Sound, few places can match the sheer splendor of western Washington. Just be sure, as you thread your way from supreme oceanfront wilderness to dense rainforests and spectacular alpine peaks, to allow time to sample crisp Washington apples, award-winning wines, and the pleasures of Northwestern cuisine.

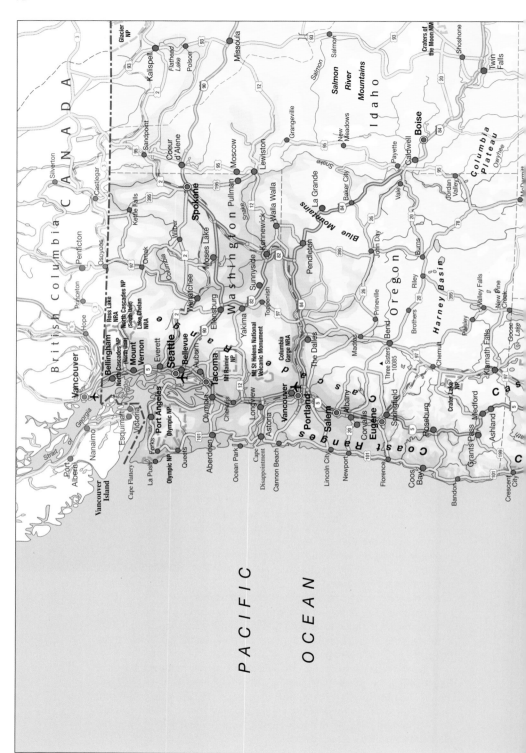

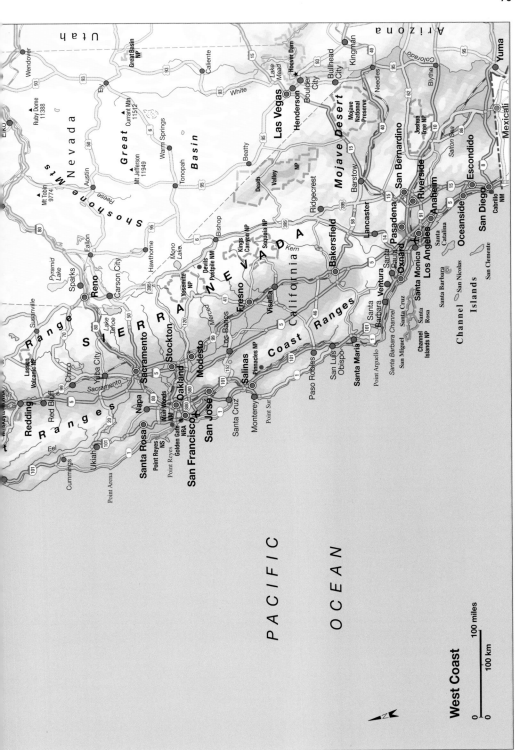

West Coast

0 100 miles
0 100 km

Seattle as seen from Kerry Park.

SEATTLE

Gorgeous, cosmopolitan, home to Microsoft and Amazon – since hitching its wagons to the Klondike Gold Rush, Seattle has never looked back.

Long and skinny, Seattle stretches luxuriantly north and south from its original core, curved around Elliott Bay on the eastern shore of Puget Sound. For its central twenty-mile (32km) stretch, Lake Washington lies just a few miles inland, sandwiching downtown between glorious expanses of water. On a clear day, you may even catch a glimpse of the snow-covered dome of Mount Rainier on the horizon.

Locals choose to live in these spectacular environs for the sheer splendor of the physical geography. For visitors, though, getting around involves bowling up and down narrow corridors where the next place of interest may be 30 miles (50km) distant – and there's usually a body of water to cross.

For all its beauty, Seattle is a dynamic, cosmopolitan city, with a fast-growing population that has rocketed to 750,000. Several global corporations have launched themselves from here, including Microsoft, Amazon, and Starbucks, plus an earlier giant, Boeing, now amazingly more than a century old.

Although Seattle started out as a logging town in 1851, it didn't blossom until the Klondike Gold Rush filled it with racy Wild West "underground" prostitution and illegal drinking dens. While it lacks the heritage architecture of older communities, Native American

culture is widely celebrated, and there's a cluster of historic attractions around Pioneer Square and Yesler Way, near the lively waterfront.

Modern Seattle was kickstarted when it hosted the Century 21 Exposition (aka Seattle World's Fair) in 1962. Elvis breezed in to shoot *It Happened at the World's Fair*, but a more lasting legacy is the Seattle Center, where the iconic Space Needle has been joined by the Gehry-designed Museum of Pop Culture and the dazzling Chihuly Garden and Glass. Seattle made an even

Main attractions
Pike Place Market
Seattle Great Wheel
Seattle Art Museum
Pioneer Square
Underground Tours
Space Needle
Chihuly Garden and Glass
Museum of Pop Culture
Museum of Flight

Map on page 96

Fresh off the boat at Pike Place Market.

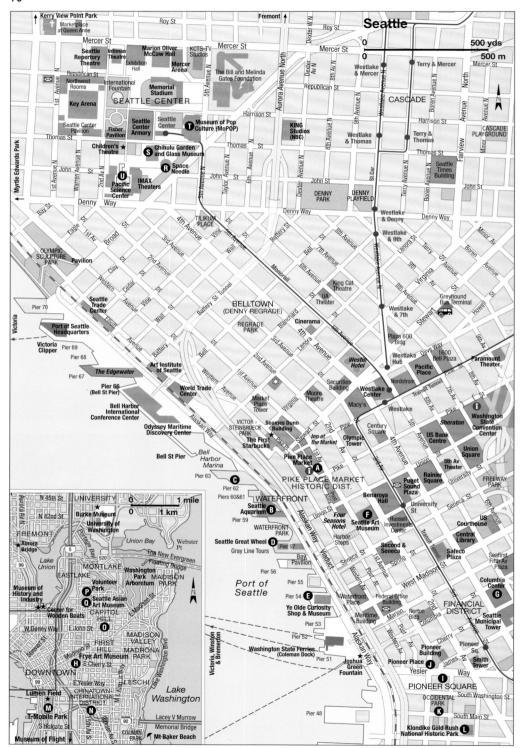

Kerry View Point Park
Marketplace at Queen Anne
Roy St
Fremont
Roy St

Seattle

0   500 yds
0   500 m

Mercer St
Mercer St
Mercer St
Mercer St
Terry & Mercer

Seattle Repertory Theatre
Intiman Theatre
Marion Oliver McCaw Hall
KCTS-TV Studios
Marion Arena
The Bill and Melinda Gates Foundation

CASCADE

Westlake & Mercer

Republican St
Republican St

Exhibition Hall

Mercer Arena

Northwest Rooms
International Fountain
Memorial Stadium

KING Studios (NBC)

Westlake & Thomas

Terry & Thomas

CASCADE PLAYGROUND

Key Arena

SEATTLE CENTER

Harrison St
Harrison St

Seattle Center Pavilion
Fisher Pavilion
Seattle Center Armory
Seattle Center
Museum of Pop Culture (MoPOP) T

Thomas St

Seattle Times Building

Children's Theatre ★
Chihuly Garden and Glass Museum S
Space Needle R
John St
John St
John St
John St

IMAX Theaters
Pacific Science Center U

DENNY PARK
DENNY PLAYFIELD

Westlake & Denny

Denny Way
Denny Way
Denny Way

Bay St
Eagle St
1st Av
Broad St
3rd Avenue
Vine St
Wall St
Battery St
TILIKUM PLACE
4th Avenue
Bell St
7th Avenue
8th Avenue
Westlake & 9th
Lenora St
Terry
Boren
Virginia
Minor Av

OLYMPIC SCULPTURE PARK
Pavilion
Clay St
2nd Avenue
Cedar St
Monorail
6th Avenue
King Cat Theatre

BELLTOWN (DENNY REGRADE)

Seattle Trade Center
Pier 70
Western
Vine St
Battery St Tunnel
REGRADE PARK
Blanchard
3rd Avenue
Lenora
4th Avenue
UA Theater

Victoria

Port of Seattle Headquarters
Elliott
Avenue
Bell St
Cinerama
Greyhound Bus Terminal
Westlake & 7th
Stewart
Howell

Victoria Clipper
Pier 69
Pier 68
Battery
Bell
2nd Avenue
4th Ave
Plaza 600 Bldg
1600 Bell Plaza
Paramount Theater

Pier 67
The Edgewater
Art Institute of Seattle
Western
1st Avenue
Virginia
Securities Building
Westin Hotel
Olive Way
Westlake Hub
Pacific Place
Nordstrom

Pier 66 (Bell St Pier)
World Trade Center
Market Place Tower
Moore Theatre
Westlake Center
Westlake
Macy's

Bell Harbor International Conference Center
Odyssey Maritime Discovery Center
VICTOR STEINBRUECK PARK
Soames Dunn Building
The First Starbucks
Pike Place Market i
Inn at the Market
Olympic Tower
Century Square
US Bank Centre
Sheraton
Washington State Convention Center i

Bell St Pier
Bell Harbor Marina
Alaskan Way
Pier 63
C
Pier 62
Piers 60&61
WATERFRONT
PIKE PLACE MARKET HISTORIC DIST.
Benaroya Hall
Puget Sound Plaza
Rainier Square
5th Av Theater
Union Square
FREEWAY PARK

Seattle Aquarium B
Pier 59
WATERFRONT PARK
Four Seasons Hotel
Seattle Art Museum F
Russell Investments Center
University St
US Courthouse
Central Library

Seattle Great Wheel D
Pier 57
Gray Line Tours
Harbor Steps
Second & Seneca
Safeco Plaza
Seafirst Fifth Ave Plaza

Pier 56
Bay Pavilion
Port of Seattle
Pier 55
Waterfront Place
Federal Office Building
Columbia Center G

Pier 54 E
Ye Olde Curiosity Shop & Museum
Maritime Building
Norton Bldg
FINANCIAL DISTRICT
Seattle Municipal Tower

Pier 53
Pier 52
Pioneer Building
Pioneer Sq.
Smith Tower

Victoria, Winston & Bremerton
Washington State Ferries (Coleman Dock)
Pier 51
Joshua Green Fountain
Pioneer Place J
Yesler Way

PIONEER SQUARE

Pier 48
OCCIDENTAL PARK
K
South Washington St
South Main St

Klondike Gold Rush National Historic Park L

Inset map (lower left)

N 45th St
UNIVERSITY
0   1 mile
0   1 km

N 42nd St
Burke Museum
University of Washington

FREMONT
Aurora Bridge
Portage Bay
Union Bay
Webster Pt
The New Evergreen Floating Bridge

Lake Union
520
MONTLAKE
Washington Park Arboretum
MADISON PARK

Museum of History and Industry
Volunteer Park
Seattle Asian Art Museum O
Lake Washington Blvd

EASTLAKE
Center for Wooden Boats
Q
P
CAPITOL HILL
MADISON VALLEY
MADRONA PARK

W Denny Way
E John St
I
FIRST HILL

DOWNTOWN
Frye Art Museum H
E Cherry St
LESCHI

E Yesler Way
CHINATOWN INTERNATIONAL DISTRICT
90
Lake Washington

Lumen Field
T-Mobile Park M
N
Lacey V Murrow Memorial Bridge

Museum of Flight
S Holgate St
COLMAN PARK
Mt Baker Beach

greater cultural impact in the 1990s, when Nirvana spearheaded the rise of grunge. Its reputation as a musical center dates back further, however; Jimi Hendrix was born here in 1942, while Ray Charles and Quincy Jones launched their careers in the city's clubs.

PIKE PLACE MARKET

Visited by more than ten million people each year, Seattle's landmark **Pike Place Market** Ⓐ (tel: 206-682 7453; www.pikeplacemarket.org; daily 9am–6pm) started out in 1907 as a simple affair. Prompted by local outrage after the retail price of onions had risen from 10 cents to $1 per pound in the previous year, Seattle City Councilman Thomas Revelle had called for an investigation. Farmers told of being cheated by middlemen and receiving bungled commissions. As a solution, Revelle proposed a public street market to sell direct to the consumer.

Propped up on stilts on the headland overlooking Elliott Bay, the new market proved popular, and the original hillside arcade soon grew into a maze of corridors, stairwells, and hidden shops. Following repeated resurrections, the market remains a vital part of the city, patronized by almost everyone in town.

In former times, "Dry Row" along the west wall had no access to running water, in contrast to "Wet Row" opposite. Now one of the nation's oldest continually operating farmers' markets allows craftspeople to sell their wares from the dry tables while local farmers sell fresh produce from the wet tables. A shallow trough still carries runoff from the farmers' tables.

A free-form conglomeration of sights, smells, sounds and characters, the market can be decidedly odiferous. Salmon periodically fly through the air as traders throw them to each other over the heads of customers. Nearby, vegetable and flower displays are turned into works of art. Countless food outlets serve up tastes of the world and the maze-like corridors are a haven for small businesses. This is the place to buy antique playing cards, opals from Australia, imported cigarettes, incense, T-shirts, and shoes – all within an old-fashioned, cozy complex with magnificent views of the harbor. Licensed street musicians play for loose change at designated spots, while the loot amassed by Rachel the Pig, the shiny cast-bronze piggy bank under the central clock, goes to charity.

Summer Sundays on **Pike Place** (Stewart and Virginia streets; June–Sept, 10am–4pm; free to watch) feature chefs giving demonstrations. To take a cooking class, or join a farm-to-table tour, head to **Atrium Kitchen** (93 Pike Street; tel: 206-829 9525; www.atriumkitchenpikeplace.com). The most famous seafood restaurant is the century-old **Athenian** (1517 Pike Place), while the open-air deck at the **Old Stove Brewing Company** (1901 Western Avenue) has great views out over Puget Sound.

The city's ferris wheel on the waterfront makes pleasant sightseeing.

Seattle Art Museum.

WATERFRONT SEATTLE

Seattle's most compelling natural advantage is its deep, scenic harbor. Arrayed north and south of **Waterfront Park**, below Pike Place Market, the promenade and piers that line Elliott Bay are in constant action, with maritime industries, stores, and restaurants jostling for custom, ferries docking, and the occasional seaplane flying overhead. The large piers of primary interest to visitors are numbered sequentially from south to north, from 48 to 70.

Waterfront Park makes the obvious starting point for pleasant waterfront strolls. On Pier 59, immediately north, the **Seattle Aquarium** Ⓑ (1483 Alaskan Way; tel: 206-386 4300; www.seattleaquarium.org; daily 9.30am–6pm) provides a fish's-eye view of life above and beneath the waves, along with a host of resident perky sea and river otters. The aquarium is a fun and friendly place to spend a few hours; in autumn it's particularly satisfying to see returning salmon making their way up its cannily positioned fish ladder.

Although the much-loved wooden decking of **Pier 62** Ⓒ, just beyond, had to be replaced with safer concrete panels in 2020, it continues to serve as a wonderful open-air park and summer concert venue. A little farther north, colossal cruise ships, belonging to the Celebrity and Norwegian lines and heading especially to and from Alaska, loom over the **Bell Street Pier Cruise Terminal** at Pier 66 (tel: 206-787 3911).

A ribbon of verdant parks line the waterfront beyond the northernmost commercially developed pier, **Pier 70**. Explore them along the green promenade of the **Elliott Bay Bicycle Path**, the highlight of which comes at the very start, a mile (1.6km) north of Waterfront Park. An offshoot of Seattle Art Museum, and named for its stunning vista of Washington's Olympic Mountains, the **Olympic Sculpture Park** (www.seattleartmuseum.org; daily dawn–dusk; free) holds monumental outdoor works including the *Father and Son* fountain by Louise Bourgeois. Relax a moment on the same artist's *Eye Benches*, nestled into enormous,

unblinking eyes. The cycle path continues 2 miles (3.2km) north to the huge **Smith Cove Cruise Terminal** at Pier 91, used by Carnival, Holland America, Royal Caribbean, and Princess Cruises.

Just south of Waterfront Park, the 175ft (53-meter) **Seattle Great Wheel** **D** (tel: 206-623 8607; https://seattlegreatwheel.com; Sun–Thu 11am–9pm, Fri and Sat until 10pm) has been towering at the tip of Pier 57 since 2012. During their 20-minute revolutions, the totally enclosed eight-passenger gondola cars dangle precariously out over the water.

If you prefer to admire all that beauty from a safer distance, join an informative and entertaining harbor tour from Pier 55 with **Argosy Cruises** (tel: 206-623 1445; www.argosycruises.com). Pride of place on **Pier 54 E** goes to the dotty oddities on display at **Ye Olde Curiosity Shop** (tel: 206-682 5844). Created during the Gold Rush days of the late 1890s, it's as much a museum as a store, with a remarkable collection of culturally significant Native American artefacts. A million visitors each year come to gawk at "Sylvester," the mummified body in the back, and buy hard-to-find souvenirs in the front. Pier 54 also holds **Ivar's Acres of Clams** (tel: 206-624 6852; www.ivars.com), where you can order a huge helping of seafood and sit undercover – but outside – while watching the boats and seagulls. Ivar's was the first in a chain of restaurants developed by the late Ivar Haglund, long known as Seattle's premier prankster, promoter, and restaurateur.

DOWNTOWN SEATTLE

Seattle's downtown and financial districts start a couple of blocks inland from the waterfront, and just south of Pike Place Market. Designed by postmodern architect Robert Venturi, the **Seattle Art Museum F** (1300 First Avenue; tel: 206-654 3100; www.seattleartmuseum.org; Wed–Sun 10am–5pm) is fronted by a massive sculpture of a manual worker, known as *Hammering Man*. The wide-ranging displays inside cover European and American works from Rembrandt to Andy Warhol, plus

The Olympic Sculpture Park.

⊘ THE FIRST SKID ROW

Seattle's Pioneer Square was located at the foot of the original Skid Road. That nickname derived from the method in which huge felled trees were "skidded" down a steep log-bed road from the nearby hilltop to be processed at Yesler Mill, a waterfront lumber mill opened by Henry Yesler in 1853.

After Seattle's business center moved uptown, early in the 20th century, Skid Road became the demarcation line between the city's rich and poor. Officially named Yesler Way, it lost its role as a place where itinerant workers could hope to find a day job. By the 1930s, though – and despite the fact that the mill employed almost half the people in town – the term, in the slightly distorted form of "Skid Row," had entered the language as a way to denote an area frequented by the homeless.

everything from ancient Greek vases to modern Aboriginal paintings from Australia. There's also a fascinating collection of Native American art and sculpture stretching back to the pre-Contact era, with an emphasis on the peoples of the Northwest. Major international temporary exhibitions are staged each year.

Across from the Art Museum, the compelling **Benaroya Hall**, which opened in 1998, boasts soaring windows and stunning chandeliers by Dale Chihuly. Its 2,500-seat Taper Auditorium provides an eloquent home for the Seattle Symphony.

Local developer Martin Selig's Darth Vader–esque **Columbia Center G** at 700 Fourth Avenue stands 76 stories high. When completed in 1985, it was at 933 feet (284 meters) the tallest building on the West Coast; it's currently the fourth tallest. Up on the 73rd floor, 360-degree views from the **Sky View Observatory** (tel: 206-386 5564; https:// skyviewobservatory.com; daily 10am–8pm) stretch as far as mounts Rainier and Baker and the Olympic and Cascade ranges, as well as across the city and Puget Sound.

A few blocks east of Columbia Center, reached by walking beneath the I-5 freeway into the First Hill neighborhood, the **Frye Art Museum H** (704 Terry Avenue; tel: 206-622 9250; www.fryemuseum. org; Wed–Sun 11am–5pm; free) nicely complements the Seattle Art Museum. Established by collectors Charles and Emma Frye from 1900 onward, whose collection centered on late 19th-century European paintings from Munich in particular, it encompasses fascinating works by Winslow Homer, John Singer Sargent, and Thomas Eakins.

PIONEER SQUARE

Seattle's oldest neighborhood, south of modern downtown, **Pioneer Square I** is a 17-square-block National Historic District where warm red-brick buildings line the streets. Spaces where speakeasies and opium dens once lurked are now occupied by shops selling wares from antiques to handmade toys, along with cafes, restaurants, and art galleries.

Memorial to Fallen Firefighters, Occidental Park.

The great pergola of ornate iron-work, shading carved wooden benches, that stands in **Pioneer Place ⑩** (First Avenue and Yesler Way), is often considered Seattle's heart. A 60ft (18-meter) totem pole and bronze bust of Chief Seattle, reminds visitors that Seattle – "Queen City of the Pacific Northwest" – first emerged into world consciousness during the Klondike Gold Rush at the end of the 19th century. Even before that, this was the site chosen by the founding settlers when they left Alki Point in the early 1850s for a superior harbor on Elliott Bay.

These days, Pioneer Square ranks among Seattle's premier neighborhoods for eating, drinking, and all-round entertainment. At night, especially on weekends or after a sports event in the huge nearby stadiums, it's truly buzzing. Favorite stopoffs for locals include **Zeitgeist Coffee** (171 South Jackson Street), with its fine coffees, succulent pies and pastries, and art-gallery vibe; **Salumi** (404 Occidental Avenue South), an Italian deli prized for its cured-meat sandwiches;

and **Bad Bishop** (704 First Avenue), an upscale contemporary pub with appealing small-plate snacks.

The handsome, 42-story **Smith Tower** (Second Avenue and Yesler) was erected in 1914 in an attempt to anchor business in the area. Formerly the pride of Seattle, this white terracotta tower long remained the tallest building west of the Mississippi. A look from its open-air observation floor (tel: 206-624 0414; www.smithtower.com; Wed–Sun 3–10pm) shows glittering skyscrapers to the north, and T-Mobile Park to the south.

If your soul needs soothing, head one block south to the **Waterfall Garden** (219 Second Avenue South), an oasis of rushing water, bamboo, and sculptured rock that lies behind slatted wooden walls. Nearby **Occidental Park ⑯** (Occidental and First avenues) displays four totem poles carved by artist Duane Pasco, including the 35ft (10-meter) *Sun and Raven*, and *Man Riding on Tail of Whale*. Two additional large figures represent *Tsonoqua*, a mythological "nightmare bringer" and *Bear*.

○ **Where**

Amazon's corporate headquarters spread across a campus a mile north of downtown. Only the Amazon Spheres (www.seattlespheres.com; first & third Sat of every month 10am–6pm), three giant conservatories along Lenora Street between Sixth and Seventh avenues, are accessible to visitors. Looking like three distinct glass globes, they're actually parts of a single building, planted with trees from around the world.

Monorail arriving at the Museum of Pop Culture.

⊙ Tip

Be sure to check out the latest in the Wing Luke Museum's ongoing series of temporary exhibitions on the life and legacy of martial arts superstar Bruce Lee (1940–73). Lee lived in Seattle as a young man, and is buried, along with his son Brandon Lee, in the city's Lakeview Cemetery.

Poor drainage after Seattle's Great Fire of 1889 necessitated raising the street line one level. As a consequence, the Square can also be explored via secret subterranean tunnels. **Underground Tours** (614 First Avenue; tel: 206-682 4646; www.undergroundtour. com; 75-minute tours; year-round) is a favorite with first-time visitors. Saucy guides entertainingly describe life in old Seattle while negotiating a maze of sunken storefronts.

Popular **Klondike Gold Rush National Historic Park** ❶ (219 Second Avenue South; tel: 206-220 4240; www. nps.gov/klse; Fri–Sun 9am–6pm; free) is a Federal-run visitor center that harks back to the crazed days when rough-and-ready gold-seekers converged on Pioneer Square in their tens of thousands. Here they purchased millions of dollars' worth of food, clothing, equipment, pack animals, and steamship tickets, before heading up to the Yukon.

Two colossal modern stadiums soar south of Pioneer Square, both of which offer spectators stunning views of the downtown skyline. First comes **Lumen Field**, used not only by the NFL's Seattle Seahawks but also the city's men's and women's soccer teams. Beyond that, **T-Mobile Park** Ⓜ, with its asymmetrical ball-park layout, is home to baseball's beloved Seattle Mariners, but also hosts occasional big-name concerts by the likes of Paul McCartney or local heroes Pearl Jam. Its retractable roof simply serves to shelter from rain; unlike similar stadiums elsewhere, there's no need for air-conditioning here. Guided tours give a close-up look at the whole intricate operation (1250 First Avenue South; www.mlb.com/mariners/ballpark/tours; tours usually Thu–Sun 12:30pm and 2:30pm).

THE INTERNATIONAL DISTRICT

The prosperous neighborhood east of Pioneer Square became home to Seattle's Chinatown late in the 19th century. In the face of white hostility, predominantly Cantonese dock workers joined with forced laborers who had been released after the completion of the

Seattle's Chinatown.

railroad to build a community of their own. Running from Fifth Avenue South to Eighth Avenue South, it's now officially designated the **Chinatown–International District** , in deference to the fact that it also holds distinct Japantown and Little Saigon areas, along with many inhabitants of other Asian descent.

The history of the Asian Pacific American experience is told at the **Wing Luke Asian Museum** (719 South King Street; tel: 206-623 5124; www.wingluke.org; Thu–Sun 10am–5pm). This pan-Asian collection is dedicated to Wing Luke (1925–65), the son of an immigrant laundryman who became the first person of Asian ancestry to be elected to office in Washington State.

The International District may be small, but it holds a multiplicity of Asian-cuisine restaurants, along with herbalists, massage parlors, acupuncturists and the like. King Street is the center of Chinese remedy activity, with shark fins, mandrake roots, trussed poultry, pungent herbs, and secret ingredients sold with a dollop of advice by shopkeepers. One favorite remedy is said to cure male "tiredness."

Dough Zone (505 Fifth Avenue South; tel: 206-285 9999) serves extremely good dumplings and noodles, while **Uwajimaya** (600 Fifth Avenue South; tel: 206-624 6248) is a vast all-Asian supermarket that also incorporates a wondrous food hall and a Japanese bookstore. A couple of blocks north, **Hing Hay Park** is the setting for martial-arts exhibitions and Chinese folk dancing. Its dragon mural and bright pagoda were donated by the City of Taipei.

CAPITOL HILL

In its original heyday the exclusive preserve of Seattle's wealthiest citizens, **Capitol Hill** , east of downtown, is now one of city's more diverse neighborhoods, peppered with impressive old mansions and home to a thriving LGBT community. Along its dynamic central artery, Broadway, you'll find stores, restaurants, clubs and cafes to suit any taste. The Seattle Architecture Foundation puts on two-hour walking

View of the Capitol Hill District.

tours of the **Harvard Belmont Historic District**, where the finest vintage treasures are concentrated (tel: 206-667 9184; https://seattlearchitecture.org).

The circling drives and manicured lawns of **Volunteer Park** , a luxurious 40-acre (16-hectare) expanse on Capitol Hill's northern crest, are topped by a conservatory and an old water tower. A fine Art Deco building here houses the **Seattle Asian Art Museum** (1400 East Prospect Street; tel: 206-654 3210; www.seattleartmuseum.org; Tues–Sun 10am–5pm), which presents magnificent artworks from all over Asia, ranging from ceramics to furniture, with some exquisite Japanese landscape scrolls for good measure.

THE SEATTLE CENTER

Designed for the 1962 World's Fair, and supposedly sketched out on the back of a napkin, the **Seattle Center** (www.seattlecenter.com) is a 74-acre (30-hectare) urban park where facilities include the signature Needle, along with several museums, amusement parks, stores, and places to eat. It's only a mile

(1.6km) northwest of downtown, and half that inland from Pier 70 on the waterfront, but for the definitive Seattle Center experience you can't beat arriving on the **monorail** (www.seattlemonorail.com), which makes a 0.9-mile (1.4km trip) from the Westlake Center mall in the Belmont neighborhood. Rather oddly, these days it feels more like a retro-tinged dip into nostalgia than the futuristic thrill described by 1962's earliest riders.

A slender, spindly column with a precarious Sputnik-age flying saucer on its summit, the **Space Needle** (400 Broad Street; www.spaceneedle.com; daily 8am–midnight) quickly established itself worldwide as the symbol of Seattle. The total structure is 605ft (184 meters) high, and is fastened to its foundation with 72 bolts, each 30ft (9 meters) long.

A 41-second elevator ride takes visitors 500ft (150 meters) above ground to reach its lower observation deck. Until 2018, this held an exclusive revolving restaurant; now, remodeled with a see-through glass floor, it's known as

The Glass Museum's striking garden artworks.

the **Loupe**, and open to all. It does continue to rotate, however. The views are utterly extraordinary, reaching beyond Seattle and Puget Sound and potentially all the way to Mount Rainier. The elevator continues beyond the Loupe – or you can take the steps if you prefer – to additional levels that hold a café and wine bar as well as floor-to-ceiling windows.

Alongside the Space Needle, the phenomenal **Chihuly Garden and Glass** ⑤ (305 Harrison Street; tel: 206-753 4940; www.chihulygardenandglass.com; daily 10am–6pm) is a permanent home for the flamboyant glass sculptures of Tacoma-born Dale Chihuly. Some of his colorful creations are visible from outside, but it's well worth paying to enter the galleries within, especially the magnificent Glasshouse conservatory.

Even more psychedelic is the nearby **Museum of Pop Culture** ❼ (325 Fifth Avenue North; tel: 206-770 2700; www.mopop.org; daily summer 10am–7pm, winter until 5pm), a spectacular tangle of ever-unfolding swathes of shimmering aluminium and stainless steel designed by Frank Gehry, of Bilbao's Guggenheim Museum fame. It opened in 2000 as the Experience Music Project (EMP), financed by billionaire Microsoft co-founder Paul Allen (1953–2018) as a no-expense-spared tribute to his musical idol, Seattle's own Jimi Hendrix. Exhibits within still honour Jimi, with guitars and personal artefacts galore, along with Nirvana and Pearl Jam. As the name change suggests, however, it's no longer solely devoted to music. It now stages also temporary exhibitions on topics such as Minecraft or horror movies, and incorporates the Science Fiction and Fantasy Hall of Fame.

The Seattle Center's new improved **Skate Plaza** opened on Thomas Street, between Fifth Avenue North and Taylor Street, in 2021. Designed to meet the needs of novices and experts alike, it spreads across a sumptuous 18,000 square feet (1672 square meters).

Two long-established, child-friendly attractions alongside the Space Needle seized the unwelcome opportunity

⊙ THE WINERIES OF WEST WASHINGTON

Although virtually all Washington's grapes are grown east of the Cascades, wineries within easy reach of Seattle mean that city visitors can enjoy tastings as part of a pleasant day's excursion. The earth's 46th parallel North, which crosses Washington from east to west, also runs through the wine-growing regions of the Bordeaux-Burgundy country in France, encouraging many comparisons between Washington wines and French ones. Additionally, the diverse climate of the Northwest, where long, warm summer days give way to cooler nights, allows Washington wineries to produce a wide range of good wines. They're also noted, incidentally, for fruit wines, like strawberry and pear.

Washington holds more than 60,000 acres (25,000 hectares) of vineyards, but much less than 1 percent of those are in the Puget Sound area. However, grapes both red and white are grown in the arid east of the state, then shipped west to be turned into wine. Thus, wine lovers head for **Woodinville**, north of Redmond, for tours, tastings, and summer concerts at the **Chateau Ste Michelle Winery** (14111 Northeast 145th Street; tel: 425-488 1133; www.ste-michelle.com; Sun–Thu 11am–5pm, Fri and Sat until 7pm). More than 250,000 visitors a year come to explore the chateau and historic 105-acre (42-hectare) grounds, once home to Seattle lumber baron Frederick Stimson, and now quite amazingly said to be the largest producer of Riesling in the world.

Wineries from all over Washington operate tasting rooms in and around Woodinville, including **Columbia Winery** (14030 Northeast 145th Street; tel: 425-488 7490; www.columbiawinery.com; Wed–Sun 11am–6pm) and **Patterson Cellars** (Hollywood Hill, 14508 148th Avenue Northeast, tel: 425-892 2964; www.pattersoncellars.com; Sun–Thu noon–7pm, Fri and Sat until 8pm). The Eastside also has its share of **breweries**, such as the Good Brewing Co Hollywood Taproom (14701 148th Avenue Northeast; tel: 425-877 1137; https://goodbrewingco.com).

For a blow-out gourmet experience, reserve well in advance to eat at Woodinville's renowned **Herbfarm** restaurant (14590 Northeast 145th Street; tel: 425-485 5300; www.theherbfarm.com). Its nine-course set menus cost hundreds of dollars per person, with optional wine pairings to sample fine local vintages.

presented by the Covid-19 pandemic to undertake extensive remodelling. The first is the **Children's Museum** (305 Harrison Street; tel: 206-441 1768; https://seattlechildrensmuseum.org; Thu–Sun 10am–5pm), which enables little visitors to explore world cultures across the globe and through time. The other is the **Pacific Science Center** (200 Second Avenue North; tel: 206-443 2844; www.pacificscience-center.org), where graceful lace-like spires crowned an impressive array of interactive science exhibits, along with a tropical Butterfly House, an IMAX theater and a planetarium. Note some areas of the Science Center are still undergoing renovation.

THE UNIVERSITY DISTRICT

Four miles north of downtown, across Lake Union, Seattle's **University District** – usually abbreviated to simply the "U" District – is a frenetic enclave of student activity. Restaurants and takeouts devoted to every imaginable global cuisine, bookstores, movie theatres, and coffeehouses (of course)

are concentrated along its main axis, University Way, similarly shortened to "The Ave."

On the campus of the University of Washington, the **Burke Museum** ❶ (4300 15th Avenue Northeast; tel: 206-543 5590; www.burkemuseum.org; Tue–Sun l0am–5pm) frames itself as a museum of natural history and culture. Exhibits honour the Native peoples and traditions of the Pacific Northwest, celebrate the various cultures that characterize contemporary Seattle, and range back through the geology and biology of Washington State, showcasing some stunning dinosaur skeletons.

THE MUSEUM OF FLIGHT

As home since 1916 to the mighty aircraft manufacturer Boeing, Seattle has played a major role in the United State's and indeed the world's aviation history. Boeing's first home, 6 miles (10km) south of downtown, now serves as the **Museum of Flight** ❷ (9404 East Marginal Way; tel: 206-764 5700; www. museumofflight.org; daily 10am–5pm).

University of Washington.

While centering on the century-old Red Barn that held the original factory, its two colossal galleries set out to cover the entire history of flight from Leonardo da Vinci's visionary drawings to the NASA space programme. As well as the sole surviving example of the Lockheed M-21 Blackbird, which by flying at three times the speed of sound in 1964 became the world's fastest plane, the museum boasts everything from a Montgolfier balloon to a Concorde. To find out what Boeing are up to these days, you can visit their current manufacturing plant which is situated just 24 miles north of downtown in Everett (see page 111).

EAST OF SEATTLE

The headquarters of Microsoft lies just outside **Redmond**, 15 miles (24km) northeast of Seattle across Lake Washington. It's an attractive little town, with tall fir trees, forested trails, snow-capped mountain vistas, and architecturally pleasing buildings, but nothing on the Microsoft campus, which covers more than 500 acres (200 hectares) and employs more than 50,000 people, is open to the public.

In **Issaquah**, 12 miles (20km) south at the opposite end of Lake Sammamish, animals and fish are the theme. Its **Cougar Mountain Zoo** (19525 Southeast 54th Street; tel: 425-392 6278; www.cougarmountainzoo.org; Wed–Sun 9.30am–5pm) specializes in the conservation of threatened or endangered animals, including cougars (also known as mountain lions) as well as gray wolves and is even home to some Bengal tigers. Each December it hosts a Reindeer Festival – cougars are not invited.

From early September through November, the grand spectacle hereabouts is watching mature chinook and coho salmon return home from the Pacific Ocean. Visitors to the free, well-developed **Issaquah Salmon Hatchery** (125 West Sunset Way; tel: 425-392 1118; www.issaquahfish.org; daily 8am–4.30pm) can view fish all year round, as well as see exhibits that explain the interesting facts around a salmon's life cycle and habits.

Aircraft displays at the Museum of Flight.

PUGET SOUND AND THE ISLANDS

Trace the convoluted shoreline of Puget Sound, and venture out to its islands, to find pretty towns, rural peace, and a leisurely life.

Sculpted by the repeated advance and withdrawal of endless glacial epochs, Puget Sound is an ocean inlet and estuary – a vast inland sea where the saltwater ocean mixes with freshwater precipitation that drains from the land. More than 10,000 rivers and streams pour into its maze of slender waterways, convoluted bays, and forked inlets. When taken as a whole, these add up to a stunning 2,354 miles (3,800km) of shoreline. There's no better way to admire all that wondrous scenery than from out on the water, be that on a kayak, a sailing ship, or simply one of the many commuter ferries.

Stretching some 100 miles (160km) south from Admiralty Inlet and Whidbey Island, and studded with islets such as Bainbridge and Vashon islands, Puget Sound defines the character of western Washington. Just beyond it to the north, the straits of Georgia and Juan de Fuca cradle the clustered island-jewels known as the San Juans. Around 75 orcas, in three family pods, reside in the San Juan Islands during the summer months. Whale-watching is a favorite local activity, and many companies offer naturalist-guided tours.

Excellent deepwater harbors, including Seattle, Tacoma, Everett, and Port Townsend, serve as outports for farmlands along the river estuaries,

The Sound is a haven for wildlife.

while Bremerton's naval shipyard adds military shipping to the Sound's already remarkable volume of local and international trade. The average depth is 450ft (140 meters).

While much of the Sound remains healthy, the growth of industry, urban development, and recreational usage have placed serious environmental pressures on certain sections. But for the first-time visitor the rewards are numerous. From the deck of a ferryboat it is easy to downshift from a bustling cosmopolitan atmosphere to

 Main attractions
Whidbey Island
San Juan Island
Orcas Island
Bainbridge Island
Museum of Glass
Mount Rainier National
 Park
Mount St Helens

Maps on pages 112, 116

timeless rural tranquility, and experience soft sea-winds moving through pine trees in the space of an hour. With the aid of a bicycle or a vehicle, explorers can travel to quaint seaside villages, via verdant farms, windswept beaches, or wildlife sanctuaries.

WHIDBEY ISLAND

Narrow **Whidbey Island** ❶ stretches up through Puget Sound, parallel to the mainland, from just off the northern reaches of Seattle up as far as La Conner. Measuring around 37 miles (60km) from north to south, it's the longest island in Washington, and the fourth longest island in the lower 48 American states. Accessible by road at its northern tip, it's also served by two separate **Washington State Ferry** routes (https://wsdot.wa.gov), one connecting Clinton on its lower eastern shore with Mukilteo near Everett, and the other sailing between Coupeville, halfway up the island, and Port Townsend on the Olympic Peninsula. Drivers can therefore use Whidbey Island as an onward route to Olympic

Admiralty head Lighthouse.

National Park and the Pacific coast. Be warned, though, that heavy commuter use can make advance ferry reservations essential.

The first stop of interest for passengers who arrive in Clinton is **Langley**, a waterfront community a short distance north that's known for its galleries and inns. **Coupeville**, 26 miles (42km) farther on by road, is the centerpiece of **Ebey's Landing National Historical Reserve** (tel: 360-678 6084; www.nps.gov/ebla), which rather strangely is the only such reserve in the country, It incorporates not only downtown Coupeville on the eastern shore, where the Victorian-era homes are filled with maritime echoes from the days of sea captains and rum runners, but also **Fort Casey State Park** (1280 Engle Road; tel: 360-678 4519; daily 8am–dusk), close at hand on the west coast. The fort itself was constructed in 1890 as part of a triangle of forts intended to protect Puget Sound; its restored **Admiralty Head Lighthouse** dates from 1903 and holds a gift shop. Note that Coupeville's **ferry** terminal

⊘ WASHINGTON FERRIES

For Washington commuters, ferries are a vital lifeline; for visitors, they make a delightful way to travel. An attractive spectacle as they power across Puget Sound or cruise among the San Juan Islands, ferries are surprisingly inexpensive, and fun to ride as they ply waters shared by orcas and seals, freighters and kayakers. Tickets for the extensive network of routes operated by **Washington State Ferries** (tel: 206-464 6400; https://wsdot.wa.gov) are sold online. If you plan to take a vehicle, it's best to book in advance; reservations for most routes open two months ahead, but some spaces are always held back until closer to the time of sailing, and ferries also accept walk-on passengers and vehicles on the actual day, on a first-come, first-served basis.

Clipper Vacations (tel: 206-443 2560; www.clippervacations.com) offers a year-round, passenger-only, high-speed catamaran connection between **Seattle** and beautiful in British Columbia, Canada. The voyage takes just under three hours, with two round trips daily between late May and early September, and one otherwise. Aim to return at sunset, a breathtaking experience as the boat winds in among the smaller islands. On summer weekends, they also put on day-trip cruises from Seattle to the **San Juan Islands**, including a two-hour lunch stop in Friday Harbor.

is not in the downtown area but alongside Fort Casey, near the tiny village of **Keystone**.

The bulk of Whidbey Island's population resides toward the north end at shabby **Oak Harbor**, a naval-base town, which is not a place with any obvious appeal for tourists. **Deception Pass State Park**, 9 miles (14km) north of Oak Harbor, is one of Washington's busiest state parks. An impressive bridge spans the rocks of Deception Pass connects Whidbey to Fidalgo Island near Anacortes. Rugged cliffs drop to meet the turbulent waters, while the park is notable for its views of Puget Sound, old-growth forests and wildlife. The **Maiden of Deception Pass**, the 24ft (7.3 meters) cedar-carved story pole of the Samish Indian Nation, is located on Rosario Beach in the north part of the park.

EVERETT AND SNOHOMISH

Several interesting stops lie on the mainland north of Seattle, en route to the border with Canada, 110 miles (176km) along. Facing west towards Whidbey Island, just offshore, and east

towards the sharp peaks of the Cascades, **Everett** ❷, 28 miles (45km) north of downtown, harks back to Washington's pioneer days with its aromatic timber mills, miles of smokestacks and floating logs, while much of the waterfront is taken by Naval Station Everett, home base for six guided-missile destroyers. It's most notable, however, for holding the current manufacturing base of Washington's own colossal Boeing corporation (although its head office moved to Chicago in 2001. In terms of both area and volume, the factory is ranked as the largest building in the world. Interactive displays here at the **Boeing Future of Flight** (8415 Paine Field Boulevard; tel: 1-800-464 1476; www.boeingfutureofflight.com; Thu–Sun 9.30am–5pm) explore potential developments in passenger aircraft, robotics, and space technology.

The community of **Snohomish** ❸, 9 miles southeast and finally beyond Seattle's urban sprawl, is a major day-trip destination for the city's antiques shoppers. Many of the 19th-century storefronts along First Street are home

Serene sunsets over the water at Whidbey Island.

⊙ PETER PUGET

Long known as Whulge, the region centering on Puget Sound had already been inhabited by Native Americans for at least 8,000 years by the time European Juan Perez encountered it in 1774. Four years later, Captain James Cook briefly imagined he'd found the fabled Northwest Passage here. The body of water was eventually named for a trusted lieutenant of Captain George Vancouver, Peter Puget, who commanded several small-boat expeditions, including a week-long tour of Southern Puget Sound. Born in London in 1765, Puget first went to sea at age 12, and served on British naval ships in the West Indies. He signed up for Vancouver's voyage when aged 26, in 1791, and was eventually promoted to captain of the *Chatham*, the small tender that sailed with Vancouver's *Discovery*.

By the time they returned from their four-year voyage in 1795, the British had lost interest in exploring the Northwest. They faced more urgent matters, such as Napoleon: Puget's distinguished naval career included action against Napoleon's navy, and he died in 1822. His memorial in Woolsey remained unremembered until it was tracked down by a local researcher in the 1970s. He shares his modern obscurity with many of those whose names are attached to the expedition's landmarks, including Rainier, Whidbey, and arguably even the skipper himself, George Vancouver.

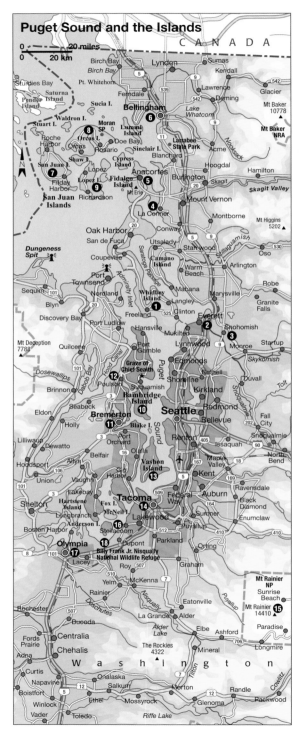

Puget Sound and the Islands

to antiques dealers, including stores specializing in old toys and fine furniture, and there's an appetizing array of restaurants and cafés.

SKAGIT COUNTY

The area around pretty **La Conner** ❹, a lively and historic little town with lovely aquatic views over Swinomish Channel, is primarily famous for its bulb farms, which burst into color each spring. Yellow daffodils bloom March and April, while tulips are best in mid- to late April.

A prime stop for tourists, it is also home to the substantial **Museum of Northwest Art** (121 South First Street; tel: 360-466 4446; www.monamuseum. org; daily 10am–5pm; free). Inspired during the 1930s and 1940s, it owes its origins to four Northwest artists who spent time in this valley: Guy Anderson, Kenneth Callahan, Morris Graves, and Mark Tobey. Drawing artistic sustenance from nature and Asian influences, they created a fresh style and a regional identity.

From January to April, thousands of snow geese from Siberia spend the winter in the **Skagit Wildlife Area** (near Ross Lake; tel: 360-902 2200; https:// wdfw.wa.gov; free). At the first signs of spring, they all leave – an awesome sight as 50,000-plus geese fly off within a timespan of just 24 hours. Take-off is no earlier than April 17 and no later than May 5. Bald eagles also gather here during the cold winter months. Join a seasonal, small-group tour with **Skagit Guided Adventures** (tel: 360-474 7479; https://skagitguidedadventures. com) to learn more.

Nearby **Anacortes** ❺ (https://anacortes.org) is the departure point for Washington State Ferries to the San Juan Islands and Vancouver Island in British Columbia. Poke around town, visit the fishing fleet and spin around Washington Park with its loop road. The downtown area has been revived with a handful of interesting shops and restaurants, while historic attractions include the **W.T. Preston** (703 R Avenue; tel: 360-293 1915), a steamboat restored as a museum.

The last sizeable town before Canada, **Bellingham** ➏ (www.bellingham.org), is the home of scenic Western Washington University, where the campus is known for its outdoor sculpture garden. A lovely stretch of accessible coastline can be found along Chuckanut Drive, which offers gratifying views of the San Juan Islands and Chuckanut Bay.

The traditional activity here is to pig out on fresh oysters. The **Oyster Bar** (2578 Chuckanut Drive; tel: 360-766 6185; www.theoysterbar.net), has indoor and outdoor seating overlooking the bay. According to its long-established slogan, "The oyster you eat today slept last night in Samish Bay!"

Set in a refurbished warehouse in the heart of downtown, and kitted out with plank floors, the **Boundary Bay Brewery and Bistro** (tel: 360-647 5593 for a tour; www.bbaybrewery.com) features unfiltered and handcrafted ales and lagers. If snack-packs of freshly smoked oysters in such flavors as jalapeno float your boat, stop by **Taylor Shellfish Farms** (2182 Chuckanut Drive; tel: 360-766 6002; www.taylorshellfishfarms.com; daily 10am–sunset). They sell big, fresh Dungeness crabs too.

The international border itself, just beyond tiny Blaine 23 miles (37km) northwest of Bellingham, is straddled by **Peace Arch Park**. The actual arch, erected in 1921, stands amid gardens that extend into both Washington and British Columbia; so long as they don't leave the park, citizens of the United States and Canada are permitted to mingle freely.

THE SAN JUAN ISLANDS

Maybe it's the eagles soaring overhead that cast a blissful spell, but whatever the reason, the **San Juan Islands**, scattered on the US side of the frontier between Washington state and Canada's Vancouver Island, are certainly compelling. Hunkering down prettily in the dry rain-shadow of the Olympic Peninsula, these islands receive more sunshine than nearby but often-cloudy Seattle.

Roche Harbor, San Juan.

Temperatures average 68°F (20°C) in summer and 34°F (1°C) in winter, with annual rainfall averaging 29in (73cm). Many of the 172 San Juans are privately owned, accessible only via private craft. **Washington State Ferries** (www.wsdot.com) stop at four of the largest islands: San Juan, Orcas, Lopez, and Shaw.

With accommodation very much in demand, reservations should be made well in advance; the San Juan Islands Visitors Bureau (tel: 360-378 9551; www.visitsanjuans.com) offers online bookings. Whale-watching and sea kayaking are hugely popular, while athletes and amateurs alike ride off to explore the far corners of the islands on readily rented bicycles.

SAN JUAN ISLAND

The commercial center for the San Juan archipelago, on **San Juan Island** ❼ itself, is **Friday Harbor**, where it's fun to stroll around the marina and village. Near the ferry terminal, the **San Juan Historical Museum** (405 Price Street; tel: 360-378 3949; www.

The Washington State Ferry service is a good way to get around.

sjmuseum.org; May–Sept Thu–Sat 10am–4pm, Sun 1–4pm; Oct–March by appointment only), presents a view of life on the island in 1894.

The non-profit **Whale Museum** (62 First Street North; tel: 360-378 4710; https://whalemuseum.org; daily 10am–4pm), encourages responsible stewardship of whales in the surrounding waters via education and research. Glimpse them between late April and Sept at designated whale-watching parks like **Lime Kiln Point State Park** (1567 Westside Road; tel: 360-378 2044; daily 8am–dusk), or hook up with a whale-watching tour boat such as **San Juan Safaris** (tel: 800-450 6858; www.sanjuansafaris.com).

Snug Harbor, 9 miles (14km) across the island from the ferry terminal, is another center for marine activities, and is home to the Snug Harbor Resort (1997 Mitchell Bay Road; tel: 360-378 4762; www.snugresort.com). Quaint little **Roche Harbor**, at the northwest corner of the island, with its cobbled streets and rose bushes, is listed on the National Register of Historical Sites.

Savor its origins as a lime and cement quarry during a stay at the comfortable 1886 **Hotel de Haro** (248 Reuben Memorial Drive; tel: 360-378 2155; www.rocheharbor.com). A traditional "Colors Ceremony" takes place at sunset every evening in summer, where flags are lowered to the sounds of various national anthems. Anyone with sensitive ears should beware the super-loud bang from the cannon. Even if you can't stay, at least be sure to take in a sunset. Both the **Duck Soup Inn** restaurant (50 Duck Soup Lane; www.ducksoupsanjuans. com), and **Friday Harbor House** (130 West Street; www.fridayharborhouse.com), which offers rooms as well as dining, serve as romantic overlooks from which to watch the light show.

ORCAS ISLAND

Orcas Island ❽ centers on the tallest mountain in the San Juan islands, mighty 2,000ft (610 meters) **Mount Constitution**. The early morning fog on its summit is pierced by a fortress built by WPA workers in the 1930s, and designed to replicate Russian watchtowers erected in the Caucasus during the 12th century. The long, winding drive up to the peak is amply rewarded by 360-degree views encompassing the Canadian Coastal Mountains, the Cascades, the Olympic Peninsula, the San Juans, and Vancouver Island. Bald eagles soar above and below. Located entirely within **Moran State Park** (tel: 1-800-452 5687; https://moranstatepark.com; camping reservations required), the mountain can boast almost 30 miles (48km) of hiking trails, which were similarly laid out by the Civilian Conservation Corps.

Enticing shops in the towns of Eastsound, Olga, and Deer Harbor brim with local crafts from the island's multitude of cottage artists: check out the pottery, the jewelry, and the weaving.

The famed **Rosario Resort** (1400 Rosario Road, Eastsound; tel: 360-376 2222; https://rosarioresort.com) and marina offers luxurious lodging with all the trimmings. The inspiration of Robert Moran, photographer, writer, and humourist, the resort's foundation is cut into solid rock, 16ft (5 meters) deep.

Patos Island Lighthouse with Mt. Baker in the backdrop.

Hewn from solid Honduran mahogany, its doors are so heavy that Moran had to invent a special butterfly-hinge. The upper three floors are paneled in mahogany with floors in teakwood, original furnishings, and Tiffany details that contribute to the overall opulence. The showcase Music Room features a stained-glass window imported from Brussels and a magnificent 1,972-pipe Aeolian Pipe Organ. Stop by the Rosario for dinner, at the very least.

LOPEZ ISLAND

Musicians and writers, boatbuilders and fishermen, sewer diggers and potters, corporate retirees and cannabis growers are said to be numbered among the odd assortment who live on **Lopez Island** ❾. It's a sleepy, rural place, prized by cyclists for its flat terrain; most rental companies will deliver bikes to your place of lodging. Contacting the Chamber of Commerce for details of camping facilities and other accommodations (265 Lopez Road; tel: 360-468 4664; https://lopezisland.com).

BAINBRIDGE ISLAND

Bainbridge Island ❿ (tel: 206-842 3700; www.visitbainbridgeisland.org), across Puget Sound west of Seattle and effectively an appendage of the Kitsap Peninsula, is easily accessible from downtown Seattle via the Washington State Ferry or by car across the Agate Pass Bridge. Predominantly a bedroom community, this semi-rural island is peppered with trim farmhouses, beach-with-a-view mansions, and half-way-finished renovations.

Winslow Way, a short walk up from the ferry terminal, is lined with small shops and restaurants, as well as tasting rooms and bistros run by various local wineries. For details of island vineyards that offer tours and tastings, visit www.bainbridgewineries.com.

Up at the northern end of the island, six miles (10km) from the ferry, **Fay Bainbridge State Park** (tel: 206-842 3931; https://biparks.org) has overnight camping with views across to Seattle. Garden lovers rave about the 150-acre (60-hectare) **Bloedel Reserve** nearby (7571 Northeast Dolphin Drive; tel: 206-842 7631; https://bloedelreserve.org; Tue–Sun 10am–5pm), a former private estate that holds fine formal gardens, nature trails, and an attractive manor house.

At the opposite, southern end of Bainbridge Island, **Fort Ward** was established during World War I to protect the Bremerton Navy Yard. There are no campsites here, but the rocky beach at sunset shows off the island's highlights: the Olympic Mountains casting their silhouettes against a deep purple sky and the lights of reflected ships across the darkened waters.

BREMERTON

Take the short ferry ride from Seattle to **Bremerton** ⓫, and you're confronted as you arrive by the **Puget Sound Naval Shipyard**. Mothballed and to-be-overhauled Navy vessels loom along the shore of Sinclair Inlet, and

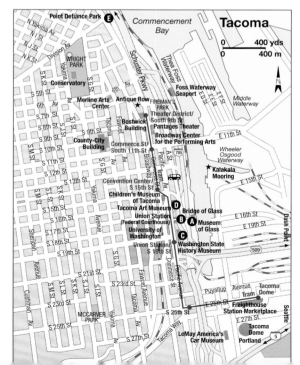

with a workforce of 14,000 this is the county's largest employer. Downtown Bremerton's waterfront park includes the Vietnam-era naval destroyer **USS Turner Joy** (300 Washington Beach Avenue; tours May–Sept; tel: 360-792 2457; https://ussturnerjoy.org; Mar–Oct 10am–5pm; Nov–Feb until 4pm).

Right where the ferries dock, the free **Puget Sound Navy Museum** (251 First Street; tel: 360-479 7447; www. pugetsoundnavymuseum.org; summer only, Wed–Mon 10am–4pm; until 7pm first Fri of every month) illustrates naval history with models of ships plus naval weapons, photographs, and memorabilia. Ten miles (16km) north of Bremerton, the **US Naval Undersea Museum** (1 Garnett Way, Keyport; tel: 360-396 4148; https://navalunderseamuseum.org; Wed–Mon 10am–4pm), houses the country's largest collection of submarines, torpedoes, and undersea mines.

POULSBO

For a scenic loop day-trip, you can cross Puget Sound north of Seattle on the Washington State Ferries connection from Edmonds to Kingston on the Kitsap Peninsula, then drive south via **Poulsbo ⑫** to reach the island via the Agate Pass Bridge, and finally return to Seattle via the Bainbridge Island ferry.

Thanks to its supposed resemblance to the famed fjords, Poulsbo itself (pronounced *pauls-bow*) has been dubbed "little Norway." To get there from Kingston, head west on State Route 104, veer left when it becomes Bond Road at Streibels Corner, and keep going to Front Street by the water.

A white-spired Lutheran church peers over the bay, and a wooden breakwater shelters the fishing fleet. Colorful murals in the traditional decorative *rosemaling* technique depict Norwegian lifestyles. The interesting **SEA Discovery Center** (18743 Front Street; tel: 360-598 4460; https://sea. wwu.edu; daily 11am–5pm) encourages visitors to get up close to the marine life of Puget Sound.

For the most attractive route east, turn right onto Fjord Drive a block up the hill from Front Street. That soon becomes

The U.S.S. Turner Joy is now a floating museum in Bremerton.

MOUNT RAINIER NATIONAL PARK

Mount Rainier, an active volcano almost permanently topped with snow, receives about 2.5 million visitors a year. Its towering summit has long attracted serious climbers.

Few Washington visitors can resist the temptation to explore glacier-clad **Mount Rainier** (14,411ft/4,392 meters). Surrounded by old-growth forest and stunning wildflower meadows, it's still an active volcano, albeit encased in snow and ice. Established as a national park in 1899, the mountain had, of course, been known for millennia by peoples including the Nisqually, Cowlitz, Yakama, Puyallup, and Muckleshoot, who hunted and gathered berries in its forests and meadows. They called it such names as Tahoma, Tachkoma, and T'chakoba; interpretations range from "nourishing breast" to "rumbling noise."

Mount Rainier National Park (tel: 360-569 2211; www.nps.gov/mora) remains open year-round, but access is limited in winter. Aim to arrive mid-week in summer, as parking is limited on the weekend. Activities range from easy ranger-guided walks to mountain climbing and car touring. Day hikers must stay on designated trails, which can be steep, but are well maintained in summer; in winter they're snow-covered and hard to follow. Winter offers

Tipsoo Lake at dawn.

cross-country skiing and snowshoeing; there are no ski areas. Bicycles are allowed on the roads.

Most drivers access the park via the year-round **Nisqually** entrance, on Highway 706 in its southwest corner. Pick up hiking and backpacking information, or wilderness permits and reservations, from the **Longmire Wilderness Information Center** (tel: 360-569 6650; May 22–Oct 15), on the site where James Longmire found mineral springs in 1883. The nearby **Longmire Museum** (daily 9am–6pm; free), holds displays on the park's natural and man-made history.

The road then winds up to the 5,400ft (1,647-meter) **Paradise** area, on Rainier's south face. Besides the stupendous view, visitors can take in the Henry M. Jackson Memorial Visitor Center (daily, weekends only in winter; tel: 360-569 6571).

Various walking trails start nearby. **Nisqually Vista Trail** is a vigorous 1.2-mile (2-km) hike, while a paved half-mile (0.8-km) section loops around the meadows on the easier **Skyline Trail**. Common flowers include the Indian paintbrush, daisies, lupins and beargrass, at their most beautiful during April, May, and June.

From Paradise, motorists can either double back or continue east along Stevens Ridge (open June–Oct) to meet Highway 123, where the **Ohanapecosh Visitor Center** (tel: 360-569 6581; late June–mid-Sept) lies a short way south.

Mountain climbers require proper equipment and training to reach the summit of Mount Rainier, a demanding ascent with an elevation gain of more than 9,000ft (2,800 meters) over a distance of 8 miles (13km). **Rainier Mountaineering Inc.** (tel: 888-892 5462; www.rmiguides.com) provide guide services including one-day instruction, two-day climbs, and five-day seminars.

Historic **Paradise Inn** (tel: 855-755 2275; https://mtrainierguestservices.com; summer only) offers the park's most prized accommodations; book months ahead. Its spacious dining room serves a celebrated Bourbon buffalo meatloaf. German carpenter Hans Fraehnke built much of its decorative woodwork, including a grandfather clock, in 1919. There's year-round in-park lodging at the **National Park Inn** at Longmire (tel: 855-755 2275; https://mtrainierguestservices.com), 6 miles (10km) in from the Nisqually entrance.

Lemolo Drive, which enjoys great mountain views as it curves around Liberty Bay, and hooks up with State Highway 305 as it approaches the bridge.

A brief detour north off the highway, just before the bridge, will bring you to the **Suquamish Museum** (15838 Sandy Hook Road; tel: 360-394 7123; https://suquamish.nsn.us; May–Sept daily 10am–5pm; Oct–Apr Fri–Sun 11am–4pm), which traces the history and culture of the Suquamish people.

Poulsbo's near-neighbor to the west, **Bangor**, is home base to eight of the country's fourteen ballistic-missile submarines.

VASHON ISLAND

The largely residential **Vashon Island ⑬**, south of Bainbridge Island, is completely dependent on the ferry system. It offers pleasant walks along beaches including Inspiration Point, which, on a clear day, enjoys a powerful view of Mount Rainier. Ferries head in three directions from Vashon: west to Southworth and east to Fauntleroy from its northern tip, and south to Tacoma from its opposite, southern end.

Just west of the Tacoma Narrows Bridge – the replacement for the infamous previous bridge that collapsed in the wind in 1940, just four months after it opened – **Gig Harbor** is a charming fishing community that lies an easy one-hour drive from Seattle. While Gig Harbor can certainly boast a wealth of galleries, shops, and restaurants, it has avoided the saccharine cuteness of other tourist towns. Local sailors consider it one of the world's most beautiful harbors. Clams, crabs, and oysters abound in **Kopachuck State Park** (10712 56th Street Northwest; tel: 253-265 3606; https://www.parks.wa.gov; daily 8am–8pm). Scuttle about at low tide, and see what you can scoop up.

TACOMA

Just 30 miles (48km) south of Seattle, and linked with its better-known neighbor by continuous urban development, the bustling commercial port of **Tacoma ⑭** is Washington's third-largest city. Lying in the shadow of **Mount Rainier ⑮**, it took its name – originally pronounced "*tahoma*" – from the peak's Native American name.

For an overview of the city's ever-busy waterfront, start by visiting the **Working Waterfront Museum** (705 Dock Street; tel: 253-272 2750; www.fosswaterway-seaport.org; Thu–Sun 10am–4pm; free), a gloriously restored warehouse that showcases its maritime heritage.

Tacoma's major attractions, however, celebrate its most famous son, world-renowned glass artist **Dale Chihuly**. The **Museum of Glass ②** (1801 Dock Street; tel: 253-284 4750; www.museumofglass.org; Wed–Sun 10am–5pm) has a ground level of glass and steel topped by a tilted glass cone encased in stainless-steel mesh. As well as its permanent Chihuly collection, it features the work of other artists, and stages live demonstrations in its Hot Shop. You don't have to enter the museum to walk across

⊘ Where

A park a couple of blocks east of the Suquamish Museum holds the grave of **Chief Sealth** (c.1786–1866), more commonly known as Chief Seattle, who smoothed relations between Native Americans and non-Natives, and gave Seattle its name. He's especially honored by environmentalists for his widely attributed statement that "The Earth does not belong to us, we belong to the Earth."

Tacoma's marina.

the stunning **Bridge of Glass ⓑ**, the 500ft (152 meters) walkway, tinkling with thousands of colored shards and open around the clock, which extends from its roof to cross Interstate 705 and link to the stimulating **Washington State History Museum ⓒ** (1911 Pacific Avenue; tel: 1-888-238 4373; www.washingtonhistory.org; Tue–Sun 10am–5pm).

Back towards the center, the fine **Tacoma Art Museum ⓓ** (1701 Pacific Avenue; tel: 253-272 4258; www.tacomaartmuseum.org; Wed–Sun 10am–5pm) features major traveling exhibitions and places a strong emphasis on contemporary Northwestern art.

Tacoma's residential districts contain many Victorian homes, decked out with turrets, gables, and leaded windows. Toward its northern end, the **Proctor** shopping district has a pleasant "small town" feel.

The prominent point of land that juts into the bay at Tacoma's northernmost tip, with the broad blue of Puget Sound as a backdrop, is home to **Point Defiance Park ⓔ**. In among its trails and gardens, the **Zoo and Aquarium** (5400

North Pearl Street; tel: 253-404 3800; www.pdza.org; summer 9am–7pm; winter Thu–Mon 9am–3:30pm), displays sharks, beluga whales, polar bears, and pachyderms.

SOUTH PUGET SOUND

Close to the southern end of Puget Sound, 42 miles (67km) south of Seattle beyond Tacoma, one of Washington state's oldest towns, **Steilacoom ⑯**, perches on a high bluff with a sweeping view of the Sound and its islands. It's a tidy little place, with a museum, a vintage drugstore complete with old-fashioned soda fountain, and streets of historic homes and retail buildings.

On the grounds of nearby Western State Hospital, volunteer craftsmen have restored the four remaining military buildings from **Fort Steilacoom** (9601 Steilacoom Boulevard Southwest, Lakewood; tel: 253-756 3928; https://historic-fortsteilacoom.org; tours first Sun of each month, 1–4pm; free), a center of regional military activity between 1849 and 1868. The officers' quarters are in front of the hospital administration building; reenactment battles from the Civil War take place here from time to time.

OLYMPIA

Washington's state capital, **Olympia ⑰**, rests at the southernmost extremity of the Sound. Attractions besides its tree-lined Capitol Campus and historic government buildings include waterfront Percival Landing park, with its humorous statues and mile-long boardwalk, and serene Capitol Lake.

Tours of the impressive, marble-lined **Washington State Capitol** (Legislative Building, Capital Way; tel: 360-902 8880; www.des.wa.gov; drop-in tours Mon–Fri 10am–3pm, Sat and Sun 11:30am–2:30pm; free) meander through a building similar in design to the United States Capitol in Washington, DC. On a clear day, it is well worth the climb up to the brick and sandstone dome. The top of the cupola is a full 287ft (87m)

The Washington State Capitol.

above ground level, making the roof of the capitol one of the tallest masonry domes in the world. From the top, it's possible to enjoy sweeping views of Mount Rainier and Mount St Helens.

Additional guided tours take in the Executive Mansion, or you can simply walk around on your own through the gardens and conservatory, or past several war memorials. A **Story Pole** that stands on a grassy slope in front of the General Administration Building on the Capitol Campus was carved by Chief William Shelton of the Snohomish Tribe.

Olympia's **Farmers' Market** (700 North Capitol Way; tel: 360-352 9096; www.olympiafarmersmarket.com; Apr–Oct Thu–Sun 10am– 3pm; Nov–Dec Sat and Sun 10am–3pm; Jan–Mar Sat 10am–3pm), on historic Budd Inlet, is the state's second-biggest open-air market and offers great produce: baby bok choy, amazing juicy berries, meats, and seafood. One choice rarity is the golden raspberry, a well-kept secret for some of the sweetest jams. It's fun to have lunch in the market and listen to live music.

The **Billy Frank Jr. Nisqually National Wildlife Refuge ⑱** (100 Brown Farm Road; tel: 360-753 9467; www.fws.gov; free), not far east of Olympia, is a relatively unpolluted coastal delta, where great blue herons, golden eagles, and hawks soar overhead. There are walking trails, but it's much more fun to rent a canoe or kayak and explore its many inlets. "Billy Frank Jr." was added to its official name in 2015 to honour a leader of the Nisqually tribe who died the previous year.

Due south of Olympia, **Wolf Haven International** (3111 Offut Lake Road Southeast, Tenino; tel: 360-264 4695; https://wolfhaven.org; daily guided tours 10am–5pm, closed Feb), is a sanctuary which at any onetime cares for around 50 endangered wolves. A captive breeding center for both the red wolf and the Mexican gray wolf, its 50-minute guided tours give more than 25,000 visitors each year a remarkable close-up wildlife experience. A short way west, **Millersylvania State Park** (12245 Tilley Road Southwest; tel: 360-753 1519; www.parks.wa.gov) is a restful park with a small lake and huge trees.

⊘ MOUNT ST HELENS

On May 18, 1980, a volcanic eruption blew the top off Mount St Helens with the force of an atomic bomb, hurtling debris into the atmosphere at 500mph (800kph). Shattered by an earthquake, the north face of this previously symmetrical mountain collapsed in a massive avalanche. An enormous slab of rock and ice slammed into Spirit Lake, crossed a high ridge, and roared 14 miles (22km) down the Toutle River. As the avalanche released pressurized gases from within the volcano, a tremendous lateral explosion developed into a stone-filled wind that swept over ridges and toppled trees. By nightfall, over half a million sq miles (1.3 million sq km) in three US states were covered in ash, and the previously 9,677ft (3,000 meters) mountain stood 1,300ft (400 meters) shorter.

In one of the largest natural disasters in US history, 57 people died, buried beneath ash and mudslides. The toll on wildlife was severe: an estimated 1,500 elk, 200 black bears, and the entire rare spotted-owl population were wiped out. **Mount St Helens National Volcanic Monument** now makes a fascinating detour en route between Seattle and Portland. For a day of exceptional viewing, turn east off I-5 at

Castle Rock, 56 miles (90km) south of Olympia. Follow Highway 504 for 5 miles (8km) to reach the **Mount St Helens Visitor Center** (tel: 360-274 2100; www.parks.wa.gov; daily 9am–5pm; closed Tue–Wed Nov–Feb) at Silver Lake. The mountain itself lies another 50 miles (80km) east, but you can see it on the horizon from the Silver Lake Wetlands Trail. From here onwards, the views grow ever more remarkable as the road climbs beside the north fork of the Toutle River.

Displays at the **Coldwater Ridge Visitor Center** (tel: 360-274 2131; www.fs.usda.gov; daily 9am–5pm), 38 miles (61km) along, explain how they're recolonizing the blast zone. The easy **Winds of Change Trail** illustrates how the forests were blasted into wastelands, and has views of the volcano.

At the far end of Highway 504, in the heart of the blast zone, the **Johnston Ridge Observatory** (tel: 360-274 2140; www.fs.usda.gov; mid-May–Oct 10am–6pm), traces the sequence of geological events that transformed the landscape. On a clear day, hikers on the short **Eruption Trail** can expect views of the lava dome, crater, pumice plain, and the landslide deposit.

THE OLYMPIC PENINSULA AND COASTAL WASHINGTON

This remote, windswept coastline is home to fantastic mountains, Native American reservations, strangely shaped rocks . . . and a kite museum.

The **Olympic Peninsula**, which encompasses Washington's coastline, juts like an oversize thumb from the fist of Washington State. There's no farther western point in the lower 48 states; as Lewis and Clark discovered, this is where the frontier ends. The relatively sheltered northern edge of the peninsula runs along the Strait of Juan de Fuca, but along the outer length of the thumb, wilderness meets the ocean in a roaring jumble of coves and bays, beaches, and foaming breakers.

Portions of this Olympic-shadowed region remained unexplored and unmapped until the start of the 20th century. Despite subsequent change and development, much of it still looks just as it did when early navigators claimed this land for the monarchies of Spain and England. And yes, it does rain a great deal, but how else could its legendary rainforests grow so lush? Try to absorb the annual rainfall figures: 137in (347cm) as reported in the Hoh Rain Forest and a significant 82in (209cm) at Long Beach. Port Angeles on the northern edge, closer to the San Juan Islands, reports a more tolerable 26in (66cm) a year.

Much of this remote, storm-swept shoreline is Native American land, where travel is restricted. Some now forms part of Olympic National Park (see page 128), most of which lies

well inland. The rest is beach, bay, and forest, though in the north especially, beaches tend to be much less accessible than along the Oregon coast. The further south you travel, the more of a tourist infrastructure you'll find, in the shape of resorts such as Long Beach and Ocean Shores.

The one north–south road that parallels the Pacific, US 101, only runs along the seashore for a single 12-mile (19km) stretch; otherwise, in those occasional places where you can drive to the ocean, you can only reach

Main attractions
Port Townsend
Hoh Rain Forest
Quinault Rainforest
Shi-Shi Beach
Rialto Beach
Ruby Beach
Long Beach
World Kite Museum

Map on page 126

New Dungeness Lighthouse.

> **Tip**

For the fastest route from Seattle to Port Townsend, take the Washington State Ferry service (https://wsdot.wa.gov) from Mukilteo, on the mainland north of Seattle (see page 98), to Clinton on Whidbey Island. From there, you can drive northwest across the island to catch another ferry onwards from Fort Casey, outside Coupeville, to Port Townsend.

it along dead-end detours before you have to double back to the highway.

PORT TOWNSEND

Poised where the waters of the Strait of Juan de Fuca and Puget Sound combine to create muscle-bound riptides, 100 miles (160km) north of Olympia, lovely **Port Townsend ❶** marks the northeast corner of the Olympic Peninsula. It could not enjoy a more picturesque setting; jagged Olympic peaks stand guard to the south, cliffs soar on nearby Whidbey Island, and the elusive "Great White Father," the Skagit name for Mount Baker, shadows the horizon.

It was the bay itself that was originally named for George, Marquis of Townshend, in 1792. An aide to General Wolfe in the Quebec campaign of 1759, Townshend commanded British forces after Wolfe was killed. He lived for 83 years, but never set eyes on the Pacific, let alone learned of the town that was established in 1851 (and somehow misplaced the "h" along the way).

Pioneers Alfred Plummer and Charles Bachelder were convinced

Port Townsend would become the greatest port on Puget Sound. However, once the Union Pacific's transcontinental railroad had failed to connect, Seattle emerged as the port of entry for the Sound. Overnight, a town designed to hold 20,000 residents was left with a mere 3,500. Seventy years later, in 1961, Port Townsend residents refurbished the Victorian homes of years past, and rekindled the town's dormant sense of civic pride.

Port Townsend is celebrated for its historic downtown district and art galleries; stately hotels and bed-and-breakfasts now occupy many of its artistically preserved Victorian buildings. Downtown centers on Water Street, and encompasses around four blocks of graceful turn-of-the-19th-century brick structures. Between glimpses of the Strait and nearby islands, you'll come across such relics of bygone years as an 1890 Bell Tower; the imposing Customs House; and the **Jefferson Museum of Art and History**, housed in the 1898 City Hall (540 Water Street; tel: 360-385 1003; www.

Port Townsend Boat Haven at sundown.

jchsmuseum.org; daily 11am–4pm). Pick up a walking tour brochure in the latter to guide your own explorations of the neighboring historic homes, redolent with juicy tales of Shanghaied sailors and underground tunnels.

Arrayed along the shoreline on the north side of town, **Fort Worden Historical State Park** (200 Battery Way; tel: 360-344 4412; www.parks.wa.gov) preserves one of three forts that were built in 1896 to protect Puget Sound from naval attack. It served as the chief location for the 1981 movie *An Officer and a Gentleman*, starring Richard Gere and Debra Winger, which also filmed in several other local spots. Overnight guests can sleep in the former officers' houses or soldiers' barracks, available as vacation rentals (tel: 360-344 4400; https://fortworden.org). On site, the educational **Marine Science Center** (tel: 360-385 5582; https://ptmsc.org; Sat and Sun noon–5pm; free) holds an aquarium and an articulated orca skeleton, while the **Coast Artillery Museum** (tel: 360-385 0373; www.coastartillery. org; daily 11am–4pm) puts on walking tours of the fortifications on summer weekends. Also, **Centrum** (www.centrum.org), an arts and education foundation based at the fort, stages musical workshops and performances, including separate festivals of jazz and fiddle music each July.

SEQUIM

Set downwind of the Olympic mountain range, the coastal area west of Port Townsend lies in a rain shadow. Pronounced *skwim*, and meaning "quiet waters," the town of **Sequim ❷**, 30 miles (50km) out from Port Townsend, has the lowest annual rainfall in western Washington, at only 11–17 in (27–43cm); climatically speaking, it's a desert island surrounded by water.

After mammoth fossils were uncovered near Sequim in 1996, persistent elementary school students persuaded the state legislature to name the Columbian Mammoth as an official state fossil. Visitors to the **Olympic Game Farm** (1423 Ward Road; tel: 360-683 4295; https://olygamefarm.com; daily 9am–dusk), can drive or ride a

Seattle's annual rainfall ensures plantlife thrives in Hoh Rain Forest.

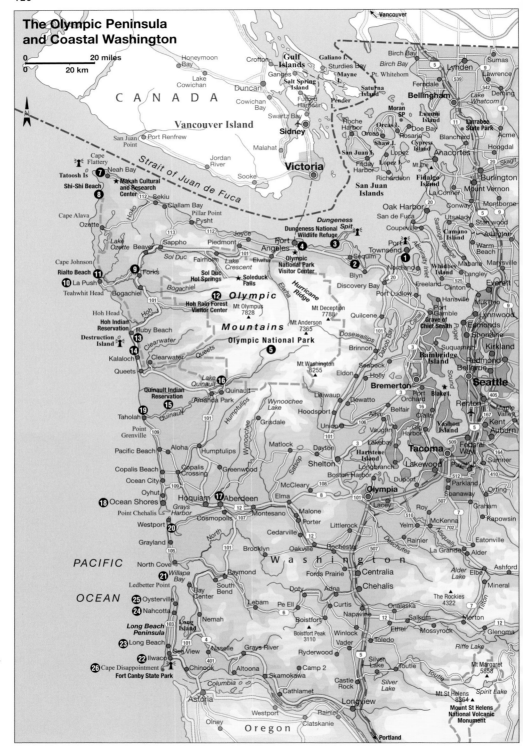

The Olympic Peninsula and Coastal Washington

0 _____ 20 miles
0 _____ 20 km

CANADA

Vancouver Island

Honeymoon Bay
Crofton
Gulf Islands
Galiano I.
Sturdies Bay
Mayne
Pt. Whitehorn
Birch Bay
Birch Bay
Sumas
Lynden
Lawrence
Deming
Ganges
Lake Cowichan
Duncan
Salt Spring Island
Fulford Harbour
Pender I.
Saturna Island
Ferndale
Bellingham
Lake Whatcom
Cowichan Bay
Swartz Bay
Roche Harbor
Orcas I.
Doe Bay
Moran SP
Lummi Island
Latrabee State Park
Acme
Hoogdal
Vancouver Island
Sidney
San Juan Point
Port Renfrew
Orcas
Rosario
Shaw I.
Cypress Island
Anacortes
Burlington
Malahat
Victoria
Jordan River
Sooke
Friday Harbor
Lopez
San Juan I.
Lopez I.
Mt. Erie
Fidalgo Island
La Conner
Richardson
Skagit
Mount Vernon
Cape Flattery
Neah Bay
San Juan Islands
Montborne
Tatoosh Is
Shi-Shi Beach
Makah Cultural and Research Center
Sekiu
Clallam Bay
Pillar Point
Pysht
Oak Harbor
San de Fuca
Coupeville
20
Conway
Utsalady
Stanwood
Arlington
Cape Alava
Ozette
Sappho
Piedmont
Joyce
Dungeness Spit
Dungeness National Wildlife Refuge
Camano Island
Warm Beach
Marysville
Lake Ozette
Beaver
Fairholm
Elwha
Port Angeles
4
Sequim
Port Townsend
1
Mabana
Langley
Everett
Cape Johnson
Rialto Beach
9
Forks
Sol Duc
Lake Crescent
Soleduck Falls
Olympic National Park Visitor Center
2
Blyn
Nordland
Whidbey Island
Freeland
Clinton
Mukilteo
La Push
10
Sol Duc Hot Springs
Discovery Bay
Port Ludlow
Hansville
Teahwhit Head
Bogachiel
Bogachiel
12
Hoh Rain Forest Visitor Center
Mt Olympus 7828 ▲
Hurricane Ridge
Mt Deception 7788 ▲
Quilcene
Port Gamble
Grave of Chief Sealth
Lynnwood
Edmonds
Shoreline
Hoh Head
Hoh Indian Reservation
Olympic
Mt Anderson 7365 ▲
Suquamish
Bainbridge Island
Kirkland
Redmond
Destruction Island
13
Ruby Beach
Clearwater
Mountains
Olympic National Park
5
Dosewallips
Brinnon
Seabeck
Poulsbo
Bellevue
Seattle
Kalaloch
14
Clearwater
Queets
Mt Washington 6255 ▲
Eldon
Holly
Port Orchard
Port Blake I.
Renton
Queets
Lake Quinault
16
Quinault
Lilliwaup
Dewatto
Bremerton
Vashon Island
Kent
Auburn
Quinault Indian Reservation
15
Amanda Park
Wynoochee Lake
Hoodsport
Allyn
Belfair
Olalla
Gig Harbor
Federal Way
Taholah
19
Quinault
Grisdale
Union
Vaughn
Lakebay
Sumner
Point Grenville
Humptulips
Matlock
Dayton
Satsop
Harstine Island
Longbranch
Tacoma
Lakewood
Puyallup
Pacific Beach
Aloha
Humptulips
Greenwood
Shelton
Boston Harbor
Dupont
Parkland
Orting
Copalis Beach
Copalis Crossing
McCleary
Elma
Olympia
Lacey
Spanaway
Graham
Kapowsin
Ocean Shores
18
Hoquiam
17
Aberdeen
Cosmopolis
Montesano
Porter
Malone
Littlerock
Rochester
Yelm
McKenna
Eatonville
Point Chehalis
Westport
20
Grayland
Cedarville
Rainier
La Grande
Alder
Ashford
Grays Harbor
Brooklyn
Oakville
Washington
Deschutes
Alder Lake
Elbe
North Cove
North River
Raymond
Fords Prairie
Centralia
The Rockies 4322
Mineral
Willapa Bay
21
Doty
Adna
Chehalis
Ledbetter Point
Bay Center
South Bend
Lebam
Pe Ell
Curtis
Napavine
Onalaska
Salkum
Morton
Glenoma
25 Oysterville
Nemah
Boistfort
Boistfort Peak 3110 ▲
Winlock
Vader
Ethel
Mossyrock
Riffe Lake
24 Nahcotta
Long Beach Peninsula
Long Island
Naselle
Grays River
Ryderwood
Toledo
Silver Lake
Mt Margaret 5858 ▲
23 Long Beach
Sea View
Camp 2
Silver Lake
22 Ilwaco
Chinook
Altoona
Skamokawa
Castle Rock
Silver Lake
Mt St Helens 8364 ▲
Spirit Lake
26 Cape Disappointment
Fort Canby State Park
Columbia
Cathlamet
Longview
Mount St Helens National Volcanic Monument
Astoria
Westport
Rainier
Clatskanie
Olney
Oregon
Portland

PACIFIC OCEAN

Strait of Juan de Fuca

tour bus though open country roamed by zebras, llamas, bison, and bears, and see captive lions and tigers in the enclosures.

Downtown, the charming century-old "Bell House" is headquarters of the **Cedarbrook Herb and Lavender Farm** (1345 South Sequim Avenue; tel: 360-683 7733; www.cedarbrooklavender. com; Mar–Dec Mon–Sat 9am–5pm, Sun 10am–4pm), which sells all sorts of lavender-scented soaps, oils, and lotions. The third weekend of July sees festivities to mark Lavender Weekend.

A certain actor often vacationed on Sequim Bay. After his death, his property was donated to the city, and now adjoins the boat basin known as the **John Wayne Marina**. Alongside, the Dockside Grill (tel: 360-683 7510; www. docksidegrill-sequim.com), serves ultra-fresh seafood. At **Sequim Bay State Park** (tel: 360-683 7510; www.parks. wa.gov), 2 miles (3km) south, you'll find rustic benches and abundant moss in a green setting of cedars and ferns. Trails lead through the trees to a beach and boat launch.

DUNGENESS

The **Dungeness National Wildlife Refuge ❸**, a favorite destination for bird-watchers, affords a 5-mile (8-km) hike along an impressive sandy hook of land, **Dungeness Spit**. Visited by British sea captain George Vancouver in 1792, it's the longest natural sandspit in the United States, and was named for Dungeness, a similar spit in southern England. Its narrowest portions measure just 50ft (15 meters) wide during high tides, and breaches have been known to occur. **Dungeness crab** – Latin name, *Cancer magister* – is native to the Dungeness Spit, and known for its distinctively sweet flavor. An 1857 **lighthouse** makes a great destination for walkers, while Cline Spit to the east is popular with windsurfers.

A short way west of Dungeness, a weather-beaten old barn is home to

one of Washington's oldest wineries. **Olympic Cellars** (255410 US 101; tel: 360-452 0160; https://olympiccellars. com; Thu–Sat 11am–5pm) welcomes visitors year-round for tastings, and hosts open-air concerts on summer evenings.

PORT ANGELES

The major stopping point along the north coast of the Olympic Peninsula, **Port Angeles ❹**, stands a mere 20 miles (32km) due south, across the Strait of Juan de Fuca, from **Victoria**, British Columbia. The **Black Ball Ferry Line** (tel: 206-622 2222; www.cohoferry. com) offers two daily car ferries each way between the two (1hr 30min). The observation tower at City Pier makes a good vantage point from which to watch them sail to and fro, along with assorted freighters and pleasure boats.

Pick up information on Port Angeles at the downtown visitor center (121 East Railroad Avenue; tel: 360-452 2364; www.portangeles.org; Mon–Fri 9.30am–5.30pm, Sat 10am–5.30pm,

Locally caught Dungeness crab for sale at the market.

OLYMPIC NATIONAL PARK

Nestled into the very heart of the Olympic Peninsula, this wilderness park of lush temperate rainforests and dazzling glacier-capped mountains remains remarkably undeveloped.

Few regions in North America can combine such natural glory, gentle wildness and infinite variety as **Olympic National Park**. Effectively three parks in one, it encompasses three ecosystems, all within a day's drive of each other. These include the central core of the Olympic Peninsula, home to magnificent stands of old-growth and temperate rainforest as well as rugged glacier-capped mountains, and a separate 60-mile (100km) stretch of Pacific shoreline to the west, protecting the last wilderness ocean beaches in mainland USA. Most of the park is designated wilderness, and inaccessible by car. No driving route crosses its central portion – though dead-end roads penetrate it from different sides, like the spokes on a wheel – and only parts of the coastal strip can be reached by road.

Native Americans having bestowed the high country with sufficient legends and mystery to discourage travel, it wasn't until 1889 that an exploration party, sponsored by the *Seattle Press*, headed west and crossed the Olympic Mountains. Spotting the

Bainbridge Island ferry dock.

opportunity, timber fellers swiftly cut their way through the low-elevation rainforests. In 1897, however, naturalists lobbied to maintain the Olympic Forest Reserve. This evolved into Olympic National Monument (1909), and then Olympic National Park (1938).

For full details and current advice, start at the main **visitor center** in Port Angeles (600 East Park Avenue; tel: 360-565 3130; www.nps.gov/olym). A sinuous, precipitous 17-mile drive from there climbs more than 5000ft (1500 meters) to the top of **Hurricane Ridge**, for a stunning panorama of snowy summits and glistening glaciers. Trails lead hikers through lush meadows to additional viewpoints.

The Olympic Mountains are a labyrinth of lofty canyons, flowered ridges and glaciated peaks. Late June through August, black-tailed deer graze belly-deep in avalanche lilies, and marmots scurry from rock to rock. The highest of the lot, **Mount Olympus** – high, icy, and rugged enough to challenge world-class climbers – stands at 7,980ft (2,430 meters) southwest of Hurricane Ridge.

The park's most visited spot, the **Hoh Rain Forest**, is only accessible from the west; turn off US 101 onto Upper Hoh Road an hour's drive south of Forks (see page 131). This 24-mile (39km) stretch of low-level temperate rainforest, along the Hoh River, is recognized by UNESCO as both a Biosphere Reserve and a World Heritage Site. The preternaturally fertile forest thrives thanks to its mild coastal climate, with infrequent winter frosts and summer temperatures that rarely exceed 80°F (25°C). Colonnades of virgin spruce and hemlock rise amid draperies of moss to form an evergreen lattice; down below, vine maples spiral from pillowy forest-floor coverings of club moss. Easy hikes include the Hall of Mosses Trail and the Spruce Nature Trail.

Another beautiful area, the **Quinault Rainforest**, can be reached by taking either the North Shore or South Shore Road northeast from US 101 in the park's southwest corner.

As well as a handful of lodges, the park holds 14 campgrounds. Three – Kalaloch, Sol Duc and Mora – can be reserved in advance (www.recreation.gov), the rest are available first-come, first-served. Arrive early in summer, especially on weekends.

Sun noon–3pm). A few blocks back from the waterfront, changing displays in the **North Olympic History Center** (933 West Ninth Street; tel: 360-452 2662; www.clallamhistoricalsociety.com; Mon–Fri 8.30am–4pm) illustrate different aspects of regional history.

Besides being a gateway to Canada, Port Angeles also holds the main visitor center for beautiful **Olympic National Park ❺**, and is the starting point for the gorgeous drive into the park's Hurricane Ridge area.

THE STRAIT OF JUAN DE FUCA

West of Port Angeles, US 101 veers inland to run through the northern reaches of Olympic National Park. For 10 stunning miles (16km), it follows the southern shore of deep **Lake Crescent**, where there are picnic sites and hiking trails. Just beyond the lake, a 12-mile (19km) detour inland climbs to one of the national park's finest lodging options, the **Sol Duc Hot Springs Resort** (12076 Sol Duc Hot Springs Rd; tel: 866-476 5382; www.olympicnational-parks.com), which boasts three naturally heated pools.

Route 112, on the other hand, continues west along the coast, crossing the scenic **Elwha River**. Native American oral traditions say that until hydroelectric dams blocked the river a century ago, it held Chinook salmon so large that a single skin could serve as a ceremonial robe. Now that those dams have been removed, in the largest such project anywhere in the world, the salmon are slowly starting to return.

This coastal stretch follows the southern shore of the **Strait of Juan de Fuca**, a dramatic glacial fjord that links Puget Sound with the Pacific Ocean. Sheltered by the huge landmass of Canada's Vancouver Island, the surf here crawls lazily ashore, unlike the wild Pacific to the west. With complex rocky shorelines, and the magical combination of soft northwest light

and water, this is a place where eagles soar above the water. Smoke from woodstoves drifts lazily, and farms and cattle dot the landscape. The Canadian island across the strait looms on the horizon, hazily green and peaked with frost.

The county park at **Salt Creek Recreation Area** (tel: 360-928 3441; www.clallam.net/parks), down a spur road 16 miles (26km) west of Port Angeles, was the site of Fort Hayden, a World War II harbor defense site that held concealed camouflaged, bomb-proof batteries. After the war, Clallam County turned it into a 92-site campground, with a marine life sanctuary and hiking trails. A great hike climbs to the summit of **Striped Peak**, for tremendous views in all directions; alternatively, you can also drive up here, via a steep, pot-holed road.

Back on Rt 112, stop off at the **Joyce General Store** (tel: 360-928 3568), which first opened its doors in 1911. Its original false front is still in place, along with a beaded ceiling and oiled wood floors, and there's a simple

Ruby Beach, Olympic National Park.

⊘ Fact

Despite having never been to Forks, novelist Stephenie Meyer used the town as a setting for her *Twilight* vampire stories, first published in 2005. The five successful spin-off movies weren't filmed here either, but that hasn't deterred hordes of young visitors from turning up, especially during September's four-day Forever Twilight festival.

museum. On an agate-strewn salt-water beach farther west, beyond the southward turn-off for Forks (see page 131), **Clallam Bay County Park** (tel: 360-417 2291; www.clallam.net/parks), offers views on a clear day of Vancouver Island and Sekiu Point. Westward again, sea stacks form wildlife refuges, which provide sanctuary for puffins, murres, guillemots, and auklets.

NEAH BAY

The Strait of Juan de Fuca reaches the ocean at the tip of the Olympic Peninsula, which is also the farthest northwestern point of the contiguous US. **Cape Flattery ❻** was named in 1778 by Captain James Cook, who spied "a small opening which flattered us with the hopes of finding an harbour."

The little fishing village of **Neah Bay ❼**, just short of the cape, is 72 miles (115km) west of Port Angeles. Home to the Makah Reservation, it also holds several motels, simple cafés, boat launches, and charter fishing companies, like **Big Salmon** (tel: 360-645 2374, bigsalmonresort.net).

Beside the highway, the excellent **Makah Museum** (1880 Bayview Avenue; tel: 360-645 2711; https://makahmuseum.com; daily 10am–5pm) traces the history of the "People of the Cape." Calling themselves Kwih-dich-chuh-ahtx or "people who live by the rocks and seagulls," the Makah have lived at this tip of land for more than 2,000 years.

Built to house ancient artefacts uncovered near Lake Ozette to the south, the museum showcases a scale model of an 18th-century Makah village, a fine whaling canoe with harpoons, samples of clothing, implements, hooks and tools, and intricate weavings of cedar, bird feathers, and animal hair. Totem poles include a thunderbird with a clever transformation mask. The museum store sells handsome baskets, carvings, and jewelry made by Makah artists, plus a wide array of prints, books, and cards.

A muddy three-quarter-mile (1.2km) trail, at times along cedar boardwalks, sets off from the end of the unpaved 5-mile (8km) access road to Cape Flattery itself. Hikers are rewarded with spectacular views of mighty waves crashing deep into cliff-carved caves. The deactivated **Cape Flattery Lighthouse** stands on tiny **Tatoosh Island** just offshore, the last speck of land before Asia.

Another scenic wonder lies south of Cape Flattery, within the national park. Reached via a convoluted drive followed by a rugged hike, **Shi-Shi Beach ❽** (pronounced *shy-shy*), sprawls for 3 sandy miles (5km) between Portage Head and Point of Arches, A true wilderness beach, it's smooth enough, dotted with myriad tide pools, but the jagged rocks out to sea make a dramatic contrast. Despite its remoteness, the beach fills up with campers on summer weekends.

FORKS

In the absence of a coastal highway beside the Pacific, drivers heading

Enjoying the serenity from the pier at Lake Crescent.

south from Neah Bay have to double back eastwards on Highway 12 for 28 miles (45km), and then turn south on Highway 113 and US 101. Another 22 miles (35km) along, **Forks ⑨** (tel: 360-374 2531; https://forkswa.com), is a run-of-the-mill lumbering community that's been suddenly transformed into a major tourist destination for the strangest of reasons – its fictional role in the blood-sucking *Twilight* Saga.

While there's precious little to see in Forks – unless you're riveted by the prominent **Timber Museum** (1421 South Forks Avenue; tel: 360-374 9663; http://forkstimbermuseum.org; May–Sept Mon–Sat 10am–5pm, Sat 11am–4pm; Oct–Apr Mon–Sat 10am–4pm, Sat 11am–4pm) – it's a comfortable base for exploring Olympic National Park.

Well off the beaten path, where the dead-end Highway 110 meets the Pacific 15 miles (24km) west of Forks, little **La Push ⑩** fronts a charcoal gray beach strewn with driftwood – the "bones of the forest, picked clean by the sea," as the descriptive panels say. High breakers roll in from the northwest, and the mournful moan of warning buoys is constant. La Push is the base of the **Quileute** (https://quileutenation.org), whose traditional tales of "shape-shifters" were distorted to provide the pseudo-mythological backstory for The *Twilight* Saga.

Picturesque spots south of La Push include **Second Beach** and the even more popular **Third Beach**, where a sea stack and rugged Teahwhit Head are striking landmarks. Be warned that neither Teahwhit Head nor Taylor Point can be rounded at any tide; people have been killed in the attempt. Most coastal streams in these parts, incidentally, have a tea-stained appearance originating from tannin leached from leaves.

RIALTO BEACH AND LAKE OZETTE

Across the mouth of the Quillayute River, just north of La Push but only accessible via a separate road that branches off Highway 110 5 miles (8km) inland, **Rialto Beach ⑪** is the oceanfront highlight of the **Mora Area**

Impressive rock formations dominate Shi Shi beach.

of the national park. The 17-mile (27-km) trail that heads northward from here, along the North Olympic Coastal Wilderness to **Sand Point**, is a hiker's dream, covering coastal forest and ocean beaches. Creeks must be forded and log jams may be slippery, so be sure to seek advice before setting out.

Inland from Sand Point, there's a seasonal park ranger station beside **Lake Ozette** (tel: 360-565 3130), the third largest lake in Washington. Boardwalks lead to the beach and lake, and can be combined as part of a longer, two-day hike, the **Lake Ozette Loop**.

DESTRUCTION ISLAND AND KALALOCH

After passing the turn-off for the **Hoh Rain Forest** ⑫ (see page 128) area of Olympic National Park, 13 miles (21km) south of Forks, US 101 continues for the same distance again to reach the Pacific at **Ruby Beach** ⑬, famed for its red pebbles, where sentinel trees and sea stacks stand guard over tiny Abbey Island. From there, it runs parallel to the ocean for another 12 miles (19km), in its only coastal stretch in Washington.

Although – or perhaps because – the history of this wild and photogenic shoreline is filled with harrowing tales, the seascape is compelling. The repetitive rumble of surf rolling over sand and stones is mesmerizing; the briny smell of the blue-gray ocean is primal and poignant; wind-twisted Sitka spruce forests line the bluffs. Oddly shaped sea stacks project from the headlands, resembling a line of gray dinosaurs marching into the ocean, while wildlife includes bald eagles, harbor seals, shorebirds, and, out to sea, migrating whales. At times, when the spruce trees creak in the wind, the entire coast seems haunted by ghosts of shipwrecked sailors, warring Native Americans, and desperate settlers. **Destruction Island** near the northern end, with its picturesque albeit decommissioned Light, was named by beleaguered 19th-century sailors, after their compatriots were murdered by less-than-welcoming Native Americans.

Kalaloch Tree or the "Tree of Life".

Seven beach access points, each a short hike from the highway, lie within 6 miles (10km) of **Kalaloch** . It might look easy to walk from one beach to the next, but it's not. Outgoing tides are hazardous, while incoming tides have caused more than one explorer to be marooned on a rock for many hours or worse. There's also a real danger of the surf torpedoing rogue logs back onshore; take the threat seriously, people die every year. To avoid such hazards, be sure to pick up a free tide table, available at local visitor centers and businesses.

The National Park offers some rather wonderful – if not exactly luxurious – accommodations here, in the form of **Kalaloch Lodge** (157151 US 101; tel: 866-662 9928; reservations required; www.thekalalochlodge.com), buffeted by the never-ending onslaught of onshore winds. Equipped with log cabins and a restaurant, the lodge overlooks the ocean while Kalaloch Creek fronts onto a dramatic section of wave-dashed shoreline. After a day hitting the beaches, visitors can return to watch the sun set as they enjoy a sumptuous salmon dinner in the dining room.

Nearby – drive along the coast past Beach 3 – the **Kalaloch Campground** (tel: 360-962 2271; summer reservations on www.recreation.gov) has 175 sites, great hiking opportunities. and a summer nature program that's open to all.

QUINAULT INDIAN RESERVATION

Four miles (6km) south of Kalalach Lodge, the highway enters the **Quinault Indian Reservation** , cross the Queets River at **Queets** itself, and veers inland. Travel on the reservation is restricted; some maps show a coastal road, but it is not passable. Visitors with a tribal permit are allowed to fish, and sometimes the **Quinault**, who are superb fishermen and boaters, take tourists for canoe trips up the Quinault River.

At the eastern edge of the reservation, 30 miles (50km) from the ocean, US 101 skirts the serene, icy-blue **Lake Quinault** . Just within the national park, the handsome 1926 **Lake Quinault Lodge** (345 South Shore Road; tel: 360-288 2900; www.olympicnationalparks.com) makes an idyllic stopover. The sweep of grassy lawn down to the waterfront is particularly wonderful. Be sure to explore the lake by kayak or canoe (rentals on site), or hike through the surrounding old-growth timber.

ABERDEEN AND HOQUIAM

Highway 101 returns to the ocean 40 miles (64km) south of Lake Quinault, when it reaches sheltered, wedge-shaped Grays Harbor. At the mouth of the Chehalis River here, the twin cities of **Aberdeen**  and **Hoquiam** were both established as logging ports. Peppered with inland waterways Aberdeen was long renowned as the home of the clamburger, but these days it's more famous as the birthplace of musician Kurt Cobain and his Nirvana bandmate Krist Novoselic – hence the "Come As

Lake Quinault Lodge.

A tribute to Kurt Cobain of Nirvana fame in Aberdeen, his hometown.

You Are" slogan, a reference to one of Cobain's best-known songs, on its roadside welcome sign.

Housed in the 26-room mansion of a timber baron, Hoquiam's **Arnold Polson Museum** (1611 Riverside Avenue; tel: 360-533 5862; www.polsonmuseum.org; summer only; Wed–Sat 10am–4pm, Sun noon–4pm), holds historic memorabilia of the Grays Harbor area. A rose garden and a 1910 Shay Three-Spot locomotive are displayed in the adjacent park.

At the **Grays Harbor National Wildlife Refuge**, in Bowerman Basin, birdwatchers can relish the spectacle of birds resting and feeding during their annual migrations. Grays Harbor has one of the largest concentrations of shorebirds on the west coast, south of Alaska. The best viewing times are two hours before and two hours after high tide. Birds of a dozen species number in the thousands in the spring, and up to half a million during the autumn.

Grays Harbor Historical Seaport (tel: 360-532 8611; https://historical-seaport.org) is home to a replica of the *Lady Washington*, the tall ship sailed by Captain Robert Gray in 1788 which became the first American vessel to land in the Pacific Northwest. This meticulously crafted replica offers afternoon and evening cruises, and occasionally makes longer trips farther afield.

OCEAN SHORES

West of Grays Harbor, Highway 115 curves through heavily logged and replanted forests to end at a wide, flat peninsula that extends southward. Along the 30-mile (48-km) stretch of coastline from **Ocean Shores** ⑱ (tel: 360-289 2451; https://oceanshores.com) at its southern tip up to Taholah, known as **North Beach**, shabby beachside resorts give way to timber-dominated lands with prominent clear-cuts.

Conceived in the 1960s as a sprawling resort development with nightclubs and wide boulevards, Ocean Shores scaled down its ambitions to become an expanse of summer homes scattered over 6 miles (9km) of ocean dunes. As well as motels and restaurants, a golf course and opportunities to fish, clam and beachcomb, it holds marked bike routes, with the best and most scenic on the bay rather than the ocean side. **North Jetty** is a great place to watch storm waves or sunsets, but be careful: winter storms can bring 25ft (8-meter) seas, and high winds can be dangerous.

At the marina marking the end of the peninsula on the bay side, the **Coastal Interpretive Center** (1033 Catala Avenue Southeast; tel: 360-289 4617; www.oceanshoresinterpretivecenter.com; summer only, Thu–Mon 11am–4pm; free) displays the area's marine life in two aquariums, with additional exhibits on birds and shellfish. **Damon Point** (aka Protection Island; Mar–Sept, parts off-limits) is a nesting site for the Snowy plover. You'll also see brown pelicans, Peregrine falcons, herons, and dozens of other species.

North of Ocean Shores, near the confusingly named Ocean City, **Ocean**

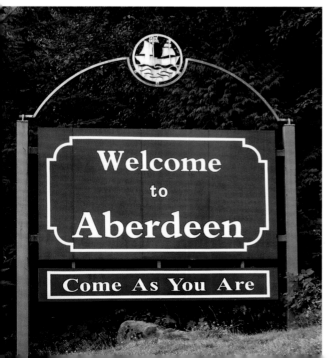

City State Park (148 Highway 115; tel: 360-289 3553; www.parks.wa.gov; daily 8am–dusk) is a large camping park with a beach, dunes, and dense thickets of shore pine. Thanks to the presence of razor clams, it's an important destination for enthusiastic diggers during the appropriate season, but permits are required. Migratory birds are prevalent and beachcombing is a popular pastime.

There are plenty of strolling opportunities along the wide-open sandy beaches that extend nearly 20 miles (32km) north from the Ocean Shores jetty to Moclips. The drive north up Highway 109 takes in a more remote section of the coastline. Piled with driftwood, the fine, dark gray sand here serves as a resting place for seagulls.

Fog and mist drift through the landscape, muting the sky against the wind-twisted dark green forests. **Pacific Beach**, a rundown village off the highway, offers decent camping facilities in a state park; otherwise it is mostly a center for oceanographic research. Its northern neighbor Moclips is a more prosperous-looking place, with homes, resorts, and restaurants perched on cliffs overlooking the sea.

Eleven miles (18km) beyond **Moclips Lighthouse**, the Native American coastal village of **Taholah** ⓳ is the last settlement accessible by road in this area.

WESTPORT

Across from Ocean Shores at the southern entrance to Grays Harbor, at the tip of a matching peninsula 21 miles (34km) west of Aberdeen, busy **Westport** ⓴ (tel: 360-268 9422; www. westportgrayland-chamber.org) is dominated by an 800-slip marina filled with sport and commercial fishing boats. The jetty here was built during the 1940s to protect the harbor; the dock area and the land on which it stands have been reclaimed from the ocean. Charter boats such as Westport Charters (tel: 360-268 0900; http://westportch-arters.com) offer tailor-made deep-sea fishing expeditions, and whale-watching cruises are also available.

Boat tours on Lady Washington take in views of Mt. Baker.

The ocean-facing side of Ocean Shores is taken up by **Westhaven State Park** (www.parks.wa.gov), also known as **Agate Beach**, which incorporates the adjoining Westport Light park. It's open during daylight hours only, for low-key activities like watching surfers and collecting shells, driftwood and agate. A concrete boardwalk traverses the main dune area.

For 12 miles (19km) along Highway 105, the coastline between Westport and North Cove is known variously as South Beach or the Cranberry Coast. Berries are grown, harvested, processed, and honored with special events.

Set among the ferns near an open beach, just north of the community of **Grayland**, itself 6 miles (10km) south of Westport, the year-round **Twin Harbors State Park** (tel: 360-268 9717; www.parks.wa.gov; daily 8am–dusk) offers 150 campsites plus rental cabins and yurts. Its half-mile (0.8km) Shifting Sands Nature Trail meanders over the dunes, through huckleberry patches and woody areas.

On the south side of town, **Grayland Beach State Park** (tel: 360-267 4301; www.parks.state.wa.us; daily 8am–dusk) has 93 campsites, 16 yurts, and a self-guided nature trail. In a nod to the local red-berry industry, the nearby **Cranberry Museum** (2395 Highway 105; tel: 360-267 3303; https://thecranzberry.com; Fri–Sun 10am–5pm) is an old cranberry warehouse that holds some funky antique equipment. The bogs themselves lie to the east, off Cranberry and Larkin roads.

Tokeland, beyond North Cove to the south, is a dreary seaside village named for Chief Toke of the Chehalis tribe, who used the area as his family summer home. Today it is home to the Shoalwater Bay Reservation.

RAYMOND AND SOUTH BEND

Broad **Willapa Bay** ㉑ fans out toward the ocean from the mouth of the Willapa River, marked by the tiny towns of **Raymond** and **South Bend**, and then stretches another 20 miles (32km) south behind the sheltering arm of Long Beach (see page 137).

Fried, stewed or eaten plain, the **oysters** from Willapa Bay are world famous for their exquisite flavor. The brisk waters here provide the ideal habitat for these tasty mollusks. In fact, an estimated one out of every six oysters consumed in the United States is grown and harvested in Willapa Bay, thereby allowing the locals to lay claim to bragging rights as the "Oyster Capital of the World." A huge waterfront statue in South Bend claims to be the "World's Largest Oyster," and local restaurants serve oysters in every imaginable form. Crab, salmon and Manila clams are also harvested in this seafood-lovers area.

Also in South Bend, the **Pacific County Courthouse** (open for self-guided tours), dubbed a "gilded palace of extravagance" when it was built in 1911, contains carvings, murals, and an illuminated stained-glass dome of green, lavender, and gold.

Fishing is an important local industry.

ILWACO

South of South Bend, US 101 follows the shoreline of Willapa Bay before finally crossing a spit of land to reach the port village of **Ilwaco** ㉒, across from Oregon at the mouth of the Columbia River. Around the end of the 19th century, it often took knives and rifles to settle the rights to fishing grounds here. Today's tourists are guaranteed less controversy, so consider taking a freshwater or sea-fishing trip. The sturgeon fishing season lasts all year round, without the need to cross the turbulent bar where the Columbia River and the Pacific Ocean collide. For a list of boat operators, contact the **Ilwaco Charter Association** (tel: 360-642 4943; https://ilwacocharterassociation.com).

SEAVIEW

In the late 19th century, the Olympic Peninsula was a summer playground for the citizens of from Portland, who would ride a steamer down the Columbia River, then board the *Clamshell*, a narrow-gauge train that ran all the way to the base of the peninsula. In 1881, promoter Jonathan Stout had big plans for the little town of **Seaview**, immediately northwest of Ilwaco. Fire destroyed his hotel during the depression of 1893, however, and real estate sales fell through. Time heals, and the 1896 **Shelburne Hotel** (4415 Pacific Way; tel: 360-642 2442; https://shelburnehotelwa.com) has thrived for over a century as the town's premier lodging and dining option.

LONG BEACH

Said to be the "world's longest beach" – even by the most generous of reckonings, it can't be more than the eighth longest – a wide uninterrupted stretch of sand extends a full 28 miles (45km) north along the peninsula north of Seaview. The beach, peninsula, and the town at its southern end are all known, of course, as **Long Beach** ㉓. The actual town of Long Beach (tel: 360-642 2400; www.visitlongbeachpeninsula.com), leans heavily on tourism with a tacky carnival touch, including go-carts, kiddy rides, miniature golf, and

Sunset at the boat basin and harbor, Ilwaco.

⊘ THE PICKLED PIONEER

Arguably the most unusual migrant ever to reach Washington Territory was 19-year-old **Willie Keil** of Bethel, Missouri. During his 2,000-mile (3,200km) trek west, in 1855, he's said to have saved the lives of many other emigrants – even though he was already dead, having succumbed to malaria four days before his party left home. Mourning the loss of his son, Wilhelm, Sr. refused to leave young Willie behind. Placed in a black, lead-lined coffin, his body was doused with Golden Rule whiskey. Carried by a wagon open at the sides, he took place of honor at the head of the wagon train. Thanks to the presence of Willie in his hearse, the company claimed to have escaped trouble at least four times. William Keil's gravestone can be seen off Highway 6, between Menlo and Raymond.

Like a set for an adventure movie – Deadman's Cove at Cape Disappointment.

bizarre attractions like the "world's largest frying pan" (there are five other claimants to that title in the US alone). Just outside the reach of the mighty Pacific, the **Long Beach Boardwalk** stretches way off into the distance. Offering displays, ocean views, and picnic areas, the boardwalk is a short stroll from most attractions.

The **Discovery Trail** winds through dune grasses from 17th Street South to 16th Street Northwest, a distance of about 2 miles (3km). Boating, beach-combing, and surf-fishing are popular pastimes, but when freshwater fish is the quarry, anglers head for Loomis Lake and its tasty rainbow trout.

The hugely enjoyable **World Kite Museum and Hall of Fame** (303 Sid Snyder Drive; tel: 360-642 4020; https:// kitefestival.com; daily 11am–5pm; closed Wed & Thu mid-Sept–mid-June) is dedicated exclusively to the history of kites. Fun facts and displays on the many scientific uses for kites are interspersed with specimens from all over the world, and the museum sponsors a major kite festival here in late August.

NAHCOTTA

The town of **Nahcotta** ㉔, named after Chief Nahcati and nestling beside Willapa Bay on the eastern side of the peninsula, grew because it received the rail terminus that its northern neighbor Oysterville had coveted. The narrow-gauge lines enabled Nahcotta to become a transportation hub for logging, fishing, and oyster shipping. Small, native oysters were once in great demand, especially in San Francisco during the Gold Rush era. For a special overnight or dining experience, reserve at the restored **Moby Dick Hotel and Oyster Farm** (25814 Sandridge Road; tel: 360-665 4543; www.mobydickhotel.com).

Although today the oyster industry in Nahcotta is "a shell of its former self," a replica of an oyster station house transports visitors back to the boom times. Known as the **Willapa Bay Interpretive Center** (3311 275th Street; tel: 360-665 4547; May–Sept Fri–Sun 11am–4pm; free), the building has walls covered with quotes and anecdotes, and shows a film about the industry and bay ecology. Visitors can

⊘ BLOOMING BERRIES

Around 550 acres (223 hectares) of **cran-berries**, yielding around 40 percent of Washington's consumption, are under cultivation on the Long Beach Peninsula. That's a lot of cranberry sauce. The industry was born at the start of the 20th century, after cranberry vines were shipped in from the state of Massachusetts. In winter, the fields take on a muted burgundy tint; by June, blossoms turn them light pink. At harvest time, in October, "blooms" containing tens of thousands of marble-sized berries paint the flooded fields a bright crimson. A former research station north of Long Beach on Pioneer Road now serves as the **Cranberry Museum** & Gift Shop (tel: 360-642 5553; http://cranberrymuseum.com; daily 10am–5pm; free).

also walk to rocky shores and the bay. Across the bay, the **Willapa National Wildlife Refuge** (daily sunrise–sunset) on the heavily forested estuarine **Long Island** is home to bears and elk, but can only be reached by boat.

OYSTERVILLE

Founded on its bivalvular namesake, today **Oysterville** ㉕ is a sleepy village on the marshlands of a bay. It was originally a booming oyster center, but harvesters exhausted the native supply, the railroad line stopped short, and South Bend got the county seat. Oysterville somehow persevered, and the entire community was placed on the National Register of Historic Places. Many of its older homes were constructed using Northern California redwood shipped in as oyster-schooner ballast.

Leadbetter Point, a mix of mudflats, marshes and dunes at the northern tip of the peninsula, is a stopover site for over a hundred species of birds, including sandpipers, yellowlegs and sanderlings. It also marks the northern limit of the breeding range of the threatened snowy plover. When this small shore bird nests on the upper ocean beach, between April and August, parts of the dunes are closed.

CAPE DISAPPOINTMENT

The southernmost point of the Washington coast, 3 miles (5km) south of Ilwaco, has been known as **Cape Disappointment** ㉖ since 1788. British fur trader John Meares gave this rain-lashed headland its name when he finally abandoned his attempts to pilot his ship across the treacherous Columbia River bar. The name seems appropriate to visitors who arrive seeking balmy weather and discover instead the endless rain of the Long Beach Peninsula.

That said, watching wind-whipped waves from the comfort of the clifftop **Lewis & Clark Interpretive Center** (Tel: 360-642 3028; April–Oct daily 10am–5pm; Nov–March Wed–Sun 10am–5pm)

can be a real thrill. Marking the spot where the explorers finally reached the Pacific on November 18, 1805, the center brings their epic transcontinental trek to life, matching original journal entries with photo murals and artwork. Also holding exhibits on local Native American tribes, it's the centerpiece of **Cape Disappointment State Park**, where yurts and cabins are available for overnight stays (tel: 888-226 7688 for reservations or 360-642 3078 for information; www.parks.wa.gov).

There are two lighthouses in the park. The 1856 **Cape Disappointment Light**, reached via a short, steep walk, is operated by the United States Coast Guard, and does not admit visitors. With 59 more wrecks occurring after it was constructed, it came to be seen as inadequate, so 42 dangerous years later, the **North Head Light** (tel: 360-642 3029; May–Sept daily 11am–3pm) was built across the peninsula to warn sailors of the treacherous sands all around. Pillow lava headlands at North Head and Cape Disappointment are stunning natural lava formations.

North Head Lighthouse.

Haystack Rock off Canon Beach.

INTRODUCTION

A detailed guide to Western Oregon, with principal sites clearly cross-referenced by number to the maps.

Black Oystercatcher.

Oregon is a state divided by mountains, but not by ideas. Although it celebrates its cultural diversity, the essence of the Oregon experience is that this is a land that delivered on its promise. Thousands came hoping to find a place of abundance at the end of the Oregon Trail, and abundance is exactly what they found. That optimism continues to imbue the spirit of the state. Perhaps that's because every Oregon schoolchild studies the words written in the tattered journals of Lewis and Clark, or sees the actual ruts of the covered wagons still etched across the landscape.

Collectively, Oregonians are not only devoted to furthering their own prosperity, but also to making that promise more generally productive. The state regularly spawns new ideas on protecting the environment and spurring urban renewal; seeks to balance individual rights with group pressures; and integrates a flourishing cultural world spanning from fine art to rodeo into everyday life. Oregonians do, however, insist on accomplishing these things their own way. Perhaps that's why they can react with a certain tension to California immigrants, and strive to avoid whatever hasn't worked for its neighbor to the south.

Seals are a common sight.

The ever-present backdrop to all this is the land. It's difficult not to wax lyrical about the Oregon's magnificent landscape, every bit as diverse as its medley of people. Within a few hours' drive of dynamic cities like Portland lie rushing rivers brimming with recreational possibilities; majestic snow-capped volcanic peaks; timbered mountain passes; verdant pastoral beauty, peppered with orchards and vineyards; and above all, the mighty Pacific shoreline, where foamy breakers crash onto sandy shores.

The response to all this beauty is an implicit protectiveness, a determination to pass on the legacy, not only of the land but also the dream of success. That's why the pioneers endured the harsh, soul-destroying Oregon Trail: not to dwell on past dreams, but to set in motion the way forward. And this is very much the way in which Oregonians are continuing to live their lives today.

Downtown Portland.

PORTLAND AND CENTRAL OREGON

Easy-going and eminently livable, Portland calls itself "the city of beers, bikes, and blooms," while verdant Willamette Valley is imbued with history and charm.

Traditionally known as "The City That Works," Portland (pop. 652,000) has learned how to enjoy itself these days. Formerly sleepy neighborhoods have become trendy, pedestrian-friendly enclaves with fun cafes, busy food carts, and glamorous galleries. Much of its recent economic success is owed to the emergence of its own "Silicon Forest," anchored by microchip giant, Intel. The city's liberal-leaning culture and history were brought to national prominence by the widespread protests that erupted in 2020 and 2021 over the killing of George Floyd.

Portland relishes a magnificent setting; on a clear day, early morning light glows pink on the West Hills as the sun rises behind Mount Hood. The Fuji-like peaks of the Cascades define the surroundings: Mounts Hood and Jefferson on the Oregon side, Adams and St Helens in Washington to the north. Truly the "City of Roses" is a beautiful place, worth saving and savoring.

To the south, the landscape around Oregon's second and third largest cities, Salem and Eugene/Springfield, combines pastoral charm with pioneer spirit. Named for the river that flows through it to meet the Columbia, the Willamette Valley (pronounced wool-am-ut) is flanked by the Coast Range and the Cascade Mountains, and holds around 70 percent of Oregon's

4.2 million inhabitants. Since humans first reached the Pacific Northwest, around 10,000 years ago, successive inhabitants have benefitted from its natural productivity. Historic cities and towns, settled by emigrants from all over the world, are now scattered everywhere, but the valley is best known for its agriculture, which includes the growing of vegetables, fruits, flowers, hops, and even Christmas trees. At one time, dense evergreen forests made the lower Willamette Valley the timber capital of the world, while its rich soil

Main attractions
Downtown Portland
Portland Saturday Market
Oregon Museum of
  Science and Industry
Eugene
Crater Lake National Park
The Wild Rogue
Oregon Caves National
  Monument

Maps on pages 144, 150

Welcome to Portland.

Portland

0   800 yds
0   800 m

NW Vaughn St

NW Front Ave

NW Fremont Bridge

Willamette River

NE Broadway Street

NORTHWEST DISTRICT

NW Thurman St

N Larrabee Avenue

N Interstate Avenue

N Williams Ave

N Weidler St

NE Weidler St

NE 2nd Ave

5

NW 20th Ave

NW Raleigh St

NW Quimby St

NW Pettygrove St

NW Overton St

NW Quimby St

NW Pettygrove St

NW Overton St

NW Naito Parkway

N Ramsay Way

Broadway Bridge

NE Clackamas St

NE Wasco Street

NW 19th Ave

NW 18th Ave

NW Marshall St

NW Lovejoy St

NW Northrup Street

NW Marshall St

NW Northrup Street

NE Multnomah St

NE Holladay Street

NW Kearney St

NW Jonson St

NW Irving Street

NW Hoyt St

NW 20th Ave

NW 17th Ave

NW 15th Ave

NW 14th Ave

NW 12th Ave

NW 11th Ave

405

PEARL DISTRICT

N

Oregon Convention Center

NE Martin Luther

NW Glisan Street

NW Glisan St

NW Flanders St

NW Everett St

NW 19th Ave

NW 18th Ave

NW 16th Ave

NW 13th Ave

NW Glisan Street

NW Flanders Street

NW Everett Street

NW Davis St

NW Couch St

NW 14th Ave

NW 13th Ave

Portland Center Stage

Powell's City of Books

NW Broadway

CHINATOWN

NW 6th Ave

NW 5th Ave

NW 3rd Ave

NW Glisan Street

NW Flanders Street

NW Everett Street

NW Davis St

NW Couch St

M

LAN SU CHINESE GARDEN

Darcelle XV Showplace

NE Lloyd Blvd

NE Davis St

NE Couch St

West Burnside Street

West Burnside Street

Burnside Bridge

East Burnside Street

Providence Park

SW 29th Ave

SW 18th Ave

SW Morrison St

SW Taylor St

SW Oak St

SW Stark St

SW Washington St

SW Alder St

SW 6th Ave

SW 5th Ave

SW Oak St

SW Stark St

SKIDMORE (OLD TOWN DISTRICT)

J

Portland Saturday Market

K

Oregon Maritime Museum

SE 2nd Ave

SE 3rd Ave

SE Stark St

First Baptist Church

SW Salmon St

SW 18th Ave

SW 17th Ave

SW Morrison St

SW Yamhill St

SW Taylor St

SW Salmon St

SW 13th Ave

SW 12th Ave

SW 11th Ave

SW Park Ave

SW Broadway

Pioneer Courthouse Square

A

SW Morrison St

SW Washington St

SW Yamhill St

I

GOVERNOR TOM McCALL WATERFRONT PARK

SW Naito Parkway

Morrison Bridge

SE Washington St

SE Alder St

SE Morrison St

SW Jefferson St

SW Columbia St

SW 10th Ave

Portland's Center for the Arts

E

Portland Art Museum

C

D

Oregon History Center

F

Portland Building

SW Salmon St

SW Main St

YAMHILL HISTORIC DISTRICT

B

U.S. Courthouse

SW Madison St

Portland Police Museum and Historical Society

MILL ENDS PARK

Eastbank Esplanade

SE Water Ave

THE EASTSIDE

SE Taylor St

SE Salmon St

SW 18th Ave

SW 17th Ave

G

City Hall

SW Jefferson St

SW Columbia St

SE Main St

SE Madison St

NE Martin Luther King Jr Blvd

NE Grand Avenue

DOWNTOWN

SW Clay St

SW Market St

SW Montgomery St

SW Broadway

SW 6th Ave

SW 5th Ave

SW 4th Ave

SW 1st Avenue

SW Naito Parkway

H

Civic Auditorium

SW Clay St

SW Columbia St

SW Market St

SOUTH PARK BLOCKS

Hawthorne Bridge

Kidds Toy Museum

SE Hawthorne Blvd

SE Clay St

SE Market Street

Portland Farmers' Market

SW Hall St

SW College St

Portland State University

SW Cardinal Drive

W Myrtle Dr

SW Myrtle Dr

405

SW Rivington Drive

SW Broadway Drive

SW Barbur Blvd

SW Sheridan St

South Harrison St

South Montgomery St

South Harbor Drive

S River Drive

S Montgomery St

South River Parkway

SW Lincoln St

Willamette River

Marquam Bridge

5

O

Oregon Museum of Science and Industry

SE Water Ave

SE Division St

SE 3rd Ave

SE 4th Ave

NE Grand Avenue

SE Caruthers St

Tilikum Crossing Bridge

moved pioneers to exclaim that "the crops never fail west of the Cascades." Further south still, the ravishing Rogue River Valley offers superb recreational opportunities, while spectacular Crater Lake makes an unmissable side-trip en route to California.

DOWNTOWN PORTLAND

Portland's compact historical **Downtown** is lively, clean, and easy to traverse on foot. At its heart, surrounded by glazed white terra-cotta towers and 1920s-style facades, **Pioneer Courthouse Square Ⓐ** is known as the city's "living room." Food carts lure a constant stream of pedestrians, while all sorts of large-scale events take place too, ranging from concerts at noon and city celebrations to political rallies and presidential speeches.

During the 19th century, this square block was the site of Portland's first public school, while upon its opening in 1890, the majestic **Portland Hotel** became the epicenter of the city's social life. At noon each day, three creatures on the mechanical 33ft (10-meter) **Weather Machine** announce the daily forecast. A whimsical Mile Post shows the distance to Portland's sister-cities, and so-called stoa columns with little sculpted roses line Yamhill and Morrison streets.

Thanks to its distinctive architecture, this neighborhood is also known as the **Terra Cotta District**. Prime specimens include the **Pioneer Courthouse** itself (555 Southwest Yamhill Street), dating from 1873 and today serving as a post office, and the lovely **Meier & Frank Building** (621 Southwest Fifth Avenue), a former department store that now holds a *Muji* outlet. The 1928 **S. H. Kress Building** (Southwest Morrison Street, Fourth and Fifth avenues) is constructed of cream-colored terra-cotta, while the 1913 **American Bank Building** (Southwest Morrison Street, Broadway and Sixth avenues), another glazed terra-cotta offering, was built

for newspaperman Henry Pittock, owner of the fabulous Pittock Mansion high above town (see page 151). The 1892 **Dekum Building** (519 Southwest Third) is a Romanesque structure with carved faces of Oregon sandstone and floral terra-cotta friezes.

In the adjoining **Yamhill Historic District Ⓑ**, around First, Second and Third avenues, the handsome Olds, Wortman and King store was remodeled as a mall in 1976, and renamed **The Galleria** (921 Southwest Morrison Street and Alder between Ninth and Tenth avenues). **Jackson Tower** (Southwest Broadway and Yamhill Street), constructed in 1912, is a glazed terra-cotta structure lit by 1,800 lightbulbs. These were switched off from World War II until 1972, when the store reopened in a blaze of glory.

Anyone serious about Portland and/ or books should head a few blocks north to **Powell's City of Books** (1005 West Burnside Street; tel: 503-228 4651; www.powells.com; daily 10am–9pm). Occupying an entire city block, it often hosts author readings and events.

The Pioneer Courthouse.

The prestigious **Portland Art Museum**  (1219 Southwest Park Avenue; tel: 503-226 2811; https://portlandartmuseum.org; Wed–Sun 10am–5pm) stands five blocks southwest of Pioneer Courthouse Square. Its various levels feature American, European, and Asian galleries, plus the Grande Ronde Center for Native American Art, which displays treasures from Central and South America as well as the Northwest. The separate Mark Building, linked by a tunnel, holds paintings by Monet, Renoir, and van Gogh.

Across the street, and the verdant open space known as the South Park Blocks, the **Oregon History Center** (1200 Southwest Park Avenue; tel: 503-222 1741; www.ohs.org; Mon–Sat 10am–5pm, Sun noon–5pm) is adorned with *trompe l'oeil* murals by Richard Haas, depicting the Lewis and Clark expedition. Permanent exhibits include the fascinating Experience Oregon and Voices of Oregon, and there are usually stimulating temporary shows, along with a good bookstore and library.

Nearby, as its typographically challenging name suggests, **Portland'5 Center for the Arts** (1111 Southwest Broadway; tel: 503-248 4335; www.portland5.com) combines five performing arts venues, even if they are confusingly located in just three adjoining buildings. These are the Arlene Schnitzer Concert Hall; the Keller Auditorium; and the Antoinette Hatfield Hall, which holds three separate auditoria.

The 15-story **Portland Building** (1120 Southwest Fifth Avenue), built in 1980, benefitted from a major overhaul in 2020. Considered the first major postmodern office building in the US, it remains the most controversial of architect Michael Graves' love-it-or-hate-it landmarks. The 36ft (10-meter) figure known as Portlandia is said to be the second largest hammered copper statue ever constructed, surpassed only by the Statue of Liberty. For a nearly eye-to-eye view of this kneeling goddess, go across the street to the Standard Plaza Building. Take the elevator up to the enclosed landing; from here the Portland Building, adorned

OMSI exhibit.

with rosettes and pink-and-blue tiling, resembles a gift-wrapped package.

Next door, **City Hall** Ⓖ (1220 Southwest Fifth Avenue) is a small, pink-marbled jewel that dates from 1895 and is listed on the National Register of Historic Places.

On hot summer days, workers eat picnic lunches on the sweeping green lawn park in front of the **Civic Auditorium** Ⓗ (Southwest Third and Clay Street), and children wade in the Ira C. Keller Fountain, a multilevel water sculpture with voluminous misty falls and rectilinear pools. The *New York Times'* architecture critic described this place as "perhaps the greatest open space since the Renaissance."

PORTLAND'S RIVERFRONT

Pioneer Portlanders strung their town along the Willamette River, and the city prospered as the first clipper ships made their way upstream carrying grain and lumber. **Governor Tom McCall Waterfront Park** ❶ (Southwest Naito Parkway from Clay to Glisan) provides up close and personal access to the river, along with grassy areas and a 2-mile (3km) jogging trail that extends Downtown's entire length. Named after the 1960s governor who gave Oregon its "green" reputation, the park is home to major summer festivals, including June's Portland Pride.

The southwest end is occupied by handsome **RiverPlace Marina** (1510 Southwest Harbor Way), which includes an elegant hotel, condominiums, a public marina, and specialty shops along an esplanade. Portland's best-known fountain, **Salmon Street Springs**, is particularly popular during hot weather. Its intermittent power-jet is forceful enough to knock down an adult; kids delight in running through its constantly changing waterspouts.

Measuring a mere 23in (58cm) across, **Mill Ends Park**, in the middle of a traffic island at Naito Parkway and Taylor Street, is officially the smallest park in the world. In theory it protects a single tree, but that keeps getting stolen and replaced – and the entire park was moved 6in (14cm) west in 2022 to make room for a new bicycle lane.

Tip

For a hugely enjoyable overview of Portland, be sure to ride the sleek Portland Aerial Tram (www.gobytram.com; Mon–Fri 5.30am–9.30pm, Sat 9am–5pm), which climbs the 500ft (152 meter) slope from downtown's South Waterfront terminal at 3303 Southwest Bond Avenue up to the Kohler Pavilion on the campus of Oregon Health & Science University.

Portland Art Museum, the oldest art museum on the West coast.

SKIDMORE

The **Skidmore Old Town District** ❿, north along the river between the Steel and Burnside bridges, is where Portland was founded in the 1840s. A fire in 1872 leveled much of the town, although it was quickly rebuilt. The district is notable for its antique road signs and early ornate buildings, several of which now hold galleries and brewpubs.

A venerable Portland tradition, **Dan and Louis Oyster Bar** (208 Southwest Ankeny Street; tel: 503-227 5906; www.danandlouis.com) was founded in 1907. The founders' descendants still run the place, preparing Louis' seafood stews, and shucking raw oysters at the famous bar.

The much-loved **Portland Saturday Market** ❿ (Southwest First Avenue and Southwest Market Street; www.portlandsaturdaymarket.com; Mar–Dec, Sat 10am–5pm, Sun 11am–4.30pm) packs the western end of the Burnside Bridge with craft stalls, street musicians, spicy foods, and lively crowds. Said to be the nation's largest open-air craft market, it's an extravaganza of craft booths, with an international food court and live entertainment. This is the best place in Portland to shop for one-of-a-kind gifts.

The **Oregon Maritime Museum** ❿ (Southwest Naito Parkway; tel: 503-224 7724; Wed, Fri and Sat 11am–4pm; www.oregonmaritimemuseum.org) is actually a boat rather than a building – it's the last steam-driven sternwheeler still functioning in the US. All sorts of models and artefacts are on display, but the real thrill comes when it ventures out on the river for regular 45-minute tours.

At Northwest Third Avenue, Old Town blends into the diminutive Chinatown. Reputed to be the largest classical Suzhou-style Chinese garden outside of China, the **Lan Su Chinese Garden** ❿ (239 Northwest Everett Street; tel: 503-228 8131; https://lansugarden.org; Nov–Mar 10am–5pm; Apr–Oct 9am–6pm) and tearoom is a wonderful walled garden occupying an entire city block. Serenity is achieved through its serpentine walkways, Moon Gate, and Garden of Awakening Orchids, reflected in ponds or arranged around rock groupings.

PEARL DISTRICT

Known as the **Pearl District** ❿, the neighborhood north of *Powell's City of Books* keeps city planners and developers hard at work, constructing offices, storefronts, and trendy loft apartments. The name may suggest an old oyster-canning factory sat amid aging warehouses, but in fact it's a modern appellation, given by gallery owner Thomas Augustine. He used to say it was because the buildings were like crusty oysters, while the galleries and lofts hidden within were like pearls; later he changed his story, claiming he'd named it in honor of an Ethiopian woman he'd met in New Orleans.

Today, the artistic infusion crackles during the first Thursday of each

Skidmore Old Town.

month when the trendy galleries along Northwest Glisan Street crack open their doors and their wine bottles until 9pm. The Pearl breathes life in the daytime too; the electrified **Portland Streetcar** (tel: 503-222 4200; https://portlandstreetcar.org), runs straight through its heart.

A few blocks west, Portland's best people-watching can be enjoyed in the **Nob Hill** neighborhood, between Burnside and Lovejoy, which got its nickname in the 1880s when a grocer likened it to San Francisco's upper-crust Nob Hill. Portland's version buzzes with activity, filled with middle-class trendies who live above retail shops or in restored homes along the nearby streets. Elegant Victorian and Georgian homes have been refurbished as one-of-a-kind stores, and the restaurants are small and fun. Parking is notoriously difficult, however, so the area is ideally visited using the streetcar.

EAST PORTLAND

Exciting plans were announced in 2021, to create a new city park on the east bank of the Willamette River, between Burnside and Morrison bridges. For the moment, though, the major attraction hereabouts is the immense **Oregon Museum of Science and Industry** (OMSI; 1945 Southeast Water Avenue; tel: 503-797 4000; Tues–Sun 9.30am–5.30pm; https://omsi.edu). Allow at least a half-day to explore it thoroughly; topics covered range from the mechanics of moving liquids to the science of lighter-than-air flight. Claustrophobic tours lead through the Navy's last non-nuclear submarine, **USS Blueback**, and there's also a 15-passenger Motion Simulator. Scenic river cruises aboard the luxury yacht *Portland Spirit* (110 Southeast Caruthers Street; tel: 503-224 3900; www.portlandspirit.com) set off just south of OMSI.

Affectionately known as Portland's own little Haight-Ashbury, the **Hawthorne District**, to the east, is a lively enclave of restaurants, shops, and specialty coffeehouses. Hawthorne Boulevard (between Southeast 32nd and 39th avenues), and Sellwood (Southeast 13th Avenue between Malden and Clatsop) teem with funky boutiques selling vintage clothes, herbal teas, and patchouli oil. Gloriously planted in precise designs, the **Ladd's Addition, Ladd Circle Park and Rose Gardens** (Southeast 16th and Harrison; daily; free) cover four neighborhood blocks and appear on the National Register of Historic Places.

WASHINGTON PARK

Up in the West Hills, a couple of miles west of Downtown, sprawling **Washington Park** (tel: 503-823 7529; https://explorewashingtonpark.org; dawn–dusk), looks out over the city and river to the Cascades. A light rail station provides access, while a free shuttle bus loops between attractions, including the famous International Rose Test Garden, which has over over 650 different varieties in bloom annually.

USS Blueback at the Oregon Museum of Science and Industry.

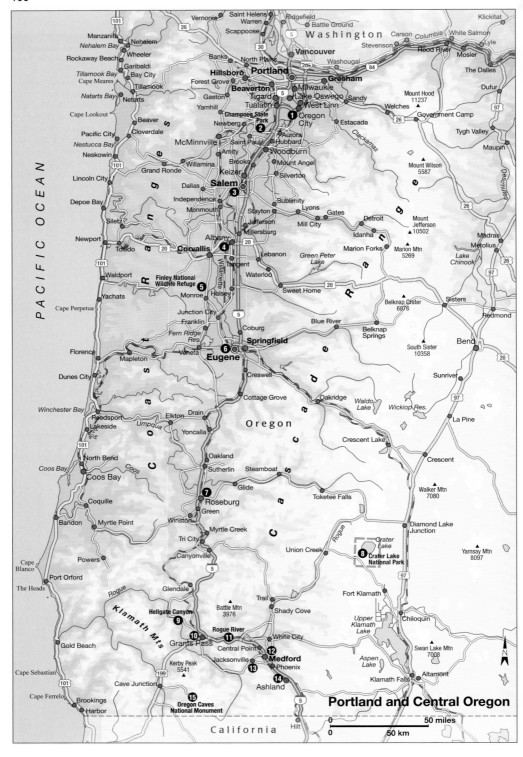

Portland and Central Oregon

At the main entrance, the **Lewis & Clark Memorial** is a granite shaft bearing the seals of the states of Oregon, Washington, Montana, and Idaho. Theodore Roosevelt laid the foundation stone on May 21, 1903.

The **Oregon Zoo** (4001 Southwest Canyon Road; tel: 503-226 1561; www.oregonzoo.org; daily 9.30am–dusk), has long been renowned for its success in breeding Asian elephants. A recent overhaul has seen the unveiling in 2021 of a Primate Forest and the Polar Passage, home to polar bears, while its much-loved miniature continues to circle the enclosures.

With 2300-plus species of trees and shrubs, **Hoyt Arboretum** (4000 Southwest Fairview Boulevard; www.hoytarboretum.org; free) is cool in summer, lush in spring and ablaze with color in the fall. Sections of its 12-mile (19km) ambling trail are paved for wheelchair access.

PITTOCK MANSION

High above Portland, just north of Washington Park, Henry and Georgiana Burton Pittock built the French chateau-style **Pittock Mansion** (3229 Northwest Pittock Drive; tel: 503-823 3623; https://pittockmansion.org; daily 10am–5pm) in 1914. Having crossed the Oregon Trail in his teens, "barefoot and penniless," Henry Pittock prospered as the owner of The Oregonian, the city's daily newspaper. He was an astute business leader, mountaineer, and family man, while Georgiana, also a pioneer, was known for her lifelong love of roses. Visitors to the mansion marvel at the view of mountains and the city below, and admire carefully crafted details like gilt mirrors, chandeliers, a china tea service, and mullioned windows.

OREGON CITY AND CHAMPOEG

As you head south from Portland into the Willamette Valley, call in at **Oregon City ❶** half an hour out, to get a sense of how it must have felt to reach the end of the Oregon Trail. This little town welcomed weary pioneer families from the 1840s onwards, along with a thousand "prairie schooners" – covered

⊘ THE CITY OF ROSES

Portland's defining image is arguably the rose-framed view of the city skyline and Mount Hood as seen from Washington Park's **International Rose Test Garden** (400 Southwest Kingston Avenue; tel: 503-823 3636; daily dawn–dusk). The oldest official public rose test garden in the US, cultivates over 10,000 rose plantings, seen at their best from May through September. Within it, the Gold Medal Garden displays each year's Portland Award winners, with national winners on view in the center aisle. Nearby, the Shakespeare Garden displays botanies mentioned by the bard.

By 1915, when nurseryman Jesse A. Currey persuaded city government to inaugurate the garden, Portland was already known as the "City of Roses," its rose-bordered streets having attracted praise during the 1905 Lewis & Clark Centennial Exposition. Though World War I was raging, hybridists from Europe and the US sent cultivars for testing, and the garden was an immediate success.

Directly uphill from here, the lovely **Japanese Garden** (611 Southwest Kingston Avenue; https://japanesegarden.org; 10am–4pm), centers on a tea house shipped over from Japan.

Consisting of five traditional gardens, it added three new structures to mark its 50th birthday in 2017. Japanese gardens are designed to offer solace year-round, and it's especially attractive during Portland's infrequent snowstorms.

Across the river, 4 miles (6km) north of Downtown, Peninsula Park's **Sunken Rose Garden** (North Ainsworth Street between Kerby and Albina; www.portland.gov/parks; daily 5am–midnight; free), is at its finest between May and September. Holding 9,000 roses on 16 acres (6 hectares) of parkland, it also has a remarkable octagonal bandstand.

The landscaped 1900s English-style **Elk Rock Garden** (11800 Southwest Military Lane at Rt 43; www.elkrockgarden.org; Mon–Fri 8am–5pm), on the impressive Bishop's Close estate 6 miles (10km) south of Downtown, is best seen in April and May for its magnolias, but its river views make it popular all summer. The magnificent **Cecil and Molly Smith Rhododendron Garden** (5065 Raybell Road Northeast, St Paul; tel: 503-771 8386; http://smithgarden.org; Apr–May Sat–Sun 11am–4pm), 27 miles (43km) southwest of the city has native trees and shrubs alongside its signature flowers.

wagons. Costumed interpreters relive the story at the **End of the Oregon Trail Interpretive Center** (1726 Washington Street; tel: 503-657 9336; https://historicoregoncity.org; daily 10am–5pm), a living history museum where authentic garden plantings complement galleries, a craft workshop, and a general store.

Beside the Willamette, another 20 miles (32km) southwest, French-Canadian and American settlers voted in May 1843 to organize a provisional government for Oregon at what's now **Historic Champoeg** (pronounced sham-*poo*-ee). Champoeg's political importance declined when Oregon City became home to this new government, and it was destroyed by floods in 1861. A visitor center at **Champoeg State Park ❷** (tel: 503-678 1251; https://stateparks.oregon.gov) tells the history of the French-Canadian fur trappers through paintings, photographs, films, and lectures.

SALEM

Oregon's capital, **Salem ❸**, dates back to 1840. The Calapooya name for this area was *chemeketa*, meaning "meeting or resting place," but as with many US cities, the missionaries opted instead for Salem, from the Hebrew word for peace, "shalom."

The **State Capitol** itself (900 Court Street; tel: 503-986 1388; www.oregonlegislature.gov/capitolhistorygateway; daily 8am–5pm; free) has an unusual cupola, topped by the gold-plated bronze statue of a bearded, axe-wielding pioneer. Ornate panels within, complemented by the neoclassical lines of the gray marble interior, illustrate wagon trails along the Willamette and Columbia rivers. A 121-step stairway spirals up to the dome, for views of the Willamette Valley, as well as Mount Hood and other distant Cascade peaks.

Past and present come together at the **Reed Opera House** in Downtown Salem, down towards the river. During the Victorian era, this was the hub of Salem's cultural and social life. Today, specialty shops thrive amid an atmosphere evocative of a gussied-up dance hall.

Immediately southeast of the Capitol is the site beside Mill Creek to which the Jason Lee Mission moved in 1840. Establishing the "Oregon Institute" there in 1842, the missionaries went on to lay out what became the town of Salem in 1844. The second- and third-oldest buildings in the Northwest, the Jason Lee House and the Methodist Parsonage, both dating from 1841, now form part of the **Willamette Heritage Center** (1313 Mill Street; tel: 503-585 7012; www.willametteheritage.org; Tue–Sat 10am–4pm). Waterpower from the Willamette meant Salem's wool and flour mills developed early, and its iron works and lumber mills subsequently helped the city to flourish.

Half a mile (1km) south, the **Deepwood Museum and Gardens** (1116 Mission Street Southeast; tel: 503-363 1825; https://deepwoodmuseum.org), preserves an 1894 Queen Anne–style mansion, and its sweetly scented gardens. The grounds include a Chinese garden and a tea garden with summerhouse,

Corvallis Courthouse.

while the house displays the original watercolor plans from when they were laid out in 1929.

A short way along Mission Street, on the grounds of a pioneer home, **Bush's Pasture Park** includes an old rose garden. Many of the cultivars were brought West by 19th-century pioneers, while the Conservatory dates from 1882. The Italianate Bush House here (600 Mission Street Southeast; tel: 503-363 4714; Tues–Sun noon–4.30pm), is also open to the public. Behind it, the Bush Barn Art Center (tel: 503-581 2228) is a showcase for local artists selling prints, ceramics, wood carvings, basketry, jewelry, and handmade cards.

South of Salem, fields of strawberries, sugar beets, beans, broccoli, and cherries alternate with regional specialties such as filberts (hazelnuts), peppermint, and, of course, acres of vineyards. Crops are nurtured by the mild climate and the blessing of gentle but persistent drizzle. Sticking to Interstate 5 spares drivers the congestion of in-town, stop-start traffic, while the slower, but more interesting Old State

99 parallels I-5, but runs through the small towns closer to the Willamette River. Both routes are distinguished by year-round greenery, hawks perched on fenceposts, sheep in the pastures, and daffodils that chart a springtime yellow brick road through what's known locally as the Emerald Empire.

Savor the bounty with a stop at the **Willamette Valley Vineyards** (8800 Enchanted Way Southeast; tel: 503-588 9463; www.wvv.com; daily 11am–6pm), just south of Salem, where the winery and underground cellar are carved into the top of an ancient cinder cone. Well-drained volcanic soils appear red due to their oxidized iron content, setting the stage for fine hillside estate vineyards that yield intensely flavored grapes, including Pinot Noir, Chardonnay, and Pinot Gris varietals.

ALBANY

The 80-square-block heart of **Albany** ❹, 26 miles (42km) south of Salem, cherishes dozens of homes in architectural styles from the 1840s through the 1920s, ranging from colorful Queen

⊙ Where

In a lonely spot 15 miles (24km) northeast of Albany, the romantic, cable-drawn **Buena Vista Ferry** (tel: 541-588 7979; daily 7am–5.30pm), carries six vehicles at a time across the Willamette River. Established in 1851 but now motorized, it's effectively just a little floating morsel of highway.

Bush House in Bush city park, Salem.

Anne-style (the "painted ladies") to Craftsman bungalows. Three neighborhoods are listed in the National Register of Historic Places – **Monteith**, **Hackleman,** and **Downtown** – reflecting the affluent era when the Willamette River and the railroad combined to export timber and agricultural produce.

Situated between the Pacific Ocean and the Cascade Mountains, 11 miles (18km) southwest of Albany, **Corvallis** is a self-absorbed college town. Home to Oregon State Center University (OSU), which specializes in agriculture and engineering and is affectionately known as "Moo U," it also has a strong high-tech presence, dominated by Hewlett Packard. Oregon's oldest institution of higher education is the focus of most local activities, including all types of college sports, and bookstores, restaurants, and craft boutiques line up along the edge of the campus. Bike lanes flank most streets, with more hiking or biking routes along the Willamette and Mary rivers.

Continue another 10 miles (16km) south on Highway 99W, and then head 4 miles (6 km) west, to reach **Finley National Wildlife Refuge ❺** (26208 Finley Refuge Road; tel: 541-757 7236; www.fws.gov; Apr–Nov dawn–dusk), where observation posts allow visitors to scout for grouse, pheasants, quail, egrets, wood ducks, herons, plovers, sandpipers, hawks, and sandhill cranes. Finley Refuge was originally established to protect the winter habitat of the Canada Goose. The short Woodpecker Loop trail leads walkers through diverse ecosystems in the hope of spotting assorted bird species.

Mary's Peak, 16 miles (26km), west of Corvallis, is the highest mountain in the Coast Range at 4,097ft (1,250 meters). The wonderful, wide-sweeping view from its summit, easily accessible by car, stretches west to the Pacific and east to the Cascades.

EUGENE

Eugene ❻ (www.eugenecascadescoast. org), Oregon's second largest city, is known as the "Jewel of the Emerald Empire." Together with its neighboring twin, **Springfield**, it rests in a garden-like setting, with the Willamette River flowing through the middle and recreational facilities on all sides, from sea level to ski level.

Life in Eugene centers on the landscaped riverside campus of the **University of Oregon** (U of O; www.uoregon.edu), where architecturally pleasing buildings include the school's first building, the 1876 University Hall. The **Jordan Schnitzer Museum of Art** (1430 Johnson Lane; tel: 541-346 3027; https://jsma.uoregon.edu; Wed–Sun 11am–5pm) is best known for its Asian collection, which incorporates ceramics, paintings, and artefacts from China, Japan, and Korea, but also has important holdings of Russian icons and American art.

A short walk east, displays in the university's **Museum of Natural and Cultural History** (1680 East 15th Avenue; tel: 541-346 3024; https://mnch.uoregon.edu; Wed–Sun 10am–5pm), range

Jordan Schnitzer Museum of Art, University of Oregon.

from geology and fossil finds to anthropology. One highlight is the oldest shoe ever unearthed, a woven sandal found at Fort Rock in eastern Oregon and thought to be 9,500 years old.

Talking of shoes, it's no coincidence that Eugene was the birthplace of **Nike**. The city acquired its status as **"Tracktown USA,"** when runner Steve Prefontaine smashed records for every distance from 2,000 to 10,000 meters, and Bill Bowerman first popularized the notion of "jogging." U of O's legendary **Hayward Field** stadium, rebuilt from 2018 onwards, hosted the World Athletics Championships in 2022.

Eugene is also home to the **Hult Center for the Performing Arts** (1 Eugene Center; tel: 541-682 5000; http://hultcenter.org) where several halls stage ballets, symphonies, and operas. June's Grammy-winning **Oregon Bach Festival** (https://oregonbachfestival.org) features an extensive program of concerts.

Downtown's **Saturday Market** (Eighth Avenue & Oak Street; www.eugenesaturdaymarket.org; Apr–mid-Nov Sat 10am–5pm), featuring craft vendors and live music, is a great chance to enjoy the city at its lively best. A few blocks north, a former chicken-processing plant now holds the **Fifth Street Public Market** (296 East Fifth Avenue; daily 11am–7pm; restaurants 7am–10pm; tel: 541-484 0383; www.5stmarket.com), offering restaurants and boutiques.

The young and the curious are sure to find something interesting in the interactive exhibits of the **Eugene Science Center** (2300 Leo Harris Parkway; Tue–Sun 10am–5pm; tel: 541-682 7888; https://eugenesciencecenter.org), which has a planetarium alongside.

Miles of cycle, walking, and jogging paths wind through parks and gardens along the Willamette River, and canoes and kayaks are available to rent.

Fifteen miles (24km) southwest of Eugene, **Silvan Ridge Winery** (tel: 541-345 1945; https://silvanridge.com; daily noon–5pm) offers daily tastings. Established in 1979, Silvan Ridge is maintained in the tradition of a small European winery, with a nicely landscaped property providing the backdrop for an afternoon picnic.

ROSEBURG AND WOLF CREEK

South of Eugene on Interstate 5, **Roseburg ❼** (www.cityofroseburg.org) lies deep within commercial forest lands, and claims the world's largest old-growth timber stand. It's also the gateway to two recreational areas – the Hundred Valleys of the Umpqua National Forest, and the Cascade Mountains – and makes the obvious launching point for visits to **Crater Lake National Park ❽**. Downtown Roseburg, located directly on the South Umpqua River, has art galleries, antique and gift shops, and a series of original outdoor murals.

A stagecoach pitstop built in the 1870s, the rustic **Wolf Creek Inn** (I-5 exit 76; tel: 541-866 2474; https://wolfcreekinn.com), 50 miles (80km) south of Roseburg, is the oldest continuously operated hotel in the Pacific

The track at Hayward Field.

CRATER LAKE NATIONAL PARK

Cradled within the collapsed volcanic caldera of Mount Mazama, this bowl-shaped mountain lake holds cobalt-blue waters and mysterious depths.

Crater Lake is so round, so blue, so perfectly tranquil that it seems unearthly. How odd that such an enchanting place is the by-product of a violent explosion, which blasted a mile off the top of Mount Mazama, 7,700 years ago. Measuring just 6 miles (10km) in diameter, Crater Lake is at 1,949ft (594 meters) the deepest lake in the US, and the ninth deepest in the world, and makes a compelling detour for any driver heading through Oregon. It's easily reached by leaving I-5 at Roseburg, and rejoining it at Medford.

On arrival at **Crater Lake National Park** (tel: 541-594 3000; www.nps.gov/crla), 100 miles (160km) east of Roseburg, get your bearings at the park headquarters, or the summer-only visitor center in nearby **Rim Village**. Then take a quick stroll to the Sinnott Memorial Overlook, for sweeping views of all that awaits. Away to your right – east – the small island poking 167ft (51 meters) out of the lake was named **Phantom Ship** by early explorers. Seen in fog

Stunning lake views from one of the lookout points.

or fading light, a ghostly image appears to be sailing straight out of *The Rime of the Ancient Mariner*.

Perched 1,000ft (300 meters) above the lake itself, the 33-mile (53km) **Rim Drive** circles the entire summit, and holds 30 scenic overlooks. Its main section typically remains open from late May until late October; the eastern half opens later and closes earlier. Taking the whole drive at a leisurely pace, setting aside time for a picnic and a few short hikes, requires a full day.

Landmarks northwest of Rim Village include the 8,013ft (2,442-meter) **Watchman** peak, overlooking the caldera 2 miles (3km) along, which can be climbed on a short, steep trail; the **Devils Backbone**, a wall of volcanic rock jutting into the water; and **Llao Rock**, an ancient lava flow dangling from the rim.

Wizard Island, a cone-shaped "volcano within a volcano," soars more than 700ft (210 meters) out of the water. Tour boats www.travelcraterlake.com) from **Cleetwood Cove** on the northeast shore can either drop you off on the island for a few hours, or take you on a longer lake cruise. Either way, allow at least an hour to drive from Rim Village to the parking area, and hike the steep trail down, equivalent to climbing 65 flights of stairs.

Back on the road, **Skell Head** is an ancient volcanic formation that bulges from the lake's eastern side. About 2.5 miles (4km) farther on, a steep trail switchbacks up through dense stands of sub-Alpine fir and clusters of wildflowers to the summit of **Mount Scott**, at 8,929ft (2,722 meters).

Crater Lake National Park doesn't end with Rim Drive. Several areas outside the caldera perimeter are well worth visiting, and offer the best prospect of catching a glimpse of such wildlife as elk, deer, pronghorn, and black bears. Many roads are closed in winter, but cross-country skiing or snowshoeing can be magical.

Rim Village holds the historic **Crater Lake Lodge** (summer only; tel: 866-292 6720; www.travelcraterlake.com; reservations required), built in 1915, some of the 71 rooms command fabulous lake views, along with a formal dining room and a casual cafe. Mazama Village (www.travelcraterlake.com), on the approach road 7 miles (11km) below the rim, holds cabins, a campground, and other facilities.

Northwest. Jack London completed his novel *Valley of the Moon* here, while the register features the signatures of Hollywood stars like Mary Pickford, Douglas Fairbanks, Clark Gable, and Orson Welles.

In Sunny Valley, another 5 miles (8km) south, the **Applegate Trail Interpretive Center** (I-5, exit 71; tel: 541-479 0253) tells the poignant story of the first emigrant wagon train, which traveled the southern route of the Oregon Trail, then known as the **Applegate Trail**, from Fort Hall, Idaho, in 1846. Its Fireside Theatre presents a dramatic reenactment of the death of 16-year-old Martha Leland Crowley, who succumbed to typhoid fever during the encampment here, and was buried beside what became known as Grave Creek.

ROGUE RIVER COUNTRY

The **Rogue River** flows 215 miles (346km), from Lost Lake in the Cascade Mountain Range and through the Coast Range to the Pacific Ocean. One of the original eight rivers included in the Wild and Scenic Rivers Act of 1968 – which now protects over 200 rivers – it's surrounded by forested mountains, rugged boulders, and rock-lined banks. Steelhead and salmon fishing and extraordinary wildlife viewing make the Rogue a national treasure. Popular activities include whitewater rafting, jet-boat tours, scenic driving, hiking, and picnicking.

To understand the river from a recreational perspective, think of it as a straight line divided into thirds. Each third, for these purposes, runs from left to right (west to east). The first third, nicknamed the **Scenic Rogue**, starts by Gold Beach on the coast, and is best seen by jetboat.

It was the more challenging 84-mile (135-km) middle section, known as the **Wild Rogue** and extending from 11 miles (18km) east of Gold Beach to 7 miles (11km) west of Grants Pass, that was designated by Congress as the "Wild and Scenic" portion. Passing through the Coast Range, it's only accessible by boat, or to experienced backpackers, with highlights including

Rafting down Rogue River.

Ⓞ STRANGER THINGS

Since the 1930s, believers and skeptics alike have been making the trek to the **Oregon Vortex and House of Mystery** (4303 Sardine Creek Road, Gold Hill; tel: 541-855 1543; http://oregonvortex.com; daily 10am–3pm), 8 miles (13km) northeast of Valley of the Rogue State Park, to observe a supposed geophysical phenomenon. Within a small spherical area – the "vortex" itself centering on a decrepit former assay office – twisted trees lean toward magnetic north, while compasses and light meters deviate from their true settings. Brooms stand on end, tennis balls and bottles roll uphill, and straight-standing people lean seven-degrees north. As a person on a level platform recedes toward magnetic south, they appear taller; as they approach, toward magnetic north, they become shorter.

the trail to roaring Rainie Falls, and the breathtaking scenery at Mule Creek Canyon and Blossom Bar.

Dozens of outfitters organize multi-day **whitewater trips** along the Wild Rogue in summer. Holding 33 miles (53km) of rapids graded Class III or less, and just two boat ramps – Grave Creek and Foster Bar – the wilderness is usually traveled in three to four days, in float boats or paddleboats. Many trips also take along inflatable kayaks, which offer greater freedom, maneuverability, and thrills, and also ensure that occupants are soaked to the skin by the first serious rapids. Both Morrisons Rogue Wilderness Adventures (tel: 800-336 1647; https://rogueriverraft.com) and Rogue Rafting Company (tel: 541-855 7080; www.rogueraftingcompany.com) offer multi-day expeditions in which participants either camp overnight beside the river or spend two nights at different luxury lodges en route.

The average hiker takes around five days to complete the 40-mile (64km) **Rogue River National Recreation Trail**, which follows the river between Illahe, north of Agness, and Grave Creek, north of Grants Pass on I-5. Hazards along the way include bears, poison oak, and rattlesnakes; for full details, visit www.blm.gov.

The final section of the Rogue, the **Hellgate Recreation Area**, ends northwest of Grants Pass. With 11 boat ramps along the 27 miles (43km) of **Hellgate Canyon** , it's accessible to all, by road or jetboat. Hellgate Jetboat Excursions (953 Southeast Seventh Street, Grants Pass; tel: 541-479 7204; https://hellgate.com) offer 1- to 5-hour jet-boat tours. Broadly speaking, the shorter tours are calm but scenic, while longer tours incorporate sections of rough water. Some trips serve dinner at an old homestead downriver.

GRANTS PASS

The so-called "whitewater rafting capital" of Oregon, **Grants Pass** ❿ (https://travelgrantspass.com), straddles the Rogue River roughly 60 miles (100 km) north of the California border. Its downtown area abounds in fine old buildings and homes, plus antique shops, ice-cream parlors and sidewalk espresso stands. The Saturday **Growers' Market** (Fourth and F streets; Mar–Nov Sat 9am–1pm; www.growersmarket.org) sells local fruits and vegetables, plus crafts made by local artisans. Riverside Park is an unhurried place to picnic and walk beside the river.

Not far from Hellgate Canyon, 12 miles (19km) northwest of Grants Pass, the **Wildlife Images Rehabilitation and Education Center** (11845 Lower River Road; tel: 541-476 0222; https://wildlifeimages.org; Jun–Aug daily 9.30am–3.30pm; Sep–May by appointment), offers fascinating hour-long tours that explain its mission to aid injured or orphaned wild animals, including bears, cougars, and raccoons.

Just east of Grants Pass, beside a placid stretch of river, the town of

Aerial view of downtown Grants Pass.

Rogue River ⑪ stands at the heart of a region where three mountain ranges meet: the Cascades, the Siskiyous and the Coast Range. Its **Palmerton Arboretum** (tel: 541-582 4401; free) displays trees and shrubs from around the world, including Mediterranean cedars and redwoods from the Pacific coast, along with trees from famous Civil War battlefields, bamboo from Hawaii, and specimens from England, Italy, Spain, and Germany.

At **Valley of the Rogue State Park** (Exit 45B off 1-5; tel: 541-582 3128; https://stateparks.oregon.gov, 21 miles (34km) east of Grants Pass, walkers can enjoy views of the river from a mile-long hiking trail.

MEDFORD

By the time I-5 reaches **Medford** ⑫ (www.travelmedford.org), an industrial, retail and professional center 26 miles (42km) southeast of Grants Pass, you're just 27 miles (43km) short of California. Here, in the heart of the attractive Rogue River Valley, orchards bloom profusely in springtime, surrounded by snow-capped peaks. Succulent pears have made the valley famous the world over.

Years ago, the Rogue River Valley was home to the Shasta, Takilma, and Athapaskan peoples. Then, in 1852, word of gold brought a throng of fortune-seekers, followed by farmers lured by the fertile soil. Small towns sprang up overnight, and the California–Oregon Stage Road grew dusty with supply wagons.

When the Oregon and California Railroad finally reached southern Oregon, in 1883, the county seat Jacksonville expected to be the main station between Portland and Sacramento. But when the railroad company requested a $25,000 "bonus" for the privilege, the town fathers refused to pay. The new station was built at Middle Ford on Bear Creek instead, swiftly spawning the town of Medford.

Medford makes a great central base for those wanting to explore the natural wonders of the region, especially Crater Lake National Park (see page 156) and Oregon Caves National Monument (see page 160). It's also a major entry point to the huge **Rogue River-Siskiyou National Forest** (tel: 541-618 2200; www.fs.usda.gov), which holds scores of campgrounds and picnic areas, plus hundreds of miles of trails for hiking, mountain biking, and horseback-riding. The **Pacific Crest National Scenic Trail** runs through the remote backcountry of Sky Lakes Wilderness along the spine of the high Cascades, and then extends westward along the crest of the Siskiyou Mountains. Other remote sections include the Rogue-Umpqua Divide Wilderness and, to the south, the Red Buttes Wilderness in the rugged headwaters of the Applegate River.

JACKSONVILLE

In 1966, the entire town of **Jacksonville** ⑬ (https://jacksonvilleoregon.org), 7 miles (11km) west of Medford, was added

Jacksonville's 19th century architecture on the corner of California and Oregon Streets.

to the National Register of Historic Landmarks. After gold was discovered at nearby Rich Gulch in 1851, saloons and gambling halls sprang up and merchants built grand mansions. After Jacksonville lost its potential as a railroad stop, however, the town remained relatively untouched and unchanged.

"Living History" is reflected in homes like the Peter Britt House, the Nunan House, and the Beekman House. Inns and bed-and-breakfasts in other historic houses reflect the elegance of bygone days, while bookstores and antiques shops pepper the streets. On California Street, the long bar of the **Bella Union** restaurant and saloon (No. 170; tel: 541-899 1770; www.bellau.com), backed by a wall mural depicting a gold-rush street scene, evokes the long-ago sound of miners' boots clumping into the boom town, while the McCully House Inn (No. 240; tel: 541-899 1942; https://mccullyhouseinn.com) is a gracious place to eat a very good brunch, lunch or dinner.

Thanks in part to its proximity to Shakespeare-crazy Ashland,

Beautiful fall foliage in Ashland's sprawling parkland.

Jacksonville enthusiastically sponsors the summer-long **Britt Music and Art Festival** (www.brittfest.org), in which stars of classical, bluegrass, and world music perform in Britt Gardens.

ASHLAND

Tacos, juicy pears, country music, and Shakespeare may seem an unlikely combination, but in **Ashland** ⑭ (https://travelashland.com), just north of the California border, that's just everyday life. The city is prettily sited 2,000ft (600 meters) above sea level, with **Mount Ashland** looming to the south, and the snow-capped Cascade Range 30 miles (48km) east. Although this attractive town has only just over 20,000 residents, it offers a quality of cultural life most small towns can only dream of: a major Shakespeare theater company, several small theater companies, art galleries, museums, and a "down-home" feeling. All that comes surrounded by mountain peaks, and a plentiful supply of tasteful bed-and-breakfasts.

With its warm summers and year-round mild climate, Ashland is an excellent place for gardens and gardeners. The climate is also conducive to growing grapes, so there are some good wineries. The 100-acre (40-hectare) **Lithia Park** (tel: 541-488 5340; daily 8am–5pm) holds native, ornamental and exotic plants, a Woodland Trail, a rose garden and a delicate, Japanese-style garden. Ashland is also on a flyway for migrating birds, and the area is home to a large concentration of bald eagles between December and February.

OREGON CAVES NATIONAL MONUMENT

Deep in Oregon's far southwestern corner, just north of California and 50 miles (80km) as the bald eagle flies inland from the ocean, the **Oregon Caves National Monument** ⑮ may be small in size – only 480 acres (194 hectares) – but it's extremely rich in diversity. Despite the name, however, there's actually just the one cave, first known to have been explored in 1874.

The monument's main visitor center (tel: 541-592 5125; www.nps.gov/orcaTues–Sat 8:30am–4pm) is down in Illinois Valley, at the western end of the Siskiyou Mountains 30 miles (48km) southwest of Grants Pass. The cave itself, another 20 miles (32km) east on OR 46, has its own seasonal visitor center (tel: 541-592 2100; April–Sept daily 8.30am–4pm).

The only way to see and understand the extraordinary marble cave and its fantastic formations, created over hundreds of thousands of years, is on the 90-minute ranger-guided **Discovery Cave Tour** (online reservations strongly advised; www.recreation.gov; April–Sept). It's a strenuous trip, which involves a lot of crouching as well as climbing more than 500 stairs.

The tour route leads through the cave via a series of interconnected "rooms" and galleries, passing pillars, stalactites, and canopies of calcite hanging from vaulted domes, along with lofty monuments like Mount Elijah. Paradise Lost is a treasure of parachute-like flowstone in a room 60ft (18 meters) high, while the draperies in the so-called Banana Groves resemble clusters of fruits. The largest formation of all, the Grand Column, was created when a stalactite fused with a stalagmite, while the largest single cavern, the Ghost Room, measures 250ft (75 meters) in length. Evaporated water leaves a residue of bumpy lumps nicknamed cave popcorn. A 7ft (2-meter) calcite column with an imprint resembling a whale's spine compliments the moon milk formation. Bats are common at night.

Above ground, three hiking trails lead deep into a green and lovely old-growth coniferous forest where plants including a celebrated Douglas fir that's said to have the widest girth of any tree in Oregon.

The rustic, cedar, six-story **Chateau at Oregon Caves** (tel: 541-592 3400; www.chateauoregoncaves.com), is a national-park lodge offering comfortable accommodations on site. Dating from 1934, it holds a huge fireplace made of local marble and a steeply pitched gable roof – a roofline as jagged as a mountain range. Non-residents are welcome to enjoy the 1930s coffee shop with its winding birch and maple lunch counter, while a mountain stream has been quirkily diverted to flow right through the dining room. Two mounds act as bridges, enabling guests to cross from one side of the room to the other.

Alternatively, you might prefer to stay at a treehouse resort, amid the woods 27 miles (43km) southwest. **Out 'n' About Treesort** (300 Page Creek Road; tel: 541-592 2208; www.treehouses.com) offers gorgeous wood cabin lodgings across its 17 suites, perched high in the trees, all connected by a labyrinth of suspension bridges. Those without a head for heights can opt for one of the on-the-ground cabins .

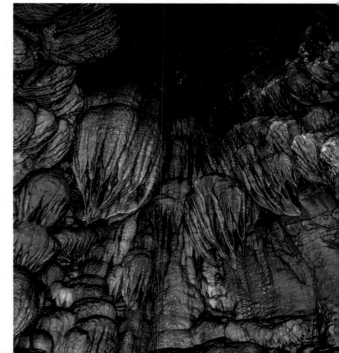

Interesting rock formations at Oregon National Caves Monument.

Natural Bridges at sunset.

COASTAL OREGON

Driving the Pacific Coast Scenic Byway along Oregon's unspoiled coastline is an exhilarating experience for any wilderness-loving traveler.

With scores of scenic overlooks, waves crashing in from the Pacific, and old-fashioned seaside towns where the streets are lined with picturesque shops, galleries, and restaurants, the Oregon coast is a vast and relatively unexplored wonderland.

The coast road, US Highway 101 – the **Pacific Coast Scenic Byway** – runs the full 350-mile (550-km) length of the state, from Astoria in the far north to Brookings in the south. Clinging to the shoreline, it skirts the beach in places, then climbs high above the rolling breakers. For most of the way, it has just two lanes; traffic moves slowly, but no one seems to mind. You could drive the whole thing in a single day, but that would leave no time to experience its breathtaking sights. Over 60 state parks lure tourists out from their cars to enjoy the beach, the trails, the hillsides, and all that invigorating fresh air.

Legislation in 1913 and again in 1967 set aside the coastline for "free and uninterrupted use." Immense beaches, often hundreds of yards wide and stretching as far as the eye can see, are public property and have numerous access points, and with billboards and advertising controled, the overall appearance is vastly different from the coastline of Washington or Southern California.

Huge piles of driftwood marking the farthest reach of storm-tossed waves testify to the ever-changing weather. The area has a marine climate, with cool summers and mild winters. Autumn often sees an Indian summer of exceptional color, with clear skies making September the best month to visit. Winter storms can be dramatic, with high winds battering the ocean bluffs. Beachcombers rise early the following day to inspect the treasures deposited by the frothing surf and ebbing tides.

◎ Main attractions

Main Attractions
Fort Astoria
Fort Clatsop
Tillamook Head
Cannon Beach
Depoe Bay
Sea Lion Caves
Oregon Dunes National
 Recreation Area

Map on page 164

Astoria's trolley travels along the waterfront.

Access to the coast is easy. Arteries head west from the Willamette Valley, while US Highway 30 links Astoria with Portland. Highway 26, the so-called **Sunset Highway**, connects Portland with the resort area of Seaside.

ASTORIA

The northernmost point of the Oregon coast is generally considered to be the city of **Astoria ❶**, close to the mouth of the Columbia River, 95 miles (140km) northwest of Portland. The eddies and cross currents formed as the broad river hurls itself into the Pacific – the infamous Columbia bar – can be felt many miles out to sea; would-be sailors are warned to seek expert advice. Said to be the most dangerous entrance to a commercial waterway anywhere in the world, it's known as the Graveyard of the Pacific, and has witnessed more than 1,500 shipwrecks. For that matter, swimming can also be treacherous, due to the undercurrents and rip tides.

The impressive **Astoria-Megler Bridge** crosses the Columbia to connect the state of Washington to the state of Oregon, and forms the entrance to Astoria itself. Considered the oldest American settlement west of the Rockies, the area was first visited by Captain Robert Gray in 1792, then served as the stopping place for the Lewis and Clark Corps of Discovery in 1805. Formally established as Fort Astoria by John Jacob Astor (J.J.) in 1811, the outpost was intended to develop Far East markets for the beaver-fur trade, but was promptly blockaded during the War of 1812. Although Astor eventually sold the post to the British, his plans were not thwarted. The man most closely associated with the American fur trade, had, in fact, become involved in the business without ever setting a trap, and he continued to monopolize it until 1834, when he retired. Thereafter, Astor's earnings, plus investments in New York real estate, made him the richest man in the United States and the country's first recorded millionaire.

By the 1870s, Astoria had become a flourishing fishing and lumber center, and was also a place where drunken patrons of saloons and bawdy-houses could find themselves shanghai-ed to crew on sailing vessels bound for the Far East.

Astoria today is a gorgeous place. Hundreds of Victorian-style homes cling to hillsides against a backdrop of misty rainforests. Astoria's sunset on the extensive waterfront begins at the Sixth Street Viewing Platform, continues to the 14th Street Riverpark, with its interpretive panels of river activity, and on to the 17th Street Pier. Fishing charter operators offer the opportunity to land salmon, sturgeon, or crab.

To learn more about the legends and lore of the river, call in at the **Columbia River Maritime Museum** (1792 Marine Drive; tel: 503-325 2323; www.crmm. org; daily 9.30am–5pm), at the heart of the waterfront. Displays explore lighthouses, shipwrecks, navigation, fishing, and naval history, with the

Coastal Oregon

0   100 miles
0   100 km

lightship Columbia, which served from 1950 until 1980 as a floating "lighthouse" for ships crossing Columbia bar, as its largest artefact.

A couple of blocks inland, the **Flavel House** (714 Exchange Street; tel: 503-325 2203; https://astoriamuseums.org) was built in 1885 by a Columbia River bar pilot and an early millionaire, Captain George Flavel. A fine example of Queen Anne–style architecture with period furnishings and artwork, Flavel House rests on park-like grounds that cover a city block. Its fourth-story cupola was designed as a vantage point to watch river traffic.

The **Astoria Riverfront Trolley** (tel: 503-325 6311; https://old300.org; Mon–Fri 3–9pm, Sat and Sun 10am–9pm), operating to the loosest of schedules, is run by an eclectic army of volunteers. Old No. 300 clickity-clacks its way along the town's tracks, and then crosses it, linking the Port of Astoria to the East End Mooring Basin.

FORT ASTORIA

It was in 1811, only five years after the departure of Lewis and Clark, that John Jacob Astor sent fur traders aboard the ship *Tonquin* to establish the trading post that they named **Fort Astoria**. The original site is commemorated by a roadside monument at what is now 15th and Exchange streets.

On December 12, 1813, as part of British naval operations in the War of 1812 – yes, sometimes history can be a little confusing – Captain Black, commanding the British *Racoon*, arrived at Fort Astoria. After dinner, the company ran up a British flag while Captain Black broke open a bottle of Madeira wine, loudly declaring that he was taking possession of the post in the name of His Royal Majesty. He followed up by changing its name to Fort George, but that didn't stick.

After Captain J. Hickley and US Commissioner J.B. Prevost arrived at Astoria aboard the British frigate *Blossom* on October 6, 1818, the British formally ceded Fort George. The Canada Northwest Company, however, continued as the sole operators of the fort, which had become a trading post rather than a military outpost of Britain.

⊙ Where

Hollywood is fond of Astoria. Movies shot here include *Kindergarten Cop*, with Arnold Schwarzenegger, and *Free Willy I* and *II*, starring Keiko as the whale hero. For the climax of *Free Willy*, filmed at the Hammond Mooring Basin, a hot tub was installed so the actors, who were spending hours in freezing water, could warm up between takes.

The Astoria Megler Bridge connects Oregon and Washington.

Atop Coxcomb Hill, half an hour's walk up from the riverfront, the handsome **Astoria Column** (tel: 503-325 2963; https://astoriacolumn.org; daily dawn to dusk; free), stands 125ft (38 meters) tall. Modeled by architect Electus Litchfield on Trajan's Column in Rome, built in AD 114, it was dedicated in 1926, and is listed in the National Register of Historic Places. A spiraling mural by Italian artist Attilio Pusterla depicts the westward expansion of Oregon settlers. Those who can bear to climb its 164 steps are rewarded with a panoramic view of the Astoria Bridge, the Pacific Ocean, the Columbia River, Saddle Mountain, and the Clatsop Plain.

FORT CLATSOP AND FORT STEVENS

Just south of Astoria, across Youngs Bay and a short way up the Lewis and Clark River, **Fort Clatsop ❷** (tel: 503-861 2471; www.nps.gov; daily 9am–6pm) is a National Park Service facility that commemorates Lewis and Clark and their Corps of Discovery. It was on the wet Christmas Eve of 1805 that the party moved into a hastily built stockade fort, measuring 50ft by 50ft (15 meters by 15 meters), and surrounded by old-growth forest.

Visitors get a good idea of where the 33-strong party lived, but have to imagine the fleas, the rotting clothing, and the rain that fell on all but 12 of the 106 days they were here. Named in honor of the local Clatsop, the fort offered much-needed refuge as the party rested from their arduous 2,000-mile (3,200km) journey, and prepared for the return trek east to St Louis.

The original fort deteriorated in the wet climate, but in 1955, using Clark's sketches, local residents constructed a replica on the same site. Furnished with hand-hewn wooden bunks and benches, the fort now serves as an open-air museum. Park rangers dress in buckskin coats, make candles, carve dugout canoes and fire flintlock muskets to reenact what life was like for the explorers.

More than 150 years ago, young soldiers dressed in Union blue stood watch over a fort at the very mouth of the Columbia. Completed during the Civil War, in 1865, it's now preserved as **Fort Stevens State Park**, (tel: 800-452 5687 or 503-861 3170; https://stateparks.oregon.gov; daily 10am–6pm), 10 miles (16km) west of Astoria, outside the town of Warrenton.

Deactivated after World War II, the fort now holds military artefacts, tours and history demonstrations. Visitors can explore abandoned gun batteries and climb to the commander's station for a strategic view of the Columbia River and the South Jetty. In summer, walking tours lead through the underground Battery Mishler, while the entire complex can be toured aboard a US Army truck. At the water's edge, the forlorn wreckage of the four-masted, iron-hulled British schooner, *Peter Iredale*, which ran aground in 1906, emphasizes the importance of

Fort Clatsop.

lighthouses along this treacherous coast.

SEASIDE

In the lively resort of **Seaside ❸** (www. seasideor.com), 14 miles (22km) south of Fort Stevens, a bronze memorial to Lewis and Clark gazes oceanward from the Promenade (the Prom). At a salt cairn here in 1806, comrades of Lewis and Clark boiled seawater to obtain salt to preserve their food for the homeward leg. The rollers from the Pacific Ocean are within walking distance of downtown Seaside with its shops, eateries, and arcades.

Underwater animals in starring roles at the **Seaside Aquarium** (tel: 503-738 6211; www.seasideaquarium. com; daily 9am–dusk), established on the Prom in 1937, include a family of 10 individually named harbor seals, a 20-ray starfish, a wily octopus, a deadly Moray eel, and a ferocious-looking wolf eel. Visitors are encouraged to stroke starfish and prickly sea urchins in the "touch tank."

TILLAMOOK HEAD

Tillamook Head ❹, the headland south of Seaside, should not be confused with the town of Tillamook, 50 miles (80km) south. Postcards of the Oregon coast often show the view from scenic **Ecola State Park** (tel: 503-812 0650; https://stateparks.oregon.gov), which wraps around Tillamook Head, where waves roll in against craggy islands and secluded beaches. Framed by lines of breakers, the beach stretches to the horizon, punctuated by the distinctive rocky outcrops known as sea stacks. Signs tell which of these unique features are safe to climb. The park's miles of clean firm sand are very walkable; old-growth Sitka spruce and a western hemlock forest are prime habitat for elk and deer.

The headland itself is a tilted remnant of a massive, 15 million-year-old Columbia River basalt flow. Incredibly,

the lava welled up near Idaho, flooded down the Columbia Gorge, and spread along the seashore to this point.

Starting from Sunset Boulevard at the southern end of Seaside, the **Tillamook Head Trail** (bring boots and waterproof jacket, even in summer) is a relatively easy hike, which switchbacks up into thick forest. As it crests Tillamook Head, not only does it follow the route of the Lewis and Clark expedition, it passes a viewpoint known as Clark's Point of View.

Walking its full 6-mile (10km) length will take you to Indian Beach, but most hikers restrict themselves to a 3.4-mile (5.5km) round-trip from Seaside, which takes anything from 2 to 5 hours. From the forest walk, there are peek-a-boo views of waves sweeping ashore.

Situated a mile out to sea, **Tillamook Rock** is a bleak island with a lighthouse that remained in operation from 1881 to 1957. Nicknamed "Terrible Tilly," the building was repeatedly swept by storms that dashed water, rocks, and fish into the lantern room 150ft (45 meters) above sea level. Funereal

The dramatic coastline by Tillamook Head.

entrepreneurs bought the island, and urns of cremated remains arrive via helicopter.

CANNON BEACH

Marked by the monolithic, picture-postcard **Haystack Rock** just offshore, the coastal village of **Cannon Beach** ❺ (www.cannonbeach.org) received its name from a cannon that washed ashore after the US Navy schooner *Shark* ran aground in 1846.

Cannon Beach is packed with coffeehouses, bungalows, and gallery-shops, and likes to see itself as the arty counterpart to "kitschy" Seaside. Creative summer festivals range from the **Earth & Ocean Arts Festival** in September to June's family-friendly **Sandcastle Day**. North by Northwest Gallery (239 North Spruce Street; tel: 503-436 0741; https://nwbynwgallery.com) offers regional artists including glass sculptors as well as painters, while White Bird Gallery (251 North Hemlock Street; tel: 503-436 2681; www.white-birdgallery.com) exhibits and sells local art-community paintings, sculpture, prints, photography, glass, ceramics, and jewelry.

South of Cannon Beach, the 1,600ft (490 meters) headland known as Neahkahnie Mountain dominates **Oswald West State Park** (tel: 503-812 0640; www.stateparksoregon.gov). The road takes hair-raising curves as it climbs to an overlook 700ft (200 meters) above the surf. Paragliders, with their usual flair for the extreme, find this daredevil place intoxicating. Native Americans considered this mountaintop a viewpoint fit for gods, and named it Ne Ekahni, "place of supreme deity." Later explorers too surrounded the peak with legend; treasure seekers sifted the beach at its base, spurred by tales of gold buried by sailors from a shipwrecked Spanish galleon. The discovery of a strangely inscribed block of beeswax fueled the speculation.

The quiet village of Manzanita stands just south of Neahkahnie, beyond it is a small river town, Nehalem, noted for its antique shops and good fishing opportunities.

Cannon Beach.

TILLAMOOK

During World War II, giant blimps were deployed at **Tillamook ❻** (tel: 503-842 2672; https://tillamookcoast.com) to patrol the coast looking for enemy submarines. The blimps themselves are long gone, but their massive hangar, 1,072ft (326 meters) long and covering over 7 acres (3 hectares), still looms over the horizon. It now houses a collection of vintage aircraft, as the **Tillamook Air Museum** (6030 Hangar Road; tel: 503-842 1130; www.tillamookair.com; daily 10am–5pm).

Tillamook is much more famous, however, for its dairy products – especially cheese and ice cream. At the north end of town, the massive **Tillamook Creamery** (4175 US 101 North; tel: 503-815 1300; www.tillamook.com; daily 10am–6pm) is a slick modern operation that attracts a million visitors each year. After the self-guided tour with free cheddar samples, customers line up in droves at the (not so free) ice cream counter. The **Blue Heron French Cheese Company** (2001 Blue Heron Road; tel: 503-842 8281; www. blueheronoregon.com; daily 8am–6pm) offers samples of its own brie, plus tasters of Oregon wines, locally-made mustards, jams, dips, and other specialty foods.

THE THREE CAPES

South of Tillamook, the **Three Capes Scenic Loop ❼** covers three jutting promontories, each of which is a state park: Cape Meares, Cape Lookout, and Cape Kiwanda. The tall forests here drop right down to the pounding surf; the huge Sitka spruce, the heartwood of which is so light and strong that it was used to make early wooden aircraft, is widely prominent.

A true highlight of the loop – no pun intended – the **Cape Meares Lighthouse** (tel: 503-842 3182; https://stateparks.oregon.gov; tours May–Sept daily 11am–4pm; free), was built in 1890 and finally switched off in 2014. Walkways lead from the parking area to the lighthouse, which may tower high above the ocean, but at 38ft (11 meters) is actually the shortest on the Oregon coast.

Military transport plane at the Tillamook Air Museum.

⊙ Tip

Be sure to heed the warnings posted at every Lincoln City beach, and watch out for larger-than-usual "sneaker" waves. You could become stranded – or worse – as the tide sweeps in. Wear shoes with grippy soles that you don't mind getting wet, and tread carefully. Many rocks are covered with sharp mussels and barnacles; look by all means, but don't touch.

Viewpoints overlook offshore islets inhabited by Steller sea lions and seabirds, common murres, peregrine falcons, tufted puffins, and pelagic cormorants, which nest on the cliff walls. Look out for the so-called Octopus Tree, a few steps south of the parking lot, with its multiple trunks. Native American tradition says this eerie, giant Sitka is a burial tree; the dead would be placed in canoes, which were then placed in turn inside specially prepared trees.

Cape Lookout holds a pleasant, year-round campground and an attractive strolling beach, while at **Cape Kiwanda** the action of wind and waves on the sandstone has created a dynamic headland. The "other" Haystack Rock, a counterpart to the more famous one near Cannon Beach, can be seen offshore.

LINCOLN CITY

Southward, the resort town of **Lincoln City** ❽ (www.lincolncity.org) is sandwiched between 7 miles (11km) of sandy beaches and scenic Devils Lake.

Situated at the start of the "Twenty Miracle Miles," a strip of somewhat tacky coastal properties, it's crowded with mom-and-pop establishments and emits a general "hey-let's-rent-a-moped" holiday feeling.

Lincoln City owes its lack of an obvious core to the fact that it was consolidated when five smaller centers decided to amalgamate in the mid-1960s. As well as its continuum of stores and motels, it holds some great locations for wave-, whale-, sunset-, and storm-watching, and there are 15 access points to the public beach. The beach is a treasure trove for driftwood, agates, shells, and floats. Large rocks emerging from the sea create ideal pockets for tide pooling during low tides, while beach hiking, surfing, and fishing challenge sun seekers. Voted the "Kite Capital of the World," Lincoln City receives steady winds; storm watching is best in winter.

Measuring 3 miles (5km) wide by 3 miles (5km) long, **Devils Lake** is deep only in terms of folklore, reaching a depth of just 22ft (7 meters). Nine species of freshwater fish lure fishermen, while water sports such as windsurfing, waterskiing, and jet skiing engage other enthusiasts. The **"D" River**, which flows from the Lake, claims to be the world's shortest river. From its source, it reaches its destination, the Pacific, in a mere 120ft (36 meters).

The delightful and colorful **Connie Hansen Garden** (1931 Northwest 33rd Street; March–mid-Dec Tues and Fri–Sun 10am–2pm; tel: 541-994 6338; www.conniehansengarden.com) features hardy species that thrive in coastal climates, such as rhododendrons, azaleas, primroses, and hybridized irises.

Lincoln also holds several galleries, some of which enable visitors to watch artisans at work. At the **Lincoln City Glass Center** (4907 Southwest US 101; Wed–Sun 10am–6pm; 541-996 2569; www.lincolncityglasscenter.com), you can learn the art of glass-blowing, or

Cape Kiwanda.

simply buy beautiful specimens created by local craftspeople. Based in a tiny farmhouse, the **Mossy Creek Pottery** (483 South Immonen Road; tel: 541-996 2415; www.mossycreekpottery. com; daily 10am–5pm), sells ceramic works by 40 regional artists.

Situated in splendid and decidedly non-tacky isolation near Gleneden Beach, 6 miles (10km) south of Lincoln City, **Salishan Coastal Lodge** (tel: 541-764 3600; https://salishan.com) was awarded a Centennial Medallion by the American Society of Landscape Architects in recognition of landscaping that preserves the natural environment. In an unspoiled 750-acre (300-hectare) forest preserve overlooking Siletz Bay, this rugged but luxurious resort offers fireplaces and balcony views of Cascade Head.

DEPOE BAY

Continuing south, **Depoe Bay** ❾ claims to be the whale-watching capital of the Oregon Coast, and for good measure the whole world. It also centers on what's said to be the world's smallest natural navigable harbor.

Each winter, between mid-December and mid-January, around 20,000 gray whales pass close to Depoe Bay as they migrate south towards Mexico. They're back again from late March through June, heading north to Alaska. On top of that, a large resident population feeds just offshore between June and mid-November. All that activity can be seen from the roadside, state-run **Depoe Bay Whale Watching Center** (tel: 541-765 3304; https://stateparks. oregon.gov; daily 9am–5pm). If you'd like a closer look, several competing charter boats offers daily whale-watching cruises, weather permitting, from the waterfront.

The extensive sea wall that runs the length of downtown Depoe Bay enables visitors to shop or dine within view of the ocean. The waves here run beneath ancient lava beds that form natural tubes. During turbulent seas, wave pressure builds to spew geyser-like sprays as high as 60ft (20 meters) into the air, a phenomenon that's particularly impressive at a spot called Spouting Horns.

CAPE FOULWEATHER

Between Depoe Bay and Otter Rock, **Cape Foulweather** is one of the highest promontories on the Oregon Coast, rising 500ft (152 meters) above the ocean. This was the point where Captain James Cook first sighted this stretch of the North American continent, in 1778. He was on his third voyage, heading north from Hawaii, when a sudden storm greeted his arrival; hence the name. News of Cook's voyage to the Pacific Northwest stimulated American interest, and contributed towards the dispatch of the Lewis and Clark Expedition. A state wayside has good views but no facilities.

Midway between Depoe Bay and Newport, the aptly named **Devil's Punchbowl State Park** (tel: 541-265 4560; https://stateparks.oregon.gov) gives

Fishing trawler coming into Depoe Bay.

a ringside seat on a frothy confrontation between rock and tide.

NEWPORT

Spread across a peninsula between the Pacific and Yaquina Bay, 25 miles (40km) south of Lincoln City, effervescent **Newport** ⑩ (www.discovernewport. com) is known for its picturesque harbor and graceful bridge, Dungeness crab and "let's-party-now" atmosphere. It's a budding upscale village, a strange slice of small-town Americana, and a coastal treasure trove all in one. Yes, it's all too easy to get lost in the crowds and tourist traps, but then again, it's not so hard to find solace on a deserted section of beach somewhere not far away.

The **Old Bay Front**, a waterfront neighborhood that offers a mix of shops, galleries, canneries, and restaurants, preserves a definite late 19th-century charm. Look out for eateries that serve local shrimp, oysters, crab, and salmon. Commercial and charter fishing boats sail from the harbor, and narrated whale-spotting tours are easy to find. **Mariner Square** on Southwest Bay Boulevard is home to a wax museum, an undersea gardens attraction, and an outpost of Ripley's Believe-It-or-Not (www.ripleys.com/newport).

South of the center, across Yaquina Bay, it takes a good three hours to explore the **Oregon Coast Aquarium** (2820 Southeast Ferry Slip Road; tel: 541-867 3474; https://aquarium.org; daily summer 9am–8pm, rest of year 10am–5pm). Four indoor aquarium galleries showcase coastal habitats, while sharks prowl against the Plexiglas of the 200ft (60-meter) underwater Passages of the Deep tunnel, and seals, sea lions, and otters play in rocky pools. There's also a giant Pacific octopus, and birds soar and dive in North America's largest walk-through seabird aviary, to the delight of all who watch them.

Within walking distance, Oregon State University's **Hatfield Marine Science Center** (tel: 541-867 0100; https://hmsc.oregonstate.edu; Thu–Mon 10am–4pm), offers another window to the ocean. As well as a public aquarium, and the chance to touch a live tentacled

Heceta Head Lighthouse.

octopus, the center houses various marine-related research projects.

On the northern edge of Newport, the **Yaquina Head Lighthouse** (tel: 541-574 3100; http://yaquinalights.org; daily 10am–4pm) has remained continuously lit since 1873. Its 93ft (28-meter) tower is the tallest on the Oregon coast; raised 162ft (50 meters) above sea level, it's visible to ocean-going vessels as much as 19 miles (30km) away. Its near neighbor, the gorgeous **Yaquina Bay Lighthouse** (daily noon–4pm, closed Mon–Tue Oct–June), guards the heart of town at the mouth of the Yaquina River. Its 40ft (12-meter) tower rises straight from a Cape Cod–style house, making it one of the few Pacific Coast lighthouses built with the lightkeeper's quarters inside the tower itself. It operated only from 1871 to 1874 before being replaced, though during that short interval it supposedly attracted hauntings by a young girl.

CAPE PERPETUA AND THE SEA LION CAVES

The highest point on the Oregon coast, **Cape Perpetua** ⑪, is 27 miles (43km)

south of Newport, just beyond the attractive little town of **Yachats** (pronounced ya-*hotz*). The magnificent panoramic view makes a stop irresistible, and the cape's visitor center (tel: 541-547 3289; www.fs.usda.gov; daily 9.30am–4.30pm; free) holds informative natural history displays.

The adjoining 2,700-acre (1,000-hectare) **Cape Perpetua Scenic Area** was set aside as part of the Siuslaw National Forest for its unique Sitka spruce rainforest. The most popular forest trail leads to the massive Giant Spruce Tree, which is more than 500 years old.

The still-functioning **Heceta Lighthouse** (tours by appointment; tel: 866-547 3696; www.hecetalighthouse.com) stands 12 miles (20km) north of the town of Florence. Built in 1894, it's the brightest lighthouse on the Oregon coast, and said to be the most-photographed lighthouse in the US. Enticingly, the keepers' cottage doubles as both an interpretive center and a bed-and-breakfast; the sea views from its porch are quite unbelievable.

Stunning sunrises can be seen at Cape Perpetua.

STELLER SEA LIONS

The world's largest sea lions gather in their hundreds in a vast grotto, hollowed from the rocks of the Oregon coast.

Steller sea lions, also known as Northern sea lions (*Eumetopias jubatus*), were once a common sight along the Oregon coast. Now, as their numbers decline, the **Sea Lion Caves** offer a rare chance to observe the largest of the sea lion species. Visitors descend unobtrusively down a 225ft (69-meter) elevator shaft, emerging at the bottom into a water-level sea grotto where these leviathans have sheltered for eons. In this vast natural cave, you may encounter an unpredictable number of wild, decidedly odiferous, Steller sea lions, many with their black pups in tow.

The Steller sea lion is named after George Wilhelm Steller, a German naturalist who accompanied Danish explorer Vitus Bering on his second Alaskan expedition in 1741. Stellers have a bulky build and a thick neck that resembles the mane of a lion. Carnivores, they feed on rock-fish, sculpins,

Sea lions basking on the rocks.

capelin, flatfish, squid, octopus, shrimp, and crabs; sometimes a Steller will even devour a Northern fur seal. Biologists often find pebble-size stones in their stomachs, but it's not known whether the stones aid digestion, or are swallowed accidentally, or even in play. Stellers use their long front flippers for propulsion, and their hind flippers for steering under water. On land, they pull hind flippers up under their body and "roll walk" on all four flippers.

Although often confused with Stellers, California sea lions, which range along the California coast and north as far as Canada's Vancouver Island, are smaller and darker in color. "Californians" do stop by the Sea Lion Caves, however, usually between late fall and early spring.

The world population of Steller sea lions has been in precipitous decline over the last fifty years, and is currently estimated at around 15,000, of which perhaps 200 are based at the Sea Lion Caves. Researchers believe that dwindling fish stocks are a significant factor. Stellers breed and bear young in May and June; gestation is nine months. It used to be assumed that much like its cousin, the Alaska fur seal, each female Steller bore a pup each year, but it's now thought that they bear every other year. Mothers stay with their pups for one or two weeks, then divide their attention between hunting and nursing. Pups typically nurse for a year, though some continue up to three years.

During the breeding season, bulls of up to 2,000lbs (900kg) lounge outside the caves, roaring and bleating. Breeding resumes 10–14 days after a pup is born. Driving weaker males away, dominant males maintain harems of 15 to 30 cows and breed with them all. Until the harem structure dissolves, dominant bulls keep constant vigil over their females; bulls do not leave their harems, even for food, for up to three months.

Females display no such loyalty. When a storm breaks up a harem, the bull may never recover all his chosen mates. Much of his work consists therefore of keeping his females together. The ordeal causes the big bulls to lose weight, and by the end of the breeding season, they are exhausted. They generally spend the remainder of the summer by themselves, resting and regaining strength.

A rookery of non-migrating Steller sea lions makes its home along the coast hereabout. Often noisy, always smelly, they congregate just north of Florence in the shelter of an enormous sea grotto known as the **Sea Lion Caves** ⑫ (tel: 541-547 3111; www.sealioncaves.com; daily 9am–4pm). Visitors access the cave via an elevator; the sea lions are wild animals, so there's no absolute guarantee they'll be present, but you'd have to be very unlucky to miss them.

A different type of natural experience can be had at the **Darlingtonia State Botanical Wayside** (https://stateparks.oregon.gov), 5 miles (8km) north of Florence. This unusual state park was dedicated solely for the protection of one specific plant, Darlingtonia, a carnivorous species commonly known as the pitcher plant. Having lured insects with its sickly, sweet smell, the plant then traps and digests them. A short loop follows the boardwalk through a boggy area, overlooking patches of Darlingtonia; they're best seen in early spring for the blossom, or in summer for the actual plants.

FLORENCE

Known as the City of Rhododendrons, **Florence** ⑬ (https://florencechamber.com) explodes with vivid pink blossoms every spring. Its tastefully restored Old Town holds interesting boutiques, along with excellent coffeehouses and restaurants, while the area is good for hiking, bird-watching, horseback riding, and dune-buggy racing. Other activities include fishing, swimming, and boating at the 17 nearby lakes, while jet-boat trips head up the Siuslaw River in summer.

South of Florence, **Jessie Honeyman State Park** (tel: 541-997 3851; camping reservations tel: 800-452 5687; https://stateparks.oregon.gov), is noted for its spring rhododendron blooms and sand dunes, which reach as high as 300ft (90 meters). It holds more than 300 camping sites, along with 10 yurts.

Another 24 miles (38km) south, **Umpqua Lighthouse State Park** ⑭ (tel: 541-271 4118; camping reservations tel: 800-452 5687; https://stateparks.oregon.gov) sits amid a stretch of towering sand dunes, though there's no direct access. It incorporates the small but very picturesque freshwater Lake Marie, open to anglers, non-motorized boaters, and swimmers. Its campground also holds eight yurts and two log cabins, while the **Umpqua River Lighthouse** itself (tel: 541-271 4631; https://umpquavalleymuseums.org; daily 10am–5pm) has a lens that emits a wonderful red-and-white flash.

OREGON DUNES NATIONAL RECREATION AREA

Stretching for 50 miles (80km) south from Florence to Coos Bay, the **Oregon Dunes National Recreation Area** ⑮ preserves the largest expanse of coastal sand dunes in the United States. Higher than those of Africa's Sahara Desert, these enormous oceanfront dunes range up to 500ft (150 meters) tall, and form long banks up to

Adrenalin-fuelled fun at Dunes National Recreation Area.

3 miles (5km) deep. Most were created during the last 10–15,000 years, from erosion sediment deposited by rivers and streams.

Pick up information on the dunes and the fabulous recreational possibilities they offer in Reedsport, 22miles (35km) south of Florence, at the **Oregon Dunes Visitor Center** (tel: 541-271 6000; www.fs.usda.gov/Siuslaw). Facilities include assorted overlooks, 14 hiking trails, 11 parking areas within walking distance of endless sandy beaches, nine day-use areas that charge fees, and three off-highway riding areas.

Sand-boarding is perhaps the most obvious attraction, but there's pounding surf, prolific estuaries, conifer forests, and lakes teeming with fish to thrill anyone who loves sports, nature, and wildlife viewing. The dunes are home to the endangered western snowy plover, as well as egrets, bald eagles, and river otters.

COOS BAY

South of the dunes, **Coos Bay** (http://coosbay.org) was founded in 1854 by J.C. Tolman of the Coos Bay Company. Sheltered within the largest natural harbor between Seattle and San Francisco, Coos Bay is more than just another quaint seaside tourist-town; nicknamed Oregon's "Bay Area," it's a shipping and manufacturing center. **North Bend**, Coos Bay's sister city, is the gateway to the fishing village of **Charleston**, 9 miles (14km) west on Cape Arago Highway.

The impressive bayfront **Coos Bay Historical and Maritime Museum** (1210 North Front Street; tel: 541-756 6320; https://cooshistory.org; Tues–Sat 11am–5pm) explores local history and cultural traditions, while the Art Deco **Coos Bay Art Museum** (235 Anderson Avenue; tel: 541-267 3901; www.coosart.org; Tues–Fri 10am–4pm, Sat 1–4pm) displays works by Northwest artists and fine art prints from further afield.

Facing the open ocean, 13 miles (20km) southwest of Coos Bay, **Shore Acres State Park** (Cape Arago Highway; tel: 541-888 3732; https://shoreacres.net; daily 8am–dusk), preserves the grand estate of pioneer lumberman

Boats docked near Coos Bay.

and shipbuilder Louis B. Simpson, who built a luxurious summer home on a scenic bluff high above the Pacific Ocean. The house was destroyed by fire in 1921, but its restored grounds today include a formal Japanese garden and beautifully tended beds of roses.

Immediately south, Cape Arago Highway comes to a dead end at **Cape Arago State Park** (tel: 541-888 3778; https://stateparks.oregon.gov; free), a fine place for whale-watching. Even if the gray ones decide not to put in an appearance, this park and its coastal views are worth checking out, with wild vistas of pounding seas and glimpses of Oregon's distinctive sea stacks.

Returning inland from Cape Arago, it's worth stopping off near Charleston on your way south to explore the 4,300 acres (1,740 hectares) of tidal marshes, mudflats, and open water channels protected at **South Slough National Estuarine Research Reserve** (tel: 541-888 5558; www.oregon.gov; daily dawn–dusk; free). Unusual species living here include great blue heron, elk, and ghost shrimp.

BANDON

Alternatively known as Bandon-by-the-Sea, **Bandon** ⑰ (https://bandon.com) centers on its renovated Old Town, next to a boat basin, and within easy walking distance of sights and shops. This is Oregon's unofficial "Cranberry Capital," so expect to encounter all sorts of cranberry products, harvested from the nearby bogs. The central **Face Rock Creamery** (680 Second Street; tel: 541-329 0549; https://facerockcreamery.com; daily 10:30am–6pm), on the site of the much-missed Bandon Cheese Factory, has revived the local manufacture of many varieties of cheddar, and has an on-site cafe.

Long **Bullards Beach** ends at the northern side of the mouth of the Coquille River, where the delightful, camera-friendly **Coquille River Lighthouse** stands sentinel. You can't walk there from Bandon itself, so the most popular coastal hikes head south of town instead. The Beach Loop, for example, winds along the shoreline, passing such formations as the Garden of the Gods, Table Rock, Cat and

The walkway down to Bandon Beach.

Kittens Rock, Elephant Rock, and the towering, monolithic **Face Rock**, supposedly the face of a Native American frozen into stone by a sea spirit.

PORT ORFORD

Just under 30 miles (48km) south of Bandon, the Oregon coast juts out to its westernmost point at **Cape Blanco** ⑱, first noted by Europeans in the records of Spanish explorer Martin de Aguilar in January 1603. The brick-built Cape Blanco Lighthouse (tel: 541-332 6774; https://stateparks.oregon.gov; Apr–Oct Wed–Mon 10am–3.30pm), has been in continuous operation since 1870. The black sand hereabouts is strikingly unlike the tan-colored sand along the rest of the coast. Just north, strong winds make Floras Lake a prized arena for windsurfers and kitesurfers.

Ten miles (16km) further on, **Port Orford** ⑲ (https://portorford.org), the most westerly city in the contiguous United States, is considered Oregon's only true ocean harbor. A friendly and unpretentious town with panoramic ocean views, it has a long history as a fishing and lumber port. As fishing boats can't moor in the unprotected harbor, there's a daily spectacle of hoisting fishing boats in and out of the wild ocean waves on a converted log boom.

A gigantic promontory known as **Battle Rock**, site of a fierce 1851 confrontation between the Quatomah and European intruders, dominates the waterfront. Steep trails lead down to the beach – a favored surfing spot – and up to the rock's windswept summit.

GOLD BEACH AND BROOKINGS

Southwards from Port Orford, the coastal communities are considered the gateway to Rogue River Country (see page 157). At the mouth of the Rogue River, 28 miles (45km) along, **Gold Beach** ⑳ (https://visitgoldbeach.com) got its start in its own short-lived 19th-century gold rush, and serves these days as a base for salmon-fishing and jet-boat trips up the river. Lodges and campgrounds line the riverbanks for several miles inland.

Ocean views along the Oregon Coast Highway make for a spectacular roadtrip.

Of the three official river classifications – wild, scenic, and recreational – the section nearest Gold Beach is classified as scenic, meaning it is accessible by water, but is not considered wilderness. Jet-boat trips travel upriver from here either 32 miles/50km to the remote village of **Agness** ㉑ (the "short trip"), or 104 miles (166km) to **Paradise** and the notorious rapids of Blossom Bar (the "long trip"). The history of the short trip belongs to postal service lore: mail boats still deliver the US mail to Agness, just as they have ever since 1895. The contractor responsible is also the major operator of sightseeing trips, Jerry's Rogue Jets (29985 Harbor Way; tel: 800-451 3645; www.roguejets.com; May–mid-Oct).

Keep heading south on US 101, and you'll soon pass three stunning state parks. **Cape Sebastian** offers tremendous ocean views plus verdant hiking trails; **Pistol River** holds some utterly amazing sea stacks; and **Samuel H. Boardman** protects a long stretch of seafront with abundant hiking and picnicking opportunities.

Serious hikers can also venture inland, into the 180,000-acre (73,000-hectare) **Kalmiopsis Wilderness**, which forms part of the Rogue River-Siskiyou National Forest (https://www.fs.usda.gov). Named for a unique flowering shrub, Kalmiopsis leachiana – one of the oldest members of the heath (*Ericaceae*) family – the wilderness is characterized by deep rough canyons, sharp rock ridges, and clear rushing streams and rivers. The Chetco, the Illinois and the North Fork Smith Wild and Scenic rivers all flow through, offering opportunities for river-based recreation.

The coastal highway reaches the California state line 34 miles (54km) south of Gold Beach, just beyond the bustling little retirement community of **Brookings** ㉒ (www.brookings.or.us). Calling itself "Oregon's banana belt," Brookings is also the nation's major producer of Easter lilies and daffodils. Historic varieties of azaleas, said to date back beyond long before Lewis and Clark reached Oregon, can be admired at Azalea City Park, east of US 101.

Close up of searchlight at Point Blanco Lighthouse.

San Francisco in the sun.

INTRODUCTION

A detailed guide to Northern California, with principal sights clearly cross-referenced by number to the maps.

Vineyards flourish in Northern California.

Towering redwoods, granite cliffs, snowy peaks, picturesque vineyards, cosmopolitan cities... Northern California is arguably home to greater natural and social diversity than any similar-sized territory in the world.

For West Coast adventurers entering California from Oregon and points north, the state's wild, mountainous and densely wooded northwestern corner may initially look somewhat familiar. Along the coast, the skyline is dominated by towering redwood trees, best admired in assorted state parks and, especially, Redwood National Park. Of the no-nonsense Pacific-edge communities, Eureka and Fort Bragg make the best stop-offs. If you follow the inland route instead, Interstate 5 swiftly brings you to snow-capped Mount Shasta, still an active volcano, south of which State Highway 299 offers a magnificent drive through Bigfoot Country to reach the ocean.

In San Francisco, its most famous city, vintage cable cars crawl up incredibly steep hills, fog rolls eerily around the Golden Gate Bridge, and boisterous sea lions bark at Fisherman's Wharf. Millions of visitors explore this open-minded metropolis every year, perusing farmers' markets and fine art museums; running, biking, paddleboating, rollerblading, swing dancing, and shooting arrows in Golden Gate Park; or heading to the world-famous Alcatraz island prison on a ferry boat.

Bigfoot Country - Mt Shasta.

San Francisco, and the vibrant Bay Area immediately east, stand at the center of a fascinating region where utterly different landscapes lie within just a few hours in either direction. One enjoyable approach from the north is via the lush Wine Country, where the rolling vineyards of the serene Napa and Sonoma valleys yield grapes that go on to produce award-winning vintages. To the south lie the kelp forests and peaceful tide pools of Monterey, the spectacular Big Sur coast, and grand Hearst Castle.

Further inland, the long, agricultural Central Valley is California's political epicenter. In the pretty state capitol, Sacramento, the historic Old Town started out during the 1849 Gold Rush, as a staging post for prospectors seeking their fortunes to the east.

Majestic redwoods.

THE NORTH COAST AND THE HIGH NORTH

California's protected northern coastline cherishes a magnificent array of redwood forests, while the soaring mountains inland shelter mysteries of their own.

Few places in America are as beautifully wild as California's North Coast. In the upper reaches of the rugged north, you can contemplate mile after mile of majestic Pacific shoreline, inland hills, and towering redwood groves without encountering a living soul. Countless parks enable visitors to penetrate the wilderness, including Redwood National Park, home to the world's tallest tree, and Humboldt Redwoods State Park on the jaw-dropping Avenue of the Giants drive.

Further south towards San Francisco, stunning coastline links together state parks and sleepy seaside towns such as Mendocino and Bodega Bay, which offer scenic bluff views along with multiple opportunities for beach-combing, hiking, and wildlife-spotting.

The refreshing absence of development along the seashore is partly due to the California Coastal Commission, formed in the 1970s, when the state seemed destined to become an endless, repetitive ribbon of private marinas and ocean-view condominiums.

If you've the time to enjoy a leisurely road trip down the full length of the West Coast, the ideal way to arrive in California is on US Highway 101, having first followed the Oregon coast. Drivers heading south from Washington and Oregon in more of a hurry, however, may well enter California along

Interstate 5. The scenery of the so-called "High North," around 80 miles (130km) inland from the Pacific, is no less dramatic. Off to the east, the Cascade Mountains slowly come to an end, with mighty Mount Shasta as their final flourish.

Continue south on I-5 to approach San Francisco via the Wine Country or Central Valley. Alternatively, **State Highway 299** offers an exhilarating route down to the Pacific via the Klamath Mountains. On its winding trek, it cuts across a remote terrain of

⊙ Main attractions
Redwood National Park
Avenue of the Giants
Mendocino
Mount Shasta
Weaverville
Trinity Alps Wilderness Area

Map on page 186

Battery Point Lighthouse, Crescent City.

mountains, valleys, volcanoes, rivers, canyons, and basins. The best time to visit is mid-April to mid-November, though even in good weather, rockslides and heart-stopping curves make driving a challenge for the timid or the impatient.

CRESCENT CITY

Just 20 miles (32 km) south of the point where US 101 crosses the Oregon state line and enters California, **Crescent City ❶** –a grim, gray gathering of plain houses and vacant lots around a semi-circular harbor – has never quite recovered from the hammering it received from a 1964 tsunami. Yet more destruction was wrought by tsunami waves generated by the 2011 earthquake off Japan.

Fifteen minutes east, on US 199 toward Grants Pass, Oregon, the last undammed river in California flows gin-clear through the 90°F (32°C) summer twilight. The **Smith River** may be wild, but its accommodations are civilized. As well as a lodge on **Patrick Creek** (www.patrickcreeklodge.com),

there are clean campgrounds, public and private, under the peeling red madronas. The attractions are simple: boulder-lined banks, clear pools, good fishing – and no redwood souvenirs.

REDWOOD NATIONAL PARK

California's North Coast owes much of its mystique to its towering, majestic redwood trees, which have survived attempts to transform them into everything from lumber and ashtrays to mulch for suburban rose gardens. Most of the state's remaining old-growth redwoods are now protected in parks.

Orick, 42 miles (67km) south of Crescent City, serves as the gateway to **Redwood National Park ❷** (www.nps. gov/redw). Established in 1968 to consolidate 40 miles (60km) of forested coastline under federal jurisdiction, the 132,000-acre (53,400-hectare) park encompasses three state parks: **Prairie Creek Redwoods**, **Del Norte Coast Redwoods**, and **Jedediah Smith Redwoods**.

The national park holds five visitor centers (most open daily 9am–5pm), and several campsites (tel: 800-444 7275; www.reservecalifornia.com). The Thomas H. **Kuchel Visitor Center** (tel: 707-464 6101), 1 mile (1.6km) south of Orick on US 101, gives out trail maps, directions, and shuttle-bus information for excursions up Redwood Creek, to the southeast, where some of the tallest trees ever identified are clustered in the **Tall Trees Grove**. Redwood National Park's very tallest tree, known as **Hyperion**, measures a towering 380ft (116 meters) high, and is the tallest known tree in the world, but it's in a remote area and not accessible to visitors.

Other notable sites include the **Lady Bird Johnson Grove**, an old-growth forest named for the former first lady. Don't raise your hopes of the scenery north of the Klamath River bridge too high, however, because you probably

Carson House, Eureka.

won't see much of it; fog can come in thick and fast, and without warning.

EUREKA

From the moment you arrive, it is obvious that **Eureka** ❸ is a good place to buy such commodities as sewer pipe, lumber, a slab of redwood burl, a life-sized statue of a lumberjack carved from a redwood log, or a fresh fish dinner. Often shrouded in fog, it's the largest Pacific Coast enclave in North America north of San Francisco. A sprawling, busy, industrial place, still home to a large fishing industry, Eureka is also the location of the North Coast's only institution of higher learning, called, appropriately enough, Humboldt State University.

The much-photographed **Carson House**, at the end of 2nd Street, exemplifies the impressive Victorian architecture of Eureka's Old Town. Visitors can't go inside, because it's now a private men's club – which makes it seem all the more Victorian. Anyone interested in this type of architecture will want to head to little **Ferndale**, 10 miles (16km) southwest, which has a fine sprinkling of well-maintained Victorian buildings.

AVENUE OF THE GIANTS

Beyond Eureka, Highway 101 curves away inland, not to return to the shoreline for another 500 miles (800km). For an honest glimpse into the spirit of the early settler life along the North Coast, stop off en route at **Scotia**, 27 miles (43km) south of Eureka. This crisp little town belonged to the Pacific Lumber Company until the company went bankrupt in 2008. Built entirely of redwood – its wooden visitor center is in the style of a classic Greek temple – it's still dominated by the world's largest redwood mill, now operated by Humboldt Sawmill.

Twenty miles (32km) south of Scotia, the breathtaking **Avenue of the Giants** ❹ is a 32-mile (51km) scenic drive that follows the South Fork of the Eel River through 55,000-acre (22,000-hectare) **Humboldt Redwoods State Park** (www.parks.ca.gov). The giants – redwood trees, otherwise known as *Sequoia sempervirens* – are breathtakingly tall and sometimes surprisingly wide. Their size can, and has been, marketed: "Drive through a living tree" is the come-on from the **Drive-Thru Tree** in the town of **Myers Flat**.

To drop back down to the Pacific, turn west off Highway 101 90 miles (144km) south of Eureka. Oceanfront **Fort Bragg**, 43 miles (69km) along Highway 1, is a down-to-earth, working-class town established in 1857 as a US military post. A mill built in 1885 served its lumber industry until 2002, when its closure dealt a huge blow to the local economy. Its unpretentious flavor is best relished in **Noyo Harbor**, a sunny inlet lined by docks, characterful boats, and seafood restaurants.

MENDOCINO

Set on a long bluff above a small bay, 10 miles (16km) south of Fort Bragg

Mendocino's ocean views.

and 156 miles (251km) north of San Francisco, **Mendocino** is a cultured town with an arts center and many galleries. A century-old former logging village, it was all but deserted in the early 20th century, but saw a cultural renaissance when artists and musicians moved in during the 1950s.

Today, it's a lovely, low-key place, much of the pleasure coming from just strolling around. Gingerbread houses cling to windswept headlands, and there are white picket fences and ancient wooden water towers. Still, with more than 20 bed-and-breakfast inns, the small town becomes hectic on weekends. Two nearby state parks, **Van Damme** and **Russian Gulch**, offer camping, hiking, bird-watching, fishing, beachcombing, and other quiet pleasures.

MENDOCINO COUNTY

The Coast Guard's **Point Arena Lighthouse** (http://pointarenalighthouse. com). 36 miles (58km) south of Mendocino, marks the closest point on the US mainland to Hawaii. Many a ship has foundered hereabouts; free brochures catalogue which vessels, and where, and what was lost as a result.

Not far south, a coastal access path leads to the eponymous community of **Point Arena**, where a tiny bayside beach comprises several dozen weathered mobile homes, two disintegrating and dangerous piers, and a few shops selling bait and fishing tackle. However, bed and breakfast inns are springing up all along the coast as former urbanites buy up Victorian homes, and surrender with relief to a lifestyle change in the countryside.

For anyone with an empty stomach and a bulging wallet, the towns of **Albion** and **Elk** make excellent places to stop as you continue south from Mendocino. Both hold upscale eateries that provide great food and good views.

SONOMA COUNTY

One compelling way to spend an afternoon in the northern reaches of **Sonoma County**, just beyond sleepy Gualala, is to explore the coastal tide pools. At **Salt Point State Park** (www.

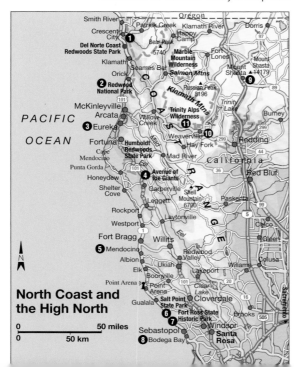

North Coast and the High North

0   50 miles
0   50 km

parks.ca.gov), a popular spot for abalone divers, visitors can inspect the rocky tide pools at low tides to see marine life up close. Additional activities include hiking, horseback riding, fishing, and diving.

In these parts, Highway 1 weaves through daily fog, rolling pastures, and sudden canyons that drop 1,000ft (over 300 meters) into the blue and foamy Pacific. Six miles (10km) southwest of Salt Point, historic **Fort Ross** ❼ (www.fortross.org; daily 10am–4.30pm), is a careful reconstruction of an original Russian trading fort from the early 19th century. There are tours, but it's more fun to stroll around on your own. The small Russian Orthodox chapel is worth a special stop.

Continuing south, most of the Sonoma coast is a state beach, with no camping but comfortable access, plenty of parking, thrilling views, and appropriate beach names like Mussel Point, Salmon Creek, Hog Back, Shell Beach, and Goat Rock. As you travel south on Highway 1 toward Bodega Bay, the prevailing scenery is atmospheric and deeply appealing with cypress trees, pines, old barns, and grazing sheep and cows, often shrouded in fog.

BODEGA BAY TO FORT ROSS

By the time you reach the coast at **Bodega Bay** ❽, named in honor of Spanish explorer Juan Francisco de la Bodega y Quadra, you're just 35 miles (56km) north of **Point Reyes National Seashore** (see page 223). Offering sweeping views from Point Reyes to Fort Ross, Bodega Bay's bluffs are a popular whale-watching spot from January through April. For further wildlife-spotting, the bird sanctuary located at **Doran Beach** is arguably the best bird-watching site in the whole of Sonoma County. Call into the **Sonoma Coast Visitors Center** (913 Highway 1; tel: 707-377 4459; www.sonomacounty.com) for more information.

MOUNT SHASTA

The first major landmark that confronts drivers who enter the High North of California on Interstate 5 comes just beyond the town of Weed, 60 miles (100km) south of the Oregon state line. **Mount Shasta** ❾ (14,162ft/4,317 meters), immediately east of I-5, is an ancient volcano that stands solitary sentinel at the head of the Sacramento Valley. Its glacier-capped peak marks the southernmost point of the volcanic **Cascade Range**, which extends all the way from Alaska. Reaching the summit is a moderately difficult all-day climb in summer, with sweeping views of the Central Valley to the south, the Trinities to the southwest, and the Sierras to the southeast. In winter, the mountain is buried in snow, but still open to enthusiastic skiers.

WEAVERVILLE

Head west on Hwy 299 at **Redding**, another 60 miles (100km) south of Mount Shasta, and you'll reach **Weaverville** ❿, the seat of **Trinity County**, after 44 miles (70km). This

The chapel at Fort Ross State Historic Park.

◉ Tip

Come summer, man-made **Shasta Lake**, south of Mount Shasta, is popular for houseboating vacations. It is possible to rent boats for a few days or an entire week (tel: 888-454 8825; www. houseboating.org/shasta/ overview.cfm).

appealing little town saw its glory days during the mid-19th century, when it was a supply post for gold prospectors. Gold hunters still haunt the creeks of Trinity County, but lumbering sustains the economy.

The central **Joss House State Historic Park** (www.parks.ca.gov; Thu–Sun 10am–4pm), pays tribute to Chinese history in California, particularly during the Gold Rush, and holds the state's oldest still-functioning Chinese temple. Nearby, the eclectic **JJ "Jake" Jackson Museum** (www.trinitymuseum.org), focuses on local history.

Weaverville is also the gateway to Trinity and Lewiston lakes, part of the expansive **Whiskeytown National Recreation Area** (www.nps.gov). A short drive north of town, these lakes were created when the upper Trinity River was dammed in the 1960s, and offer such recreation as fishing, hiking, boating, and camping.

Trinity County's population breaks into two groups – true locals and incomers since the 1960s. Generally, old-timers tend to be conservative,

newcomers less so – but both groups share an individualism and a jealous regard for the natural environment. While Trinity tends to vote Republican, it also displays an abiding sensitivity to ecological issues.

Many residents hunt for their own food and draw water directly from springs, rivers, and creeks. The bedrock of granite and serpentine is too impermeable for aquifers. When locals tried to stop the federal government from spraying Trinity's woodlands with a herbicide many feared would end up in water supplies, no politicians – Democrat or Republican – openly opposed the grassroots effort.

THE KLAMATH MOUNTAINS

On its 100-mile (160km) route west of Weaverville to meet the Pacific Coast at **Arcata**, north of Eureka, State Highway 299 crosses the wilderness realm of the Klamath and Trinity rivers. These two principal rivers drain both the **Klamath Mountains** and the Coast Range beyond. Comprising a series of smaller ranges – the Siskiyou, the Trinity, the Trinity Alps, the Marble, the Scott Bar, the South Fork, and the Salmon mountains – the Klamaths cover 12,000 sq miles (31,000 sq km) of Northern California and southern Oregon, with Mount Hilton as the highest peak.

There's something very wild about the Klamaths: receiving more than 70in (1,800mm) of annual rainfall in some parts, they sustain a lush forest of ferns, hemlocks, pines, and spruce. Except for the highest of the Trinity Alps, glaciers are rare, so most peaks retain a raw, jagged quality, and river canyons lack the graceful horseshoe shape of their glaciated Sierra Nevada counterparts.

Native American tribes still inhabit the area. The **Hoopa** and **Klamath** own ancestral fishing rights and set their traps and dip their nets at the foot of **Ishi Pishi Falls**. Guides with graceful

The Chinese temple at Joss House State Historic Park.

rowboats, called "MacKenzies," will lead you to the finest holding pools. Stealthy visitors may spot eagle, river otter, great blue heron, duck, fox, bobcat, and the occasional great bear.

The rivers and streams bear names that blend Native American mythology with the whims of 19th-century prospectors: Klamath, Ukunom, Trinity, Salmon, Smith. Fishing and floating on these rivers is by no means limited to natives; the streams are big and cool in hot summers, and rafting and fishing guides take visitors down inviting canyons. Salmon and steelhead trout still spawn, and the fall run is unparalleled in the state.

The three national forests that contain most of California's Klamaths – Klamath, Shasta, and Trinity – hold more protected wilderness areas. The best-known and most popular, the vast **Trinity Alps Wilderness Area ⓫** with its high, craggy peaks and sparkling lakes, is laced with trails for hiking and camping. Ranger stations along State Highway 299 at **Weaverville**, **Big Bar**, and **Burnt Ranch**, and at **Trinity Center** on State Highway 3, issue free permits, and advise on current conditions.

Redwood trees can especially be found in the old-growth state parks of these northern coastal mountains. Some of these mighty giants, 1,000 years old and reaching 300ft (90 meters) into the sky, are the largest living things on earth. Sun filtering through the redwood canopy as if through leaded glass, the cool enveloping shade, and the imposing sense of age often draw comparisons to the cathedrals of Europe.

About 10 miles (16km) east of the Trinity River bridge that marks the Humboldt–Trinity county line, near the community of Burnt Ranch, State Highway 299 passes just south of **Ironside Mountain** (5,255ft/1,602 meters). Ironside's sheer, scenic face is the eroded, exposed tip of a much larger piece of granite. About 165 million years old, it's typical of other such intrusions in the Sierra Nevada and Klamaths, which distinguish the Klamaths from the neighboring Coast Range.

⊙ Fact

California's far northern corner, still partly populated by Native Americans, is home to the legendary **Sasquatch**, or, as he's more widely known, **Bigfoot**. This huge, reclusive, ape-like creature has red fur that camouflages him among the towering redwood trees and river canyons. Multiple sightings are attributed by the scientific community to deliberate hoaxes or cases of animal misidentification.

California poppies bloom from mid-February often until well into May.

Napa Valley.

THE WINE COUNTRY AND CENTRAL VALLEY

Spending a day or two in the gorgeous Napa and Sonoma valleys is not to be missed, while the fertile Central Valley, just east, is redolent of Gold-Rush history.

For drivers heading south toward San Francisco, taking a detour through California's legendary Wine Country makes a wonderful alternative to either following the Pacific Coast or barrelling down the Central Valley. If you're approaching on I-5, sticking to the interstate sweeps you inexorably into state capital Sacramento; to reach the Wine Country, turn off west at Williams.

As seen from the definitive Wine-Country viewpoint, the summit of Mount St Helena, a vast, rolling expanse of emerald vineyards stretches for miles below. Supported by a temperate climate and rich, drainable soil, the grape vines blanket the beautifully bucolic Napa, Sonoma, Mendocino, and Lake counties, which together form one of the world's premier wine-growing regions. While visiting individual wineries to sample their product is the prime attraction for visitors – just remember, someone has to stay sober to drive you away afterwards – but the Wine Country also boasts a renowned farm-to-table restaurant scene, spas fed by hot springs, and abundant opportunities for biking, hiking, and camping.

To the east, the 450-mile-long (720km) Central Valley is a vast, flat, basin that came to the world's attention

in 1848, when James Marshall discovered gold in the Sierra foothills nearby. Gold-seekers flocked here in the late 1800s, and the Gold Rush continues to shape much of the region's identity. That's especially true in Sacramento's Old Town and along the Mother Lode, California's richest mineral vein, where towns have been expensively restored to their former pioneer glory. The Great Depression saw another influx of migrants, in the shape of thousands of families driven west from the Dust Bowl.

 Main attractions
Silverado Trail
Napa Wine Train
Yountville
Downtown Sonoma
Old Sacramento
Sutter's Fort

Map on page 196

The veins in the vine leaves feed the grapes.

◎ Eat

Before the **Culinary Institute of America** (CIA) was founded, many cooks were so secretive about recipes that it was hard for a novice to break into the profession. Today, the California branch works to preserve knowledge and share it with the public. Expect tasty tidbits, paired wines, and up-and-coming chefs at the teaching school (The Gatehouse Restaurant; 2555 Main Street, St Helena; tel: 707-967 2300; www.ciarestaurantgroup.com/gatehouse-restaurant; Tue–Sat lunch and dinner).

Today, the Central Valley is still making a major contribution to the wealth of California, albeit with agriculture rather than gold. The San Joaquin Valley produces more than half of the state's annual $40 billion-plus in farm goods, and Fresno County alone accounts for a significant proportion of that, making it the number-one farming county in America.

CLEAR LAKE

If you plan to approach the Wine Country from the north, you can either turn inland from the coast at Fort Bragg (see page 185), or head west from I-5 at Williams, 100 miles (160km) south of Redding. Bold, friendly, visitor-seeking wineries are scattered all around **Clear Lake ❶**, California's largest natural lake, which is also ringed by resorts and campgrounds. There's good walking in **Clear Lake State Park** at the foot of conical Mount Konocti, an extinct volcano.

NAPA VALLEY

California's most famous wine-producing region, rural Napa Valley, has a wealthy and genteel aura. Catapulted to prominence when it defeated the finest French wines in a hugely publicized 1976 blind tasting, this 30-mile (50km) thrust of flat land nestles between the pine-forested Mayacamas Mountains and the buff-colored Howell Mountains, pinched off in the north by Mount St Helena. State Highway 29 and the **Silverado Trail** run parallel through the valley, passing long expanses of vineyards broken up by farmhouses, stone wineries, and a series of small towns. Simply choose which wineries you want to visit and hit the road (with a designated driver, of course).

CALISTOGA

The one-street spa town of **Calistoga ❷**, south of Clear Lake on Highway 29 and the northernmost Napa Valley community, is a little gem. Wooden hangings shading the shopfronts give it a Wild West feel, while treatment centers including Indian Springs, Calistoga Spa Hot Springs, and Solage make use of mineral springs and hot, therapeutic mud to soothe and rejuvenate.

Idyllic hot air balloon flight territory.

Calistoga is surrounded by wineries. Enjoying a lakeside setting with a Chinese feel, the 1882 **Chateau Montelena** (tel: 707-942 5105; www.montelena. com), produces classic Chardonnay and Cabernet Sauvignon. Reservations are advised for the picnic sites on Jade Lake, in view of the pagoda.

Two miles (3km) north of town, **Old Faithful Geyser** (tel: 707-942 6463; www.oldfaithfulgeyser.com; daily, 8.30am–7pm, until 5pm in winter) spouts jets of boiling water 60–100ft (18–30 meters) into the sky every half-hour. Just to the west, the redwoods of the **Petrified Forest** (4100 Petrified Forest Road; www.petrifiedforest. org), were turned to stone three million years ago. Docent-led tours discuss local geology, flora, and fauna.

Mount St Helena itself stands within **Robert Louis Stevenson State Park**, 7 miles (11km) north of Calistoga and named for the author of *Treasure Island*, who honeymooned here in 1880. The 5-mile (8km) hike to the top passes a marker noting where his cabin once stood. On clear days, Mount Shasta can be seen 192 miles (309km) to the north.

Atop a knoll just south of Calistoga, **Sterling Vineyards** (tel: 800-726 6136; www.sterlingvineyards.com) – part Spanish mission, part sheer fantasy – reigns over the upper valley. A sky tram whisks visitors 300ft (91 meters) up for a self-guided tour. Close by, the sleek, modern **Clos Pegase** (tel: 707-942 4981; www.clospegase.com) is known almost as much for its art collection as for its wines.

To take a break from wine tasting, visit the **Bale Grist Mill State Historic Park** (tel: 707-963 2236; Fri–Mon 10am–4pm), 5 miles (8km) south of Calistoga. At one time the center of Napa social activity, the historic 1846 mill is where settlers used to grind their corn and wheat into flour or meal. Tours and milling demonstrations are held on weekends.

ST HELENA

St Helena ❸, the undisputed capital of the Napa Valley, is noted for its dozens of wineries, historic stone buildings,

Shopping in Castiloga.

⊘ THE SILVERADO TRAIL

Quieter and more scenic than State Highway 29, the **Silverado Trail** was built to connect Mount St Helena's cinnabar mines with Napa's river docks. Running parallel to the highway, above the valley floor, this elevated, two-lane road links Calistoga and Napa, offering panoramic views, wineries, and hidden valleys deep in the Howell Mountains. Popular stops include the **Rutherford Hill Winery** (www.rutherfordhill.com), an ark-like structure with picnic grounds, and **Auberge du Soleil** (https://aubergeresorts.com), where the dining terrace overlooks verdant vineyards.

Stag's Leap, a rocky promontory near Yountville where a 16-point Roosevelt elk once plunged to its death, overlooks the award-winning **Stag's Leap Wine Cellars** (www.cask23.com) and **Clos du Val** (www. closduval.com).

Eat

A one-of-a-kind fine-dining experience, with exceptional Napa wines, awaits passengers on the year-round Wine Train (tel: 800-427 4124; www.winetrain.com). Lavishly restored 1915 Pullman dining and lounge cars whizz past wineries on its three-hour, round-trip tour through the heart of the Napa Valley, between St Helena and Napa. Packages range from champagne brunches to winemakers' dinners and murder mystery rides. Optional excursions head to the Raymond Winery and Grgich Hills Estate.

picnic parks, chic shops, pricey hotels, and the CIA (no, not that CIA; see page 194). The **Robert Louis Stevenson Museum** (1490 Library Lane; tel: 707-963 3757; http://stevenson-museum.org; Tue–Sat noon–4pm), is stuffed with Stevenson memorabilia and collectables, like first editions of his works and souvenirs of his global jaunts.

Two historic wineries lie at the north end of town. Jacob and Frederick started the **Beringer Vineyards** (tel: 707-257 5771; www.beringer.com) in 1876, modeling the Rhine House (1883) after their ancestral estate in Mainz, Germany. They dug limestone caves for aging wine. Today's winery, owned by Foster's (yes, the Australian beer people), features Fumé Blanc and Cabernet Sauvignon in the mansion tasting room. Outside spread spacious lawns and a regal row of elms.

The building of the other founding father, **Charles Krug Winery** (tel: 707-967 2200; www.charleskrug.com), dates from 1874. The lavish Greystone structure nearby was the world's largest stone winery when it was erected in 1889 by mining magnate William Bourn; today, the mansion is run by the California headquarters of the **Culinary Institute of America**, a brilliant cooking school complete with restaurant.

South of the center, and run by one of the valley's oldest winemaking clans, the **Louis M. Martini Winery** (tel: 800-321 9463; www.louismartini.com), offers reasonably priced wines in an unpretentious setting. A little farther along, the **Robert Mondavi Winery** (tel: 888-766 6328; www.robertmondaviwinery.com), is a sleek operation, as befits such a famous name.

YOUNTVILLE

In what must surely be one of history's most lucrative contracting deals, George Yount received his huge land grant for roofing the Petaluma adobe of General Vallejo. The renovated brick and stone buildings in **Yountville ④** are home to exceptional restaurants, from Thomas Keller's world-renowned **French Laundry** (www.thomaskeller.com) to the more relaxed **The Girl and the Fig** (www.thegirlandthefig.com). Across from the city park, the pioneer center holds the grave of George Yount.

Of course, the focus in Yountville is also on wine. **Domaine Chandon Winery** (tel: 888-242 6366; www.chandon.com), just west of town, is owned by Chandon of Moët and Chandon fame, and produces sparkling wine in the *méthode champenoise*; that is, fermented in the same bottle from which it is poured.

NAPA

The southernmost Napa Valley town, and thus the first you enter if you're approaching from San Francisco, is **Napa ⑤** (www.visitnapavalley.com). The charming small town (whose name means "plenty") is a compact collection of shops, country inns, wineries, and eateries. Peruse boutiques on the

Rhine House, Beringer Vineyards, Napa.

main street through the quaint Downtown, grab a bite at an upscale restaurant, then get on the road to taste your way through wineries like Darioush, Paraduxx, Ceja, Frogs Leap, Vintners Collective, and Schramberg. If you'd rather not drive, consider taking a tour on the Napa Valley Wine Train.

At the popular **Oxbow Public Market** (610 and 644 First Street; www.oxbow-publicmarket.com; daily 7.30am–9.30pm), hungry customers can choose from dozens of restaurants and specialty food purveyors, including Hog Island, dishing out fresh oysters; Gott's Roadside, for burgers, hot dogs, and poke tacos; and Ritual Coffee Roasters, pouring some of the Bay Area's best coffee. On Tuesdays and Saturdays, the **Napa Farmers' Market** is held at 105 Gasser Drive (https://napafarmers-market.org; Tues and Sat 8am–1pm).

ALEXANDER, DRY CREEK, AND RUSSIAN RIVER VALLEYS

Slow-paced and rustic, **Sonoma County** is a patchwork of country roads, towns, orchards, ridges, and hills. West of Napa, Sonoma is at its southern end an hour's drive (without traffic) from San Francisco. US 101, the Wine Country's only freeway, runs the length of Sonoma County north to south, entering it near Cloverdale, on the Mendocino County border, and continuing on through Healdsburg and Santa Rosa.

Healdsburg ❻, 24 miles (38km) west of Calistoga, stands at the junction of the Alexander, Dry Creek, and Russian River valleys. There's a tree-shaded, Spanish-style plaza, and a beach on the Russian River encourages swimming, fishing, and canoeing. The **Healdsburg Museum** (221 Matheson Street; www.healdsburgmuseum.org), housed in the former Carnegie Library, displays Pomo tribal artifacts and 19th-century exhibits.

More than 60 wineries lie within half an hour's drive of Healdsburg, attracting almost a million visitors a year to this pretty town. The tasting room of the **Simi Winery** (tel: 800-746 4880; www.simiwinery.com) is on Healdsburg Avenue, opposite the 130-year-old **Belle du Jour Inn** (tel: 707-431 9777; www.belledujourinn.com). Alongside a sketch of himself in its 1942 guestbook, Alfred Hitchcock noted "The port here is far too good for most people."

To the north, east of US 101, the picturesque **Alexander Valley** holds another concentration of wineries. State Highway 253 snakes westward from US 101 just south of Ukiah to join northbound State Highway 128 at Boonville. This narrow, often-wooded country road meanders through the valley past grazing sheep, vineyards, and orchards all the way to Navarro and beyond to the coast.

Winemaking here began well over a century ago, when frustrated gold-seekers settled and planted vineyards. **Boonville** ❼ is a delightful little place. You can eat well and stay comfortably at the Boonville Hotel (tel: 707-895 2210; www.boonvillehotel.com), which calls itself a "roadhouse," defined in

○ Drink

Don't drive after a wine tasting; it's best to have a non-drinking designated driver. Quite apart from the very real risks of getting in an accident, police frequently set up mandatory checkpoints along the main roads, where they stop all cars to ensure that drivers are sober. The penalties if you are not are liable to be severe.

Ripe for harvest.

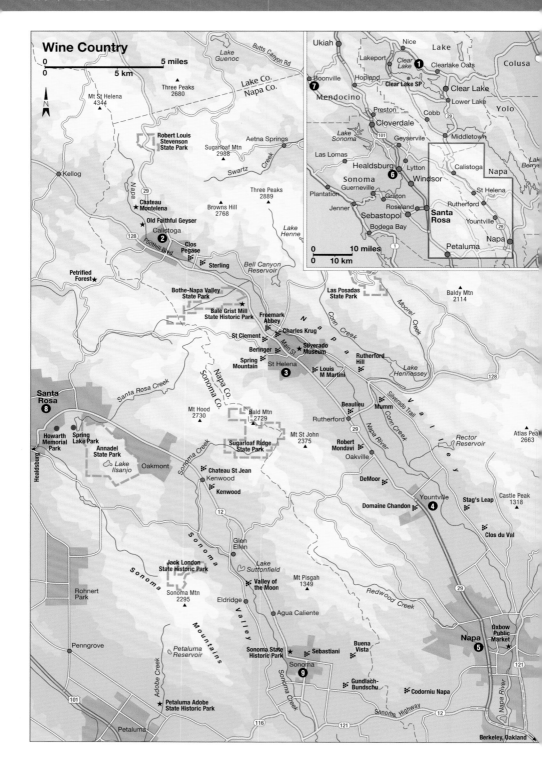

Wine Country

0   5 miles
0   5 km

N

Lake Guenoc
Butts Canyon Rd
Three Peaks 2680
Lake Co.
Napa Co.
Mt St Helena 4344
Robert Louis Stevenson State Park
Aetna Springs
Sugarloaf Mtn 2988
Swartz   Creek
Kellog
Three Peaks 2889
Chateau Montelena
Browns Hill 2768
Old Faithful Geyser
Calistoga
Lake Henne
Clos Pegase
Bell Canyon Reservoir
Sterling
Petrified Forest
Bothe-Napa Valley State Park
Las Posadas State Park
Baldy Mtn 2114
Bale Grist Mill State Historic Park
Freemark Abbey
Charles Krug
St Clement
Silverado Museum
Beringer
Spring Mountain
St Helena
Louis M Martini
Rutherford Hill
Lake Hennessey
Santa Rosa Creek
Mt Hood 2730
Bald Mtn 2729
Beaulieu
Mumm
Santa Rosa
Mt St John 2375
Rutherford
Howarth Memorial Park
Spring Lake Park
Sugarloaf Ridge State Park
Robert Mondavi
Rector Reservoir
Atlas Peak 2663
Annadel State Park
Lake Ilsanjo
Oakmont
Chateau St Jean
Oakville
DeMoor
Castle Peak 1318
Kenwood
Kenwood
Yountville
Stag's Leap
Domaine Chandon
Clos du Val
Jack London State Historic Park
Glen Ellen
Lake Suttonfield
Valley of the Moon
Mt Pisgah 1349
Rohnert Park
Sonoma Mtn 2295
Eldridge
Redwood Creek
Penngrove
Agua Caliente
Petaluma Reservoir
Napa
Oxbow Public Market
Sonoma State Historic Park
Sebastiani
Buena Vista
Sonoma
Petaluma Adobe State Historic Park
Gundlach-Bundschu
Petaluma
Codorniu Napa
Sonoma Highway
Berkeley, Oakland

Ukiah
Nice
Lake
Colusa
Lakeport
Clear Lake
Clearlake Oaks
Boonville
Hopland
Clear Lake SP
Clear Lake
Mendocino
Preston
Lower Lake
Yolo
Cloverdale
Cobb
Lake Sonoma
Geyserville
Middletown
Las Lomas
Healdsburg
Lytton
Calistoga
Napa
Sonoma
Windsor
Guerneville
Graton
St Helena
Plantation
Roseland
Rutherford
Jenner
Sebastopol
Santa Rosa
Yountville
Bodega Bay
Napa
0   10 miles
0   10 km
Petaluma

Central Valley

0   20 miles
0   20 km

Lincoln

Placer

Auburn State
Recreation Area

Rocklin
Auburn

Roseville

El Dorado

Citrus Heights
Coloma

11 Sutter's Fort

Marshall Gold
Discovery
State Historic
Park

Placerville

10 Sacramento

Sacramento

Sloughhouse

Cosumnes

Cosumnes

Clay

Plymouth

Amador

Sutter
Creek

Indian Grinding Rock
State Historic Park

Lone

Jackson

West Point

Lockeford

Mokelumne
Hill

Railroad Flat

Lodi

Camanche
Res.

Calaveras
Big Trees
State Park

San Andreas

San
Joaquin

Mercer
Caverns

Stockton

Angels Camp

Murphys

Calaveras

New Melones
Lake

Columbia State
Historic Park

Mark Twain's Cabin

Columbia

Manteca

Sonora

Riverbank

Stanislaus

Tuolumne

Oakdale

Modesto
12

Don Pedro
Res.

Moccasin

Ceres

Ticolumne

Blanchard

islaus

Coulterville

Turlock

Snelling

Livingston

Merced

Mariposa

Winton

Catheys
Valley

Atwater

Mariposa

Gustine

Bear Cr.

Merced

Owens

El Nido

Los Banos

Planada

Red Top

Chowchilla

Raymond

Merced

Dos
Palos

Chowchilla

Fresno

Madera

Firebaugh

Madera

Mendota

San Joaquin

Panoche

Clovis

Whites
Bridge

Fresno

13
Fresno

an
nito

Kerman

Bakersfield

Los Angeles

Funk and Wagnall's 19th-century dictionary as "an inn or restaurant in a rural locality which caters especially to transient pleasure-seekers."

SANTA ROSA

Botanist Luther Burbank picked the area around **Santa Rosa** **8**, 15 miles (24km) south of Healdsburg, as "the chosen spot of all the earth" to conduct his experiments in hybridization, from 1875 onward. Although he developed more than 800 new plants, including many fruits, vegetables, and flowers, aside from asparagus he relished hardly any. Visitors can tour the **Luther Burbank Home and Gardens** (tel: 707-524 5445; www.lutherburbank. org).

Santa Rosa's trinity of adjoining parks form a 5,000-acre (12,000-hectare) urban oasis, with a children's amusement park and lake in Howarth Park; camping, picnicking, and boating in Spring Lake Park; and hiking and equestrian trails in Annadel State Park.

SONOMA VALLEY

The **Sonoma Valley** is steeped in wine and wineries, as well as literary and political

Sacramento's summer highlight is the colourful, family-friendly **California State Fair** (1600 Exposition Boulevard; https://calexpostatefair.com), which runs for around 18 days through the second half of July. Packed with concerts, exhibits, and events ranging from a simultaneous food festival to thoroughbred horse races, it attracts thousands of visitors from all over the county.

El Paseo de Sonoma has a variety of shops to browse.

history. Sonoma is a native Patwin word meaning "Land of Chief Nose," after a Native leader with a prominent proboscis. Founding father Mariano Vallejo romanticized Sonoma Valley as the "Valley of the Moon," an appellation later borrowed by author Jack London for his 1913 novel about frazzled urbanites rejuvenated by country living.

KENWOOD

To reach Sonoma Valley from Santa Rosa, head 11 miles (18km) west on State Highway 12, to the town of **Kenwood**. The **Kenwood Vineyards** (tel: 707-282 4281; www.kenwoodvineyards.com) features Zinfandel, Cabernet Sauvignon, and Chenin Blanc, while Chardonnay lovers head for **Château St Jean** (tel: 707-257 5784; www.chateaustjean.com), with its beautiful backdrop of the Sonoma Mountains and excellent whites.

SONOMA

Father Altimira founded California's last mission, **San Francisco de Solano**, in 1823. General Vallejo set up the town in 1835, making **Sonoma ⑨** the northernmost outpost of a Catholic, Spanish-speaking realm that, at its peak, extended all the way to the tip of South America. It briefly became a republic after the Bear Flag Revolt in 1846, when Americans stormed Vallejo's home. Although Vallejo and the missionaries dabbled in winemaking, local residents only really appreciated the region's vinicultural potential after Hungarian political refugee Count Agoston Haraszthy founded **Buena Vista Winery** in 1957.

Today, downtown Sonoma is picturesque, relaxed, and well-heeled. Upscale restaurants and art galleries encircle its tree-shaded **Sonoma Plaza**. Here you'll come across **El Paseo de Sonoma**, an enclave of shops in a courtyard setting that makes for pleasant browsing. Restored adobes scattered around the plaza and on nearby streets include the **Mission** itself (tel: 707-938 9560); Vallejo's old house, Lachryma Montis (tel: 707-938 9559); and the Sonoma Barracks (tel:

707-939 9420), all part of the Sonoma State Historic Park (20 East Spain Street; daily 10am–5pm; www.parks.ca.gov).

Three blocks east of the plaza, **Sebastiani Vineyards** (tel: 707-933 3200; www.sebastiani.com), occupies land once cultivated by the people of the San Francisco de Solano Mission. A little farther east, the **Buena Vista Winery Tasting Room** (tel: 800-926 1266; www.buenavistawinery.com) retains connections with Count Haraszthy; his original cellars are still standing and his image adorns the label of the winery's Founder's red wine.

SACRAMENTO

California's state capital, **Sacramento** ⑩, nestles in the heart of the Central Valley 90 miles (144km) northeast of San Francisco. In contrast to its glamorous coastal neighbor, the city is a blazing furnace in midsummer; temperatures often exceed 100°F (38°C) for days at a time. But the weather can still be pleasant, as humidity is low, it seldom rains for long, and marine breezes from San Francisco Bay cool the nights.

OLD SACRAMENTO

Along the Sacramento waterfront, beneath the impassive mirrored facades of office buildings, the historic **Old Sacramento** district was where steamers from San Francisco deposited gold-seeking passengers from 1849 onward. Today, wooden buildings, horse-drawn carriages, and cobblestone streets convey a distinct image of the Old West. The **Delta King**, a permanently moored 1920s paddle steamboat, now operates as a hotel-restaurant.

For an overview of historic sites, stop off at the **Visitor Center** (1000 Second Street; tel: 916-808 7644). The city was the western terminus of both the Pony Express overland mail service and the Transcontinental Railroad. The station now forms part of the **California State Railroad Museum** (111 I Street; www.californiarailroad.museum; daily 10am–5pm), which delights kids and adults alike with its 50-plus restored

⊙ **Where**

Half an hour west of Stockton, en route to the Bay, Interstate 580 crests **Altamont Pass**. One of the West Coast's windiest spots, it's a fine example of California's dedication to alternative energy – a wind farm producing electricity, with overhead power lines and dairy cows peacefully coexisting. Incidentally, Altamont Raceway Park, just east, was the site of the infamous 1969 rock festival.

West Sacramento is postcard pretty.

locomotives. Nearby, exhibits in the **Sacramento History Museum** (101 I Street; tel: 916-808 7059; http://sachistorymuseum.org; daily 10am–5pm), focus on Native American heritage, celebrate the Pony Express, and commemorate the role Chinese immigrants played in the Gold Rush.

The oldest art museum west of the Mississippi, the **Crocker Art Museum** (216 O Street; tel: 916-808 7000; www.crockerart.org; Wed–Sun 10am–5pm), boasts a great collection of Californian art, with works from the Gold Rush to the present.

DOWNTOWN SACRAMENTO

Downtown Sacramento is dominated by the restored **California State Capitol** (between 10th and 16th and L and N streets), which offers daily tours (tel: 916-324 0333; daily 9am–5pm). The surrounding **Capitol Park** serves as an arboretum, with a vast collection of California flora as well as plants from different climates and continents. Not far away, the **California Museum** (1020 O Street; tel: 916-653 7524;

www.californiamuseum.org; Tue–Sat 10am–5pm, Sun noon–5pm), holds a fascinating array of treasures and cutting-edge multimedia displays, all designed to illuminate California's history and influence on the world.

SUTTER'S FORT

Now all but engulfed by suburbs, **Sutter's Fort** ⓫ (2701 L Street; tel: 916-445 4422; www.suttersfort.org; daily 10am–5pm) was once one of the West's most important outposts. Eleven years before one of John Sutter's employees discovered gold in 1848, Sutter had established the fort as a rest stop and refueling station for immigrants crossing the frontier from the east. The reconstructed site, which includes a prison and a bakery, paints an authentic picture of pioneer life and makes for a pleasant afternoon's sightseeing.

SACRAMENTO RIVER DELTA

When temperatures get too hot to handle, take a cue from recreational houseboaters, water-skiers, anglers, and sailors, and head south toward the

Riverboat tours are a relaxing way to do some sightseeing.

Sacramento River Delta, where hundreds of miles of interconnected river channels percolate slowly toward San Francisco Bay and the Pacific Ocean. This river country contains hundreds of islands, many only accessible by water. Still, even landlocked car passengers can choose from a variety of charming olde-worlde towns. **Locke**, created by Chinese laborers brought in to build the railroads, has a porticoed street with wooden sidewalks straight out of the Old West. The deepwater port of **Stockton**, the "Gateway to the Delta," holds 1860s homes, the **Haggin Museum** (1201 North Pershing Avenue; www.hagginmuseum.org; Sat and Sun noon–5pm, Wed–Fri 1.30–5pm), which is full of local history, and several popular wineries.

SAN JOAQUIN VALLEY

Though its name is often mistakenly applied to California's entire Central Valley, the San Joaquin Valley only comprises its southern two-thirds. It follows the course of the San Joaquin River, flowing northward to the Sacramento–San Joaquin Delta, where both rivers empty into San Francisco Bay.

Covering more than a million irrigated acres (405,000 hectares) of hugely productive farming land, the San Joaquin Valley is the lifeline of California. Interstate 5 runs its full length, linking Los Angeles and the Bay Area, while east–west routes cross to Lake Tahoe and the Sierras. Several great rivers also flow through the region – the San Joaquin, the Stanislaus, the Tuolumne, the Merced, the Kings, and, farther south, the Kern. Most are renowned for their outstanding – and occasionally terrifying – stretches of whitewater rafting.

LODI TO FRESNO

Just 37 miles (60km) south of Sacramento, **Lodi** is a major center of wine production, especially the renowned Zinfandel label. Owner Robert Mondavi

grew up here, and his Woodbridge winery is nearby.

Another 45 minutes south, **Modesto** ⓬ is yet another creation of Leland Stanford's Central Pacific Railroad, and is a major access point to Yosemite. The Tuolumne River runs almost unnoticed through its southern fringes, and food production is king – look out for an almond exchange, a mushroom farm, a cheese processor, and more wineries.

The sleeping giant of central California, **Fresno** ⓭ claims to be the only community in the US within little more than an hour's drive of three national parks. From a simple train station by the edge of a wheat field, it's grown to become the financial, cultural and commercial center of the San Joaquin Valley. Fresno's extraordinary **Forestiere Underground Gardens** (tel: 559-271 0734; www.undergroundgardens. com; closed mid-Dec–mid-March), were once home to sculptor-horticulturist Baldasare Forestiere, a Sicilian immigrant, who spent 40 years carving out a spectacular maze.

> **⊙ Tip**
>
> In December and January, dense tule fog – a thick ground fog – blankets the area around the Sacramento and San Joaquin valleys for days at a time, making driving hazardous.

Re-enactments at Sutter's Fort.

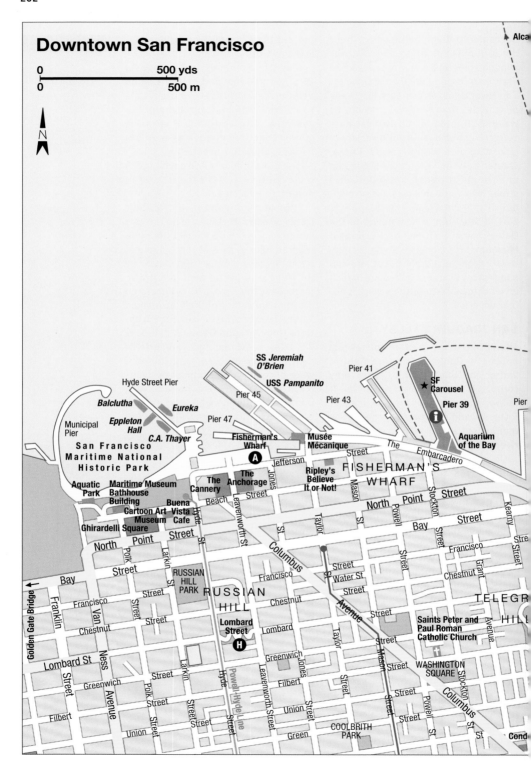

Downtown San Francisco

0 — 500 yds
0 — 500 m

N

Alca

Hyde Street Pier

SS *Jeremiah O'Brien*

USS *Pampanito*

Pier 41

SF Carousel

Pier 39

Pier

Balclutha

Eureka

Pier 45

Pier 43

Municipal Pier

Eppleton Hall

Pier 47

C.A. Thayer

Fisherman's Wharf

Musée Mécanique

The Embarcadero

Aquarium of the Bay

San Francisco Maritime National Historic Park

Jefferson Street

FISHERMAN'S WHARF

Aquatic Park

Maritime Museum Bathhouse Building

The Cannery

The Anchorage

Ripley's Believe It or Not!

Jones

Mason

North Point Street

Stockton

Kearny

Ghirardelli Square

Cartoon Art Museum

Buena Vista Cafe

Beach

Street

Leavenworth St

Powell

Bay Street

Francisco

Stre

North Point Street

Polk

St.

Taylor

Columbus

Francisco

Water St

Street

Chestnut

Grant

TELEGR

Bay Street

Larkin

RUSSIAN HILL PARK

RUSSIAN HILL

Chestnut

Avenue

Street

WASHINGTON SQUARE

Saints Peter and Paul Roman Catholic Church

HILL

Avenue

Stockton

Golden Gate Bridge

Franklin

Van

Francisco

Street

Lombard Street

Lombard

Taylor

Street

Powell

Columbus St

Chestnut

Ness

Street

Larkin

Hyde

Greenwich

Jones

Street

Mason

Street

Lombard St

Avenue

Greenwich

Polk

Powell-Hyde Line

Filbert

Union

Street

Filbert

Street

Union

Green

COOLBRITH PARK

Cond

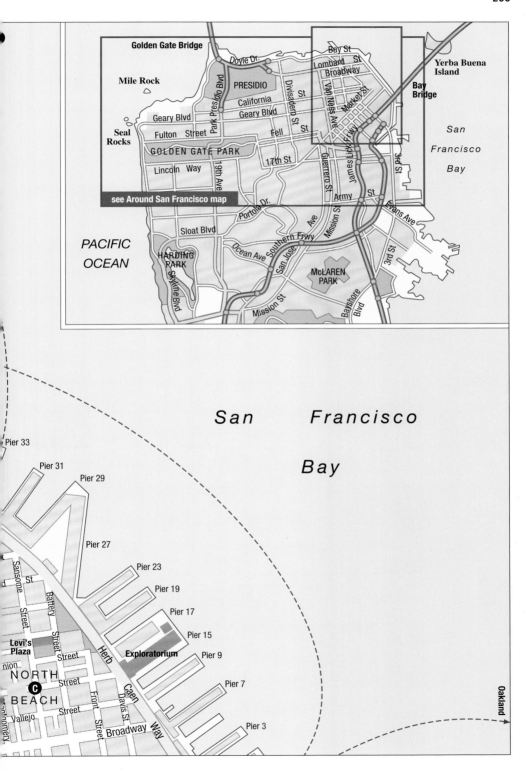

The City by the Bay.

SAN FRANCISCO AND THE BAY

Tony Bennett sang it like it is. Despite cool temperatures and foggy summers, the "City by the Bay" still wins every visitor's heart.

San Francisco ranks among the most beautiful, vibrant, and diverse cities on the planet. Sitting like a thumb at the end of a 32-mile (50km) peninsula, this city of seven hills is bordered by water on three sides and blessed by one of the world's greatest natural harbors. It is joined to the mainland by two master-pieces of bridge design, one of which, the magnificent Golden Gate Bridge, glitters on those nights when the lights are not blurred by a blanket of fog.

Beyond the iconic San Francisco – the grand bridges, rattling cable cars, and barking sea lions – you'll encoun-ter much greater depth than you might expect from a city of just 49 sq miles (127 sq km). It's easy to get caught up in the excitement of Downtown and Union Square, but there are dozens more distinct and wonderfully original neighborhoods to explore, each with its own appeal. And whether it's innova-tive cuisine, fine art, music and dance, sprawling parks, or boisterous street festivals you're after, you will be sure to find it.

This truly endless variety of things to do is in many ways driven by the social and economic diversity of San Franciscans themselves. The more than 870,000 residents of this charmed city, the nation's 17th largest, form an impressive demographic bouilla-baisse (or should that be cioppino?).

Streetcars are the easiest way to get around.

The descendants of early Italian, Ger-man, and Irish families are still to be found in snug neighborhood enclaves, but their numbers have fallen as many have moved to the rapidly developing suburbs, replaced by an influx of Asian and Latino people.

Regardless of their heritage, San Franciscans are generally known for being left-leaning, environmentally conscious, gay-friendly, and very open-minded – eccentricity seldom raises an eyebrow. Embracing the beauti-ful and eclectic makes San Francisco

Main attractions
Fisherman's Wharf
Coit Tower
Chinatown
SFMOMA
Golden Gate Bridge
Mission Dolores
Golden Gate Park
Sausalito
Muir Woods National Monument
Jack London Square, Oakland

Maps on pages 202, 218, 220

the vibrant city it is today, and one that draws more than 25 million visitors a year to discover its magic.

From the sequoias of Muir Woods to Jack London's Oakland, the Bay Area, surrounding San Francisco, holds as many delights as the city itself. Mountains, redwood forests, and wonderful Pacific beaches beckon, as well as intriguing Silicon Valley, Oakland, and Berkeley. Travel is easy: several bridges span the bay; an underground train system (BART) links the East Bay, South Bay and the San Francisco International Airport (SFO) with the city; ferries crisscross the water; and trains run up and down the peninsula. Getting around by car, though, is the most attractive way to explore the coasts, hills, and valleys.

FISHERMAN'S WHARF

Pier 39 is home to the city's colony of sealions.

Among San Francisco's most visited spots, the touristy **Fisherman's Wharf** Ⓐ is a bright, family-oriented carnival of attractions. Despite the crowds and occasional tackiness, it also holds tons of seafood restaurants, good little

stores tucked between the souvenir stands, and two garden parks with open space for picnicking.

In summer, when the narrow boardwalks are jammed with sightseers, it's easy to forget this is a major historic site. Along with hundreds of sailboats and yachts, and the ferries packed with visitors and office commuters, much of San Francisco's maritime past is moored here.

A fleet of vintage vessels is docked at the **Hyde Street Pier**, including a sidewheel ferry and three schooners that carried heavy freight in the days of sailing ships. The tall masts and rigging at water's edge belong to the graceful Scottish-built *Balclutha*, a 301ft (81-meter) clipper built in 1886 that made 17 trips around Cape Horn. All these ships are operated by the **Maritime Museum** (900 Beach Street; tel: 415-561 5000; www.nps.gov/safr; daily 10am–4pm; free), which displays intricate models of boats and muralist Hilaire Hiler's surrealist vision of Atlantis. One block away, the **Cartoon Art Museum** (781 Beach Street; tel: 415-227 8666;

www.cartoonart.org; Thu–Tue 11am–5pm) offers great views over the bay plus a library, bookstore, and ample gallery space.

To the south, occupying an entire block, the **Ghirardelli Square** shopping center (www.ghirardellisq.com) was built as a wool mill during the Civil War and became a chocolate factory in 1893. It now holds a retail outlet, candy store, and ice cream shop. If you're in the mood for something warmer, stop at the **Buena Vista Café** (www.thebuenavista.com) on the corner of Hyde and Beach streets, for an Irish coffee (it was invented here) and watch the busy cable-car activity at the Powell-Hyde Cable Car Turnaround.

An appetite for fruits of the sea can be satisfied by strolling down **Jefferson Street**, the main drag of Fisherman's Wharf, where sidewalk vendors boil and steam shellfish all day long. Walk toward the waterfront to Pier 45, which remains as much of a working site as the wharf can offer. Fishermen depart before dawn and return with sand dabs, scallops, Dungeness crabs, and sea bass. Historically, Italians skippered and manned the boats and ran the restaurants. Not all that much has changed; most restaurants here either serve Italian-inspired fare or fresh fish. Fisherman's Wharf is also a perfect place to sample San Francisco's legendary sourdough bread, which pairs perfectly with sweet butter, Dungeness crab, and a glass of crisp Chardonnay.

Moored at Pier 45, the **SS Jeremiah O'Brien** is a World War II Liberty Ship. Also on Pier 45, the nostalgic **Musée Mécanique** (tel: 415-346 2000; www.museemecaniquesf.com; daily 10am–8pm), displays coin-operated pianos, antique slot machines, and a 1910 steam-driven motorcycle.

To see the city's famous sea lions sunbathe and bark, head to **Pier 39** (www.pier39.com). This 45-acre (18-hectare) assortment of shops, arcades, restaurants, and other diversions lures tourists by the thousands to places like the **7D Experience** (www.theflyer-sanfrancisco.com/7dexperience/) and the **Aquarium**

⊙ Eat

Cioppino is San Francisco's own brand of catch-of-the-day seafood stew. Its name is derived from *ciuppin*, which means "to chop" in the Ligurian dialect that was spoken by the Italian fishermen who created the dish from the bounty of the bay; typically, Dungeness crab, clams, scallops, shrimp, squid, mussels, and fish with fresh tomatoes in a wine sauce.

Pier 45 along Fisherman's Wharf.

Alcatraz looms loney at sea, the iconic former prison is regularly shrouded in fog.

of the Bay (Embarcadero at Beach Street; tel: 415-623 5300; https:// aquariumofthebay.org). The oldest thing at Pier 39 is the **Eagle Café** (www. eaglecafe.com), long favored by fishermen and longshoremen.

ALCATRAZ ISLAND

Set in the spellbinding harbor, and accessible only by ferry, **Alcatraz Island ⑧** (tel: 415-981 7625; www. alcatrazcruises.com and www.nps. gov/alca; daily tours depart from Pier 33), and its tales of legendary inmates, have fascinated visitors since the days of Prohibition.

Just over a mile offshore, the hump of rock was sighted in 1775 by Spanish Lieutenant Juan Manuel de Ayala. Back then, the only occupants were pelicans, so Ayala named it La Isla de los Alcatraces – the Island of Pelicans. Its strategic location suited it to military purposes and it was garrisoned with soldiers in the 1850s. Because escape was a remote possibility, requiring a 1.5-mile (2-km) swim through frigid waters and swift currents, renegade servicemen were incarcerated on Alcatraz, later followed by Apache captives seized in Arizona during the 1870s, and then prisoners from the Spanish-American War.

Alcatraz evolved into a federal prison that housed such hardened criminals as mobster Al Capone and the notorious Machine Gun Kelly. Those few desperate inmates who managed to escape their cells in bids for freedom perished in the cold surrounding waters. Finally closed in 1963, when the costs of repairing the constant ravages of wind and weather grew too great, the prison is now part of the Golden Gate National Recreational Area. Rangers give guided tours of safe parts of the island, including a peek at the cell blocks, while the evocative audio tour features voices of original prisoners.

NORTH BEACH

North Beach ⑨ is many neighborhoods in one; the Little Italy of San Francisco (though nobody calls it that), the former haunt of Beat poets like Jack Kerouac, the city's strip club hub, and a destination where young nightowls mingle at bars and dance clubs.

While the once tawdry **Broadway** strip has been somewhat gentrified, strip clubs still beckon with promises of lap dances and naked girls. One survivor, the historic **Condor** (560 Broadway; https://condorsf.com), became famous one night in 1964, when a waitress named Carol Doda peeled to the waist and ushered in the topless boom. The venerable Doda descended nightly from the ceiling atop a piano, wearing only a G-string.

The neighborhood has also long been congenial to writers, artists, and deep thinkers. A favorite haunt of wordsmiths is the still-thriving **City Lights** bookstore at 261 Columbus Avenue (www.citylights.com; open late), which was run by poet Lawrence Ferlinghetti, a luminary of the 1950s Beat era, from

1953 until his death aged 101 in 2021. Across Kerouac Alley – where quotes from Jack Kerouac, Ferlinghetti, Maya Angelou, Confucius, and John Steinbeck can be found on the sidewalk – is **Vesuvio** (www.vesuvio.com), an eclectic bar full of Beat nostalgia. Nearby, on Columbus, the old **Tosca Café** (http://toscacafesf.com), is a bar where opera records play on the jukebox.

Columbus Street, running north from Broadway, is the real heart of North Beach. With the flavor of an old-fashioned Italian neighborhood, it's full of little cafés, Italian restaurants, and a few working-men's bars where elderly Italians sip red wine and muse about life. At the intersection of Columbus and Union, **Washington Square** is a grassy expanse for pick-up sports games, a morning Tai chi location, and an ideal picnic spot. Outside the Romanesque **Saints Peter and Paul Church**, overlooking the square, Joe DiMaggio and Marylin Monroe posed for their wedding pictures.

TELEGRAPH HILL

Above North Beach, **Telegraph Hill** is crowned by the 210ft (55-meter) **Coit Tower** D (tel: 415-249 0995; summer 10am–6pm, winter 10am–5pm). Built in 1934 on the site of an early telegraph station and funded by heiress Lillie Hitchcock Coit, it lures visitors with momentous views and WPA frescoes in the style of Diego Rivera.

The lovely Filbert and Greenwich street staircases drop down the east side of Telegraph Hill, flanked by attractive and lush private gardens. If you're lucky, you'll hear and spot the flock of wild red-headed parrots who live there.

CHINATOWN

The largest such enclave outside Asia, San Francisco's 24-block **Chinatown** is the quintessential city within in a city. Its official entrance, the green pagoda-topped **Chinatown Gate** E at

the corner of Bush Street and Grant Avenue, was gifted by the Republic of China in 1969. Dragon-topped lampposts and crisscrossing lines of red lanterns run the length of **Grant Avenue**, the main tourist street, and shop windows entice with displays of silk, porcelain, hand-painted vases, teak furniture, and cheap tchotchkes. Food ranges from tiny cafés and obscure eateries to popular dim sum lunches, for which waitresses push along carts of dumplings and pastries from table to table.

Two blocks north along Grant Avenue, the city's main Catholic cathedral from 1853 to 1891, **Old St Mary's Church**, is now a parish church. Until the 1906 fire destroyed most of its commercial establishments, this area was renowned for a seedy array of brothels, gambling houses, and opium dens.

It's on the narrow streets intersecting Grant that Chinatown truly comes to life. Turn left on Clay Street to find **Waverly Place** F, a colorful alley that lent its name to a character in Amy

○ Tip

With parking very scarce near Coit Tower, it's best not to drive to Telegraph Hill. If you want to avoid the steep climb by foot, therefore, catch the No. 39 bus near Saints Peter and Paul Church on Washington Square, and ride it all the way to the tower.

San Francisco's Chinatown is immense and a must-visit.

⊘ Shop

Gump's (135 Post Street, www.gumps.com) started out selling mirrors to bars and bordellos during the Gold Rush. When the store was rebuilt after the 1906 earthquake, it sought inspiration for new stock from the east; one acquisition, a Qing dynasty Buddha, still surveys the first floor. More akin to a museum, the present-day store sells the best in jade, glassware, silks, and antiques.

Tan's *The Joy Luck Club*. After admiring the bright curved roofs and ornate balconies, climb three flights of stairs at No. 125 to visit the **Tin Hou** temple, dedicated in 1852 to the Goddess of the Seven Seas, where hundreds of red-and-gold paper lanterns flood the ceiling and incense fills the air. Other such Chinatown alleys include Spofford Alley – notable for its cameo in *The Maltese Falcon* – and Ross Alley, home to an *erhu*-playing barber and a one-room fortune cookie "factory," where you can watch fresh fortune cookies being made.

On Washington Street, tiny, cluttered herb shops offer powders and poultices promising everything from rheumatism relief to the restoration of sexual prowess. Outdoor produce and pastry shops also vie for your nose. A little farther west all of Chinatown comes to grocery shop on **Stockton Street**.

When you're done exploring, head south of Grant to reach **Portsmouth Square**, Chinatown's small urban park, where Tai chi devotees practice their balletic movements in the morning, children clamber on play structures, and men gather to bet over mah-jongg and Chinese cards. Here Robert Louis Stevenson used to watch the ships come in, waiting for the married woman he loved to divorce her husband. Across Kearny Street, inside the Hilton Hotel, the **Chinese Culture Center** (www.cccsf.us; Tue–Sat 10am–4pm), offers art shows, cultural events, and guided tours.

UNION SQUARE

Considered the city's geographical center in pioneer days, **Union Square** ⑥ and the surrounding blocks today comprise San Francisco's downtown hub for shopping, entertainment, and tourism. Set aside for public use in 1850, the land received its name a decade later when Union sympathizers rallied here before the Civil War. A 90ft (27-meter) Corinthian column topped by a bronze winged Victory statue commemorates another conflict, Commodore George Dewey's naval victory over the Spanish in 1898.

⊘ THE BARBARY COAST

During the California Gold Rush, from 1848 to 1855, modern-day **Jackson Square** was a place of unparalleled vice. The **Barbary Coast**, as it was then known, was a vast marketplace of flesh and liquor, where sailors and miners found fleeting pleasures, fast money, and, just as likely, a violent end. Gambling and shoot-outs were favored sports, and fortunes rode on the wink of an eye. Barbary Coast businessmen trafficked in human bodies, selling sex to miners and kidnapped sailors to the captains of hell ships. Both enterprises returned high profits, and local politicians turned a blind eye for a piece of the action. Red lights burned on almost every block, from high-class "parlors" to squalid "cribs," where prostitutes worked in rooms barely big enough to hold a bed.

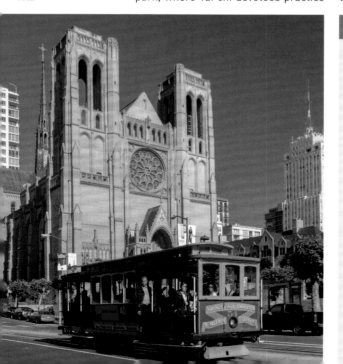
Grace Cathedral, Nob Hill.

West of the Union Square area, San Francisco's theater (mostly spelled *theatre* here) district begins along Geary and Sutter streets. The **Geary Theatre** is home to the **American Conservatory Theater**, (www.act-sf.org), one of the nation's finest repertory companies. Next door, the **Curran** (https://sfcurran.com) offers big hits and stars from New York. Theatres on Sutter Street include the **Lorraine Hansberry Theatre** (www.lhtsf.org), and the nearby **Marines' Memorial Theatre** (www.marinesmemorialtheatre.com), which specializes in Broadway musicals.

In the other direction, cross Stockton Street to wander down chic **Maiden Lane**, a quiet pedestrianized street of high-end boutiques that was named for the female company to be found here during the tough Gold Rush era. No. 140 is the only Frank Lloyd Wright-designed building in the city.

NOB HILL AND RUSSIAN HILL

The cable cars from Fisherman's Wharf and Union Square climb one of the city's best-known slopes, **Nob Hill**. Called the "Hill of Palaces" by Robert Louis Stevenson, the hill is celebrated for the size and elegance of its century-old mansions and hotels.

The **Intercontinental Mark Hopkins Hotel** (www.sfmarkhopkins.com), holds the 19th-floor *Top of the Mark* bar (tel: 415-616 6916). Sampling its 100-martini menu while enjoying spectacular views of the city and bay is a romantic and time-honored tradition.

Lavish edifices encircle the neo-Gothic **Grace Cathedral**, inspired by Paris' Notre Dame. Its doors are cast from Lorenzo Ghiberti's original *Doors of Paradise* in Florence, while the rose window was inspired by the blue glass of Chartres Cathedral. The acoustics are superb when the organ is played and the boys' choir sings. Northeast, the **Cable Car Museum** (1201 Mason Street; tel: 415-474 1887; www.cablecarmuseum.org; Tue–Thu 10am–6pm, Fri–Sun 10am–5pm; free), exhibits the city's transit history as well as the massive machinery and cables that still haul the cars through town.

Tip

Buy cable car tickets at the booth at the corner of Market and Powell Streets, or in cash on the cable car when you board ($8 for a single, regular ride; Muni 1-, 3- and 7-day Passports are much better value). If the line is long, try walking a half dozen blocks up to a stop further along the route.

The column commemorates Admiral G. Dewey's victory against the Spanish in the 1800's.

⊘ THE FERRY BUILDING

Once a thriving terminal, San Francisco's Ferry Building is now an upscale emporium designed to satisfy the local passion for food.

Before the rise of the automobile and the construction of bridges over the Bay, this long and graceful building was one of the most active transit terminals in the world. Constructed in 1898 on the site of the original wooden ferry house at the foot of Market Street, it received thousands of daily commuters from Marin County and the East Bay.

When speedier alternatives came on the scene, during the 1930s, passengers abandoned the ferries. By the mid-1950s, the once-airy Grand Nave was clogged with offices, sealing out the natural light. Next, the building was walled off by the Embarcadero Freeway. But after the freeway was damaged by the 1989 earthquake, and subsequently demolished, the Ferry Building returned to full view. Meticulously restored, it now holds a food hall that's open daily with artisan shops, restaurants, and cafes, and a farmers' market twice a week. The ferries with their cross-bay commuters have returned, too.

Free walking tours are conducted on most Saturday and Tuesday mornings (www.sfcityguides.org).

The Financial District brings a dash of modernity to the city skyline.

Russian Hill, next to Nob Hill, is known for magnificent views, stately homes, hidden bistros, and a labyrinth of secret streets, stairways, and alleys like **Macondray Lane**, which provided the setting for writer Armistead Maupin's much-loved *Tales of the City*. Russian Hill is also home to **Lombard Street** ⓗ, the so-called "crookedest street in the world." Located between Hyde and Leavenworth streets, this one block takes cars on eight hairpin turns along a cobblestone roadway.

THE FINANCIAL DISTRICT

The original forty-niners' sailed into San Francisco Bay, dropped anchor, and set off north to pursue their dream of striking gold. Soon the city's shoreline burgeoned, contributing to the birth of today's soaring **Financial District**. Brokers, bankers, marketers, and software engineers now pursue wealth on acres of landfill on and around Montgomery Street.

When the landmark **Transamerica Pyramid** ⓘ (no visitor access) was completed on Montgomery Street in 1972, many were appalled by its pointed, unorthodox appearance. These days almost everyone has come to appreciate its architectural eccentricity. A little farther north, **Jackson Square**, with its acclaimed restaurants, architectural shops, and high-end antiques dealers, is the focus of the beautiful brick-lined **Barbary Coast** neighborhood.

The sprawling **Embarcadero Center** (http://embarcaderocenter.com) takes up four square blocks; bridges connected its shops, restaurants, and high-rise apartments. Conspicuous from any part of town, the **Bank of America** building (555 California Street) is so tall its roof sometimes disappears in the fog.

Where Market Street ends, the bay begins, with the **Ferry Building** ⓙ, whose clocktower was influenced by the Giralda in Seville, Spain. Still the gateway for ferry riders from all over the bay, it's also the site of a popular farmers' market and upscale food esplanade. Foodies converge here on Saturday mornings for breakfast at

⦿ SFMOMA

Completed in 1995, and designed by Swiss architect Mario Botta, the San Francisco Museum of Modern Art, otherwise abbreviated to and known as **SFMOMA**, was both San Francisco's answer to New York's Museum of Modern Art, and a bid to regain cultural supremacy over Los Angeles. A major expansion of the museum in 2016 almost trebled its previous size, adding the Doris and Donald Fisher Collection, one of the world's greatest private collections of contemporary art, as well as the Pritzker Center for Photography, the largest space in the whole of the United States dedicated to photography. Overall, the museum contains a collection of more than 30,000 works, covering most of the major movements in modern art.

Paintings by American and European expressionists, such as Max Ernst, Picasso, Paul Klee, and the Californian artist Richard Diebenkorn, are exhibited on the first floor, while the second floor holds the architecture and design sections, and stages temporary touring exhibitions. Interesting displays of experimental 1920s and 1930s photography can be found on the third floor, and the fourth floor is devoted mainly to contemporary works of art. On the fifth, sixth, and seventh floors, you'll find a sculpture garden, German art, and special exhibitions.

its mobile kitchens, or to buy fresh produce, artisan cheese, bread, and chocolates.

SOUTH OF MARKET (SOMA)

Stretching in wide blocks south of Market Street to the bay, the forward-looking **SoMa** neighborhood is fueled by artistic and entrepreneurial energy. As well as the locale for nightclubs, restaurants, and museums, it's the city's high-tech district, home to many innovative Internet, design, and programming firms. Its biggest attraction is the bold **San Francisco Museum of Modern Art** Ⓚ (151 Third Street; tel: 415-357 4000; www.sfmoma.org; Fri–Tue 10am–5pm, Thu 1–8pm).

Across the street, a waterfall monument honors Martin Luther King, Jr., in the **Yerba Buena Gardens**. The **Yerba Buena Center for the Arts** (www.ybca.org), stages plays, modern art exhibitions, and multimedia performances, while the innovative **Children's Creative Museum**, (https://creativity.org), is a visual arts facility geared toward young people.

Neighbours on Mission Street include the museum of the **California Historical Society** (No. 678; 415-357 1848; www.californiahistoricalsociety.org; Tue–Sun 11am–5pm), and the **Museum of the African Diaspora** (No. 685; tel: 415-358 7200; www.moadsf.org; Sun noon–5pm, Wed–Sat 11am–6pm), which explores the culture, history, and art of people of African descent.

Nearby, the **Contemporary Jewish Museum** (736 Mission Street; tel: 415-655 7800; www.thecjm.org; Fri–Tue 11am–5pm, Thu until 8pm), designed by Daniel Libeskind, houses one of the world's leading collections of Jewish art and artifacts.

A couple of blocks away on 5th Street, **San Francisco's Old Mint** (http://thesanfranciscomint.com) dates from the days when the city was still a Wild West town. Silver from Nevada was converted into dollars here, then stored in huge safes in the cellar.

CIVIC CENTER

San Francisco's most historic buildings are focused around the **Civic Center**,

> ### ⏱ Tip
> The largest structure in the heart of SoMa, the **Moscone Convention Center**, (www.moscone.com), is the latest site of the **San Francisco Visitor Information Center** (749 Howard Street; tel: 415-391 2000; www.sftravel.com; Mon–Fri 9am–5pm, Sat and Sun until 3pm, Nov–Apr closed Sun), offering maps, brochures, and transportation passes. Ask for details of the **CityPASS** (www.citypass.com/san-francisco), a discount pass for city attractions.

The Ferry Building's clocktower has strong Spanish architectural influences.

bisected by Van Ness Avenue, the city's widest street. West of the large central square, beautiful **City Hall** ❶ (tel: 415-554 6139; http://sfgov.org/cityhall; tours Fri 1pm), was designed by Arthur Brown, an architect so young and so unknown that he figured he might as well shoot for the moon in the early-20th-century competition to design the building. To his surprise, Brown and his partner, John Bakewell, won with a scheme that called for the lavish use of marble, and a neoclassical dome influenced by Brown's time in Paris studying at the Ecole des Beaux-Arts. The full effect is best experienced from its Polk Street entrance, which faces the plaza. The magnificent stairway inside leads to the second-floor Board of Supervisors' chambers.

It was in this building that supervisor Dan White shot and killed Mayor George Moscone in 1978 for refusing to reappoint him to the seat White had resigned, and then killed gay supervisor **Harvey Milk**. After White was convicted of manslaughter and given a remarkably lenient sentence, protestors descended on City Hall.

Opposite City Hall, on Van Ness Avenue, both the **War Memorial Veterans Building**, which houses the Herbst Theatre, and the **Opera House** alongside, were built in 1932. The opera company stages a regular season from September to December and a summer festival, and shares quarters with the **San Francisco Ballet**. Across the street, the sumptuous **Louise M. Davies Symphony Hall** has a separate wing containing **Harold L. Zellerbach Rehearsal Hall**. All these venues make up the War Memorial and Performing Arts Center (**SFWMPAC**; www.sfwarmemorial.org).

ASIAN ART MUSEUM

Occupying 1917 Beaux-Arts style premises, the **Asian Art Museum** (200 Larkin Street; tel: 415-581 3500; www.asianart.org; Fri–Mon 1–5pm, Thu until 8pm) is one of the largest museums of its kind outside Asia. Its galleries are replete with Japanese paintings, ceramics, and lacquer; Chinese bronzes and jade; and sculpture from Korea and India. At the south end of the

City Hall.

plaza, the 1913 **Bill Graham Civic Auditorium**, (www.sanfranciscoauditorium.com), was renamed in honor of the city's late, great rock entrepreneur.

PACIFIC HEIGHTS

South of Union Street, the massive hills of the wealthy **Pacific Heights** neighbourhood provide unparalleled views of the bay and are home to local luminaries like romance novelist Danielle Steele and the prestigious Getty oil family. Stunning mansions line every steep-and-wide street. One stellar example of Victorian Queen Anne architecture is the beautiful **Haas-Lilienthal House** (2007 Franklin Street; tel: 415-441 3000; www.haas-lilienthalhouse.org; one-hour guided tours Sat–Sun noon, 1pm and 2pm).

JAPANTOWN

To the south, the hill crests at Jackson Street to mark the start of Fillmore Street. Farther south lies the heart of **Japantown**, at Post Street. The neighborhood's focal point, the **Japan Center** (www.sfjapantown.org), is an Asian-oriented shopping center that stretches three blocks. It's filled with affordable Japanese restaurants and little stores featuring everything from kimonos to bonsai trees. The handsome, distinctive five-tiered **Peace Pagoda**, designed by the Japanese architect Yoshiro Taniguchi, stands as a monument of goodwill between the Japanese people and those of the United States.

THE MARINA

The waterfront **Marina District**, much loved by young urban dwellers, encompasses the area from Fort Mason to the Presidio, and inland to Chestnut and Union streets. By day, Chestnut acts as one big outdoor café where the next generation of yuppies congregates in workout gear, when not shopping in the trendy boutiques. After dark, they reconvene in a plethora of tasty and inexpensive restaurants, then head to the bars. Union Street is a chic stretch of boutiques, antiques stores, gourmet shops, delicatessens, and classy restaurants.

⊙ Tip

Stretching east of Civic Center to Union Square, bordered by Market and Sutter streets, the gritty **Tenderloin** neighborhood is notorious for drugs, crime, and homelessness, and can be dangerous. Various stories account for its name; one stems from the eponymous cut of meat, the "soft underbelly" of the city, relating to the vice, corruption, and harsh realities of street life hereabouts.

Victorian splendor.

On the waterfront, long huts in decommissioned **Fort Mason** (https://fortmason.org) now house art galleries, ethnic museums, workshops, and a harbour-view vegetarian restaurant, **Greens** (www.greensrestaurant.com).

PALACE OF FINE ARTS

Heading for the bridge, follow the waterfront **Golden Gate Promenade**. A few blocks inland, across Marina Boulevard, stands the classic rococo rotunda of the **Palace of Fine Arts** (https://palaceoffinearts.com). Built of plaster of Paris for the Panama-Pacific Exposition of 1915, the "Plaster Palace" wasn't expected to last, but somehow it did, until it was strengthened and made permanent in 1967.

Just west on the waterfront, **Crissy Field** is an airfield-turned-picnic area belonging to the **Presidio**. Established by the Spanish in 1776, later owned by the US Army, and decommissioned in 1992, the Presidio is a very unwarlike military installation. Its manicured grounds include stands of pine and eucalyptus and even a lake.

Palace of Fine Arts.

GOLDEN GATE BRIDGE

The full splendor of the vast, reddish-gold **Golden Gate Bridge** can be appreciated from a viewpoint near the access road on its south aide. Many engineers originally argued that no such span could ever be built at this point, due to the depth of the water and the powerful tidal rush. The city authorized the first studies in 1918, and the bridge was completed it in 1937, at a cost of $35 million and the lives of 11 construction workers.

THE MISSION

The **Mission** is San Francisco's great melting pot of Latin American cultures. In the latter part of the 20th century, thanks to accessibility and low rents, artists and musicians moved in too, earning the Mission an easy-going reputation as the city's new bohemia. These days, its trendy restaurants and hip nightspots attract an eclectic mix.

The district takes its name from **Mission Dolores** (3321 16th Street; tel: 415-621 8203; www.missiondolores.org; Tue–Sun 10am–4pm). The sixth in the chain of Spanish mission settlements that stretched 650 miles (1,050km) from San Diego to northern California, Mission Dolores was founded less than a week before the Declaration of Independence was signed in 1776, and its thick adobe walls still form San Francisco's oldest building. Its cemetery holds the graves of many early pioneers, and thousands of Costanoan.

Valencia Street is full of boutiques, restaurants and bars, while **Mission Street** a block east has an entirely different feel, with discount shops, pawnbrokers, and produce stands. At vast **Dolores Park**, families gather for birthday celebrations and twenty-somethings camp out on weekend afternoons.

THE CASTRO

The **Castro** neighborhood is home to the world's most celebrated gay community. Its streets are filled with same-sex couples, rainbow flags, hopping bars, and whimsical novelty shops, especially on Castro Street between 17th and 19th streets. **Harvey Milk Plaza**, in front of a Muni bus stop, is dedicated to Harvey Milk who was shot and killed in 1978, along with Mayor Moscone. The **Castro Theatre** (www.castrotheatre.com) is a beautiful work of Spanish Baroque design features classic and cult films.

The **SF LGBT Center** (1800 Market Street; tel: 415-865 5555; www.sfcenter.org), may be closer to the Mission than the Castro, but it's the nexus for community events, classes, support groups, and information. In this one spot, you might attend a Mensa bisexual support group, view a show of Robert Rauschenberg, or obtain personalized legal services.

THE HAIGHT

Heading north, back toward Downtown, are lively **Haight-Ashbury** Q and tranquil Golden Gate Park. Stanyan Street bordering the park's eastern edge, intersects **Haight Street**, which became world famous in the 1960s, when a new generation set about creating an alternative lifestyle characterized by long hair, tie-dyed fabrics, hallucinogens, and a belief in the power of love and peace. These "hippies" openly smoked marijuana, took up Eastern mysticism, declined to fight in foreign wars, and became a thorn in the sides of their elders. At times, police in riot gear stormed into the Haight-Ashbury district to clean it up.

Haight Street was once so gaudy and bizarre that tour buses full of goggle-eyed tourists ran up and down it. Like most such radical departures from the social norm, the hippie experiment fell victim to time and fashion. Half a century later, the neighborhood retains its anti-establishment roots, but today there are more families and homeless youngsters than hippies on the streets, and flower power has been replaced by piercing shops and tattoo parlors. It's still a vibrant, colorful stretch, however, with great shopping plus good, inexpensive restaurants, cafés, and vintage boutiques.

⊘ GOLDEN GATE BRIDGE

On opening day in 1937, the *San Francisco Chronicle* described the Golden Gate Bridge as "a thirty-five million dollar steel harp." Ever since, the bridge has weathered political detractors, powerful wind, and even an earthquake.

Romantic as the bridge may be, the hard facts are undeniably impressive. Including its freeway approaches, the Golden Gate Bridge is 1.7 miles (2.7km) long, with the main suspended span stretching for 4,200ft (1,280 meters). When completed, it was the longest suspension bridge in the world, while its Art Deco towers, looming 746ft (227 meters) above the water, were the tallest structures in the West. Its distinctive vermilion color, called International Orange, was chosen to stand out in the famous Bay fog.

Dolores Park.

ALAMO SQUARE

Nine blocks south, at the corner of Fulton and Steiner streets, **Alamo Square** preserves a very different history. Countless thousands of photographs have immortalized the perfectly maintained Victorian houses that surround this grassy square, with skyscrapers peeping over the top. Known as "Painted Ladies," these harmonious beauties are characterized by pointed gables and tiny oriel windows.

GOLDEN GATE PARK

Measuring 3 miles (5km) long by half a mile (1km) wide, **Golden Gate Park** (https://goldengatepark.com) consists of groves of redwoods, eucalyptus, pine, and countless other tree species from all over the world. It is dotted with lakes, grassy meadows, and sunlit dells. Even with thousands of people within its borders, Golden Gate Park is so large one can easily find solitary tranquility in a misty forest grove or by a peaceful pond. More than a century ago, the park was painstakingly reclaimed from sand dunes through the Herculean efforts of Scottish landscape architect John McLaren. He so disliked statuary that he shrouded all human likeness in dense vegetation. Most statues remain "lost" today.

Along John F. Kennedy Drive, seven blocks into the park, the incredible glass **Conservatory of Flowers** was built in 1878, and modeled after the Palm House at London's Kew Gardens. Housing wonderful collections of rare palms and other tropical flora, the atmosphere inside is one of color unleashed.

The park has feasts for the mind as well as the eyes. Farther along JFK Drive, a road branches off to the left for the **Music Concourse**, an 1894 esplanade offering Sunday concerts. To one side, the **California Academy of Sciences** (tel: 415-379 8000; www.calacademy.org; daily 9.30am–5pm, from 11am Sun), designed by Renzo Piano, is among the world's greenest museums, with a "living" roof of native grasses, porthole skylights, and solar panels to supply its power. The complex also includes the **Steinhart**

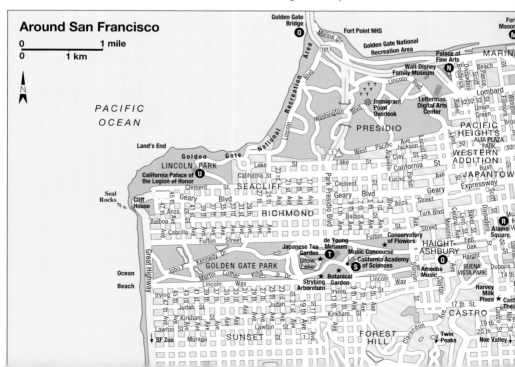

Around San Francisco

0   1 mile
0   1 km

PACIFIC OCEAN

Golden Gate Bridge

Fort Point NHS

Golden Gate National Recreation Area

Palace of Fine Arts

MARIN

Walt Disney Family Museum

Fort Mason

Beach St

Lombard

Immigrant Point Overlook

Letterman Digital Arts Center

PACIFIC HEIGHTS

Union

Green

PRESIDIO

Land's End

Golden Gate

ALTA PLAZA PARK

WESTERN ADDITION

LINCOLN PARK

California Palace of the Legion of Honor

Lake St

West Pacific Ave

Jackson

Clay St

California St

Euclid Ave

Bush

JAPANTOWN

Seal Rocks

Cliff House

Clement St

Geary Blvd

SEACLIFF

California St

Clement

Geary

Geary Expressway

RICHMOND

Balboa St

Turk Blvd

Anza

Balboa

Alamo Square

Cabrillo Ave

Fulton Street

de Young Museum

Conservatory of Flowers

HAIGHT-ASHBURY

Haight

Ocean Beach

Great Highway

John F. Kennedy Dr

GOLDEN GATE PARK

Martin Luther King Jr. Dr

Japanese Tea Garden

Stow Lake

Music Concourse

California Academy of Sciences

Amoeba Music

BUENA VISTA PARK

Duboce

14th

Lincoln Way

Strybing Arboretum

Botanical Garden

Lincoln Way

Harvey Milk Plaza

CASTRO

Irving

Judah St

Irving St

17th St

SUNSET

Kirkham St

Lawton St

Judah

Kirkham St

Lawton St

19th

20th St

FOREST HILL

Twin Peaks

Noe Valley

SF Zoo   Moraga

Aquarium, the **Morrison Planetarium**, coral reef exhibits, and a live rainforest with orchids, macaws, butterflies, bats, scorpions, turtles, and an enormous anaconda.

The fabulous **de Young Museum** ❶ (50 Hagiwara Tea Garden Drive; tel: 415-750 3600; https://deyoung.famsf.org; Apr–Nov Tue–Sun 9.30am–5.15pm) was severely damaged in the 1989 earthquake. To withstand future seismic incidents, the new building – a bold, monolithic structure with a copper skin that will slowly turn green – can move up to 3ft (90cm). As well as a great collection of American paintings it displays art from Oceania, Latin America, Africa, and Meso-America.

Next door, the beautiful 1894 **Japanese Tea Garden** (http://japaneseteagardensf.com) is a harmonious blend of architecture, landscaping, and pools. A renowned Japanese gardener, Makota Hagiwara, planted traditional dwarf bonsai conifers, elms, and cherry trees, and also laid out the winding brooks with their moss-covered rocks, irises, and carp pond.

Across from the tea garden, the extraordinary **San Francisco Botanical Garden** (tel: 415-661 1316; www.sfbotanicalgarden.org; daily from 7.30am) is an urban oasis that entrances the senses with some 7,500 plant species. Limestone walls in its Succulent Garden warm giant aloe plants and cactus, while magnolias, Japanese maples, and camellias surround a reflecting pond in the Moon Viewing Garden.

THE BEACHES AND NORTHERN COAST

Although **Ocean Beach**, at the far western end of Golden Gate Park, has dramatic ocean views, only hardy souls and little kids dip their toes into the ice-cold water. In verdant Lincoln Park to the north, the stunning neoclassical **California Palace of the Legion of Honor** ❶ (100 34th Avenue; tel: 415-750 3600; Tue–Sun 9.30am–5.15pm), is a spectacular fine-art museum. One of five existing bronze casts of Rodin's *The Thinker* stands at the entrance.

The cliffs wind east along the world's largest urban park, the **Golden Gate**

> ⚲ **Drink**
>
> In the delightful Tea House of the Japanese Tea Garden in Golden Gate Park, visitors can enjoy a refreshing cup of green tea along with some rice cookies, each bowl of which also contains a fortune cookie. You might also catch an authentic Japanese tea ceremony.

Funky fishnets at the Piedmont Boutique.

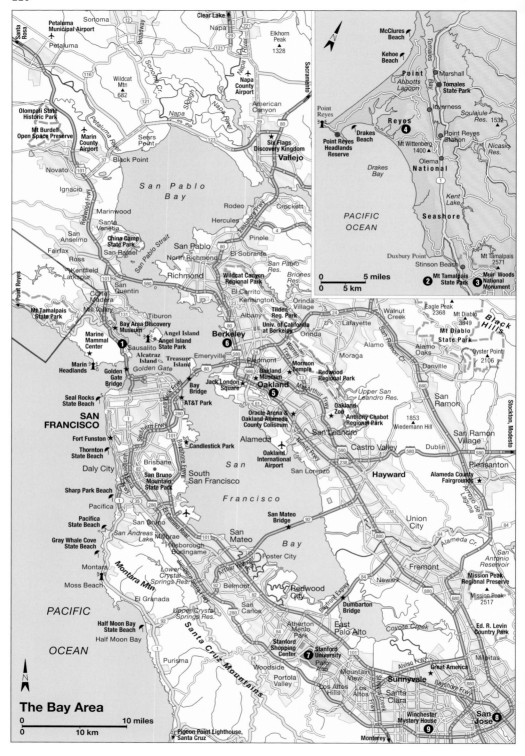

Santa Rosa
Petaluma
Municipal Airport
Sonoma
Clear Lake
Napa
Elkhorn
Peak
1328

McClures
Beach

Petaluma
Kehoe
Beach

Point

Marshall

Abbotts
Lagoon
Tomales
Bay State
Park

Napa
County
Airport

Inverness

Soulajule
Res. 1532

Olompali State
Historic Park

American
Canyon

Point
Reyes

Reyes

Point Reyes
Station

Mt Burdell
Open Space Preserve
Marin
County
Airport
Sears
Point

Drakes
Beach

Mt Wittenberg
1400

Nicasio
Res.

Novato
Black Point

Point Reyes
Headlands
Reserve

Olema

National

Ignacio

Drakes
Bay

Kent
Lake

San Pablo
Bay

Seashore

PACIFIC
OCEAN

Marinwood

Santa
Venetia

Duxbury Point

Mt Tamalpais
2571

Rodeo
Crockett

San
Anselmo
China Camp
State Park

Stinson Beach

Fairfax
Ross
Kentfield
Larkspur

Hercules
Pinole

Mt Tamalpais
State Park

Muir Woods
National
Monument

San Rafael

San Pablo

San Pablo
Res.

El Sobrante

0   5 miles
0   5 km

Point Reyes

Corte
Madera
San
Quentin

North Richmond

Briones
Res.

Eagle Peak
2368

Mt Diablo
3849

Black

Mt Tamalpais
State Park

Mill Valley

Richmond

Wildcat Canyon
Regional Park

El Cerrito

Orinda
Village

Walnut
Creek

Mt Diablo
State Park

Hills

Tiburon

Bay Area Discovery
Museum

Kensington

Tilden
Reg. Park

Lafayette

Oyster Point
2106

Marine
Mammal
Center

Angel Island
Angel Island
State Park

Albany

Berkeley

Univ. of California
at Berkeley

Orinda

Alamo

Alamo
Oaks

Danville

San
Ramon

Sausalito
Alcatraz
Island

Emeryville

Piedmont

Moraga

Marin
Headlands

Treasure
Island

Mormon
Temple

Upper San
Leandro Res.

San Ramon
Village

Golden
Gate
Bridge

Golden Gate

Oakland
Museum

Oakland

Redwood
Regional Park

680

Seal Rocks
State Beach

Bay
Bridge

Jack London
Square

Oakland
Zoo

1853
Wiedemann Hill

Stockton, Modesto

AT&T Park

Oracle Arena &
Oakland Alameda
County Coliseum

Anthony Chabot
Regional Park

SAN
FRANCISCO

Alameda

San Leandro

Castro Valley

Dublin

Fort Funston

San Lorenzo

Pleasanton

Thornton
State Beach

Oakland
International
Airport

Hayward

Alameda County
Fairgrounds

Daly City

Candlestick Park

Brisbane

San Bruno
Mountain
State Park

South
San Francisco

San
Francisco
Bay

Union
City

Sharp Park Beach

Pacifica

San
Antonio
Reservoir

Pacifica
State Beach

San Bruno

San Mateo
Bridge

Fremont

Gray Whale Cove
State Beach

Millbrae

Newark

Mission Peak
Regional Preserve

Montara

San Andreas
Lake

Hillsborough
Burlingame

San
Mateo

Foster City

Mission Peak
2517

Moss Beach

Lower
Crystal
Springs Res.

Belmont

Redwood
City

Ed. R. Levin
Country Park

El Granada

Upper Crystal
Springs Res.

San
Carlos

Dumbarton
Bridge

Coyote Creek

PACIFIC

Half Moon Bay
State Beach

Atherton

Menlo
Park

East
Palo Alto

Milpitas

OCEAN

Half Moon Bay

Santa Cruz Mountains

Stanford
Shopping
Center

Stanford
University

Palo
Alto

Mountain
View

Great America

Purisma

Woodside

Santa
Clara

San
Jose

Portola
Valley

Los Altos
Hills

Los Altos

Sunnyvale

N

Winchester
Mystery House

Monterey

The Bay Area

0   10 miles
0   10 km

Pigeon Point Lighthouse,
Santa Cruz

National Recreation Area, under the Golden Gate Bridge.

MARIN COUNTY

Encircling San Francisco Bay from the north, **Marin County** abounds in pristine coastline, unspoiled redwood groves and mountain meadows, and pretty beaches. This luxurious green belt offers limitless options for hikers and nature-lovers, while old-fashioned towns and charming bed and break-fasts lend themselves to relaxed week-end getaways.

SAUSALITO

The first – or last – stop for most Marin visitors, **Sausalito ❶** is tucked inside the bay to the east behind the Golden Gate, and served by ferries from San Francisco. The waterside shops, the warrens of pricey but perfect bou-tiques, and the houses perched on the hillside behind invite comparisons to the Mediterranean Riviera. That said, there's precious little to do in Sausalito except stroll around, have a meal, and admire the boats and pretty people.

MOUNT TAMALPAIS

Even though **Mount Tamalpais ❷** can be a weekend traffic jam of hikers, mountain bikers, and runners, there's still enough beauty to go around. Miles of trails wind around its contours, and through the contiguous watershed lands. Mount Tam's lower elevations, often shrouded in fog, hold stands of virgin redwood. Above, its chaparral-covered high slopes jut proudly into the sunshine, overlooking San Francisco Bay and the Pacific. It's a fantastic spectacle.

MUIR WOODS

At the very base of Mount Tamalpais is wonderful, woodsy **Muir Woods National Monument ❸** (www.nps.gov/muwo). A century ago, the Marin Water District planned to condemn a prop-erty called Redwood Canyon, cut its timber on it, and build a dam and res-ervoir. The scheme so appalled wealthy Marinite William Kent that he bought the land, then deeded the redwood stand to the government, who turned it into a national monument named after Kent's friend, naturalist John Muir.

The bridge can be enjoyed from many vantage points.

⊘ HIPPIES IN THE HAIGHT

For several hot months during the first **Summer of Love**, 1967, life became a costume party in a wonderland setting of brightly painted Victorian buildings with peace, love and freedom of speech being the core values of its outspoken inhabitants. San Francisco's Haight-Ashbury neighborhood became immersed in a swirl of colors as the "flower children" painted storefronts, sidewalks, posters, cars, and vans, along of course with their own bodies, with Day-Glo. The days and nights were filled with free love, fuelled by sex, drugs, and a pot-laced breeze, and a psychedelic soundtrack provided by artists such as Janis Joplin, Jefferson Airplane, and the Grateful Dead, all of whom lived in Haight-Ashbury pads during this iconic free-spirited time.

SAN FRANCISCO'S CABLE CARS

Much more than just a means of transport, San Francisco's cable cars are an iconic feature of the city. They've been designated a National Landmark, starred in countless movies and TV shows, and featured on a postage stamp.

Ever since their earliest days, San Francisco's iconic cable cars have been impressing visitors. "They turn corners almost at right angles, cross over other lines and for aught I know run up the sides of houses," wrote Rudyard Kipling, who visited the city in 1889 on his way to India. And they're still going strong today.

Streetcars on California Street.

Operating on three routes – the Powell–Mason, Powell–Hyde and California lines – San Francisco's cable cars are among the last in the United States. At least a hundred cities have abandoned them for buses. Underestimating their appeal to visitors, San Francisco tried to get rid of the cars in 1947, but a vigorous local campaign saved them by a City Charter.

Today the cable cars transport over 9 million passengers a year, more than half of them local commuters. It's the tourists, of course, who buy the engraved knives, belt buckles, posters, and T-shirts emblazoned with pictures of the beloved cars, or dig into their wallets to pay for genuine cable car bells. The most enjoyable routes for visitors are the Powell–Mason and Powell–Hyde lines, which share a terminus at Powell and Market and then diverge in Nob Hill on different routes to Fisherman's Wharf. Powell–Hyde is more scenic, passing through Russian Hill and the top of Lombard Street.

ANDREW SMITH HALLIDIE

The cable-car system was created in 1873 by Andrew Smith Hallidie, a British-born engineer with a reputation for building suspension bridges and a background in mining engineering. Seven years before, it's said, he saw a horse slip, breaking a chain on the overloaded streetcar it was pulling uphill. Hallidie set about devising a system that would eliminate such accidents.

Although Hallidie and his friends put up $20,000 to get the cable cars operating, it was Benjamin Brooks, the son of a local lawyer, who was awarded a franchise in 1870 to operate a similar system, but he ultimately failed to raise the necessary financing.

When the Hallidie plan came to fruition, skepticism was the order of the day. "I'd like to see it happen," said realtor L.C. Carlson, "but I don't know who is going to want to ride the dang thing."

Critics of the system still abide today. Although the cars run at only 9.5mph (15kph), they can't duck potential collisions and their braking system has been called "unimprovable" or "blacksmith shop crudity at its worst" by columnist Dick Nolan.

Over 1 million tourists a year visit the giant sequoia trees that spread through Muir Woods, growing to 200ft (60 meters) in height and 16ft (5 meters) in diameter, and living up to 1,000 years. Energetic walkers can leave the cars behind and climb the Ben Johnson Trail through deeply shaded glens rife with ferns and mushrooms, past ever-changing groves of bay, tan oaks, madrona, and nutmeg.

THE MARIN HEADLANDS

Beyond Mount Tam, Marin County's green belt extends some 50 miles (80km) to the distant tip of **Point Reyes National Seashore**. The coastal country, known as the Marin Headlands (easily accessible off Highway 1 just north of the Golden Gate Bridge; www.nps.gov), holds miles of coastal and beach-bound trails. Stellar views can be had by driving up the Fort Baker Road.

Stinson Beach, at the foot of Mount Tamalpais, is San Francisco's favorite playground, popular among anglers and bird-watchers. When the fog pulls back, it also attracts hordes of sunbathers.

POINT REYES

A triangular peninsula, **Point Reyes ❹** is separated from the rest of the world by the main fissure line of the San Andreas fault, which is nudging it northeast at an average rate of 2in (5cm) a year. Drawing over 2 million visitors a year, this 65,000 sq mile (105 sq km) National Seashore is one of the country's busiest national parks. Add quaint inns and diners in the little towns of Inverness and Point Reyes Station, and it seems as close to untouched paradise as you can get.

To reach the park headquarters, and most of its trailheads, in the National Seashore, drive up Highway 1 past the town of Olema to Bear Valley Road. This spot is just a half-mile from the epicenter of San Francisco's 1906 earthquake. The quake moved one old stone fence, seen on today's Earthquake Trail, at least 15ft (5 meters).

The park is open only to those prepared to walk or ride a horse. The terrain is varied, much of it very steep. Gloomy forests open abruptly onto lush, sweeping meadows, while the coast is rockbound with occasional pocket beaches. Hikers may see owls, foxes, raccoons, bobcats, deer, and almost every kind of bird imaginable, especially herons, egrets, and ducks.

A hike up wind-whipped, 1,400ft (427-meter) **Mount Wittenberg** rewards out-of-breath hikers with a truly breathtaking view of the California coast: green-black forests and golden meadows that roll down to a coastline where the eye can track for miles without seeing a soul. Below is **Drakes Beach**, where Elizabethan navigator Sir Francis Drake is said to have set ashore in 1579 for ship repairs.

A lighthouse at the tip of the Point Reyes promontory warns ships away from the treacherous coast. This foggy spot usually has no view at all;

Red wildflowers form a carpet over the cliffs at Drakes Bay.

when the fog lifts, though, it's a great vantage point for spotting migrating whales.

Pierce Point Road meanders around the seashore's northern edge to several beaches – Abbotts, Kehoe, and the most ruggedly dramatic, McClures. Due to sharks, undertow, and rip tides, none of the latter are recommended spots for swimming; head instead for sheltered Drakes Beach on the southern side.

THE EAST BAY

From the Black Panthers to Chez Panisse, the East Bay is as revolutionary as San Francisco. Built around the ports and the University of California, Oakland and Berkeley offer a slightly slower pace than their sister city, as well as Craftsman-style homes and leafy, winding neighborhoods. But don't mistake this for suburbia: the lively political culture, widely diverse demographics, museums, and intellectual centers make these cities thriving metropolitan centers with a distinctly urban edge.

Cathedral of Christ the Light, Oakland.

OAKLAND

Despite author Gertrude Stein's infamous quip that "there is no there there," **Oakland** ❺ long ago emerged from the shadow of its older sister to the west. Its reputation as an affordable haven for artists, teachers, and the like has become threatened, though, since the tech boom that so dramatically escalated San Francisco's rental and real estate prices has crept into Oakland too.

Oakland's version of Fisherman's Wharf is the restaurant and shopping pedestrian walk called **Jack London Square**. The author of *The Call of the Wild*, who died in 1916, might not be impressed by its overpriced restaurants and souvenir stores, but at least he'd be able to munch crab, listen to live music, and watch the sailboats pass by. The First and Last Chance Saloon, which London frequented, is popular with tourists, and nearby you can visit his sod-roofed Yukon cabin, transplanted from Alaska to the waterfront in tribute to Oakland's most famous son.

Moored in the harbor, the **USS Potomac**, President Franklin D. Roosevelt's "floating White House," is now a National Historic Monument (www.usspotomac.org). On Sundays a farmers' market is held in **Old Oakland** (around Washington Street at 8th Street), a neighborhood with stores, restaurants, and shops in its renovated buildings.

Not far from saltwater Lake Merritt, a wildlife refuge on the eastern edge of town, the terraced **Oakland Museum of California** (1000 Oak Street; tel: 510-318 8400; www.museumca.org; Wed–Sun 11am–5pm), is a wonderful resource for information on California's art, history, and natural science.

Oakland's newer attractions include the City Center, a pedestrian mall with quaint restaurants, jazz concerts, and art exhibits; Preservation Park, a restored Victorian village with lush gardens; and the African American Museum and Library at 659 14th Street (www.oaklandlibrary.org). Oakland has a special significance for Black Americans, as the place where the Black Panther Movement was founded in the 1960s.

BERKELEY

Just north of Oakland, **Berkeley ❻** remains famous for social experimentation and the birth of the Free Speech movement, though in recent times, it's become slightly less flamboyant and slightly more commercial.

As you approach Berkeley from Oakland, two buildings catch the eye. The fairy-tale white palace on a hillside, the **Claremont Club & Spa** (tel: 510-843 3000; www.fairmont.com/claremont-berkeley), which, like San Francisco's Palace of Fine Arts, was finished just before the Panama-Pacific Exposition of 1915. The other landmark is tall, pointed **Sather Tower**, known as "the campanile" because it's modeled after St Mark's campanile in Venice, Italy. It's the bell tower of the University of California (www.universityofcalifornia.edu), known simply as "Cal."

To get the feel of Berkeley at its liveliest, walk down Telegraph Avenue from Dwight Way to the university.

A typical foggy day in the Bay.

Students, townspeople, and "street people" pick their way between street vendors offering jewelry and pottery, and stores catering to modern students.

Berkeley's climate (it can be foggy in San Francisco but sunny across the bay) produces sweet scents in the **University Botanical Gardens** in Strawberry Canyon. Over 12,000 species thrive in its research facility.

THE PENINSULA

A 55-mile (89km) swath of high hills, tall trees, and beautiful estates, the **San Francisco Peninsula** is wedged between the Pacific Ocean and San Francisco Bay. To its north is San Francisco. At its southern end lies the sprawl of **Silicon Valley** – which until they started harvesting computers and silicon chips here, rather than apples and pears, was known as the Santa Clara Valley. In the valley, the peninsula's highlands segue into the affluent, high-tech communities of Palo Alto, Los Altos, Sunnyvale, Santa Clara, and San Jose. As the drive south

on El Camino Real will prove, the only true borders between peninsula cities seem to be stoplights. Where the commercial and spartan-finish industrial strips end, the wealthy suburban homes begin.

The style of the peninsula is sophisticated, shamelessly commercial, and contemporary. Stanford University is the hub of academic and cultural activity. New and old money alike shop at the impressive Stanford Shopping Center (www.simon.com/mall/stanford-shopping-center).

STANFORD UNIVERSITY

What's now the campus of renowned **Stanford University** ❼ (www.stanford.edu) was a blue-blooded horse ranch 150 years ago, when Leland Stanford and photographer Eadweard Muybridge began to experiment with moving images, thus paving the way for motion pictures. Today, it's the academic lifeblood of the peninsula, in the northwestern corner of Palo Alto. Architecturally, Stanford's handsome, rough-hewn sandstone buildings are

Pigeon Point Lighthouse.

Romanesque in style, though the red-tiled roofs, the burnt adobe color of the stone, and the wide arches give the university a Spanish mission look. The exception to the overall prosaic qualities is beautiful Memorial Church, which dominates the Inner Quad.

SAN JOSE

San Jose ❽ was the first pueblo founded by the Spanish in Northern California, in 1777. Until 1956, this area supplied America with half its prunes; those long-vanished orchards have now sprouted condominiums and industrial parks. San Jose has become the third largest city in California, with a million-strong population that has absorbed tech personnel and like-minded groupies from around the world.

Artworks, new media, and installations in the **San Jose Museum of Art** (110 South Market Street; tel: 408-271 6840; www.sjmusart.org; Tue–Sun 11am–5pm) include glass sculptures by Dale Chihuly and photographs by Ruth Bernard. The sprawling, red-roofed **Winchester Mystery House**

❾ (near Interstate 280 and State Highway 17; tel: 408-247 2101; www. winchestermysteryhouse.com; daily 9am–5pm) in downtown San Jose is touristy but fascinating. Local eccentric Sarah L. Winchester, who inherited the namesake gun-manufacturing fortune, believed she'd live as long as she kept adding to her house. Sixteen carpenters worked on the mansion for 36 years, adding stairways to nowhere and doors without rooms.

The West Coast's largest collection of Egyptian, Babylonian, and Assyrian artifacts can be admired in the **Rosicrucian Egyptian Museum and Planetarium** (1660 Park Avenue; tel: 408-947 3635; www.egyptianmuseum.org; Fri 10am–5pm, Sat and Sun 11am–6pm), along with a recreated walk-in tomb from 2000 BC.

Anyone longing for fresh air and the sound of the sea should nip over to Highway 1 west of San Jose near the little town of **Pescadero**, where there is a particularly atmospheric site – **Pigeon Point Lighthouse**, the second-tallest lighthouse on the West Coast.

⊙ Where

While in San Jose, take a look at the city-center **Tech Museum of Innovation** (201 South Market Street; tel: 408-294 8324; www. thetech.org; daily 10am–5pm). "The Tech" is a hands-on museum with galleries documenting innovations in areas like health and biotechnology, energy, exploration, and the development of local industry. Don't miss Body Worlds Decoded, a high-tech opportunity to explore the human body in all its complexity.

"Gay Liberation" bronze sculptures by George Segal at Stanford University.

Bixby Bridge.

THE MONTEREY PENINSULA AND BIG SUR COAST

Between Santa Cruz and Big Sur, scenic State Highway 1 passes beautiful state parks, rustic inns, and fabulous surf spots.

South from San Francisco, Highway 1 – also known as the Pacific Coast Highway (PCH) – has to count as one of the most spectacular routes in America. A series of razor-sharp switchbacks hug hills, plunge into valleys, and skirt the coast the entire way. Steep, rugged mountains loom to the left, while to the right there's nothing but a sheer drop to the wild, crashing waves below. The climate changes every few miles, from fog to rain to blinding sunshine. No doubt about it, this is the real California that every visitor wants to see.

Highlights along the northern stretch of the highway include Santa Cruz, a delightful blend of seaside resort, surfers' hangout, and college town, complete with vintage boardwalk and a century-old rollercoaster; the former fishing community of Monterey, overflowing with historical charm and home to a world-class aquarium; and Carmel-by-the-Sea, site of the 1771 Carmel Mission and now an artists' haven that has attracted creative types from Robert Louis Stevenson to former mayor Clint Eastwood.

It's south of Carmel, however, that the Pacific Coast Highway really gets into its stride, crossing spectacular bridges as it carves a circuitous and enticing course between the mountains to the east and the awesome ocean to the west. For the next 90 miles

(140km), as far as San Simeon – site of fabled Hearst Castle – the Big Sur coast is never short of breathtaking.

As you first set off south, beyond the delightful town of Pescadero, it's well worth taking the time to stop off at the **Año Nuevo State Reserve** , just off Highway 1, 20 miles (32km) north of Santa Cruz. This is the place to encounter whiskered, roly-poly elephant seal pups. The pups are born in January, when entire seal families are visible from beachfront lookout points, though seals can be viewed

Main attractions

Map on page 232

Elephant Seals at Ano Nuevo State Reserve.

⊙ Tip

At parking garages on both Front and Cedar streets, it's possible to park for three hours for free in Santa Cruz.

in different phases of their lifecycle throughout the year.

SANTA CRUZ

At the northern end of Monterey Bay, 77 miles (120km) southeast of San Francisco, **Santa Cruz ❷** is a cool, green, redwood-shingled beach. Within a few years of the **University of California** opening its Santa Cruz campus in 1965, this previously tranquil backwater town had been transformed into an activist community. Santa Cruz was rejuvenated with excellent restaurants, cafés, pastry shops, and bookstores. Old buildings were refurbished, with cement block and aluminum replaced by natural redwood and hanging ferns.

Sunny Santa Cruz enjoys sparkling clean air, and is seldom affected by the fog and chilly winds that hover off the coast, north and south. Popular beaches include Natural Bridges State Beach, Bonny Doon, Pleasure Point Beach, and Twin Lakes State Beach. Surfing is very popular; to learn more, visit the **Santa Cruz Surfing Museum**, set in an appealing little lighthouse (701 West Cliff Drive; tel: 831-420 6289; www.santacruzsurfingmuseum. org; Thu–Tue 10am–4pm, until 5pm in summer). Santa Cruz Pier is the place for all things fishy – fish restaurants, fish markets, and fishing facilities. The much-loved **Santa Cruz Beach Boardwalk** (www.beachboardwalk.com), is adorned with an 1911 carousel with hand-carved horses, the thrillingly rickety Giant Dipper rollercoaster built in 1924, an old-fashioned arcade containing shooting galleries, and a giant Ferris wheel. In summer, the Beach Bandstand hosts free concerts on Friday nights, and there are free beach movie screenings on Wednesday nights (end of June–mid-Aug).

Leaving Santa Cruz, Highway 1 follows the coast in a beautiful arc around Monterey Bay. During the springtime, marigolds carpet the high sand dunes. After passing near the beach town of Capitola, the road stretches dramatically toward Big Sur. Break at produce and peanut stands for snacks, or at wineries in the mountains behind Santa Cruz for tastings (www.scmwa.com).

The Sky Glider ride on the boardwalk in Santa Cruz.

⊙ AÑO NUEVO RESERVE

On the wild and undeveloped shores of the Año Nuevo State Reserve, northern elephant seals come ashore every winter to give birth to pups and breed. Starting in mid-December, the 2.5-ton bulls fight for breeding access to females. Pregnant females then come on shore to have pups in late December and January, and then nurse for about a month before weaning, mating, and departing to sea. In March, pups learn to swim in the tide pools before heading out to sea.

For a chance to watch the action, reserve tickets for the 2.5-hour naturalist-led tours (tel: 1-800-444 4445; www. parks.ca.gov). To see them up close in a more subdued state, visit between April and August when they spend time on land molting. Weather can be extreme here, so come prepared for rain and muddy trails.

MONTEREY

During World War II, the city of **Monterey ❸**, at the northern end of Monterey Peninsula, was the sardine capital of the western hemisphere, processing some 200,000 tons a year. After the war, for reasons variously blamed on overfishing, changing tidal currents, and divine retribution, the sardines suddenly disappeared from Monterey Bay and all the canneries went broke.

Cannery Row, located along the waterfront on the northwest side of town just beyond the Presidio, has become a tourist attraction, its old buildings filled with bars, seafood restaurants, a wax museum, dozens of shops, and food vendors. It's also home to one of the world's premier aquariums: the **Monterey Bay Aquarium ❹** (886 Cannery Row; tel: 831-648 4800; www.montereybayaquarium.org; daily 10am–5pm). The enormous building, with its outdoor pools overlooking the sea, stands on the site of what was Cannery Row's largest cannery, the Hovden Cannery. Showcasing the incredible diversity of marine life from near and far, more than a hundred galleries and exhibits include over 350,000 specimens, from sea otters, leopard sharks, bat rays, and giant octopuses, to towering underwater kelp forests. Although always crowded – the biggest aquarium in the US, it attracts two million visitors each year – this spectacular sanctuary is worth any amount of waiting time.

The main attraction in downtown Monterey is **Fisherman's Wharf**, lined with restaurants and shops, and complete with fish markets, an organ grinder plus monkey, and noisy sea lions that swim among the pilings. The real working wharf is two blocks east.

To see the rest of Monterey, a 3-mile (5km) **Path of History** walking tour leads past key historical buildings and sites. These include California's oldest public building, the Customs House, now a museum (www.mshpa.org); Pacific House, a two-story adobe with a Monterey balcony around the second floor; and impressive exhibits from the Spanish, Mexican, and early American eras.

⊙ Tip

To rent boats in the Santa Cruz area, check out Capitola and Santa Cruz Boat Rentals, tel: 831-462 2208 and 831-423 1739; http://capitolaboatandbait.com). Offering the only motorized ocean skiffs for rent on Monterey Bay, they're located on the Santa Cruz and Capitola wharves, perfect spots to start an adventurous day on the water. Both rent boats, fishing gear and other equipment, and the Capitola shop has kayaks too.

Cannery Row.

⊙ CANNERY ROW

During the heady heyday of Monterey's canning industry, the beaches were so deeply covered with fish guts, scales, and flies that a sickening stench engulfed the entire town. When the fishing boats came in heavy with their catch, canneries blew whistles and residents streamed down the hill to work amid the rumbling, rattling, squealing machinery of the canning plants. Once the last sardine was cleaned, cut, cooked, and canned, the whistle blew again, and the wet, smelly workers trudged back up the hill. John Steinbeck famously described the former Ocean View Avenue, now Cannery Row, as "a poem, a stink, a grating noise, a quality of light, a tone, a habit, a nostalgia, a dream." Today, thankfully, the beaches are bright and clean, and the air is sparkling fresh.

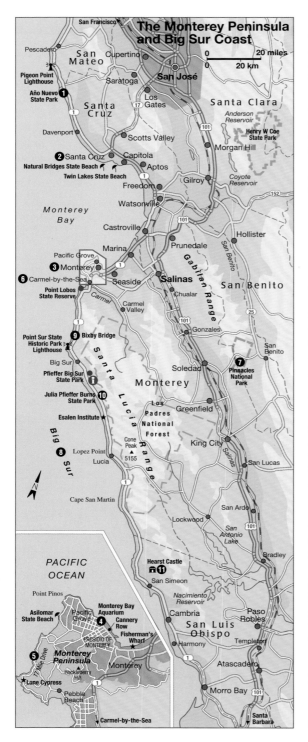

The Monterey Peninsula and Big Sur Coast

Other points of interest include **Colton Hall**, a two-story building with a classical portico that hosted the state's first (1849) constitutional convention; Stevenson House, a smaller former hotel where the romantic (and sickly) Robert Louis Stevenson lived for a few months while courting his wife; and the **Royal Presidio Chapel**, in use since 1794. The **Presidio** itself, founded in 1770 by Gaspar de Portolá, was one of a series of "royal forts" built on the west coast by Spain, and now serves as the US government's Defense Language Institute Foreign Language Center.

The **Monterey Museum of Art** (559 Pacific Street; tel: 831-372 5477; www.montereyart.org; Thu–Sat 11am–5pm), focuses on Californian art and photography from the 19th century onwards, while the **Museum of Monterey** (5 Custom House Plaza; tel: 831-372 2608; www.museumofmonterey.org; Tue–Sun 10am–5pm), displays models of sailing ships and boats, photographs, and decorative objects. In mid-September each year, the hugely popular **Monterey Jazz Festival** (tel: 831-373 3366; www.montereyjazzfestival.org) attracts the biggest names in music to the Monterey Fairgrounds; this is where Jimi Hendrix made his American debut, in 1967.

Diving is popular in Monterey, as is kayaking, which offers a delightful opportunity to get out among the otters and sea lions. The Monterey County Convention and Visitors Bureau (787 Munras Avenue, suite 110; tel: 888-221 1010; www.seemonterey.com) lists tour-boat operators that enable passengers to see the gray whales on their migration between Alaska and Baja California.

17-MILE DRIVE AND PEBBLE BEACH

Leaving Monterey, head south on Route 1 (PCH) toward Carmel-by-the-Sea. Pay to access the famous **17-Mile**

Drive ❺ through one of five guarded gates. The route hugs the coast, meandering around the Peninsula, passing the **Del Monte Forest**, mansions, and the world-famous **Pebble Beach Golf Links**, which has hosted six U.S. Opens, on the way to Pacific Grove. At the scenic attraction known as Cypress Point, you can see the eerie **Ghost Tree** and the **Lone Cypress**, a single gnarled and wind-sculpted Monterey Cypress near the top of a huge wave-battered rock.

While 17-Mile Drive is undeniably beautiful, the attitude of the Pebble Beach Company toward tourists can be condescending to say the least; the landscape is littered with "no trespassing" signs threatening fines and imprisonment.

CARMEL-BY-THE-SEA

Chance factors made **Carmel-by-the-Sea ❻**, the southern gateway to the Monterey Peninsula, what it is today. Starving writers and unemployed painters fled here the devastation of the 1906 San Francisco earthquake, while canny property developers, to reduce their taxes, covered the treeless acres with a thick, lush carpet of Monterey pines.

The result is one of the most charming seaside towns on the West Coast, one that has attracted artists and celebrities such as Sinclair Lewis, Ansel Adams, Robert Louis Stevenson, and Clint Eastwood (who served as mayor for two years). When the evening fog rolls in from the bay, the lights inside the cozy houses, combined with the faint whiff of wood smoke from roaring fires, give Carmel the peaceful feeling of a 19th-century European village. That said, Carmel has grown from the affordable artist haven it once was, and now has a definite air of preciousness.

Carmel's most noteworthy historical site, the large **Carmel Mission** (https://carmelmission.org), dates from 1771, and is the burial place of Father Junípero Serra. Masses are still conducted daily, and self-guided or docent-led tours of the church and grounds are available.

⊙ **Where**

The town of Gilroy, east of Santa Cruz, stages an annual Garlic Festival (www.gilroygarlicfestival.com), held every July. Garlic bread, fries, popcorn, seafood, ice cream – everything here is seasoned with garlic. Gilroy's other claim to fame, the Gilroy Yamato Hot Springs (www.gilroyhotspringsconservancy.org) was a renowned center of healing from the 1880s to the 1920s. Since fallen into disrepair, it's now being slowly refurbished by volunteers.

Shopping in Carmel.

Despite its millions of visitors, Carmel has resisted neon signs, fast-food franchises, and even street numbers. Its plazas and little shopping malls attract pedestrians to wine shops and antiques stores, art galleries, and over 500 boutiques, especially on Ocean Avenue between San Antonio and Junipero avenues.

Streets in the residential neighborhoods meander through the forest, sometimes even splitting in two to accommodate an especially praiseworthy specimen of pine. Sandy Carmel beach, at the bottom of the hill and within easy distance of town, is undeniably stunning. For tours, contact Carmel Walks (tel: 831-223 4399; www.carmelwalks.com).

Rocky **Point Lobos State Reserve**, overlooking the ocean south of Carmel, is crisscrossed by nature trails. Big natural rock pools are home to lolling sea lions. Bring water and a picnic: there are no food facilities.

South again, Highway 1 starts to swoop and curve in dramatic fashion. The Santa Lucia Mountains soar to one side, while the foamy, raging sea to the other endlessly changes shape and color. Only the two-lane highway separates the two, so the curling ribbon of road has its own weather pattern. Although the sun may be shining brightly on the other side of the mountains, and can often be seen through the trees, Highway 1 can be distinctly chilly, and the fog comes on very quickly so caution driving this route is advised.

PINNACLES NATIONAL PARK

Roughly 50 miles (80km) inland from Carmel and Monterey, and accessible via US 101, **Pinnacles National Park ❼** (www.nps.gov/pinn), is a compelling destination for hikers, climbers, campers, and bird-watchers. Named for its unusual eroded rock formations – massive monoliths and spires – it's also a release site for endangered California condors, the largest land birds in North America. During the 1980s, the wild condor population sank to just 22 but today, thanks to the success of a captive breeding program, the wild population now numbers more than 300, of

The high peaks at Pinnacles National Park before sundown.

which around half live in the state of California.

BIG SUR

Arguably California's most beautiful expanse of coastline, **Big Sur** ❽ stretches 90 miles (140km) from Carmel to San Simeon, between the Santa Lucia range and the Pacific Ocean. Halfway to Big Sur village, 15 miles (24km) south of Carmel, the stunning **Bixby Bridge** ❾, one of the world's highest single-span concrete bridges, crosses Rainbow Canyon.

Until 1945, Big Sur was mainly populated by ranchers, loggers, and miners. Then literary sorts began arriving, attracted by the idea of living cheaply, growing marijuana in remote canyons, and communing with what longtime resident Henry Miller called "the face of the earth as the creator intended it to look." The **Henry Miller Memorial Library** (https://henrymiller.org/), near the **Nepenthe** restaurant (www.nepenthe.com), where everyone goes to enjoy a sunset over dinner, has works by and about this local hero.

Big Sur village is really little more than a huddle of shops and a post office. Places to stay are scarce; book early if you're planning a weekend visit. Besides a handful of campsites, motels, and inns, there are a few luxurious rustic resorts, notably the **Ventana Inn** (tel: 800-628 6500; www.ventanabigsur.com) and the **Post Ranch Inn** (tel: 831-667 2200; www.postranchinn.com).

A gem among the parks and wilderness areas that lie south of Big Sur village, the stunning **Julia Pfeiffer Burns State Park** holds twisting nature trails and a silvery waterfall. Not far beyond, Highway 1 passes the entrance to 1960s alternative haven the Esalen Institute (www.esalen.org), which has famous hot spring baths on a ledge over the ocean, before ending 16 miles (25km) north of **Hearst Castle** ⓫ (see page 236).

Beyond Hearst Castle, Highway 1 branches off to hug the coast, passing close to dramatic **Morro Bay**, dominated by a 576ft (176-meter) rock just offshore.

Big Sur.

HEARST CASTLE AT SAN SIMEON

Tycoon William Randolph Hearst, the media magnate, was larger than life – and so is his mansion home. It's so lavish that it's often referred to as Hearst Castle, but he just used to call it "the ranch."

The massive, Baroque Hearst Castle was built by media tycoon William Randolph Hearst, who was the model for Orson Welles' 1941 movie *Citizen Kane*.

It was Hearst's father George, a multimillionaire from his gold, silver, and copper mines, who first acquired the 275,000-acre (111,300-hectare) ranch. On his parent's death, the younger Hearst hired his favorite architect, Julia Morgan, to design the highly ornate twin-towered main house, which ended up with 38 bedrooms, a Gothic dining room, two swimming pools, and three sumptuous guest houses.

Guest bedroom at Hearst Castle.

Next, he stocked the grounds with exotic animals and filled the buildings with carvings, furnishings, and works of art from European castles and cathedrals. To conceal a water tank on the adjoining hill from view, Hearst planted 6,000 pine trees. All in all, craftsmen labored for 28 years to create La Cuesta Encantada, "the Enchanted Hill," with its acres of gardens, terraces, pools, and walkways, and four grand buildings holding a total of 46 rooms and almost as many fireplaces.

Hearst lived in his 130-room hilltop mansion at San Simeon for 20 years – now a State Historical Monument – until ill health caused him to move to Beverly Hills in 1947. At his death in 1951, he stood at the helm of a media empire including the country's largest newspaper chain, 14 US magazines, and 11 radio stations.

Hearst Castle, 750 Hearst Castle Road, San Simeon; tel: 800-444 4445; www.hearstcastle.org; tours daily from 9am; advance reservations are required.

HOLLYWOOD HIGHLIFE

Hearst Castle frequently welcomed the elite of moviedom. A special train with a jazz band and open bar brought party guests 210 miles (340km) from Hollywood to San Luis Obispo; limousines then transported them through the estate's grounds filled with lions, bears, ostriches, elephants, and leopards. Guest were free to wander, except during the mandatory late-night dinner. There were also special occasions: the hundred guests at a covered-wagon party included the Warner Brothers, the Gary Coopers, and William Powell.

"The society people always wanted to meet the movie stars so I mixed them together," wrote actress Marion Davies, Hearst's longtime mistress. "Jean Harlow came up quite frequently. She was very nice and I liked her. She didn't have an awful lot to say ... all the men used to flock around her. She was very attractive in an evening dress because she never wore anything under it." Clark Gable was another regular guest. "Women were always running after him but he'd just give them a look as if to say 'how crazy these people are' and he stayed pretty much to himself."

The Neptune Pool at Hearst Castle.

Pismo Beach.

INTRODUCTION

A detailed guide to Southern California, with principal sights clearly cross-referenced by number to the maps.

Balboa Park Bell Tower in San Diego.

Southern California has to be one of the few places on the planet where a few hours' drive can transport the wide-eyed visitor from gorgeous sun-drenched beaches to majestic snow-capped mountains, and from fertile green farmland to parched desert landscapes.

The diversity of the geography is mirrored by the varied cities and attractions packed into the region. Modern Los Angeles, a sprawling, thriving, and often smoggy metropolis, is home to the birthplace of popular cinema, Hollywood, which continues to attract stars, fame-seekers, and fans in their thousands, as well as the blockbuster attractions of Disneyland and Universal Studios, a string of oceanfront communities, and, throughout the many neighborhoods that make up the entire urban cityscape, constantly evolving restaurant, nightlife, and cultural scenes.

To the north of LA, California's Central Coast is lined with appealing towns like San Luis Obispo and Santa Barbara, interspersed with spectacular beaches such as Pismo Beach with its massive sand dunes. Just offshore, the Channel Islands are havens for unique wildlife species, while a very short way inland the Santa Ynez and Santa Maria valleys produce some high-quality wines, and the Ojai Valley is renowned for its extraordinary sunset pink

Vineyards around Santa Barbara.

skies. To the south, the state's second-largest city, sunny San Diego, boasts surfer-packed coastlines, a charming historic core, an amazing array of museums set in the Spanish-style buildings in Balboa Park, and one of the best zoos in the world. For a memorable south-of-the-border day trip, it also offers easy access to Tijuana, Mexico.

On the whole, balmy weather is the norm for the coastal regions of Southern California; it seldom rains between April and November. That sunny climate not only feeds the thriving agricultural sector that has made California the United State's agricultural powerhouse, but it has also helped to create the healthy, upbeat attitude that Southern California is famed for.

Downtown Solvang.

THE CENTRAL COAST

From beautiful beaches to its own increasingly popular Wine Country, California's central coast and its small, relaxed towns make lovely escapes for city folk.

Stretching southeast for around 200 miles (320km) from San Luis Obispo to Los Angeles, California's central coast holds a lovely assortment of small seafront communities and scenic attractions.

San Luis Obispo itself is a sleepy college town with an appealing old town and a Spanish-era mission, while nearby Pismo Beach is a surfing center that's famous for its towering sand dunes and migratory monarch butterflies. Highway 1 then heads inland, skirting the enormous oceanfront Vandenberg Space Force Base, to reach the Santa Ynez and Santa Maria valleys. Set just a few miles back from the Pacific, these are home to over a hundred wineries – increasingly visited these days, ever since they featured in the 2004 movie *Sideways* – along with quaint towns like Scandinavian-influenced Solvang, all decked out in Danish trimmings, and flower-filled Lompoc.

Then comes Santa Barbara, a beautiful coastal city that boasts Spanish-style architecture – including one of California's most beautiful missions – along with a relaxed, prosperous vibe. Not for nothing has it been nicknamed the "American Riviera." For a detour, head inland to artsy Ojai, redolent of yet more Spanish charm, or take a boat trip out from seaside Ventura to explore the uninhabited Channel Islands, home to many unique wildlife species though

San Luis Obispo de Tolosa Mission Church.

sadly no longer its extinct local herd of pygmy mammoths.

The entire central coast can be explored easily by car – driving directly from San Luis Obispo to Los Angeles takes about 3.5 hours, though as ever it's worth allowing much longer to appreciate the region to the full. Both Santa Barbara and San Luis Obispo hold small regional airports.

SAN LUIS OBISPO

Halfway between San Francisco and Los Angeles, the pleasant town of **San**

Main attractions
San Luis Obispo
Guadalupe-Nipomo Dunes
  Preserve Solvang
Santa Barbara
Mission Santa Barbara
Ojai
Channel Islands National
  Park

Map on page 242

⊙ Where

Bubblegum Alley, between 733 and 734 Higuera Street, is a colorful, if somewhat gross, San Luis Obispo landmark. For at least fifty years, visitors have been covering its walls with wads of bubble gum. In places they've attempted to make patterns or even pictures, but mostly it's as bad as it sounds. The narrow alley is 70ft (21 meters) long, and its walls 15ft (5 meters) high.

Luis Obispo ❶ owes its beginnings to the 1772 mission, and its development to the arrival of the Southern Pacific Railroad in 1894. A frequent stopover for visitors to the nearby Wine Country, it's also home to the students at Cal Poly (California Polytechnic State University).

On Thursday nights, the pedestrian-friendly downtown hosts a popular farmers' market on Higuera Street that turns into a proper street festival, with entertainment and barbecues plus stalls selling produce such as flowers, herbs, nuts, honey, and marmalades.

The Victorian homes in the **Old Town** neighborhood around Buchon and Broad streets are worth exploring; download self-guided historic walking tours at www.historycenterslo.org. Visitors to the 1772 **Mission San Luis Obispo de Toloso** (751 Palm Street; tel: 805-781 8220; daily 9am–5pm; www.missionsanluisobispo.org), can view Chumash artifacts in the museum and explore the grounds. The **San Luis Obispo Children's Museum** (1010 Nipoma Street; tel: 805-545 5874; www.slocm.org) caters to those with shorter attention spans.

PISMO BEACH

For anyone craving beach time, **Pismo Beach ❷** delivers. The only real shore community on US 101 between San Francisco and Santa Barbara, it's ideal for sunning and surfing. The stunning **Guadalupe-Nipomo Dunes Preserve** (tel: 805-343 2455; www.dunescenter.org), incorporates the Mussel Rock Dunes, California's highest coastal dunes.

From late November through February, hordes of colorful Monarch butterflies come to winter in groves of eucalyptus and Monterey pines. The groves are accessible from State Highway 1 at the southern city limits of Pismo Beach (daily guided walks 11am and 2pm).

If time permits, leave US 101 50 miles (80km) southeast of Pismo Beach to view the virtually one-block town of **Los Alamos ❸**, with its antiques stores and frontier-style buildings. The **1880 Union Hotel** (https://1880union.com) has a wonderful saloon and pool room as well as bedrooms and a restaurant furnished completely in 19th-century style. Even more unusual rooms are

Santa Barbara County Courthouse.

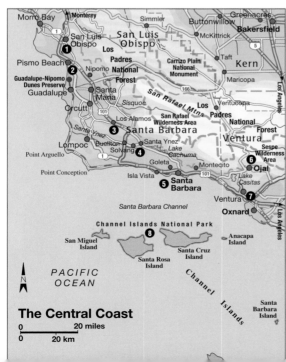

offered by the famously pink and kitschy **Madonna Inn** (tel: 805-543 3000; www.madonnainn.com).

SANTA YNEZ AND SANTA MARIA VALLEYS

Napa and Sonoma may be California's best-known wine-producing regions, but the increasingly respected wineries of **Santa Ynez** and **Santa Maria** valleys are well worth a visit. Spotlighted in the movie *Sideways*, this rural region is home to such wineries as the high-profile Firestone Vineyard (tel: 805-688 3940; www.firestonewine.com) and the Fess Parker Winery (tel: 805-688 1545; www.fessparker.com). For full details of local wineries, see www.sbcountywines.com.

The most notable town hereabouts, **Solvang** ❹, is an amusing and slightly camp replica of a Scandinavian town complete with horse-drawn streetcars, windmills, and Danish bakeries. The Hans Christian Andersen Museum (1680 Mission Drive; tel: 805-688 2052; daily 9am–6pm) has first, early, and illustrated editions of Andersen's works, while the Elverhøj Museum (1624 Elverhoy Way;

tel: 805-686 1211; www.elverhoj.org; Wed–Sun 11am–4pm) traces the history of Solvang and its Danish heritage.

Continuing south on US 101, the highway skirts gorgeous beaches before passing through **Goleta**, home of a University of California branch, and then arriving in Santa Barbara.

SANTA BARBARA

Beautiful **Santa Barbara** ❺ first attracted attention as a health resort after New York journalist Charles Nordhoff glowingly touted its mineral springs in the 1870s. The sunny "American Riviera" remains an alluring getaway destination, boasting a Mediterranean climate, picturesque white stucco buildings topped with red-tiled roofs, and five miles (8km) of palm-tree-lined beaches, perfect for leisurely jogging, biking, rollerblading, and sunbathing.

At the landmark **Stearns Wharf**, the oldest pier on the West Coast, visitors choose among seafood stands, restaurants, wine tasting, and fishing. Jellyfish in the **Sea Center** here (tel: 805-962 2526; www.sbnature.org; daily

⊙ Fact

Pismo Beach is famous for its clams. In theory they grow to almost 8in (20cm), but they've almost disappeared because of overharvesting. Nevertheless, a Clam Festival is still held every October. To try clamming, you must have a saltwater fishing license and a caliper to check their size (legal minimum 4.5in/11.5cm). There's a limit of 10 per day, taken between a half-hour before sunrise and a half-hour after sunset.

Pismo Beach.

⊙ Tip

On man-made Cachuma Lake in the Santa Ynez Valley, park naturalists lead guided cruises (Fri–Sun). In winter you can view a rare flock of migrating bald eagles; in spring and summer, resident birds can be seen building their nests.

10am–5pm), mesmerize visitors with their graceful undulations, while small sharks patrol a touch pool. Looking for larger marine life? Whale-watching boat trips depart from Stearns Wharf most days from February through September in search of the heavyweight mammals heading north from the Baja coast with their offspring.

Take a short diversion to Chapala and Montecito streets to admire a massive **Moreton Bay fig tree**, native to Australia and said to be the largest of its kind in America. Planted in 1914, its branches have grown to cover, at their widest spread, a length of 160ft (49 meters) and often shade the city's homeless community. A bit farther along the harbor, the Santa Barbara Maritime Museum (www.sbmm.org; Thu–Tue 10am–5pm), displays ship models and floating exhibits.

At the eastern end of the shore, expensive hotels line the waterfront. The multicolored 21ft (6-meter) **Chromatic Gate** here was created by Herbert Bayer, last survivor of the seminal Bauhaus school, who spent his final years in the town. Nearby, the petite Santa Barbara Zoo (500 Ninos Drive; tel: 805-962 5339; www.sbzoo.org; daily 10am–5pm) houses 146 species – including gorillas, snow leopards, tropical birds, and giant anteaters – along with a small train and a petting zoo.

To explore downtown Santa Barbara, head up State Street, the main thoroughfare that runs northwest from the coast through Downtown. Turn right at East De La Guerra Street to admire the 1827 **Casa de la Guerra** (www.sbthp.org/casa-de-la-guerra), the original home of the Presidio's commander and his family. Here the city council first met in 1850, an event still celebrated every August with a fiesta. The enticing cobbled area, **El Paseo** ("the walk" in Spanish), is an attractive place to shop and sip coffee at outdoor cafés around the fountain.

The next block of East De La Guerra, bordered by the **Canedo Adobe** (1782), is where the city began, centered around the **Presidio** with its chapel, restored adobes, and the **Historical Society Museum** (www.sbhistorical.org). Continue up Anacapa Street and

Stearns Wharf.

turn left on Carrillo to visit the **Hill-Carrillo Adobe**. The city's first home with a wooden floor, it was built by Daniel Hill in 1826 for his Spanish bride.

Farther up Anacapa, the lobby of the handsome 1929 Spanish-Moorish **Court House** (1100 Anacapa Street; tel: 805-962 6464; Mon–Fri 8am–5pm, Sat and Sun 10am–5pm) holds splendid mosaics and murals. Ride the elevator up the tower for a lovely 360-degree view of gently sloping roofs and the multi-level lawn below. The Santa Barbara Public Library is around the corner on Anapamu Street and the **Museum of Art** (www.sbma.net; Tue–Sun 11am–5pm, Thu 5–8pm) close by on State Street.

A short drive up State Street and right on East Los Olivos Street brings you to **Mission Santa Barbara** (Laguna and Los Olivos streets; tel: 805-682 4713; www.santabarbaramission. org; daily 9am–5pm), among the most beautiful of California's surviving missions. Founded in 1786, it was damaged by major earthquakes in 1812 and 1925, but lovingly restored, and is still in use as a parish church. The museum displays relics from the days when the Chumash lived and worked at the mission.

Just two blocks north, the **Museum of Natural History** (2559 Puesta del Sol; tel: 805-682 4711; www.sbnature. org; daily 10am–5pm), shares more about Native American, and, in particular, Chumash life, and also focuses on animals, birds, reptiles, and fish. Highlights include a blue whale skeleton, the Nature Trail along Mission Creek, the Space Lab, and Gladwin Planetarium.

A mile to the west up Mission Canyon Road, trails at the **Botanic Garden** (tel: 805-682 4726; www.sbbg.org/explore-garden) meander through 78 acres (32 hectares) of native flowers, shrubs, and cacti.

OJAI

Hidden away on the edge of the Los Padres National Forest, **Ojai** ❻ (pronounced Oh-hi) is a sleepy but happy town full of artists and writers. From the Pacific Coast Highway, take state Highway 33 for 15 miles (24km), or

Inside El Presidio de Santa Barbara Historic Park.

⊘ MONTECITO

The seaside community of Montecito, on the eastern outskirts of Santa Barbara, has long been a great place to spot celebs. The charming Montecito Inn (1295 Coast Village Road; tel: 805-969 7854; www.montecitoinn.com) was popular with refugees from Hollywood in the 1920s; one of its original owners was Charlie Chaplin. At Montecito's other legendary hotel, San Ysidro Ranch (900 San Ysidro Lane; tel: 800-368 6788; www. sanysidroranch.com), John F. Kennedy honeymooned with his wife, Jackie; Lauren Bacall fell in love with Humphrey Bogart; and Laurence Olivier and Vivien Leigh exchanged wedding vows at midnight in 1940. These days Butterfly Beach, at Olive Mill Road across from the posh Biltmore Hotel, is often frequented by celebrities.

head inland 35 miles (56km) from Santa Barbara on US highway 101 then State Highway 150.

On the main street, a graceful tower offsets a row of shops behind a covered arcade. The predominantly Spanish-style architecture owes its origins to glass tycoon Edward Drummond Libby, who in 1917 built the elegant **Oaks Hotel** opposite the library. Bart's Books (302 West matlija Street; www.bartsbooksojai.com) is worth a stop.

To see exhibits on the environmental, cultural, and historical factors that shaped this locale, visit the **Ojai Valley Museum** (130 West Ojai Avenue; tel: 805-640 1390; www.ojaivalleymuseum.org; Tue–Sat 10am–4pm, Sun noon–4pm). Located in the St Thomas Aquinas Chapel (c.1918), it doubles as the **Ojai Visitor Center**.

Major annual events in Ojai include a spring tennis tournament, an arts festival in May, a classical music festival in June, and a film festival in October.

West of Ojai, you can take State Highway 150 to wind along the attractive shoreline of **Lake Casitas**, but there's no great point; the scenery is even more spectacular along the coast.

VENTURA AND THE CHANNEL ISLANDS

Just north of Los Angeles, **Ventura** ❼ is dominated by an ostentatious city hall perched on the hillside. The grand civic giant is outshone in style and grace, however, by the 240-year-old **Mission San Buenaventura** (211 East Main Street; tel: 805-648 4496; www.sanbuenaventuramission.org) with its pretty garden. Founded by Father Junípero Serra in 1782, it sits on the edge of a restored "Olde Towne" area filled with antiques shops.

Ventura also serves as a departure point for the **Channel Islands National Park** ❽, which encompasses Anacapa, Santa Cruz, San Miguel, Santa Rosa, and Santa Barbara islands. Desolate Santa Barbara Island is popular, with its 640 acres (260 hectares) a haven for birds, sea lions, and seals. For trip planning, see the National Park Service Visitors Center (1901 Spinaker Drive; tel: 805-658 5730; www.nps.gov/chis).

☉ THE CHANNEL ISLANDS

One of America's least visited national parks, attracting fewer than 250,000 annual visitors, the isolated Channel Islands have often been called the "North American Galapagos." Over 150 endemic or unique species are found here, including the island fox, island spotted skunk, and island night lizard. The pygmy mammoth once lived here too, standing just 4–8ft (1–2 meters) high at the shoulders, compared to the 12–14ft tall (3.5–4-meter) mainland mammoths. Why so much smaller? Separated from their wide-roaming counterparts, this isolated population evolved due to food scarcity.

Today, 99 percent of Southern California seabirds nest and feed here, including bald eagles and peregrine falcons, while sea lions, whales, dolphins, and giant black sea bass swim the surrounding waters.

Shopping in Ojai.

Inspiration Point, Anacapa Island.

📷 EARTHQUAKES AND OTHER DISASTERS

Life in California does have its downsides: the state is prone to natural disasters like earthquakes and fires. Most Californians, though, say that's a small price to pay for living in paradise.

California lies within a major earthquake zone. In 1769, Gaspar de Portola's expedition was shaken by the first quake to be recorded in the state, 30 miles (48km) southeast of Los Angeles. Today, Southern California alone is hit by a staggering 10,000 or so earthquakes per year, although only 15 to 20 of these quakes reach a magnitude greater than 4.0 on the Richter Scale.

It's all because the southern portion of the state straddles the boundary between the Pacific plate (extending as far west as Japan) and the North American plate (eastwards to Iceland). The former moves northwest at a rate of 1.25in (45mm) per year, about as fast as fingernails grow; in another 15 million years, if that rate continues, San Francisco and Los Angeles will be next-door neighbors.

The shift is neither gradual nor steady but a process where the earth stores up the energy before releasing it, along one of scores of fault lines with the enormous burst that we know as an earthquake. The San Andreas fault, considered one of California's major fault lines, is in fact a fault zone with many segments, in some parts reaching up to 10 miles (16km) deep and stretching for more than 800 miles (1300km). Although earthquakes have been recorded since the 18th century, it was not until 1935 that Charles F. Richter devised the scale by which seismographs are used to plot today's temblors.

Aerial view of the San Andreas Fault line.

Firefighters working hard to dispel the flames in the aftermath of the 1906 earthquake.

A destroyed car dealership in Santa Monica after the Northridge earthquake in 1994 - buildings can be razed to the ground from the tremors of an earthquake.

A camp set up in the Presidio after the April 18, 1906 Earthquake and fire. 16,000 refugees were sheltered and fed in 3,000 tents.

The Red Cross provide essential relief work.

Support workers providing water after the 1994 earthquake.

The Big Ones

The most disastrous earthquake in Californian history was the cataclysmic 8.25-magnitude quake that struck San Francisco on April 18, 1906, at 5.12am. Although more than 300 deaths were reported, modern estimates put the toll at over 3,000, while 225,000 people lost their homes.

When will the next major earthquake hit? Scientists and California residents have for many years been anticipating the "Big One," a massive earthquake along the San Andreas fault. Research shows the southern portion of the San Andreas is long overdue a large quake, leading some scientists to predict an 8.1 magnitude "wall-to-wall" quake running from the Salton Sea, a rift lake sitting directly on the fault line southeast of Palm Springs, to Monterey. Such a quake would release twice the energy of California's 1857 7.9-magnitude earthquake. Northern California's Hayward fault, which averages a major quake every 140 years, is also overdue an earthquake. Its last one occurred in 1868, so 2018 was the 150-year mark.

If you do experience an earthquake, stay indoors and find shelter under something sturdy such as a piece of furniture or a door frame, and stay away from glass windows. If outside, avoid trees, power lines, buildings, and bridges.

A statue of Louis Agassiz imploded in the pavement after the 1906 earthquake, falling from the Zoology building at Stanford University.

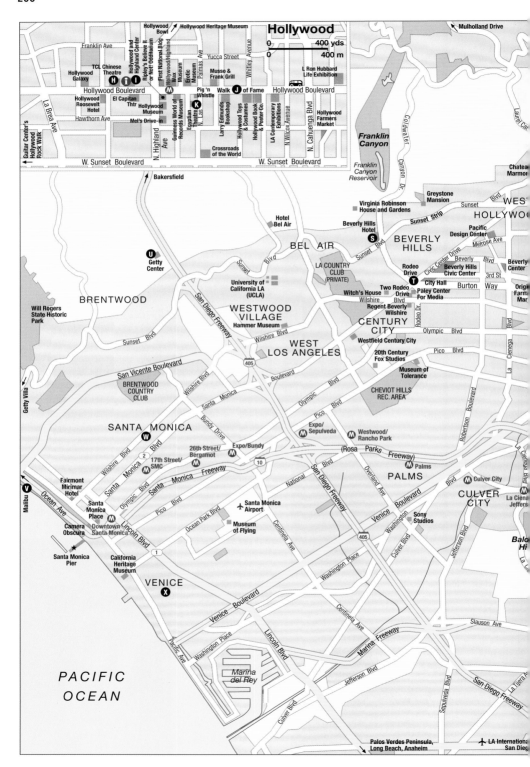

Hollywood

Franklin Ave

Hollywood Heritage Museum
Hollywood Bowl
Hollywood and Highland Center
Ripley's Believe It or Not! Odditorium
First National Bldg
Hollywood/Highland
Hollywood Wax Museum
Erotic Museum
Yucca Street
Whitley Avenue
Musso & Frank Grill
L. Ron Hubbard Life Exhibition
Palmas Ave

TCL Chinese Theatre
Hollywood Galaxy

Hollywood Boulevard

0   400 yds
0   400 m

Pig 'n Whistle
Walk of Fame
Hollywood Boulevard

Hollywood Roosevelt Hotel
El Capitan Thtr
Hollywood Museum
Hawthorn Ave
Mel's Drive-in
Guinness World of Records Museum
Egyptian Theatre
N Las
Larry Edmunds Bookshop
Hollywood Toys & Costumes
Hollywood Book & Poster Co.
LA Contemporary Exhibitions
Hollywood Farmers Market

N Highland Ave
N Wilcox Avenue
N Cahuenga Blvd

Crossroads of the World

La Brea Ave

Guitar Center's Hollywood Rock Walk

W. Sunset Boulevard
W. Sunset Boulevard

Bakersfield

Franklin Canyon
Franklin Canyon Reservoir
Coldwater Canyon Dr.
Laurel Can
Mulholland Drive
Chatea Marmor
WEST HOLLYWOO

Greystone Mansion
Virginia Robinson House and Gardens
Sunset Strip
Sunset Blvd
Melrose Ave
Pacific Design Center
Beverly Center
Orig Farm Mar
Beverly Blvd
3rd St
Burton Way

Hotel Bel Air
Beverly Hills Hotel
BEVERLY HILLS
Rodeo Drive
Beverly Hills Civic Center
Beverly Hills Civic Center
City Hall
Two Rodeo Drive
Paley Center For Media
Witch's House
Wilshire Blvd
Regent Beverly Wilshire

BEL AIR
LA COUNTRY CLUB (PRIVATE)

Getty Center

University of California LA (UCLA)
WESTWOOD VILLAGE
Hammer Museum

San Diego Freeway
Sunset Blvd

BRENTWOOD

Will Rogers State Historic Park

Sunset Blvd

Wilshire Blvd
WEST LOS ANGELES
CENTURY CITY
Westfield Century City
20th Century Fox Studios
Museum of Tolerance
CHEVIOT HILLS REC. AREA
Olympic Blvd
Pico Blvd
La Cienega
Robertson Boulevard

San Vicente Boulevard
BRENTWOOD COUNTRY CLUB
Wilshire Blvd
Santa Monica Blvd
Boulevard
Olympic Blvd
Pico

Getty Villa

SANTA MONICA
Wilshire Blvd
Santa Monica Blvd
26th Street/Bergamot
17th Street/SMC
Expo/Bundy
Santa Monica Freeway
Expo/Sepulveda
Westwood/Rancho Park
National
San Diego Freeway
Overland Ave
Palms
Venice Boulevard
PALMS
CULVER CITY
Culver City
La Ciena Jeffers
Balo Hi

Malibu
Ocean Ave
Fairmont Mirimar Hotel
Santa Monica Place
Camera Obscura
Downtown Santa Monica
Lincoln Blvd
Ocean Park Blvd
Pico Blvd
Santa Monica Airport
Museum of Flying
Centinela Ave
Washington Blvd
Sony Studios
Culver Blvd
Jefferson Blvd

Santa Monica Pier
California Heritage Museum

VENICE
Venice Boulevard
Washington Place
Lincoln Blvd
Centinela Ave
Slauson Ave
Marina Freeway

PACIFIC OCEAN

Pacific Ave
Marina del Rey
Culver Blvd
Jefferson Blvd
Sepulveda Blvd
San Diego Freeway
La Tijera

Palos Verdes Peninsula, Long Beach, Anaheim
LA International San Dieg

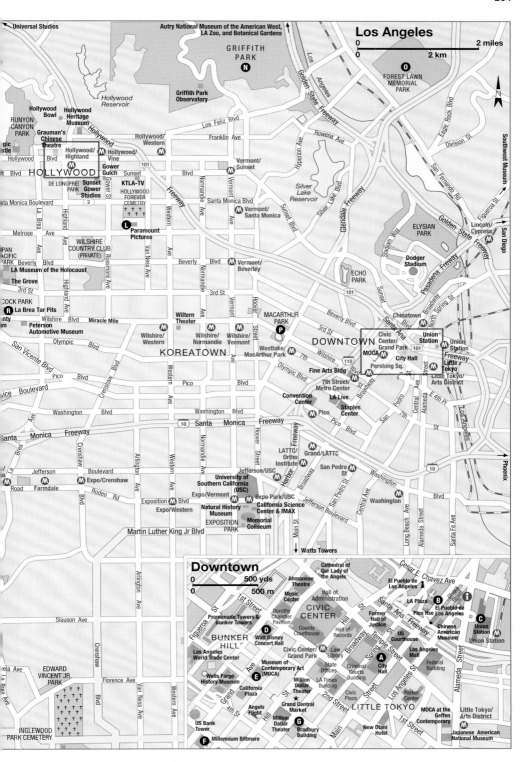

251

Los Angeles

0 ————————— 2 miles
0 ————————— 2 km

Universal Studios

Autry National Museum of the American West, LA Zoo, and Botanical Gardens

GRIFFITH PARK

N

FOREST LAWN MEMORIAL PARK

O

Griffith Park Observatory

Hollywood Reservoir

Los Feliz Blvd

Hollywood Bowl

Hollywood Heritage Museum

RUNYON CANYON PARK

gic Canyon stle

Grauman's Chinese Theatre

Hollywood Blvd

Hollywood/ Highland **M**

HOLLYWOOD

Franklin Ave

Hollywood/ Western **M**

Vermont/ Sunset **M**

Rowena Ave

Eagle Rock Blvd

Southwest Museum

Hollywood/ Vine **M**

Gower Gulch

Sunset

101

DE LONGPRE PARK

KTLA-TV

Sunset Gower Studios 2

HOLLYWOOD FOREVER CEMETERY

L Paramount Pictures

Silver Lake Reservoir

ELYSIAN PARK

Dodger Stadium

Division St

Lincoln/ Cypress **M**

San Diego

Santa Monica Boulevard

MAP AN PACIFIC ARK Beverly

LA Museum of the Holocaust

The Grove

La Brea

Highland

Melrose Ave

Blvd

3rd St

Van Ness Ave

Rossmore Ave

Beverly Blvd

Normandie Ave

Vermont/ Beverley **M**

ECHO PARK

101

Chinatown

North Spring St

North Broadway

OCK PARK nty m

R La Brea Tar Pits

Wilshire Blvd

Miracle Mile

Wiltern Theatre

Vermont St

MACARTHUR PARK

P

3rd St

Beverly Blvd

DOWNTOWN

Civic Center/ Grand Park

Union Station

M Union Station

Peterson Automotive Museum

Wilshire/ Western **M**

Wilshire/ Normandie **M**

Wilshire/ Vermont **M**

Wilshire

110

M MOCA

City Hall **M**

Pershing Sq.

Freeway

Little Tokyo/ Arts District

Olympic Blvd

San Vicente Blvd

Pico

KOREATOWN

Westlake/ MacArthur Park **M**

7th

Olympic Blvd

Fine Arts Bldg

7th Street/ Metro Center **M**

4th St

Little Tokyo

Pico Boulevard

Washington Blvd

Western Ave

Washington Blvd

10 Santa Monica Freeway

Convention Center

Pico **M**

LA Live

Staples Center

San Pedro St

Central Ave

Alameda St

Phoenix

Santa Monica Freeway

Jefferson

Boulevard

Crenshaw

Arlington Ave

Western Ave

Normandie Ave

Hoover Street

LATTC/ Ortho Institute

Grand/LATTC **M**

San Pedro St

Harbor Freeway

San Pedro St

Broadway

Washington

10

M Expo/Crenshaw

Rodeo Rd

Exposition Blvd **M**

University of Southern California (USC)

Jefferson/USC

Expo/Vermont **M**

Expo Park/USC **M**

Jefferson Boulevard

Central Ave

Washington

Long Beach Ave

Alameda Street

Santa Fe Ave

Road Farmdale

Expo/Western

Exposition Blvd

Natural History Museum

EXPOSITION PARK

California Science Center & IMAX

Memorial Coliseum

Martin Luther King Jr Blvd

Main St

↓ Watts Towers

Downtown

0 ————————— 500 yds
0 ————————— 500 m

Cathedral of Our Lady of the Angels

Ahmanson Theatre

Music Center

Hall of Administration

CIVIC CENTER

Dorothy Chandler Pavilion

El Pueblo de Los Angeles

Cesar E. Chavez Ave

LA PLAZA **B** El Pueblo de Los Angeles

Pico Hse Los Angeles

i

1st Street

Santa Ana Freeway

Former Hall of Justice

US Courthouse

Chinese American Museum

C Union Station

Union Station

Promenade Towers & Bunker Towers

Figueroa

County Courthouse

Hall of Records

Temple Street

BUNKER HILL

Walt Disney Concert Hall

Civic Center/ Grand Park **M**

Law Library

Spring Street

State Offices

Criminal Courts Building

Los Angeles Mall

Federal Building

Slauson Ave

Los Angeles World Trade Center

Museum of Contemporary Art (MOCA) **E**

A City Hall

Los Angeles Street

Wells Fargo History Museum

Grand Ave

California Plaza

Million Dollar Theater

LA Times Building

2nd Street

Parker Center

EDWARD VINCENT JR. PARK

Florence Ave

Angels Flight

4th St

Grand Central Market

Civic Plaza

LITTLE TOKYO

MOCA at the Geffen Contemporary

Little Tokyo/ Arts District

ela Ave

US Bank Tower

Million Dollar Theater

G Bradbury Building

Main St

New Otani Hotel

INGLEWOOD PARK CEMETERY

F Millennium Biltmore

Japanese American National Museum

The City of Angels.

LOS ANGELES AND AROUND

Sun-drenched beaches, Hollywood glitz, fabulous food, blockbuster theme parks ... La La Land comprises many identities, and many cities, within one vast whole.

A huge, sprawling city that's home to more than 18 million residents, Greater Los Angeles is a metropolis with multiple (and often contradictory) personalities. There's the MOCA's modern art and the cliff-side Getty Center, innovative fine dining from celebrity chefs and street-side food carts, slick clubs and hipster dives, and designer Rodeo Drive and tiny vintage shops. Movie buffs can soak up Hollywood and television show tapings, while beach lovers have plenty to keep them busy: from the exclusive Malibu colony to the roller-blading boardwalk of Venice, Los Angeles wouldn't be Los Angeles without its photogenic beaches. A forward-looking city from the start, Los Angeles has enticed the young and hopeful since the 1950s, and it is still a magnet for the adventurous, for those seeking to begin a new life, and especially anyone looking to become a star – or, failing that, at least see one.

The whole of downtown Los Angeles lies surrounded by hills in the low-lying Los Angeles Basin (which explains why it's notoriously prone to smog, with all that sunshine beating down on emissions that don't get blown away). Various valleys radiate away from the center, each with its own character. The most noteworthy is the San Fernando Valley to the north, encircled by the Traverse Ranges, and universally

City Hall, Downtown LA.

known as simply "the Valley." Effectively a city in its own right, it's home to beautiful gardens, historic missions, plenty of malls, and some 1.8 million people. To the east, Pasadena boasts further delightful gardens at the Huntington Library, not to mention a New Year's Day parade featuring elaborate floats made entirely of flowers.

Several of LA's most important visitor attractions lie beyond the bounds of the city proper, including, to the south, the original Magic Kingdom. The opening of Disneyland in 1955 transformed

 Main attractions

El Pueblo de Los Angeles
Museum of Contemporary Art
Hollywood Walk of Fame
LA County Museum of Contemporary Art
La Brea Tar Pits
Getty Center
Venice Beach Boardwalk
Huntington Library
Universal Studios
Disneyland

Maps on pages 250, 262

Avila Adobe house is the oldest house in LA, built in 1818.

the community of Anaheim, and for sheer year-round entertainment, it remains unsurpassed, despite the many rivals that have followed in its wake.

DOWNTOWN LA

While it may not be the bustling central hub you might expect, LA's Downtown district represents both new and old faces of the city. Millions of dollars have gone into sprucing it up with modern architecture, cultural institutions, and high-end lofts, now interspersed among the ornate movie palaces and other unforgettable fixtures of the city's past.

One such historic landmark is **City Hall Ⓐ**, which was built using sand from every California county and water from every mission. The Los Angeles Conservancy (tel: 213-623 2489; www.laconservancy.org) offers fascinating walking tours, taking in the magnificent rotunda.

A few blocks northeast, **El Pueblo de Los Angeles Ⓑ** marks where LA's story began in 1780, with the founding of El Pueblo de Nuestra Señora a la Reina de Los Angeles. Lively Olvera Street, a pedestrian marketplace, teems with craftspeople, Mexican stands, and strolling mariachi who serenade diners sipping frozen margaritas under the sidewalk awning of La Golondrina, the city's first brick building (c.1855). Next to the marketplace, **LA Plaza de Cultura y Artes** (LA Plaza; www.lapca.org) features interactive exhibits, a re-creation of 1920s-era Main Street, a short film series, and a large public garden. Other preserved buildings nearby include the Avila Adobe, the home of a rancher who died in 1832; Pico House, the city's first three-story building and once its finest hotel; and the Hellman Quon building, originally a Chinese store but now managed by the Parks Department, who run morning neighborhood tours.

Nearby, the majestic 1939 **Union Station Ⓒ** is one of the country's last grand railway stations. Its leather seats, marble floors, and stratospheric ceiling were seen in scores of old newsreels. The mural- and fountain-filled Gateway Transit Center, just behind, is the region's transportation hub today.

Not far away, the exterior of the austere **Cathedral of Our Lady of the Angels** (555 West Temple Street; tel: 213-680 5200; www.olacathedral.com) is all jutting angles, while inside, daylight seeps through thin alabaster panes into a cavernous, polished space. A block and a half on, the LA Philharmonic performs at Frank Gehry's striking, stainless-steel **Walt Disney Concert Hall Ⓓ** (111 South Grand Avenue; tel: 323-850 2000; www.laphil.com; tours most days. The main auditorium comes as a bit of a surprise: it's warm and inviting with golden-hued Douglas fir panels and an enormous organ centrepiece.

Another block along Grand Avenue, the postmodern **Museum of Contemporary Art (MOCA) Ⓔ** (tel: 213-626

6222; www.moca.org; Mon, Wed and Fri 11am–6pm, Thu 11am–8pm, Sat and Sun 11am–5pm), harbors American and European art from the 1940s to the present, including work from Mark Rothko, Diane Arbus, and Franz Kline. Its permanent collection is also displayed in the **Geffen Contemporary at MOCA** in Little Tokyo (152 North Central Avenue; tel: 213-625 4390), and West Hollywood's **MOCA Pacific Design Center** (8687 Melrose Avenue; tel: 310-289 5223).

A few blocks away up Bunker Hill are the LA Central Library at 5th and Grand streets, and Pershing Square, flanked by the awe-inspiring **Millennium Biltmore F**, with its ornate lobby and photographs of attendees at the 1937 Academy Awards. It was here that MGM's art director is said to have sketched a design for a still-unnamed Oscar statue on a napkin.

At 811 West 7th, the **Fine Arts Building** has a medieval-style lobby with 15 chandeliers and a tiled fountain, and hosts exhibitions. The stepped, white form of the **777 Tower** was created by Argentine-born César Pelli, also responsible for the distinctive Pacific Design Center ("the Blue Whale") in West Hollywood. A few blocks away, adjacent to the **Staples Center**, is the **LA Live** entertainment complex, where you can catch a show at the Nokia Theatre, or peruse the four-floor **Grammy Museum** (www.grammymuseum.org).

Opposite the **Bradbury Building G**, lively **Grand Central Market** (www.grandcentralmarket.com), adjoins the **Million Dollar Theater** (www.milliondollar.la) at 307 South Broadway. Founded by showman Sid Grauman, its gala opening in 1918 had Charlie Chaplin, Mary Pickford, and Lillian Gish in attendance. The last of the grand movie palaces, S. Charles Lee's **Los Angeles Theatre** (https://losangelestheatre.com), which opened with the premiere of Charlie Chaplin's *City Lights* in 1931, is still operating down the street.

Head east to explore **Little Tokyo**, where you'll encounter interesting shops in Little Tokyo Square, lush Japanese gardens, Buddhist temples, and the **Japanese American National**

The Frank Gehry designed Walt Disney Concert Hall.

⊘ THE WATTS TOWERS

The major landmark of the downtown suburb of Watts, in Los Angeles' South Central area, is one of the most astonishing sculptures in the nation: The Watts Towers (1727 East 107th Street; tel: 213-847 4646; www.wattstowers.org). Created between 1921 and 1954 by Simon Rodia, a penniless Italian tiler, this trio of lacy columns was intended as an affectionate tribute to his adopted land. Composed of broken bottles, pottery shards, tiles, pebbles, and steel rods, all stuccoed together and covered with 70,000 seashells, the towers are a set of sculptures so far ahead of their time that they remained unappreciated for years: vandals did their utmost to destroy them, and the city planned to pull them down.

The towers, the highest of which reaches 100ft (30 meters), were eventually reprieved after a 1959 attempt to dismantle them using steel cables pulled by a tractor – in full view of TV cameras – proved unsuccessful. In time, the towers started to accumulate the adulation they had long deserved, but by then Rodia had died in poverty in 1965 at the age of 86, 10 years after deeding the site to a friend and leaving town. The towers can be seen behind the fence even when the adjoining Watts Towers Arts Center, which displays works by African American artists, is closed.

⊙ Tip

Parking in Downtown LA is difficult, unless you leave your car on the periphery, for example in the lot opposite The Original Pantry, at 9th and Figueroa streets. For those on foot, a bus runs along 7th every few minutes, from 6.30am on weekdays and 10am on weekends. Between Grand, Hill, 3rd, and 4th streets, the old-fashioned Angels Flight funicular (www.angelsflight.com) takes just 70 seconds to ride up steep Bunker Hill.

The Academy Awards - "the Oscars" - are held in the Dolby Theatre.

Museum (100 North Central Avenue; tel: 213-625 0414; www.janm.org; Tue, Wed, and Fri–Sun 11am–5pm, Thu noon–8pm).

HOLLYWOOD

Start your explorations of Los Angeles' most iconic neighborhood at the landmark **TCL Chinese Theatre** ⊕ (formally Grauman's Chinese Theatre), notable for its forecourt of famous footprints. Nearby, the glamorous Hollywood Roosevelt Hotel (www.the-hollywoodroosevelt.com), hosted the first public Oscars ceremony in 1929. These days, the Oscars are staged in the **Dolby Theatre** (tel: 323-308 6300; www.dolbytheatre.com), in the **Hollywood & Highland Center** ⊕. On 30-minute guided tours, visitors get access to VIP areas and the low-down on all the gossip and glitz.

The old Max Factor building (a former speakeasy) on Highland just south of Hollywood is now the **Hollywood Museum** (tel: 323-464 7776; http://thehollywoodmuseum.com; Wed–Sun 10am–5pm), where costumes, movie posters, and artifacts include Cary Grant's Rolls-Royce.

Across the street, the 18,000-seat **Hollywood Bowl** (www.hollywoodbowl.com) stages "Symphonies Under the Stars" concerts all summer, not to mention jazz, world music, and rock performances.

Most modern visitors think of the **Hollywood Walk of Fame** ⊕ (www.walkoffame.com) as the heart of Hollywood: the celebrated brass and terrazzo stars run west along Hollywood Boulevard from Vine Street, with Marilyn Monroe's star outside a McDonald's. Since 1958, when stars including Burt Lancaster, Ronald Colman, and Joanne Woodward were first cemented into the sidewalk, well over 2,500 have followed.

On Hollywood Boulevard, the magnificent, century-old **Egyptian Theatre** ⊕ (tel: 323-461 2020; www.egyptian-theatre.com; monthly tours), is now jointly programmed by Netflix (Mon–Thu) and the American Cinematheque (Fri and Sun).

Steep Whitley Terrace heads up to Whitley Heights, a cluster of elegant

mansions favored by movie stars of the Gloria Swanson era, preceding the rise of Beverly Hills. Access is easier, off Highland Avenue, just before the big yellow barn that served as the original de Mille and Lasky studio, now the **Hollywood Heritage Museum** (tel: 323-874 2276; www.hollywoodheritage.org; Fri and Sun 11am–3pm).

THE STUDIOS

While most of Hollywood's legendary movie studios are long gone, the famous gate seen in *Sunset Boulevard* still guards the entrance to **Paramount Pictures ❶** (5555 Melrose at Van Ness Avenue; tel: 323-956 1777; www.paramount. com), where *The Ten Commandments* and the Godfather movies were also made. Fans seek out the graves of Rudolph Valentino, Douglas Fairbanks, Cecil B. de Mille, and Marion Davies in the adjoining Hollywood Forever Cemetery.

Northwest, on Sunset Boulevard itself, Columbia Square stands where Hollywood's first film studio, the Nestor Film Company, paid just $40 to rent a defunct tavern in 1911.

Four blocks east, the KTLA TV station replaced the Warner Brothers studios, where, in 1927, Al Jolson emoted in *The Jazz Singer*.

WEST HOLLYWOOD

Tourists often assume that "Sunset Strip" refers to the entire length of Sunset Boulevard. In reality, it begins and ends at West Hollywood's city limits. One of LA's hippest neighborhoods, "WeHo" has a large gay community and a stylish outlook. Its chic crowd glides from art gallery to bohemian clothing store to intimate café by day, and between classy bistro, slick lounge, and pulsating club by night.

At the eastern edge of the Strip near Laurel Canyon, the castle-like **Chateau Marmont ⓜ** www.chateaumarmont. com), once welcomed guests like Greta Garbo and Howard Hughes, and retains a laid-back but starry ambience. From here, temples of cool march down the boulevard on ever-higher heels, the roll-call including the Comedy Store, the Whiskey a Go-Go, the Viper Room, and the Roxy.

The Walk of Fame, Hollywood Boulevard.

GRIFFITH PARK

Immense **Griffith Park**  (tel: 323-644 2050; www.laparks.org/griffithpark) extends from Los Feliz Boulevard all the way to the Ventura freeway. The nation's largest park, at 4,000 acres (1,620 hectares), it's home to a zoo, an open-air theater, a train museum, and the excellent **Autry Museum of the American West** (tel: 323-667 2000; www.theautry.org; Tue–Fri 10am–4pm, Sat and Sun 10am–5pm), which focuses on the culture and history of the American West, and incorporates a huge collection of Native American art. Perched on the south-facing slope of Mount Hollywood, the wonderful **Griffith Park Observatory** (2800 East Observatory Road; tel: 213-473 0800; www.griffithobservatory.org; Tue–Fri noon–10pm, Sat and Sun 10am–10pm; free) offers star parties and planetarium shows.

Forest Lawn Memorial Park – the park literature studiously avoids the word "cemetery" – has two peaceful locations flanking Griffith Park: **Glendale** and the **Hollywood Hills** (tel: 800-204 3131). The inspiration for Evelyn Waugh's *The Loved One*, the must-see Glendale location is the final resting place of stars including Clark Gable, Carole Lombard, Nat King Cole, and Jean Harlow, while the Hollywood Hills site holds Buster Keaton, Stan Laurel, and Liberace.

WESTLAKE, MIRACLE MILE, AND LA BREA

West of Downtown, Wilshire is showing its age these days, although the Metro Line subway has brought life to otherwise seedy **MacArthur Park** . The Ambassador Hotel once stood at 3400 Wilshire Boulevard, drawing showbiz types to its Coconut Grove; it became infamous in 1968 as the site of Robert Kennedy's assassination.

On Miracle Mile's Museum Row, on Wilshire near Fairfax, the **LA County Museum of Art** (LACMA; www.lacma.org; Mon, Tue, Thu 11am–5pm, Fri 11am–8pm, Sat and Sun 10am–7pm), is the largest art museum in the Western United States. Established in 1961, and housed in a massive complex,

Griffith Observatory Park.

it treasures more than 135,000 objects from ancient times to the present. Particular strengths include its Asian art, with a comprehensive collection of Korean works as well as Tibetan and Nepalese paintings, sculpture, furniture, and decorative arts. European holdings range from Georges de la Tour and Rembrandt van Rijn to Edgar Degas, Paul Cézanne, Pablo Picasso, and Alberto Giacometti.

For well over a century, scientists at the extraordinary **La Brea Tar Pits** Ⓡ (5801 Wilshire Boulevard; tel: 323-934 7243; www.tarpits.org; daily 9.30am–5pm), have been excavating the skeletons of an amazing array of animals that became trapped in a natural asphalt lake between 11,000 and 15,000 years ago. Remarkable fossils on display include mammoths, saber-toothed tigers, dire wolves, and giant sloths.

In Pan Pacific Park, the **Los Angeles Museum of the Holocaust** (www.lamoth.org; Mon–Thu and Sat and Sun 10am–5pm, Fri 10am–2pm), holds the largest archive of documents, relics, and other materials from the Holocaust period.

BEVERLY HILLS

It was drilling for oil on the former Rancho Rodeo de las Aguas that led to the birth of **Beverly Hills**; the unsuccessful prospectors decided to develop the land instead, offering one-acre lots along Sunset Boulevard for under $1,000. In 1912, Burton Green built the **Beverly Hills Hotel** Ⓢ as the focal point of the new community.

Filmdom's elite built ever-larger homes in this elegant area, fanning out into the hills and canyons, and around **Mulholland Drive**, the spectacular highway that runs for 50 miles (80km) along the crest of the Santa Monica Mountains to reach the coast just north of Malibu. Greta Garbo and John Gilbert shared idyllic poolside afternoons together in a mansion at

Seabright and Tower Grove Drive; Rudolph Valentino luxuriated in Falcon's Lair at 1436 Bella Drive; and the home of Roman Polanski and Sharon Tate at 10050 Cielo Drive witnessed the 1969 "Manson family" murders. Along immaculate **North Roxbury Drive**, at the canyon's lower end, lived Marlene Dietrich (No. 822), Jimmy Stewart (No. 918), Lucille Ball (No. 1000), and Jack Benny (No. 1002).

City Hall, with its handsome tiled dome, is a splendid sight, part of the Spanish Renaissance–style Beverly Hills Civic Center. The intriguing **Witch's House**, at 516 Walden Drive, began life as a 1921 movie set designed to evoke the home of the witch in Hansel and Gretel, and was later moved to this site. Beverly Hills' informed, active Visitors Bureau is at 9400 South Santa Monica Blvd (tel: 310-248 1015; www.lovebeverlyhills.com; Mon–Fri 9am–5pm, Sat and Sun 10am-5pm).

Santa Monica and Wilshire boulevards intersect not far west of **Rodeo Drive** Ⓣ, beside the **Electric Fountain**, which caused sightseeing traffic jams

Rodeo Drive, Beverly Hills.

⊙ Shop

The three iconic blocks of **Rodeo Drive** (https://rodeodrive-bh.com), between Santa Monica and Wilshire in the heart of Beverly Hills, are lined with designer stores such as Gucci, Hermès, Chanel, Fendi, and Cartier. Novelist Judith Krantz described it as "the most staggering display of luxury in the western world."

Manhattan Beach.

when it was first installed in the 1930s. Santa Monica Boulevard heads west past the skyscrapers of Century City to terminate at Santa Monica. Century City's 180-acre (73-hectare) site once formed part of the studio back lot of 20th Century Fox.

WESTWOOD, BEL-AIR, AND BRENTWOOD

Wilshire Boulevard swerves slightly northwest heading out of Beverly Hills, alongside **Westwood Village**. Once the headquarters of William Fox's newsreel operations, this shopping complex is now home to the interesting Hammer Museum (10899 Wilshire Boulevard; tel: 310-443 7000; www.hammer.ucla.edu; Tue–Fri 11am–8pm, Sat–Sun until 5pm), exhibiting European paintings, da Vinci drawings, and traveling art shows. Westwood also adjoins the tree-shaded **University of California** (UCLA) campus. UCLA's 130 buildings include Schoenberg Hall (named after the composer who taught here), Bunche Hall Library, and the New Wight Gallery.

The ultra-chic gated community of **Bel Air** is north of Sunset, the road up through Stone Canyon passing LA's most beautiful hideaway hotel, the **Hotel Bel Air**. Grace Kelly lived here for much of her movie career.

Back on Sunset, the boulevard begins a series of dizzying loops and curves passing through Brentwood, site of the impressive **Getty Center** Ⓤ (see page 261). Sunset continues through Pacific Palisades before sweeping down to the Pacific Coast Highway.

MALIBU

Head west on Pacific Coast Highway (PCH) to reach the wealthy seaside community of **Malibu** Ⓥ, with its free state beach. **Malibu Pier**, built by Frederick Rindge, Malibu's founder and major landholder, in 1905, makes a fun place to while away an amusing hour or two. Just southwest of the pier, the oceanfront **Adamson House** (tel: 310-456 8432; www.adamsonhouse.org; Thu–Sat 11am–3pm) was built in 1929 by Rindge's daughter Rhoda Adamson.

⊙ BEVERLY HILLS HOTEL

The Beverly Hills Hotel, the famous pink palace, is an LA legend. Elizabeth Taylor honeymooned in a bungalow here, while reclusive resident Howard Hughes ordered pineapple upside-down cake from room service almost every night. Katharine Hepburn took lessons from the hotel's tennis pro and one day, after six sets, dove in the pool fully clothed. She was also known to curl up outside Spencer Tracy's locked door, waiting for him to let her in after a drinking bout. Greta Garbo chose the hotel as a hideaway in 1932 and Clark Gable checked in to dodge the press after separating from his wife, Rita. At the Fountain Café, Marilyn Monroe and Yves Montand romanced over afternoon tea in 1959.

The world's then richest man, Hassanal Bolkiah, Sultan of Brunei, bought the hotel for $185 million in 1987. The hotel became Beverly Hills' first historic landmark in 2012, but the Sultan's continued ownership has attracted controversy in recent years, with widespread calls for it to be boycotted on account of Brunei's repressive human rights policies.

Some things, of course, have stayed the same. The menu of the Polo Lounge, where Will Rogers and Darryl Zanuck dropped in after their matches, still features the McCarthy Salad, named for the polo-playing millionaire Neil McCarthy, who died in 1972.

THE GETTY CENTER

More than a dozen years in the making, the billion-dollar Getty Center, comprising art collections, gardens, a research center, and more, was likened to a Tuscan hill town by its award-winning architect, Richard Meier.

Like so many examples of 20th-century architecture, the white city on the hill high above the intersection of the Santa Monica and San Diego freeways provoked both praise and criticism. Detractors have suggested it resembles an oversize refrigerator or a strip mall, while one admirer claims it is "too good for Los Angeles." Richard Meier, winner of architecture's highest honor, the Pritzker Prize, was chosen for the commission in 1984, after a worldwide search. He described the site as the most beautiful he had ever been invited to build upon, one whose light, landscape, and topography provided the cues for his design. The center, he says, "is both in the city and removed from it ... evok[ing] a sense of both urbanity and contemplation."

The collections of the J. Paul Getty Museum include European drawings, paintings, illuminated manuscripts, sculpture, French 17th- and 18th-century decorative arts, and photography, all displayed in a series of five interconnecting buildings. However, the Getty Center site also includes six other buildings, including a research institute, a library, an auditorium, and a restaurant, most offering breathtaking views of the city, the sea, and the mountains. The playful and imaginative central garden between the museum and the research institute was designed by artist Robert Irwin.

THE RECLUSIVE BILLIONAIRE

Minneapolis-born oil billionaire J. Paul Getty, who refused to fly and lived his last years as a virtual recluse in England, never saw the museum that bears his name. When his Malibu ranch house opened to the public to exhibit his art and antiquities, he was no longer in the country. From the oilfields of Kuwait in May 1954, he telegraphed regrets that he could not attend the opening: "I hope this museum, modest and unpretentious as it is, will give pleasure ..."

Later, he remotely directed the construction of a new site, an elaborate reproduction of a Pompeian villa (now called the Getty Villa), which opened in 1974. When Getty died two years later, aged 83, Getty oil stock was left to the museum; this $700-million endowment has ballooned into billions. Planning for the ambitious Getty Center began almost immediately, but family lawsuits (eventually running up $26.4 million in legal fees) delayed progress until 1982.

With five marriages and innumerable mistresses, Getty had 26 children, but only one – his third son, Gordon – maintained a lasting connection with the museum.

The terrace offers great views of the city.

⊙ Where

Broad Beach, like so much of the Malibu coastline, is private but only down to the mean high-tide line – so long as you stay on wet sand, you have every right to be there. Access is in the 3100 and 3200 block of Broad Beach Road. Zuma Beach and Point Dume State Beach are public and often crowded.

The house is as attractive outside as it is inside, and even when it's closed you can drive or walk up the lane to admire the tiled terrace, lovely fountains, bottle-glass windows, and well-kept gardens. In the lagoon alongside, you may spot ducks, herons, and pelicans.

SANTA MONICA

At one time, it took a full day's stage-coach ride to get from Downtown LA to **Santa Monica** ⓦ. When the freeway opened in 1966, the trip was cut to half an hour, and Los Angelenos discovered the beach. Previously the city's seashores had been the preserve of fishermen and the wealthy owners of oceanfront bungalows; now everyone was sporting a tan and hanging ten. Today Santa Monica is the largest coastal town in the 100-mile (160-km) stretch between Oxnard and Long Beach.

This deceptively casual town embraces both metropolitan sophistication and a beach-town atmosphere. Almost every LA visitor under the age of 35 chooses to visit or stay here. It's a great place to walk around and, so unusual for LA, no car is necessary. The Visitor Information Kiosk at 1400 Ocean Avenue, open daily 9–5pm, is a great place to start.

The century-old **Santa Monica Pier** holds several amusement arcades, a carousel you might recognize from *The Sting* and *Forest Gump*, and eating places and fishing stands with gorgeous views of Pacific sunsets and beaches curving gently around the bay. Unfortunately, though, the ocean tends to be too polluted for safe swimming.

Eucalyptus-fringed **Palisades Park**, overlooking the pier, was given to the city in 1892 for use "forever" by Santa Monica's founders, Colonel Robert Baker and his partner, silver tycoon John P. Jones. Jones's house at the corner of Wilshire was where the **Fairmont Miramar Hotel** now sits; the enormous fig tree outside the lobby was planted more than a century ago. Greta Garbo spent three years living at the Miramar, while the pool was seen in the "Bermuda" sequence of *That Touch of Mink* with Cary Grant and Doris Day.

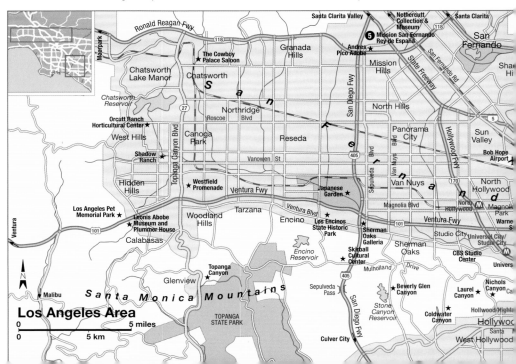

Los Angeles Area

South of the pier, a walkway and bicycle path extends all the way down to Venice. The local visitor center is at 2427 Main Street (tel: 310-393 7593; www.santamonica.com; daily 9am–5pm).

Poised above the Pacific Coast Highway 5 miles (8km) northwest of the pier, on the other hand, the beautiful, clifftop **Getty Villa** (www.getty.edu; Wed–Mon 10am–5pm; timed ticket required; free) makes an evocative and highly appropriate home for the Getty Museum's Greek and Roman treasures.

VENICE

The closer you get to **Venice ❽**, the odder the ambiance. An early favorite of moviemakers like Charlie Chaplin and Carole Lombard, **Venice Boardwalk** is now jammed around the clock with characters who appear to be auditioning for some unannounced contemporary epic. Sights and sounds might include guitar-bearing rollerbladers in robes and turbans, bikini-clad beach bunnies, rainbow-haired punks, lunatic dreamers, outrageous con men, barely dressed cyclists, psychics, chain-saw jugglers, and the bicep-bound boasters of Muscle Beach.

Another, less-explored Venice lies a few blocks east. What remains of Venice's original network of canals now form a charmingly tranquil area of shallow waterways lined with houses in myriad styles, mostly with gardens full of flowers that thrive in the hot sunshine, and where ducks and geese roam the walkways.

MARINA DEL REY

Close to Los Angeles international airport (LAX), **Marina del Rey** is a good place for a stopover. The marina's tourist attraction is the charming but phony Fisherman's Village (the "lighthouse" is a fast-food stand) with its multitude of restaurants, overlooking a harbor that holds berths for 6,000 boats. At the end of Basin D is a shallow-water family beach known as **Mother's Beach**.

PASADENA AND ENVIRONS

Beyond Los Angeles proper, east of the San Fernando Valley and almost

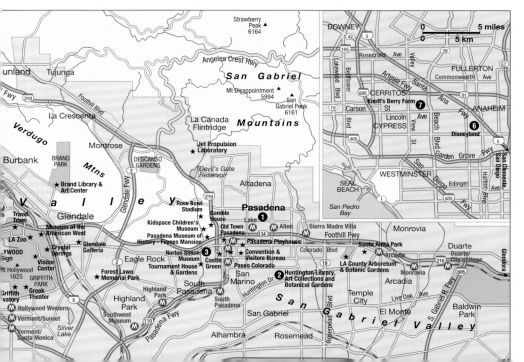

bordering on the San Gabriel Mountains, **Pasadena**  comes fully alive once a year during the Rose Bowl football game and the famous Tournament of Roses Parade, both held on New Year's Day. Any other day, the city's houses, museums, and gardens take center stage.

Pasadena's prime attraction is the **Huntington Library, Art Collections, and Botanical Gardens** ❷ (1151 Oxford Road, San Marino; tel: 626-405 2100; www.huntington.org; Wed–Mon 10am–5pm), created by railroad magnate Henry Edwards Huntington. World-famous paintings here include Thomas Gainsborough's *Blue Boy* (c.1770), Sir Joshua Reynolds' *Sarah Siddons* (1784), and John Constable's *View on the Stour* (1822). Among rarities displayed in the library are a 1410 edition of Chaucer's *Canterbury Tales*, a Gutenberg Bible, an early Shakespeare folio, and Audubon prints. Beyond the lily pond there are a series of tranquil gardens, including the colorful Subtropical Garden, the Australian Garden, and the Japanese and Zen gardens.

Near the freeway, the 18-room Fenyes Mansion (1905) is home of the **Pasadena Museum of History** (tel: 626-577 1660; https://pasadenahistory. org; Wed–Sun noon–5pm). Half a block away, the impressive 1908 **Gamble House** (tel: 626-793 3334; http://gamblehouse.org; guided tours), a California-style "bungalow," was built for David Gamble of the Procter & Gamble soap company. Its interior is a knock-out, but its impressive exterior makes it worth seeing even when the house is closed.

Just south of the freeway, the **Norton Simon Museum** ❸ (411 West Colorado at Orange Grove; tel: 626-449 6840; www.nortonsimon.org; Thu–Mon noon–5pm), preserves a remarkable collection of both European and South and Southeast Asian art amassed by industrialist Norton Simon (1907–93). Museum highlights include Raphael's *Madonna and Child with Book* (c.1502–03), Rembrandt's *Portrait of a Boy* (c.1655–60), van Gogh's *Mulberry Tree* (1889), and Picasso's *Woman with a Book* (1932).

Sunset over Santa Monica beach.

Ø LA DETECTIVES

Los Angeles has long been popular as the setting for crime novels. The "Bay City" setting that features in so many of Raymond Chandler's detective novels centers on the area where Wilshire and Sunset boulevards meet the ocean. Discussing the locale, Chandler's biographer Frank MacShane said he felt the detective story was an entirely appropriate form for LA because such stories "could involve an extraordinary range of humanity from the very rich to the very poor and can encompass a great many different places."

Chandler, who spent his childhood in suburban London but became the revered documenter of Los Angeles of the 1940s, felt LA was a city "rich and vigorous and full of pride ... a city lost and beaten and full of emptiness."

SAN FERNANDO VALLEY

Were it a city unto itself, the San Fernando Valley would be the fifth largest in the whole of the USA, topped only by New York, Chicago, Houston, and Los Angeles. Despite sporadic efforts to secede, the valley is not officially its own city – with the exception of holdouts Burbank and Glendale which are cities onto themselves. All the other differently designated areas are merely neighborhoods in the City of Los Angeles, and hold one-third of LA's burgeoning population.

Measuring 24 miles (39km) wide and 12 miles (19km) north to south, the staggeringly flat valley is bounded by the Ventura county line on the west, the San Gabriel mountains to the north, the Verdugo range on the east, and the Santa Monica Mountains and Hollywood Hills on the south. The west and south sides, home to cities like **Encino**, **Tarzana**, **Woodland Hills** and **West Hills**, are the more affluent, with industry concentrated farther north, around Pacoima, Sylmar, and San Fernando.

UNIVERSAL STUDIOS

West of Griffith Park, in the Cahuenga Pass, **Universal Studios ❹** (Hollywood 101; tel: 800-864 8377; www.universalstudioshollywood.com), is indeed a working movie studio, but visitors experience it entirely as a theme park. A 60-minute tram ride visits King Kong and the giant shark from *Jaws*, negotiates the perils of a flash flood, and goes past the Bates Motel from *Psycho*. Other attractions include Jurassic World: The Ride, the DreamWorks Theatre, The Wizarding World of Harry Potter, and the climactic 120mph (200kph) car chase on the Fast & Furious Supercharged set.

FROM VAN NUYS TO ENCINO

West along the Ventura Freeway, great homes and gardens dot the valley neighborhoods. Tours of the **Japanese Garden** (6100 Woodley Avenue, Van Nuys; tel: 818-756 8166; http://thejapanesegarden.com), visit three distinctly different areas: a dry *karesansui*, a wet garden, and an authentic tea ceremony garden with a tatami mat tea room.

⊘ Where

Seven miles (11km) northwest of Pasadena, off the Angeles Crest Highway exit on Interstate 210, the fragrant **Descanso Gardens** (1418 Descanso Drive, La Cañada Flintridge; tel: 818-949 4200; www.descansogardens.org; daily 9am–5pm), take several hours to explore. Splendid oak and camellia woodlands are augmented by winding trails, a lilac garden, the International Rosarium, and the Japanese Garden and Teahouse.

The elite Venice canals.

⊘ VENICE

When tobacco magnate Abbot Kinney (1850–1920) invested millions in creating his Venice from worthless marshland in the early 1900s, he lined the canals with Japanese lanterns, imported gondolas, encircled the project with a miniature railroad, and sold scores of housing lots. Visitors who paid 25 cents to take the railroad from Downtown ended a busy day on the (now-abandoned) pier watching an armored trumpeter serenade the sunset from a replica of Juan Cabrillo's medieval flagship before retiring for the night in the St Mark's Hotel, modeled after the Doge's Palace in Venice, Italy.

Kinney's ambitious plans included hiring Sarah Bernhardt and the Chicago Symphony Orchestra for his 3,500-seat auditorium, but as other entrepreneurs began to cater to less high-flown tastes, the area became known as the "Coney Island of the Pacific." Kinney managed to rename what had been Ocean Beach as Venice, but the collapse of his project was speed up by the discovery of oil (the area held 163 wells by 1931) and a shortage of fresh water. Like so many neighboring communities, Venice was forced under the aegis of Los Angeles to ensure a regular water supply. With incorporation came less tolerance. Moreover, the envisaged water circulation system proved unworkable and the canals became stagnant. Extensive renovations since have restored them.

The infamous Mickey Mouse is synonymous with Los Angeles.

Orcutt Ranch Horticultural Center (23600 Roscoe Boulevard, Canoga Park; tel: 818-346 7449; www.laparks.org) evokes a vanished moment in California history, with citrus groves bounded by ancient, majestic, and stately oaks. The Orcutts, who bought the estate in 1917, named it Rancho Sombra del Roble, "ranch in the shadow of the oak." One magnificent valley oak, 33ft (10 meters) in circumference, is thought to be at least 700 years old. The orange groves open to the public on one July weekend each year.

Near the junction of Interstates 5 and 405 in Mission Hills, the **Mission San Fernando Rey de España ⑤** (tel: 818-361 0186; www.missionscalifornia.com; daily 9am–4.30pm), California's 17th mission, was founded in 1797, and devastated by earthquakes in 1806 and 1971. Tours of its working, sleeping, and recreation areas vividly recreate day-to-day early mission life. Nearby, the **Andres Pico Adobe**, San Fernando's oldest home, was built by San Fernando Mission Indians in 1834, and now houses the **San Fernando Valley Historical Society** (www.sfvhs.com).

DISNEYLAND: THE MAGIC KINGDOM

There's nothing quite like the original **Disneyland ⑥** (1313 Harbor Boulevard, Anaheim; tel: 714-781 4000; https://disneyland.disney.go.com), which opened with the tagline "Magic Kingdom" in 1955. And there's no successful way to avoid the crowds and the lengthy line-ups, especially in summertime. If you have the scope to plan ahead and visit when there are fewer visitors, come Tuesday to Thursday during mid-September through mid-November, mid-January through mid-March, or mid-April through mid-May. Otherwise, it helps to arrive as soon as the gates open and head straight for the most popular rides, taking the park one "land" at a time.

One Disney designer, John Hench, pinpointed Walt's knack for putting "little touches of humanity" in everything he did. Hench said Mickey Mouse's appeal has something to do with his body shape – all circles, all round, harmless and non-threatening. In fact, because of a height restriction – you

can't have Mickey towering too much over his fans – most of the besuited Mouse persons in Disneyland are actually girls.

THE DISNEY LANDS

Main Street is the place to get information and maps (City Hall), hire a stroller or wheelchair, and stash your surplus items in a locker.

Fantasyland is a favorite for younger children, for Sleeping Beauty's Castle and rides like the It's A Small World cruise, the 68-horse King Arthur Carrousel, and Mad Hatter's Tea Party. Some of its other rides, though, like Peter Pan's Flight, Mr Toad's Wild Ride, and Alice in Wonderland, are aimed as much at adults. Fantasyland is also a key place for little ones to meet Disney princesses like Snow White, Aurora, Cinderella, and Mulan.

Adventureland holds the popular Indiana Jones Adventure, a ride into an ancient temple full of giant snakes and screaming mummies. The Jungle Cruise, Tarzan's Treehouse, and the Enchanted Tiki Room are tamer but still fun.

In **Critter Country**, paddle along the Rivers of America in a canoe, then cool off on Splash Mountain, a water flume ride that finishes with a five-story plunge.

Frontierland centers around the hokey Big Thunder Mountain Railroad, Mark Twain Riverboat, and the Pirate's Lair on Tom Sawyer Island. Immediately north, in **Star Wars: Galaxy's Edge**, the in-demand Rise of the Resistance incorporates multiple death-defying rides.

Pointing the way to **Tomorrowland**, Astro Orbitor allows visitors to pilot spaceships through animated constellations. Tomorrowland is also home to the thrilling Space Mountain roller coaster, a pioneer of the "dark rides" concept. Relax afterward on the Disneyland Railroad, and don't miss **New Orleans Square**, with its spooky

Haunted Mansion and the nearby Pirates of the Caribbean.

KNOTT'S BERRY FARM

Knott's Berry Farm ❼ (8039 Beach Boulevard, Buena Park; tel: 714-220 5200; www.knotts.com; hours vary), a recreated 19th-century gold town a few miles north of Disneyland, started out as a roadside snack bar operated by farmer Walter Knott and his wife Cordelia. Predating its more famous rival by a few years, it's just as interesting but a little funkier.

The Ghost Town offers panning for gold, a stagecoach ride, a watery log ride, and stunt and vaudeville shows, while more contemporary theme areas include stomach-dropping rides such as the 20-story-freefall Supreme Scream. Thrill-seekers will also enjoy GhostRider, Silver Bullet, Supreme Scream, Xcelerator, and the spinning coaster Sierra Sidewinder. There's also a water park and surf-inspired dual roller coaster, Rip Tide. Meanwhile kids love the cartoon-themed Camp Snoopy with its miniature train and other rides.

⊙ Tip

In theory you can buy tickets to visit **Disney's California Adventure Park**, which adjoins Disneyland, on the same day that you go to the original park, but trying to do that won't give you time to do signature attractions like its Spiderman and Guardians of the Galaxy rides justice.

Sleeping Beauty's Castle.

Vincent Thomas Bridge, San Pedro.

SOUTH BAY AND ORANGE COUNTY

Pristine beaches, ecological preserves, and a Surfing Walk of Fame are just a few of the coastal attractions south of Los Angeles.

Driving down the coast from Los Angeles towards San Diego may take a little longer than simply whizzing down the freeway, but the seaside route along the Pacific Coast Highway – known to all as the "PCH" – makes a much more beautiful and interesting alternative.

As you head south from the South Bay neighborhood of Palos Verdes, you get to explore a string of beach towns – Long Beach, Seal Beach, Huntington Beach, Newport Beach, Laguna Beach – before eventually hitting Del Mar. Along the way, a boat trip out to Catalina Island, and a visit to San Juan Capistrano, with its venerable mission, make delightful detours.

PALOS VERDES PENINSULA

The Palos Verdes Peninsula is home to magnificent seaside houses as well as natural attractions. Exhibits in the **Point Vicente Interpretive Center** ❶ (31501 Palos Verdes Drive West; tel: 310-544 5375; www.rpvca.gov; daily 10am–5pm), next to a lighthouse, focus on the peninsula's natural and cultural history. Look through telescopes to spot passing whales (December to spring), then pick up a leaflet identifying plants along the Botanic Trail, or picnic on the grassy grounds. Yet more nature fun can be enjoyed at **Abalone Cove** beach, west of Narcissa Drive, which is an ecological preserve perfect for diving and exploring tidepools.

Wayfarers Chapel, Rancho Palos Verdes.

Two miles (3km) farther on, the wood-and-glass **Wayfarers Chapel** (5755 Palos Verdes Drive; tel: 310-377 1650; www.wayfarerschapel.org; daily 9am–5pm), was designed by Frank Lloyd Wright's son, Lloyd, and inspired by Northern California's majestic redwood trees. In its peaceful gardens, songbirds warble and a fountain and stream gurgle. Services are held in the chapel every Sunday.

SAN PEDRO

Eastward along the coast is **San Pedro**, headquarters of Southern California's

Main attractions
Queen Mary
Aquarium of the Pacific
Santa Catalina Island
Laguna Beach
San Juan Capistrano
    Mission

Map on page 270

fishing fleet. All the authentic old parts of what was once a genuine fishing port are long gone, replaced in the 1960s by the ersatz New England fishing village **Ports O' Call** (torn down in 2018). Multimillion-dollar redevelopment plans include a 42-acre shopping and entertainment complex and a 6,200-seat amphitheater.

A few miles south, **Cabrillo Beach** ➋ is a great place to windsurf; beginners favor the sheltered waters inside the harbor breakwater. Visitors also relish the nearby **Cabrillo Marine Aquarium** (3720 Stephen M. White Drive; tel: 310-548 7562; www.cabrillomarineaquarium.org; Tue–Fri noon–5pm, Sat and Sun 10am–5pm) and elevated coastal trail. Palos Verdes Drive segues into 25th Street, from which a left turn on Gaffey and up to State Highway 47 over the **Vincent Thomas Bridge** takes you straight ahead through Long Beach on Ocean Boulevard.

Out in the bay, take a close look at the palm-fringed island topped by tall towers that are illuminated at night. This is in fact one of four man-made islands that were created by a consortium of oil companies, to hold (and conceal) the working oil derricks that tap one of the richest offshore fields in the United States.

LONG BEACH

The most famous attraction in the town of **Long Beach** is the wonderful, historic *Queen Mary* ➌ (1126 Queens Highway; tel: 562-499 1739; https://queenmary.com), a retired ocean liner that was launched in 1936 and crossed the Atlantic Ocean 1,001 times. Tours explore its beautifully restored Art Deco halls, restaurants, and lounges.

On the Rainbow Harbor across the water, the top-quality **Aquarium of the Pacific** ➍ (100 Aquarium Way; tel: 562-590 3100; www.aquariumofpacific.org; daily 9am–6pm) houses more than 500 ocean species, from mesmerizing jellyfish to leopard sharks and barracuda.

SANTA CATALINA ISLAND

A temperate outcrop 26 miles (42km) offshore, scenic **Santa Catalina Island** ➎ is home to rugged canyons and 54

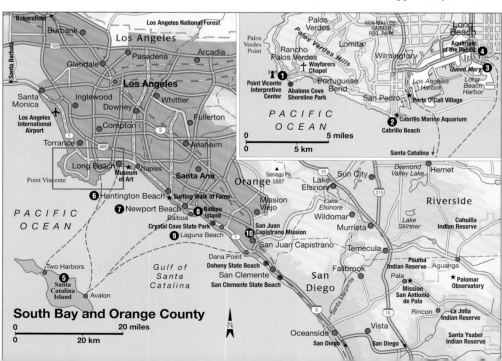

South Bay and Orange County

miles (87km) of coastline, and makes a quiet weekend excursion, or day trip if time is short.

Start by taking the *Catalina Express* (tel: 800-613 1212; www.catalinaexpress.com), which takes an hour to zip across to the island from Long Beach; ferries also depart from San Pedro, Newport Beach, and Dana Point. The five-minute walk from the dock into the charming capital of **Avalon** passes rental outlets for bicycles or golf carts, which are the island's main personal transportation.

The Art Deco ballroom of the landmark **Casino on Avalon Bay**, at the far end of the harbour, achieved national fame in the 1930s, when the likes of Count Basie and Kay Kyser would play broadcast shows for up to 6,000 dancers at a time. Unveiled in 1929 as the first movie theatre built especially for the new talking pictures, complete with a pipe organ, the ground-floor theater still screens films nightly.

Book water and island tours on the **Pleasure Pier**. A 45-minute trip in a glass-bottomed boat traverses shallow waters where multicolored fish – mostly olive or blue, with the occasional orange garibaldi – dart in and out of a seaweed "garden." Fronds of kelp sway to the motion of the glass-bottomed boat, while at night the little fish are replaced by nocturnal creatures, including "wimpy" lobsters that lack the formidable claws of their Maine cousins.

Inland motor tours stop at **El Rancho Escondido**, an Arabian horse ranch, before following an old stagecoach route to ancient sites and secluded bays. The best parts of Catalina are these wilderness areas, popular with campers and walkers. You may even spot a couple of bison, descendants of a herd brought over for the filming of Zane Gray's *The Vanishing American* in 1925. Obtain permits for day hiking and mountain biking from the Catalina Island Conservancy (www.catalinaconservancy.org).

HUNTINGTON BEACH

You may have to slow down in busy **Huntington Beach** ❻ to avoid surfers

The Queen Mary is moored in Long Beach.

⊙ SANTA CATALINA ISLAND

When "discovered" by Portuguese navigator Don Juan Rodríguez Cabrillo in 1542, and claimed for Spain 60 years later, Catalina Island had already been inhabited by Native Americans for thousands of years. However, sadly within two centuries, the Native Americans had been all but eliminated by Russian hunters trawling the area in search of sea-otter pelts.

Descendants of General Phineas Banning, who operated the earliest legendary stagecoach routes across the West, once owned most of Santa Catalina Island and began the process of turning it into a tourist resort, building the luxury Hotel St Catherine at Descanso Beach. Chewing-gum tycoon William Wrigley continued this development when he acquired the island after the great fire of 1915. He built the Casino, the Hotel Atwater (now reopened following centenary renovations), and a mansion on Mount Ada. The Wrigley family still owns about 11 percent of the island, having donated the remainder to the non-profit Island Conservancy.

Since the Conservancy took over, much of the damage caused by logging has been repaired. Fauna such as bald eagle, wild boar, and the endemic Catalina gray fox have been protected and their numbers expanded.

carrying their boards across the road to white-sand beaches fronting great waves. North and south of the 1,800ft (540-meter) **Huntington Pier** is the three-mile (5km) **Huntington City Beach**, which has lifeguards, changing rooms, concessions, and parking. To the north, the **Bolsa Chica State Beach** is less crowded, while bird-lovers in the salt marshes of the **Bolsa Chica Ecological Reserve** opposite may spot such species as great blue herons.

Many communities around here stake claims to the title of "Surf City," but Huntington Beach may have the best case. It hosts the professional US Open surf competition each July, while the **Surfing Walk of Fame** lines Main Street at the Pacific Coast Highway, and the **International Surfing Museum** (411 Olive Avenue; tel: 714-465 4350; www.huntingtonbeachsurfingmuseum.org displays classic boards and memorabilia.

NEWPORT BEACH

The mission at San Juan Capistrano.

In chic **Newport Beach ➐**, the Balboa peninsula's six miles (10km) of sandy shore enclose Newport Harbor. From **Balboa Pier**, you see kite flyers, frisbee-throwers, body-surfers, and sunbathers.

On Main Street, it's hard to miss the 1906 **Balboa Pavilion**, built as a railroad terminal, with its superfluous steeple. Behind it, fishing boats unload their catch in early morning. Alongside, ferries make the three-minute crossing to **Balboa Island ➑**, where you can gawk at million-dollar cottages then shop and relax in cafés.

South of Newport, **Corona del Mar** has gorgeous beaches. En route to Laguna Beach, Crystal Cove State Park is a spot for beachgoers, tide pooling, hiking, and mountain biking.

LAGUNA BEACH AND DANA POINT

Ten miles south of Newport Beach, **Laguna Beach ➒** is a beautiful coastal community, with a creative streak. In the early 1900s, the California Plein Air art movement, advocating painting outdoors, began here, as celebrated in the Laguna Art Museum (307 Cliff Drive;

☉ SAN JUAN CAPISTRANO SWALLOWS

Legend has it that the famous cliff swallows first came to San Juan Capistrano Mission after a shopkeeper destroyed their gourd-shaped mud nests. They traditionally arrived on or around March 19th, St Joseph's day, to be greeted with a festival. "Scout swallows" tip off their return, arriving a few days before the rest of the flock. Come autumn, they would leave the mission around the Day of San Juan, October 23rd, flying 6,000 miles (10,000km) south to winter in Argentina.

The swallows became truly famous after Leon Rene recorded "When the Swallows Come Back to Capistrano" in 1940. The hit song was also recorded by Glenn Miller, Elvis Presley, and Pat Boone.

While an innkeeper may have driven the swallows here, they likely stayed because of the mission's location near two rivers, which provided plenty of insects for them to feast on. These days many of the swallows have relocated farther from town, as development has reduced the insect population.

Town and mission still celebrate their return each year with a festival and Swallows Day Parade (www.swallowsparade.com), and the city prohibits destroying their nests, both in the church ruins and elsewhere in the Capistrano Valley.

tel: 949-494 8971; www.lagunaartmuseum.org; Thu–Tue 11am–5pm).

Before turning inland, the harbor at **Dana Point** is worth a stop to browse in the shops. Then it's off on Del Obispo Street to Camino Capistrano to visit a historic mission.

SAN JUAN CAPISTRANO

The so-called "Jewel of the Missions," **San Juan Capistrano Mission** ⑩ (26801 Ortega Highway; tel: 949-234 1300; www.missionsjc.com; daily 9am–5pm) was founded by Father Junípero Serra in 1776, the seventh of the chain of 21 missions that were set up by the Franciscan order in California. Serra's statue stands beside the ruins of the Great Stone Church, to the right as you enter. Behind it, what's now known as Serra's Chapel, constructed in 1782, is the oldest still-in-use church in California.

In the far left corner of the mission, tanning vats, metal furnaces, and tallow ovens can still be inspected. Archaeologists based in the field office here still uncover old relics from time to time. The lovely gardens were added during the last century, but the main courtyard was always the mission's central focus. It also used to serve as the site of rodeos; eager spectators would watch from the surrounding roofs, including that of the west wing, which now houses the museum.

SAN CLEMENTE TO RINCON SPRINGS

Just north of the controversial San Onofre Nuclear Generating Station (which permanently closed down in 2013), in the town of **San Clemente**, San Clemente state beach allows camping for a small fee. Former US president Richard Nixon operated his "Western White House" from San Clemente; to learn more about his life and times, head 40 miles (65km) north to the Nixon Presidential Library and Museum (18001 Yorba Linda Boulevard; tel: 714-983 9120; www.nixonfoundation.org; daily 10am–5pm), in

Yorba Linda.. Farther south, an interesting drive follows State Highway 76 inland from near Oceanside to the village of **Pala**, notable for the Mission San Antonio de Pala, an *asistencia* (extension mission) built in 1816. Located on the Pala Indian Reservation, it's the only California mission still serving Native Americans and has celebrated its Corpus Christi Festival, with an open-air mass, dances, and games, on the first Sunday of every June since 1816.

The road continues southeast to **Rincon Springs**, north of Escondido on Road S6, which is the gateway to **Palomar Mountain**. Rising 5,500ft (1,700 meters) above sea level and stretching for 20 miles (32km), this is the home of the Hale Telescope and the Oschin Telescope, contained inside **Palomar Observatory** (tel: 760-742 2119; www. astro.caltech.edu/palomar; self-guided tours daily 9am–3pm, until 4pm in summer). Check current conditions before you set out, as the observatory is closed during bad weather.

Off State Highway 76, you can catch Interstate 15 south toward San Diego.

⊙ Tip

Each March, the Dana Point Festival of Whales (http://festivalofwhales.com) celebrates the migrating gray whales. The town of Dana Point puts on a great show, complete with concerts, a weekend street fair, educational hands-on activities, and giant whale-shaped balloons. The biggest attraction, in every sense, is the sheer quantity of whale-watching tours available, in all sorts of vessels.

The Pacific Ocean off Corona de Mar.

The Botanical Building, Balboa Park.

SAN DIEGO

Sunny and relaxed, San Diego attracts families, surfers, and culture-hounds with its beautiful beaches, world-class zoo, museum-filled Balboa Park, and trendy Gaslamp Quarter.

Basking in its 77 miles (124km) of beautiful Pacific coastline, the busy, elegant harbor town of San Diego has to be considered the birthplace of California. Although the bay itself was claimed for Spain as early as 1542, two more centuries were to pass before four separate parties of Spanish settlers arrived from Mexico in 1769. One group established the Presidio in May, just above the pueblo that formed the nucleus of the historic Old Town, while Franciscan friars led by Father Junípero Serra founded California's first mission in July. San Diego's population today exceeds 1.4 million, making it the second largest city in the state, ranked only behind Los Angeles.

San Diego is a vibrantly modern and evolving place, with a growing roster of cultural attractions in the 1200-acre (490-hectare) Balboa Park and a revitalized Gaslamp Quarter with a hip shopping and nightlife scene. Active travelers love the city for its surfing, diving, and hang-gliding opportunities, while families come to explore SeaWorld, nearby Legoland, and the world-class San Diego Zoo.

OLD TOWN

The six-block **Old Town** area (bounded by Juan, Twiggs, Congress, and Wallace streets) is where San Diego's original pueblo once stood.

Now you'll find old adobes, restored Victorian homes, open-air stands, museums and galleries, and charming patio restaurants that offer fine dining. Mariachi groups entertain in the Bazaar del Mundo, a Spanish-style plaza flanked by craft shops and Mexican restaurants.

Of special historical interest are the **Thomas Whaley House Museum** (2476 San Diego Avenue; tel: 619-273 5824; www.whaleyhousesandiego.com; daily 10am–4.30pm) – allegedly one of America's most haunted houses – and

Main attractions
Old Town
SeaWorld
Balboa Park
Timken Museum of Art
San Diego Zoo
Hotel del Coronado
La Jolla
Legoland

Maps on pages 276, 278

Sailing is a popular pastime.

the Robinson-Rose house, which now serves as the **Old Town State Historic Park Visitor Center** (4002 Wallace Street; tel: 619-220 5422; www.parks. ca.gov). Stop in to pick up detailed maps.

PRESIDIO HILL

Up the hill from Old Town's historic center, **Presidio Hill** and its sprawling park make an historic oasis in a sea of traffic (Interstates 5 and 8 are just to the west and north). Here, Father Junípero Serra conducted a mass on July 16, 1769, dedicating first the **Mission Basilica San Diego de Alcalá** and then the military settlement that surrounded it. After its original structures were burned during an uprising by the local Kumeyaay in 1775, the mission moved to its present site in Mission Valley (10818 San Diego Mission Road; tel: 619-283 7319; www.missionsandiego.org; daily 9am–4pm), where you can view original records in Father Serra's handwriting.

Take the curving road east of the Old Town to see, on the hillside, the elegant **Junípero Serra Museum** (2727 Presidio Drive; tel: 619-232 6203; www.

sandiegohistory.org), which displays documents of early California life. Although it looks like a mission, it was actually built in 1929.

MISSION BAY AND SEAWORLD

The **Mission Bay area** combines parkland, beaches and inner lagoons with extensive outdoor leisure activities. One of the world's largest marine parks, **SeaWorld ⑧** (500 SeaWorld Drive; tel: 619-222 4SEA; https://seaworld.com/san-diego; daily), is filled with aquariums, live-animal shows, and rides. Its most famous inhabitants are the orca whales; you can experience the natural behavior of these powerful predators up close. Other attractions include bottlenose dolphins, sharks, polar bears, and 300 penguins. On a hot day the Shipwreck Rapids ride will cool you off.

Ocean Beach lies south of the channel leading into Mission Bay. To the north, locals shop and dine in **Pacific Beach**, where activities center around Crystal Pier and the area along Mission Boulevard and up Garnet Avenue. There are wonderful beaches along

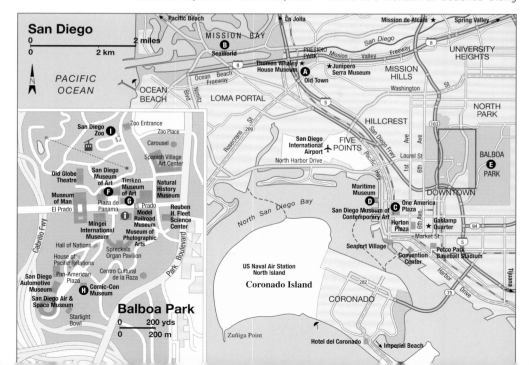

most of this coast – 25 miles (40km) of them form an unbroken line between Del Mar and Oceanside.

DOWNTOWN SAN DIEGO

Toward the top end of the vast bay discovered by Cabrillo is downtown San Diego. A complex adjoining the former Santa Fe railroad station now holds the 34-story **One America Plaza tower** and the downtown branch of the **San Diego Museum of Contemporary Art ⓒ** (1001 Kettner Boulevard; tel: 858-454 3541; www.mcasd.org; Thu–Sun 11am–5pm), displaying world-class modern art, with rotating exhibitions and interesting programs.

Along the Embarcadero just north, historic vessels at the large **Maritime Museum ⓓ** (1492 North Harbor Drive; https://sdmaritime.org; daily 10am–5pm), include the 1863 *Star of India*, one of the last steel-hulled merchant sailing ships still afloat. The USS Midway, moored at Navy Pier in 2003, now serves as the **USS Midway Museum** (tel: 619-544 9600; www.midway.org; daily 10am–5pm).

The harbor centers around the carefully landscaped **Seaport Village**, with its cafés and live entertainment. The **Convention Center** alongside faces the **Gaslamp Quarter**, where the brick-paved sidewalks are flanked by restored Victorian buildings serving as galleries, trendy boutiques, and cafés. A hub for nightlife and shopping, and a magnet for artists and young entrepreneurs, this refurbished section has also become the breeding ground of a flourishing theater movement.

BALBOA PARK

At the northeast edge of town, the 1,400-acre (570-hectare) **Balboa Park ⓔ** (www.balboapark.org) is the nation's largest urban cultural park. Many people enjoy simply strolling or picnicking here – note, though, that it's no place to venture after dark. Several museums are housed here in Moorish- and Spanish-style buildings, many dating back to international expositions staged here in 1915 and 1935. Other attractions include a science center, an arts center, several theaters, and the city's famous zoo.

Reconnaissance radar propeler aircraft on the USS Midway CV-41 Aircraft Carrier.

The Gaslamp Quarter extends from Broadway to Harbor Drive, and from 4th to 6th Avenue.

To learn about space and aviation history, visit the **San Diego Air and Space Museum** (2001 Pan American Plaza; tel: 619-234 8291; www.sandiegoairandspace.org; daily 10am–4.30pm), which houses artifacts and aircraft, including the actual Apollo 9 command module, and a replica of *The Spirit of St Louis* in which Charles Lindbergh crossed the Atlantic.

The **San Diego Museum of Art ⓕ** (1450 El Prado; tel: 619-232 7931; www.sdmart.org; Mon, Tue and Thu–Sat 10am–5pm, Sun noon–5pm) is the region's largest and oldest art museum. In addition to 19th- and 20th-century American art, the collection features treasures of European and Asian art and growing collections of contemporary and Latin American work.

Just next door, the white marble **Timken Museum of Art ⓖ** (1500 El Prado; tel: 619-239 5548; www.timkenmuseum.org; Tue–Sat 10am–4.30pm, Sun noon–4.30pm) exhibits works by such European masters as Rembrandt, Rubens, and Pieter Bruegel the Elder, as well as American paintings and Russian icons.

Other museums of note include the anthropology-focused **Museum of Us** (1350 El Prado; tel: 619-239 2001; https://museumofus.org; daily 10am–5pm), formerly the Museum of Man; the **Natural History Museum** (1788 El Prado; tel: 619-232 3821; www.sdnhm.org; daily 10am–5pm); and the **Comic-Con Museum ⓗ** (2131 Pan American Plaza; www.comic-con.org; Wed–Sat 10am–6pm, Sun 11am–7pm), unveiled in 2022, which celebrates the role of comics in popular culture.

SAN DIEGO ZOO

Giant pandas, Bornean sun bears, jaguars, California condors, and the largest colony of koalas outside Australia can all be found on the western side of Balboa Park in the huge and acclaimed **San Diego Zoo ❶** (tel: 619-234 3153; http://zoo.sandiegozoo.org; daily 9am–5pm). With the aim of replicating natural conditions, the zoo eschews cages in favor of moats wherever possible. Admission includes the Children's Zoo and a ride on Skyfari, an aerial tramway overlooking uncaged elephants, lions, tigers, giraffes, and bears in their canyon habitats.

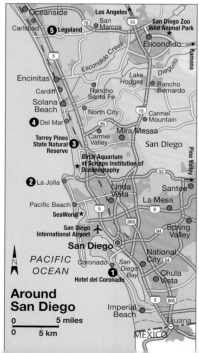

TIJUANA, MEXICO

Rancho Tía Juana (Aunt Jane's Ranch) became an international border town in the 1840s, following the Mexican–American War. Today, it can claim to be the "most crossed border in the world."

By the early 1900s, Tijuana was enticing countless North Americans with its diverse marketplaces, live bullfights, horse races, thermal baths, and other unique attractions. These days, Tijuana is fun, but can be dangerous, and visitors come as much for the nightclubs and duty-free bargains on jewelry, pottery, perfume, and fine art as they do for historic sites.

Crossing to and from San Diego into Baja California is relatively easy, but time-consuming. Be sure that you have valid passports, proper health coverage, and, if you're driving, Mexican auto insurance. As you drive into Tijuana or cross the footbridge, you'll soon enter the tourist zone of Tijuana. While there are tourist information offices at the border the main Tourist Assistance Office is in the **Viva Tijuana Shopping Center**, located on Calle Vía de la Juventud.

Avenida Revolución is lined with bars, nightclubs, crafts stores, and clothing and jewelry shops mixed up along with the traditional ponchos and leather sandals. Behind the Plaza Revolución, eclectic subjects in the **Wax Museum** (daily 10am–6pm), range from Laurel & Hardy to Michael Jackson, and the Pope to Cortés and an Aztec priest holding the bloody heart of a prostrate victim.

A few blocks down Revolución, past the former **Jai Alai Fronton** (an open-walled playing area for the Basque sport of Jai Alai), turn left on 10th Street to head towards the river. The **Plaza Río Tijuana** mall here is the largest shopping center in northwestern Mexico.

The main street continues south, seguing onto the Boulevard Agua Caliente and running past the city's old **bullring**, its finest hotels, Caliente Hipódromo, and the Sports Arena where concerts and most big events take place.

The famous old **Caliente Hipódromo** still has its marble floors, ornate decoration, mirrored elevators, and a lobby filled with sculptured cowboys, caged birds, and an incongruous pair of playful anteaters, but retains little of the glamor that once caused it to be regarded as the American Monte Carlo. In the days when the track's regular clientele included Charlie Chaplin, Jean Harlow, and heavyweight champion Jack Dempsey, fortunes were won and lost at dice, blackjack, and roulette.

Head eastward along 10th Street, watching out for the giant globe (indicating a "world of culture") housing the concert hall and the 85ft (26-meter)-high **Omnitheater**. Adjoining is the ultra-modern **Tijuana Cultural Center**, whose historical survey embraces Olmec stone heads, Aztec charts showing the god of the hour, a meticulous model of the 16th-century Aztec capital, Tenochtitlan, plus skilfully embroidered Indian costumes.

On the Pacific Coast, 13 miles (22km) southwest of central Tijuana, the lovely beaches of **Rosarito** have provided the backdrop for movies like *Titanic*, *Pearl Harbor*, and *Pirates of the Caribbean*. If you visit, you'll soon understand why. As a resort area, it's a popular retirement getaway for Americans, but thanks to the drinking age being 18 in Mexico. it doubles as a party place for the younger set. Keep your wits about you when you're out and about.

The Millennial Arch.

CORONADO

Set on a peninsula, with stately Victorian homes scattered among its cottages and condos, **Coronado** is the wealthiest of the communities along the lower end of San Diego Bay. It's best known for the superlative 1888 **Hotel del Coronado** ❶, where a dozen presidents have stayed since Thomas Edison personally installed the electric lighting. Britain's future Edward VIII met his wife, the notorious Mrs Simpson, here – she lived in a still-extant bungalow on the grounds – while Charles Lindbergh was honored both before and after his first trans-Atlantic flight, and author L. Frank Baum used it as an inspiration for *The Wizard of Oz*. Such milestones are memorialized in the **Museum of History and Art** (1100 Orange Avenue; tel: 619-435 7242; https://coronadohistory.org; daily 10am–4pm).

LA JOLLA, TORREY PINES, AND DEL MAR

Wealthy, charming **La Jolla** ❷ is home to the San Diego campus of the University of California, the highly regarded **Salk Institute**, the cliff-top **Birch Aquarium at Scripps** (2300 Expedition Way; tel: 858-534 3474; www.aquarium.ucsd.edu; daily 9am–5pm), and the iconic **San Diego Museum of Contemporary Art** (700 Prospect Street; tel: 854-454 3541; www.mcasd.org; Thu–Sun 10am–4pm).

The San Diego-La Jolla Underwater Park Ecological Reserve is a popular destination for kayaking, diving, swimming, and snorkeling; snorkelers should head for the **La Jolla Caves**.

Just beyond the northern outskirts of La Jolla, stop off to walk through the groves of twisted trees at **Torrey Pines State Reserve** ❸ (www.parks.ca.gov), and watch daredevil hang-gliders soar from 300ft (90-meter) cliffs. Immediately past the reserve, **Del Mar** ❹ offers a sweeping hillside view of the Pacific. The **Del Mar National Horse Show** (https://delmarnational.com) takes place each spring, while the **San Diego County Fair** (https://sdfair.com) follows in June and July. The summer season begins a week after the end of the fair, and runs well into September. **Legoland** ❺ is another 15 miles (24km) north.

Historic Hotel del Coronado.

Sailboats at sunset.

The Golden Gate at night.

WEST COAST USA

TRAVEL TIPS

TRANSPORTATION

GETTING THERE

By air

Seattle-Tacoma International Airport (SEA)

Tel: 206-787 5388 or 1-800-544 1965; www.portseattle.org/sea-tac.

Located 13 miles (21km) south of downtown, Seattle's airport is connected with the city in 45 minutes via Link Light Rail (tel: 1-888-889 6368; www.soundtransit.org), which departs frequently from a station in the parking garage, and costs $3. Premier Airport Shuttle offers a shared door-to-door service (tel: 206-244 0011 or 1-800-962 3579; https://premierairport-shuttle.com), starting at $20 to downtown, while a taxi ride downtown will cost around $40.

Portland International Airport (PDX)

Tel: 503-460 4234 or 1-877-739 4636; www.flypdx.com.

Portland's airport is 12 miles (19km) northeast of downtown. It's a 40-minute ride to or from the city on the Red Line of the Tri-Met MAX light rail system (https://trimet.org), which departs every 15min from the south end of the ticket lobby on the airport's main level, and costs $2.50. Cabs charge around $40 for the trip downtown. Visit Groome Transportation (https://groometrans-portation.com/portland-airport) for information on airport shuttle service.

San Francisco International Airport (SFO)

Tel: 650-821 8211 or 1-800-435 9736; www.flysfo.com.

The airport is 14 miles (23km) south of downtown San Francisco, near San Mateo. Bay Area Rapid Transit (BART; www.bart.gov) connects the Garage G/BART Station at SFO, via Metro rail, to San Francisco, for $9.65 each way. SamTrans (tel: 800-660 4287; www.samtrans.com) operates a 24-hour bus service to San Mateo County and parts of the city, while Caltrain Commuter Rail (www.caltrain.com) runs trains between San Francisco and San Jose on weekdays (connect via BART's Millbrae station). Taxis to downtown San Francisco cost around $50. Airport Express (tel: 415-775 5121; www.airportexpresssf.com) run shared-ride shuttles into town, costing from $17.

Oakland International Airport (OAK)

Tel: 510-563 3300; www.oaklandair-port.com.

Much smaller and less crowded than SFO, Oakland Airport is well served by public transportation, with its own BART station across from Terminal 1. AC Transit (www.actransit.org) run buses to Oakland downtown and other local destinations, and private shuttles are also available.

Los Angeles International Airport (LAX)

Tel: 310-646 5252; www.flylax.com.

LAX, close to the ocean 14 miles (22km) southwest of downtown, is California's busiest airport. A free, frequent shuttle bus "C" links it with Metro's Green Line Light Rail (Metropolitan Transportation Authority; www.metro.net), for onward connections throughout the city. The LAX FlyAway bus service provides frequent nonstop transportation to Van Nuys Bus Terminal and Union Station downtown. Door-to-door shuttle vans and taxis ($40–50 to the city center) are also available.

San Diego International Airport (SAN)

Tel: 619-400 2404; www.san.org.

San Diego's airport is 3 miles (5km) northwest of downtown. Taxis charge from $20, while bus route 992, operated by the Metropolitan Transit System (www.sdmts.com), connects both terminals with downtown destinations including the Amtrak station.

By rail

Amtrak

Tel: 1-800-872 7245; www.amtrak.com

Amtrak, the major rail passenger carrier in the US, is more useful as a way to reach the West Coast than to explore once you're there. Four cross-country routes connect the region with the rest of the nation. The Empire Builder runs parallel to the Canadian border from Chicago via Minneapolis to Spokane, where passengers can choose to continue to either Seattle or Portland. The California Zephyr heads from Chicago to San Francisco via Denver, Salt Lake City, and Sacramento. The Southwest Chief links Chicago with Los Angeles via Albuquerque and Flagstaff, while the Sunset Limited runs a more southerly route between New Orleans and Los Angeles, stopping at Houston, San Antonio, and Tucson.

The most useful north–south route on the West Coast is the Coast

⊘ Airlines

Major airlines that fly into the US West Coast include:
Air Canada, www.aircanada.com
Air France, www.airfrance.com
American Airlines, www.aa.com
British Airways, www.britishairways.com
Delta Airlines, www.delta.com
jetBlue, www.jetblue.com
KLM, www.klm.com
Qantas Airways, www.qantas.com
Southwest, www.southwest.com
United, www.united.com
Virgin Atlantic, www.virginatlantic.com

Starlight, which takes 35 hours to run all the way from Los Angeles to Seattle. Despite the name, its only major coastal stretch comes in southern California, between Santa Barbara and Pismo Beach. North from there, it continues to Oakland, then heads via Sacramento and Redding to Eugene, Salem, and Portland in Oregon, and Olympia, Tacoma, and Seattle in Washington and across the Oregon border.

By bus

Greyhound Lines

Tel: 800-231 2222; www.greyhound.com

The national bus line, Greyhound Lines, as well as a number of smaller charter companies, offer daily service to major towns and cities throughout the West Coast region, with connections to the rest of the country. Routes and schedules are subject to change; check all arrangements with local stations, in advance. Seattle, Portland, San Francisco, Los Angeles, San Diego, and other large towns all have municipal bus systems.

By road

When it comes to exploring the West Coast, three north–south roads invariably prove crucial. Your basic choice lies between sticking close to the ocean, in which case you'll enjoy a gloriously scenic ride but risk making slower progress than your schedule allows, or racing along the I-5 interstate highway inland, which can whisk you from Seattle to Portland and all the way to Los Angeles, without ever coming within 50 miles (80km) of the Pacific.

If it's the sea you've come to see, reckon on spending as much time as you can on US 101 in Washington, Oregon, and the northernmost part of California, and on California State Highway 1, which hugs the coast from 200 miles (320km) north of San Francisco all the way south of Los Angeles.

GETTING AROUND

Public transportation

Seattle

Metro buses run throughout Seattle (tel: 206-553 3000; www.metro.king-county.gov; Mon–Fri from 5–5.30am until midnight–1am, Sat and Sun 6–6.30am until 11am–midnight; some late-night services; fares $2.75–3.25). Link Light Rail operate a north–south route that passes through downtown and continues to Sea-Tac airport (tel: 1-888-889 6368; www.soundtransit.org; Mon–Sat 5am–1am, Sun 6am–midnight, every 6–15min; fares $2.25–3.25). ORCA cards, valid on buses, trains and ferries, cost $5, and can be loaded with additional funds (www.orcacard.com).

In addition, Seattle's famous 1.3-mile (2km) monorail route connects the Westlake Center mall, 400 Pine St, with the Seattle Center (tel: 206-905 2600; www.seattlemonorail.com; hours vary: summer Mon–Fri 7.30am–11pm, Sat and Sun 8.30am–11pm, every 10min; $3).

Portland

Portland's public transit is coordinated by MAX (tel: 503-238 7433; https://trimet.org; 1 trip $2.50, all-day pass $5). Buses radiate through the city from a downtown transit mall on 5th and 6th avenues, while four colour-coded light rail lines channel riders around central downtown and Old Town, and out to the suburbs. The Portland Streetcar runs three routes through the city centre, covering both sides of the river (tel: 503-222 4200; https://portlandstreetcar.org).

San Francisco

San Francisco's excellent Muni network of buses, street cars, and historic cable cars make getting around a snap (tel: 415-701 2311; www.sfmta.com; 6am–late, with some night service; 1 trip $2.50, all-day pass $5). The "owl" – late-night service – runs every 30 minutes from midnight–5am.

The modern and efficient Bay Area Rapid Transit subway system (BART; tel: 415-989 2278; www.bart.gov; Mon–Fri 4am–midnight, Sat 6am–midnight and Sun 8am–midnight) connects San Francisco with the East Bay via a tunnel under the bay. It serves 45 stations in three counties, from San Francisco to Millbrae and throughout the East Bay.

Oakland and Berkeley are serviced by East Bay Transit (tel: 510-891 4777, www.actransit.org), while Caltrain (tel: 1-800-660 4287; www.caltrain.com) runs passengers from a terminal at Fourth and King streets in San Francisco to San Jose, with several stops along the peninsula.

For visitors, the city's commuter ferries, traveling to Angel Island and throughout the North and East Bay areas, make a great scenic alternative to driving:

Blue and Gold Fleet, Pier 41 Marina Terminal, The Embarcadero at Beach St; tel: 415-705 8200; www.blueandgoldfleet.com.

Golden Gate Ferry, Ferry Building, The Embarcadero at Market St; tel: 415-455 2000; www.goldengateferry.com.

Los Angeles

LA's main public transportation provider, known as the Metro or MTA, runs both a comprehensive bus system and a newer Metro and light rail system (tel: 323-466 3876; www.mta.net; $1.75, day pass $7). The Red Line operates between Downtown, North Hollywood, and Universal City; the Purple line overlaps part of it. The Blue Line operates between Downtown and Long Beach. The Green Line runs all the way to Redondo Beach, crossing the Blue Line just north of Compton. The Gold

Taking off from LAX airport.

Line, travels between Downtown and Pasadena, and the Expo Line goes out to Culver City.

A handy tool for public transportation in California is NextBus (www.nextbus.com). Also available as a mobile phone application, it provides real-time arrival information so you can find out whether your bus is coming in 5 minutes or 35.

San Diego

San Diego's Metropolitan Transit System (tel: 619-233 3004; www.sdmts.com), offers bus and trolley routes throughout the San Diego area, from Old Town to Mission Beach and Mission Valley. One-way bus tickets are $2.25, trolley tickets are $2.50; an all-day pass for either is $5. The system also provides access to neighbouring towns including Coronado, Del Mar, Escondido, Oceanside, Borrego Springs, and Tecate.

Private transportation

Driver's license and insurance

Drivers are required to carry a valid license at all times. Visitors from English-speaking countries are allowed to use their full domestic licenses; it's not necessarily sufficient, however, to carry an International Driving Permit (IDP).

Be sure to also have a certificate proving you have liability insurance with you at all times. It is illegal to drive without these items, and you're required to show them to any law enforcement officers who stop your car.

Historic cable cars on California Street.

Laws for safety

Belts and child seats: State laws in California, Oregon and Washington require that every passenger wear a seat belt. Youth or infant seats are required for babies and small children under 60lbs or 6 years of age.

Cell phones: It is illegal to talk on a cell phone while driving unless you are able to listen and talk hands-free.

Emergency vehicles: When a fire truck, ambulance, or police vehicle approaches from either direction with flashing lights and/or a siren, you must immediately pull over to the side of the road.

Helmets: All motorcycle riders are required to wear helmets.

Hitchhiking: Hitchhiking is illegal on all highways and Interstates and on many secondary roads as well. Because traffic is sparse in some regions, it can also be quite difficult. Everywhere in the United States, hitchhiking can be dangerous and unpredictable, and is not recommended. If you do decide to hitch, it is best to do it from an exit ramp (if legal) or a highway rest stop, rather than on the road itself. To find the safest situations, check ride services and bulletin boards for posted rideshares.

Roadside assistance: The Highway Patrol cruises the highways, not just monitoring speed limits but also looking for drivers in trouble. If you have any emergency that won't allow you to continue the trip, signal your distress by raising the hood. Motorists are often advised that it is safest to stay in

the car with the doors locked until a patrol car stops to help.

Motoring advisories

If you plan to drive any significant distance, it's a good idea to join the American Automobile Association (tel: 1-800-222 4357; www.aaa.com). In addition to emergency road service, AAA offers maps, guidebooks, and insurance. There are reciprocal arrangements with many international AAA organizations, such as those in Great Britain, Germany, and Australia.

Parking

Parking lots and garages are scattered through all major cities. In addition, metered parking is also available, with specific spots dedicated to two-hour, four-hour and longer stays. As a general rule, meters do not need to be fed on Sundays or major holidays. It's always possible to pay with a credit card, and usually with a mobile phone app too, though the fact that each city tends to use its own app makes that inconvenient for travellers. Often but not always, it is possible to pay in cash.

When you're looking for a parking space, note the color of the curb, which corresponds to the following limitations:

No color: No specific limitations; follow guidelines on nearby signs or meters.

White: You may stop only long enough to pick up or drop off passengers.

Green: You may park for a limited time; look for a sign nearby with the time limit, or a time limit painted on the curb.

Yellow: Stop no longer than the time posted to load or unload passengers or freight; drivers of non-commercial vehicles usually must stay in the car.

Red: No stopping or parking.

Blue: Parking is permitted only for a disabled person who displays a special placard or license plate.

Rules of the road

Those roads that are restricted to one-way traffic only are identified by a black and white sign with an arrow pointing in the permitted direction of travel. At an intersection with a four-way red stop sign, motorists must completely stop and then proceed across the intersection following the order in which they arrived at the stop. If you arrive at the same time, the person to the right has the right of way, but usually one person just waves on another.

In California, Oregon, and Washington, it is legal to make a right turn on a red light after making a full stop, unless signs indicate otherwise.

Speed limits for roads and highways are posted on white signs to the right, as are all other road signs. Unless otherwise indicated, the speed limit is 65mph (105kmh) on freeways, 55mph (88kmh) on two-lane highways, 25mph (40kmh) near schools and in residential or business districts.

Watch for white signs warning that you will be in a different "Speed Zone Ahead." Be prepared to slow to the lower speed you will soon see posted on upcoming white signs. Some very small towns are notorious for catching and fining drivers who have not slowed down quickly enough from the highway speed to the (much lower) in-town speed limit.

Taxis

Taxis are an easy, though expensive, way to get about major cities. They hover around popular tourist or nightlife spots, but in out-of-the-way locations it's best to call a radio-dispatched taxi. Your fare will be displayed on the meter and will

Los Angeles' dizzying intersections.

⊘ Renting a car

National car-rental companies are located at all airports and large towns. To secure the best rates, it's always advisable to book your car rental in advance; if you're flying in with a major airline, check to see whether they offer discounted car rental. You must be at least 21 years old to rent a car (often 25) in the US, and you must have a valid driver's license that you have held for at least a year already, along with a major credit card to guarantee your booking. Foreign travelers should always expect to have to show a license from their home country; an international driver's license will not be enough. Standard rental vehicles have automatic transmissions; expect to pay extra if you require a manual (stick-shift) car. Be sure to take out collision and liability insurance, which may not always be included in the base price of the rental. If you're embarking on any sort of road trip, be sure your rental rate includes unlimited mileage: given the vast area of the West Coast, any extra mileage costs will add up quickly. And consider waiting to rent a vehicle until a day or two after any long international flight.

Alamo: Tel: 1-844-354 6962; www.alamo.com

Avis: Tel: 1-800-633 3469; www.avis.com

Budget: Tel: 1-800-218 7992; www.budget.com

Dollar: Tel: 1-800-800 5252; www.dollar.com

Enterprise: Tel: 1-855-266 9565; www.enterprise.com

Hertz: Tel: 1-800-654 3131; www.hertz.com

National: Tel: 1-844-382 6875; www.nationalcar.com

Thrifty: Tel: 1-800-847 4389; www.thrifty.com

include a flag-drop charge plus a per-mile and/or a per-hour charge. Fares follow standard rules by city. A 10 percent tip, rounding up to the next dollar, is standard.

Seattle

After an initial "drop charge" of $2.60, taxis in Seattle charge $2.70 per mile, or 50¢ per minute of waiting time when the vehicle is stationary. Local companies include Yellow Cab (tel: 206-622 6500) and Seattle Town Car (tel: 206-369 9199).

Portland

To the minimum charge of $3.50, Portland cabs add $2.90 per miles plus 66¢ per minute of waiting, and there's an additional $3.50 airport charge. Taxi companies include Flat Cab (tel: 503-970 0033) and PDX Yellow Cab (tel: 503-841 6328).

San Francisco

Standard charges are $3.50 for the first one-fifth mile or flag, 55¢ each additional one-fifth mile or fraction thereof, 55¢ each minute of waiting or traffic time delay, plus a $5.50 airport surcharge.

Eco-Taxi: Tel: 415-970 1300

Green Cab: Tel: 415-626 4733

Lucky Cab: Tel: 415-681 6888

Yellow Cab: Tel: 415-333 3333

For a full list of San Francisco taxi firms, see www.sfmta.com. All cabs authorized by the city (look for the metal "license plate" on the dashboard, and the driver's ID, visible from the back seat) are obligated to let passengers pay by credit card, though some drivers may complain that their machine is "broken" as they prefer cash, to avoid paying a surcharge to the credit card companies.

Los Angeles

Look for the Official City of Los Angeles Taxicab Seal before boarding – this means the taxi driver is insured, well trained, and authorized by the city to operate. Fare is $2.85 for the first one-ninth mile or flag, 30¢ for each additional one-ninth mile ($2.70 per mile), and 30¢ for each 37 seconds waiting ($29.19 per hour). There's also a $4 airport surcharge.

San Diego

Standard charges are $2.80 for the first one-sixth mile, $3 for each additional mile, and $24 per hour of waiting time.

Taxi alternatives – mobile app ride request companies

Driving companies that can be accessed through apps often work out less expensive that taxis. These mobile app companies are extremely popular, reliable, and easy to use. Prospective customers need to be set up their own personal account using a credit card, and download the app to a smart phone in order to request service. Most offer ride-share possibilities that further cut down on transportation costs.

Among the best-known companies are:

Uber: www.uber.com
Lyft: www.lyft.com
Flywheel: www.flywheel.com

Driving in the wilderness

A word of caution for anyone driving in remote areas: the single most important precaution you can take is to tell someone your destination, route, and expected time of arrival. Check your tires carefully before you set out, and make sure you're carrying plenty of water, for passengers as well as for vehicles. Ideally, you should have at least 1 gallon (4 liters) per person. Keep an eye on the gas gauge; it's a good idea to have more than you think you need. Follow the latest weather forecasts, and ask about the road ahead when you can, at visitor centers and information offices. Winter storms in the mountains can close major roads, and at times chains are required for tires. Remember, if you should have car trouble or become lost, do not strike out on foot. A car, visible from the air and presumably on a road, is easier to spot than a person on their own, and it affords shelter from the weather. Just be patient and wait to be found.

Traveling to Mexico

All US citizens – including children – are required to present a valid passport or passport card for travel into Mexico, and so too are all other nationalities (along with their Green Card, if they have one, for re-entry to the US.)

US citizens do not require a visa or a tourist card for tourist stays of 72 hours or less within the 12–19-mile (20–30km) "border zone." US citizens traveling as tourists beyond this zone, or entering Mexico by air, must pay a fee to obtain a tourist card, also known as an FMM, available from Mexican consulates, Mexican border crossing points, Mexican tourism offices, airports within the border zone, and most airlines serving Mexico. Proof of nationality must accompany the visa.

Mexican law requires that any non-Mexican citizen under the age of 18 departing Mexico must carry notarized written permission from any parent or guardian not traveling with the child to or from Mexico. This permission must include the name of the parent, the name of the child, the name of anyone traveling with the child, and the notarized signature(s) of the absent parent(s).

US insurance is not valid in Mexico and it is definitely a wise move to obtain short-term insurance, obtainable at innumerable sales offices just north of the border.

Crossing the border into Tijuana, Mexico, at busy San Ysidro, 18 miles (29km) south of downtown San Diego, is easy. Most visitors do not take their cars – if you really want to take a rental vehicle into Mexico, check with your rental company in advance – and simply park in San Ysidro and cross into Tijuana via the elevated pedestrian walkway. There's an all-day secure lot off the "Last Exit US parking" ramp – turn right at the stop sign to the Tijuana side. Cheap taxis and buses are also available.

The return to California can be a bit tenser than the entry into Mexico, as US Border Patrol officers take far more interest in who's coming into the country (hence those passports and Green Cards). Waiting several hours to cross back into the US is not uncommon.

Traveling to Canada

Crossing into Canada from Washington is straightforward. All foreign nationals must carry valid passports. US citizens do not need a visa or an eTA (Electronic Travel Authorization). Note other visa-exempt foreign nationals require an eTA, which can be obtained online and costs CA$7. For full details, visit www.canada.ca.

A

Accessible Travel

US legislation requires public buildings and most public transportation be made accessible to travelers with disabilities. There are also some special concessions: all Greyhound buses offer priority seating to disabled persons (tel: 1-800-752 4841), while many are equipped with wheelchair lifts, and the railway system, Amtrak, offers discounted tickets and accessible rooms. For more information, visit www.greyhound. com or www.amtrak.com.

In theory, major car-rental companies offer automobiles with hand controls at no extra cost, but that's on their full-size – most expensive – vehicles.

Accommodation

The Western United States offers the complete spectrum of accommodation, from elegant European-style hotels to inexpensive motels that can be rented by the week.

Both Seattle and Portland offer imposing and impressive hotels in their historic central districts, while in San Francisco, the most expensive hotels are generally located in Nob Hill, the Financial District, and Union Square. These grand hotels are particularly well suited to the international traveler, and many are attractive landmarks in their own right. In Los Angeles, the most expensive are situated Downtown and in Beverly Hills, with the best access to shopping and public transportation.

Everywhere you go, you'll also find a large number of smaller hotels and hotel chains, which usually offer all of the essential comforts without the high prices of the grand hotels. The West Coast is also well endowed with cheap hostels and campgrounds.

Admission charges

Most large museums charge entrance fees, which these days tend to range from $10 to $25. Smaller art galleries tend to be free. Special exhibitions usually cost extra, but many museums have free general admission on certain days each month or once a week in the evenings. Such free days are always indicated on the museum's website. Some attractions, like LA's Getty Center, are always free. Plays, concerts, and sporting events are often expensive, as are theme park tickets. You can sometimes get free tickets to live TV shows, especially sit-coms, if you call in advance.

Age restrictions

In Washington, Oregon, and California, the legal age to consume alcohol and marijuana is 21. The legal age for driving is 16 in Washington and California, 17 in Oregon.

B

Budgeting for your trip

If you're looking for a hotel room with an acceptable minimum level of comfort, cleanliness, and facilities, a reasonable starting point for the price of a double room is $85 in budget-class hotels; upping your budget to at least $150 will make a significant difference in quality. For between $150 and $300 a whole range of hotels opens up, from bland but functional business traveler places to hip little boutique hotels. Beyond this, and certainly beyond $350, you're moving into deluxe territory; though you don't really arrive at "discreet hideaway for celebrities" status until $700 and above.

Food costs range from $3 to $10 for a perfectly acceptable hot dog, burrito or Asian delicacy, to $50 for a two- or three-course meal at a cute contemporary-cuisine type restaurant. Expect to pay $100-plus at a fine restaurant. A glass of house wine is usually under $10, a beer around $6.

Getting around by public transportation can cost as little as $3–5 a day. Bus or train tickets typically cost around $2.50, but in most cities you can get an all-day pass for around $5. Car rental costs $40 or more per day. A taxi to or from the airport can cost $50 in the larger cities, like San Francisco and Los Angeles.

C

Children

From the Space Needle in the north to Disneyland and the San Diego Zoo in the south, the West Coast is a great place to bring kids, and a popular destination for family vacations. Playgrounds are plentiful, and children pay a reduced fee for admission to museums, other attractions, and on public transportation.

Children's menus are common (some restaurants even provide crayons), although young children rarely make an appearance at fancy restaurants.

Childcare is not usually offered by hotels, but reputable baby-sitting services can be recommended by hotel concierges. It's best to call in advance to arrange this.

Climate

When to visit

Washington and Oregon: A mild, humid climate predominates in the western area of both states, west of the Cascade mountains, with moisture-laden clouds moving in from the Pacific to bring considerable rainfall.

In Seattle, the average maximum temperature in July is 72°F (21°C), while the average low in January is 36°F (2°C). The average annual rainfall of 38in (96cm) is not that high really, but it comes in a constant drizzle, and visitors can anticipate some fog, mist or at minimum, cloud. Portland and the Willamette Valley receive much the same rainfall, but tend to be somewhat warmer, with daily high temperatures in July reaching 81°F (27°C), dropping to 57°F (14°C) at night, while the equivalent averages for January, the coldest month, are 46°F (8°C) in the day, and 37°F (3°C) at night. Both Seattle and Portland get around 80 percent of their annual rainfall between October and April, but even when the climate is at its best, between June and September, it's a good idea to come expecting rain.

While average temperatures on the coastal side of Washington's Olympic Peninsula are similar to those in Seattle, the area receives as much as 160in (406cm) of precipitation annually, making it the wettest spot in the 48 contiguous US states. The contrast is not so great in Oregon, but Gold Beach on the coast, for example, gets an average of 81in (205cm) of rain per year, while inland Grants Pass receives only 31in (78cm).

Pike Place Market, Seattle.

Typical October through April weather conditions in the valley were described by the Washington Post's Joel Garreau as a "difficult-to-define balance that is moister than mist but drier than drizzle." Unappealing as that may sound, locals are quick to point out that the Willamette Valley's 40in (101cm) average yearly rainfall does not appreciably exceed that of Miami. The average January low is 32°F (0°C); the average July high, 82°F (27°C).

Northern California: San Francisco's climate is typical of the Northern California coast. Daytime temperatures average in the mid-50s Fahrenheit (12–14° C) and drop as much as 10°F (6°C) at night. Average temperatures are significantly higher in the South Bay and inland valleys. Summers tend to be warm and dry. Winters are generally rainy; temperatures rarely go below freezing along the coast. Note that San Francisco can be chilly and foggy in summer, even though the sun might be shining across the bridge in the Bay Area. The ideal time to visit the city itself is in the fall, when the weather is often perfect.

Southern California: This is one of the few places in the world where you can ski in the morning and surf in the afternoon. It is not uncommon for the temperature to vary by 30–40°F (17–22°C) as you travel from mountains to deserts to the beach. The change of seasons is not all that dramatic. The winters are mild, with a rainy season that lasts from January through March. In summer, the humidity is usually low, so discomfort is rare. LA's famous smog is at its worst in August and September.

Crime and safety

Much like urban centers anywhere, the major cities have dangerous neighborhoods. Common sense is an effective safeguard. Do not walk alone at night. Keep a careful eye on belongings. Lock valuable possessions in a safe. Never leave your car unlocked. Never leave children by themselves.

When driving, never pick up anyone you don't know. Always be wary of who is around you. If you have trouble on the road, stay in the car and lock the doors, turn on your hazard lights and leave the hood up in order to increase visibility and alert police cars.

Hotels usually warn that they do not guarantee the safety of belongings left in the rooms. If you have any valuables, you may want to lock them in the hotel safe.

Customs regulations

Whether or not you're carrying anything to declare, all travelers entering the country must fill out a US Customs form (usually provided on the airplane) and go through US Customs. This can be a time-consuming process, but, in order to speed things up, be prepared to open your luggage for inspection and try to keep the following restrictions in mind:

There is no limit to the amount of money you can bring with you. If the amount exceeds $10,000, however, you must fill out a report.

Anything you have for your own personal use may be brought in duty- and tax-free.

Adults are allowed to bring in one quart (1 liter) of alcohol for personal

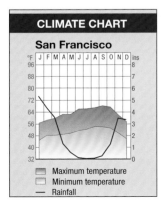

CLIMATE CHART

San Francisco

- Maximum temperature
- Minimum temperature
- Rainfall

The Georgian Hotel, Santa Monica has welcomed many a celebrity.

use; 100 cigars or 4.4lbs of tobacco or 200 cigarettes; and $100 worth of gifts.

Agricultural items – including fruits, plants, and vegetables – may not be brought into the US.

Dogs, cats, and other animals may be brought into the country with certain restrictions. For details, contact the US consulate nearest you or the US Department of Agriculture.

Automobiles may be driven into the US if they are for the personal use of the visitor, family, and guests.

For a full list of prohibited or restricted items, see: www.cbp.gov/travel/international-visitors.

US Customs & Border Protection, 1300 Pennsylvania Avenue NW; Washington, DC 20229; tel: 1-877-227 5511; www.cbp.gov.

E

Eating out

The West Coast is a food-lover's delight, and has the statistics to prove it. San Francisco alone has more than 3,000 restaurants and bars, said to be more per capita than anywhere else in the nation.

There is an endless variety of cuisines to try, from classic American and "California Cuisine," to all manner of ethnic food. From Europe you'll find Italian trattorias, French bistros, German beer halls, and Mediterranean eateries with hookah lounges. As for Asian foods, Washington and California alike offer the opportunity to sample curries from India, Vietnamese pho, Korean BBQ, sushi, and dim sum, plus Americanized fusion fare

from several regions. From Central America, California in particular has whole-heartedly adopted Mexican favorites such as burritos, quesadillas, and tacos al pastor, especially in San Diego and in San Francisco's Mission District. South America is represented as well, from Brazilian steakhouses to Peruvian restaurants serving savory lomo saltado and fresh ceviche. And don't forget the extraordinary array of ultra-fresh seafood that's available in the Northwest especially. In short, the region offers some of the most wonderfully diverse menus in the world. Of course, the drink menu has the best local wines in the country, too.

Electricity

The standard electric current in the United States is 110 volts, and outlets are generally for flat-blade, two-prong plugs. Foreign appliances usually require a converter and an adaptor plug. Many hotel bathrooms have plugs for electric shavers that work on either current.

Embassies and consulates

Australia: 575 Market St, San Francisco. Tel: 415-644 3620; http://usa.embassy.gov.au
Also: 2029 Century Park E, Suite 3150, Los Angeles. Tel: 310-229 2300
Canada: 580 California St, 14th Floor, San Francisco. Tel: 415-834 3180; http://international.gc.ca
Also: 550 S. Hope St, Los Angeles. Tel: 213-346 2700
Also: 1501 4th Ave, Seattle. Tel: 206-443 1777
Great Britain: 1 Sansome St, Suite 850, San Francisco. Tel: 415-617 1300; www.gov.uk

Also: 2029 Century Park East, Suite 1350, Los Angeles. Tel: 310-789 0031
Ireland: 1 Post St, San Francisco. Tel: 415-392 4214; www.dfa.ie
Also: 6380 Wilshire Blvd, Suite 1205, Los Angeles. Tel: 310-424 5538
Also: 7511 210th St SW, Seattle. Tel: 425-582 2688
New Zealand: 2425 Olympic Blvd, Suite 600E, Santa Monica (Los Angeles). Tel: 310-566 6555; www.mfat.govt.nz
South Africa: 6300 Wilshire Blvd, Suite 600, Los Angeles. Tel: 323-651 0902; www.dirco.gov.za

Emergency

In the case of an emergency, dial 911 from any telephone for the police, fire department, or ambulance service.

Etiquette

People usually address each other in friendly, rather than formal, terms. Mr. and Ms. are used in business and formal settings if the person is a superior. Mrs. is rarely heard or used. When meeting someone, a handshake is expected. Occasionally, the European kiss on the cheeks is seen, but the "air kiss," as it is often called, is not common. If you are invited to someone's home, a bottle of wine, a box of candy, or a small personal token is thoughtful. Flowers are less popular. Discussing politics can lead to nasty arguments. It's best to avoid the topic, although you may be asked how things are viewed in your country. Gender etiquette can be a minefield. The best advice is to treat everyone with the same level of respect that you want for yourself.

F

Festivals and events

Here are just a few of the most popular festivals and events up and down the West Coast.

January

Tournament of Roses Parade and Rose Bowl Football Game, Pasadena, CA
Tel: 626-449 4100
www.tournamentofroses.com

Kick off New Year's Day alongside 100,000 happy spectators at this massive, float-filled parade in Pasadena.

February

AT&T Pebble Beach National Pro-Am Golf Tournament, Pebble Beach, CA
www.attpbgolf.com

First hosted in 1937 by Bing Crosby in Santa Fe, the high-profile Pro-Am is now held in scenic Pebble Beach, where celebrities and professional golfers team up on the links to raise money for hundreds of non-profits.

Chinese New Year Fireworks, parades with dancing dragons, and Miss Chinatown pageants mark the start of the Chinese New Year. Especially large celebrations are held in Seattle, Portland, San Francisco, Los Angeles, and San Diego.

Clam Chowder Cook-Off, Santa Cruz, CA
Tel: 831-423-5590
http://beachboardwalk.com/Clam-Chowder-Cook-Off

A fundraiser for the City of Santa Cruz Parks and Recreation Department, this 30-year-old cook-off event draws individuals and restaurants – who whip up their best Boston- and Manhattan-style chowders – plus the public who gets to taste them!

Oregon Shakespeare Festival, Ashland, OR
Tel: 541-482 4331
www.osfashland.org

Running from late February until October, Ashland's celebrated festival honors the Bard with as many as seven plays being staged at any one time, both indoors and outside.

March

Academy Awards, Los Angeles, CA
www.oscars.com

"And the Oscar goes to..." Before the rest of the country watches the Oscars on television, those in Los Angeles can brave the crowds and see the stars walk the red carpet live.

Return of the Swallows, San Juan Capistrano, CA
www.swallowsparade.com

Celebrate the mid-March return of the swallows to San Juan Capistrano on St Joseph's Day (March 19) with the Fiesta de las Golondrinas and Swallows' Day Parade, the country's biggest non-motorized parade.

Saint Patrick's Day Don something green and drink to the luck of the Irish on March 17th. Parades and celebrations are held in all major cities, including Seattle, Portland, San Francisco, Los Angeles, and San Diego.

April

Cherry Blossom Festival, San Francisco, CA
Tel: 415-563 2313
www.sfcherryblossom.org

A 55-year Japantown tradition, the Cherry Blossom Festival is a celebration of Japanese heritage and traditions – including martial arts, music, and dance – that draws 200,000 people each year.

Doo Dah Parade, Pasadena, CA
Tel: 626-590 1134
www.pasadenadoodahparade.info

In the mood for a crazy frolic? This outrageous parade is full of off-beat floats and eccentric performers.

San Francisco International Film Festival, San Francisco, CA
Tel: 415-561 5000
https://sffilm.org

The country's longest-running film festival showcases around 200 films from all over the world.

May

Cinco de Mayo With music and margaritas, Seattle, Portland, Los Angeles, San Diego, Santa Barbara, and San Francisco all commemorate Mexico's May 5, 1863, victory over the French.

Kinetic Grand Championship, Arcata to Ferndale, Humboldt County, CA
Tel: 707-786 3443
www.kineticgrandchampionship.com

Transportation meets art at this three-day race; participants ride human-powered sculptures over a 38-mile (61km) course.

Bay to Breakers, San Francisco, CA
https://capstoneraces.com

This long-running footrace sees thousands of costume-clad runners converge in San Francisco for an entertaining 12km dash from Ferry Building to Ocean Beach.

June

Ojai Music Festival, Ojai, CA
Tel: 805-646 2094
www.ojaifestival.org

Drawing an eclectic group of performers, this music celebration features everything from bluegrass and rockabilly to classical.

Hollywood Bowl Jazz Festival, Los Angeles, CA
Tel: 323-850-2000
www.hollywoodbowl.com

At the Hollywood Bowl, this long-time jazz fest, formerly known as the Playboy Jazz Festival, now features both classic styles (New Orleans, swing, bebop) and jazz-rock fusions, over two days.

San Francisco Pride, San Francisco, CA
Tel: 415-864 0831
www.sfpride.org

An annual highlight ever since 1970, this huge LGBTQ celebration includes a two-day festival culminating with a Sunday morning parade.

Oregon Bach Festival, Eugene, OR
http://oregonbachfestival.org

Classical music concerts and performances in a wide-ranging program that's by no means exclusively devoted to Bach.

July

Comic-Con International, San Diego, CA
www.comic-con.org

The largest comic book and popular culture convention in the world.

Fourth of July Fireworks explode throughout the country, celebrating America's Independence Day.

Gilroy Garlic Festival, Gilroy, CA
Tel: 408-842 1625.
www.gilroygarlicfestival.com

Everything from traditional garlic fries to the more innovative garlic ice cream can be tasted at this celebration of Gilroy's major industry.

Pageant of the Masters, Laguna Beach, CA
Tel: 1-800-487 3378
www.foapom.com

This long-standing festival wows audience with its tableaux vivants ("living pictures") – incredibly faithful live depictions of classical and contemporary artworks, complete with intricate sets.

California State Fair, Sacramento, CA
Tel: 916-263 3000
www.castatefair.com

This 18-day state fair features competitions in livestock, wine and beer, and cheese; dozens of rides, and tons of food, music, and live entertainment.

August

Nisei Week, Little Tokyo, Los Angeles, CA
Tel: 213-687 7193
www.niseiweek.org

One of the country's oldest Japanese-American festivals, Nisei Week includes a karate tournament, gyoza-eating competition, parade, and numerous other sport competitions.

Washington State International Kite Festival, Long Beach, WA
tel: 360-642 4020
https://kitefestival.com
This gloriously windswept and colourful celebration features kites from all over the world, some battling in fierce one-on-one competition, others participating in breathtaking mass ascensions.

Seafair Weekend Festival, Seattle, WA
Tel: 206-728 0123
www.seafair.org
Part air show, with displays by the US Navy's Blue Angels, part boat race, with the world's fastest racing boats in competition, this annual extravaganza sees the Seattle waterfront come alive.

Old Spanish Days Fiesta, Santa Barbara, CA
Tel: 805-962 8101
www.oldspanishdays-fiesta.org
Take your pick from folk dancing, a market, a carnival, a rodeo, and a parade.

September

Monterey Jazz Festival, Monterey, CA
Tel: 831-373 3366
www.montereyjazzfestival.org
Co-founded by Jimmy Lyons and Ralph J. Gleason in 1958, this is the world's longest-running jazz festival. Among other renowned performers, it has presented Louis Armstrong, Billie Holiday, Dave Brubeck, Miles Davis, Diana Krall, Wynton Marsalis, and Terence Blanchard.

Forever Twilight, Forks, WA
tel: 360-374 2531
https://forkswa.com
Devotees of Stephenie Meyer's Twilight vampire saga descend on their fictional setting for four days of fan events and frolicking.

Sausalito Art Festival, Sausalito, CA
www.sausalitoartfestival.org
Over 250 artists converge in Sausalito on Labor Day weekend, showcasing everything from ceramics and sculpture to photography, watercolor, glass, and mixed media.

October

Art and Pumpkin Festival, Half Moon Bay, CA

Tel: 650-726 9652
www.miramarevents.com
At the World Pumpkin Capital you'll find gigantic pumpkins, a Haunted House, harvest-inspired crafts, pie-eating and costume contests, an enormous jack-o-lantern, and pumpkin ale.

California Avocado Festival, Carpinteria, CA
Tel: 805-684 0038
www.avofest.com
Described as "three days of peace, love, and guacamole," this eco-friendly festival features music, recipe contests, and the world's largest vat of guacamole.

Fleet Week, San Diego and San Francisco, CA
www.fleetweeksandiego.org;
https://fleetweeksf.org
Contests, air shows, and ship tours are held in honor of the US military.

Hardly Strictly Bluegrass Festival, San Francisco, CA
www.hardlystrictlybluegrass.com
Conceived and patronized by late philanthropist Warren Hellman in 2001, this free, annual music festival held every first weekend of October in Golden Gate Park draws crowds in the hundreds of thousands.

November

Dia de los Muertos Festival, Los Angeles, CA
Tel: 323-469 1181
www.ladayofthedead.com
The Mexican Day of the Dead is celebrated with processions, masks, face-painting, and other rituals that pay homage to the dearly departed.

December

Parade of Lights, southern CA
http://sdparadeoflights.org
Beautifully illuminated boats parade through Southern California harbors, including Newport Beach and San Diego; contact local tourist bureaus for information.

H

Health and medical care

There is nothing cheap about being sick in the United States. It is essential to have adequate medical insurance and to carry an identification card or policy number at all times.

In the event that you need medical assistance, consult the local Yellow Pages for the physician or pharmacist nearest you. In large cities, there is usually a physician referral service number listed. If you need immediate attention, go to a hospital emergency room.

Some medicines that are available over the counter in your home country may require a prescription in the US. Walgreens drugstores (pharmacies) have 24-hour locations in major cities.

Hospitals

Large hospitals with 24-hour emergency services on the West Coast include the following:

Seattle, WA
Harborview Medical Center, 325 9th Avenue; tel: 206-744 3074; www.uwmedicine.org.
UW Medical Center, 1550 115th Street North; tel: 206-668 0500; www.uwmedicine.org.

Portland, OR
Providence Portland Medical Center, 4805 Glisan Street Northeast; tel: 503-215 6079; www.providence.org.

San Francisco, CA
California Pacific Medical Center, with buildings at 3700 California Street, 3898 California Street, 2333 Buchanan Street, and at Castro and Duboce streets; tel: 415-600 6000; www.sutterhealth.org.
Saint Francis Memorial Hospital, 900 Hyde Street (Downtown); tel: 415-353 6000; www.dignityhealth.org.
UCSF Medical Center, 505 Parnassus Avenue (Richmond); tel: 415-353 1037; www.ucsfhealth.org.
Zuckerberg San Francisco General Hospital, 1001 Potrero Avenue; tel: 628-206 8000; https://zuckerbergsanfranciscogeneral.org.

Los Angeles, CA
California Hospital Medical Center, 1401 South Grand Avenue (Downtown); tel: 213-748 2411; www.dignityhealth.org.
Cedars-Sinai Medical Center, 8700 Beverly Boulevard (Beverly Hills); tel: 310-423 3277; www.cedars-sinai.org.
LAC+USC Medical Center, 2051 Marengo Street; tel: 323-409 1000; https://dhs.lacounty.gov.
Saint John's Health Center, 2121 Santa Monica Boulevard (Santa

Monica); tel: 310-829 5511; www. providence.org.

UCLA Medical Center, 757 Westwood Plaza; tel: 310-825 2111; www.uclahealth.org.

Internet

Pretty much every coffee house in the US gives customers free wi-fi access, though it's becoming rarer for them to provide computers for public use. Many local and state visitor centers also have free wi-fi, but although it would be very rare to find a hotel that didn't offer wi-fi access in its guestrooms and common areas, it's not always free. Most public libraries have free terminals, while FedEx Office, a national chain with locations in every state (www. fedexoffice.com), rents out space on terminals, scanners, and printers by the minute or by the hour.

LGBTQ+ travelers

San Francisco is one of the most welcoming places in the world for gay men and lesbians. The best sources for up-to-date information on new clubs, shows, films, events, and gay news are the free newspapers, notably the Bay Times and the Bay Area Reporter (BAR; www.ebar.

The go-to publication for entertainment listings.

com) found in cafés or street-corner boxes. The online newspaper Bay Guardian (www.sfbg.com) and SF Weekly (www.sfweekly.com), also have useful listings and information.

The Center, a vital nexus for the LGBTQ+ community at 1800 Market Street, has numerous flyers and listings for events. The Women's Building, www.womensbuilding.org, houses various non-profit organizations and you'll find newspapers, bulletin board postings, and information here too.

In Los Angeles, West Hollywood (www.visitwesthollywood.com) contains Southern California's largest homosexual population, and sponsors LA's annual Gay Pride Parade. Also check out the ONE National Gay & Lesbian Archives (909 West Adams Boulevard; https://one.usc. edu), the world's largest research library on lesbian, gay, bisexual, and transgender issues.

Seattle too is a welcoming city for LGBTQ+ residents and visitors. Its best source for local information is the weekly Seattle Gay News (www. sgn.org).

Portland ranks second only to San Francisco in the nation, in terms of the percentage of its residents who identify as LGBTQ+, but the city has no specifically gay neighbourhood. The local tourism authority maintains good listings of LGBTQ+ events and resources (www.travelportland.com).

Lost luggage

File claims for damaged or missing luggage with the relevant

airline, before leaving the airport. For queries and complaints, contact the Office of Aviation Consumer Protection (tel: 202-366 2220; www. transportation.gov/airconsumer).

Maps

State and local visitor centers throughout the region are invaluable sources of free maps, while commercial maps are of course widely available. Insight Flexi Map: San Francisco and Insight Flexi Map: Los Angeles are laminated, easy-to-fold maps that combine detailed cartography with pictures and essential information. As you explore San Francisco, bear in mind that Muni bus shelters often display detailed maps of the city, including a close-up map of Downtown.

Media

Television & radio

Television and radio are invaluable sources of up-to-the-minute information about weather, road conditions, and current events. Television and radio listings are published in local newspapers. Sunday editions usually carry a detailed weekly guide to events and activities.

Newspapers, magazines, and websites

In San Francisco, the major daily newspaper is the San Francisco Chronicle (www.sfchronicle.com), while websites such as www.7x7. com and www.sanfranmag.com keep up to date with events and activities.

The Los Angeles Times (www. latimes.com) is among the most widely read papers in the country, and its Sunday "Calendar" section is an excellent source of entertainment information.

The Seattle Times (www.seattletimes.com) plays much the same role in Seattle, with a Sunday edition that incorporates the glossy and informative Pacific NW magazine.

First published in 1850, Portland's Oregonian (www.oregonlive.com) has the largest circulation of any Oregon newspaper.

Some of the free local weekly newspapers, available in cafés and newspaper boxes on the street, are excellent sources of up-to-the-minute information on what's going on in a particular town. Check out the Stranger in Seattle (www.thestranger.com); LA Weekly in Los Angeles (www.laweekly.com); SF Weekly (www.sfweekly.com), East Bay Express (https://eastbayex-press.com), and San Francisco Bay Guardian (www.sfbg.com) in the San Francisco area; and the bi-weekly Portland Mercury (www.portlandmer-cury.com).

Money

Cash: Most banks belong to a network of ATMs (automatic teller machines) which dispense cash 24 hours a day.

Credit cards: Not all credit cards are accepted everywhere, but most places accept either Visa, American Express, or MasterCard. Major credit cards can also be used to withdraw cash from ATMs; look for those that use one of the banking networks indicated on the back of your credit card, such as Plus, Cirrus, or Interlink. Most likely there will be a charge, but at least you can avoid high interest charges by paying money into your account before you set off on a road trip.

Traveler's Checks: With the popularity of ATMs, credit cards, and debit cards, traveler's checks are becoming increasingly rare. Still, banks, stores, restaurants, and hotels generally accept US dollar-denominated traveler's checks. If yours are in foreign denominations, they must be changed to dollars. Banks readily cash large traveler's checks, although be sure to take along your passport. When lost or stolen, most traveler's checks can be replaced; record the checks' serial numbers in a separate place to facilitate refunds of lost or stolen checks.

O

Opening hours

Standard business hours are 9am–5pm weekdays. Most department stores open at 10am; many stores, especially those in shopping malls, stay open until 9pm; and major cities tend to hold a handful of 24-hour restaurants. A few supermarkets and convenience stores are also open around the clock. Bank hours usually run from 9am to 5pm, although some stay open until 6pm. Some branch offices keep Saturday morning hours. However, most banks are equipped with 24-hour ATM machines on the outside of their buildings, which you can use for simple transactions at your convenience. Be careful at night.

During public holidays, post offices, banks, government offices, and many private businesses are closed.

P

Postal services

Post offices open between 9am and usually close at 6pm, Monday–Friday. Many also open for a few hours on Saturday morning, but they're closed all day on Sunday. If you don't know where you will be staying in any particular town, you can receive mail by having it addressed to General Delivery at the main post office in that town. You must pick up General Delivery mail in person and show proper identification.

You can buy stamps in most convenience stores, although you may have to buy a book of stamps. You can also buy them at post offices.

Public holidays

National US holidays are:
New Year's Day (January 1)
Martin Luther King Jr. Day (3rd Monday in January)
Presidents' Day (3rd Monday in February)
Memorial Day (Last Monday in May)
Independence Day (July 4)
Labor Day (1st Monday in September)
Columbus Day (2nd Monday in October)
Veteran's Day (November 11)
Thanksgiving (4th Thursday in November)
Christmas Day (December 25)

R

Religious services

There is no official religion in the US. The majority of Americans identify themselves as Protestant or Catholic. Non-Christian religions (including Judaism, Islam, Buddhism, and Hinduism) collectively make up about 5 percent of the adult population.

S

Senior travelers

Senior citizens (65 and older) are entitled to many benefits, including reduced rates on public transportation and for entrance to museums. Seniors who want to be students should contact Road Scholar (tel: 1-800-454 5768, www.roadscholar.org) for information on places that provide both accommodations and classes. Its "Elderhostel" lodging options, of which there are a number in the Bay Area, have recently been rebranded under the name Exploritas.

Shopping

The cities of the West Coast are a true shoppers paradise. From exclusive boutiques on Rodeo Drive in Los Angeles to large malls in the San Fernando Valley, California in particular is ready to satisfy all tastes and suit every pocket, but all the states covered in this book have their fair share of small-town art galleries, quirky craft shops, and farmers' markets brimming with artisan food products.

Smoking

The West Coast does not extend its famed tolerance to smokers. State laws throughout the region ban smoking in almost all indoor public places and workplaces including bars, clubs, restaurants, and, outdoors, within slightly varying distances of playgrounds, sandboxes, and all public buildings. On some public beaches, too, cigarettes are illegal. You may find it difficult to reserve a smoking room in a hotel; check when you book.

Student travelers

With a current school ID, a student traveler can take advantage of discounts at some museums, in movie theaters, and on public transportation.

Check out colleges in the summer for dormitory accommodation.

T

Tax

In principle, you can expect sales tax to be added to your bill at shops and restaurants. When calculating a tip at restaurants, do so using the pre-tax total.

With each state choosing whether or not to set a sales tax, however, and each local community free to add its own surcharge, West Coast tax rates vary enormously. In California, they range 7.25 to 10.75 percent; in Washington the standard rate of 6.5 percent is only subject to small local variations; and in Oregon there's no sales tax.

In addition, separate hotel room taxes can add as much as 15.6 percent (in Seattle) or 14 percent (in both San Francisco and Los Angeles), while even in Portland they amount to 8 percent.

Telephones and faxes

Local US phone numbers are seven-digit numbers. To make a long-distance call, dial "1," then the three-digit area code of the place you're calling, and then the seven-digit local number. Make use of toll-free numbers when possible (indicated by 1-800, 855, 866, 877 or 888).

Foreign travelers hoping to use their cellphones in the US should check with their service providers; it's very likely that your phone will work, but calls may well incur substantial roaming charges. Ideally, if possible, try to use online services such as Skype (www.skype.com), Zoom, or Facetime. Alternatively, it's possible to buy pay-as-you-go phones from major electrical stores in the US, or prepaid SIM cards from the likes of https://triptel.com and www.telestial.com.

Coin-operated telephones are becoming rare, but can usually be found in hotels, gas stations, or lighted booths on street corners.

Helpful dialing information:

US calls outside your area code: Dial 1 plus area code plus local number.

International Calls: Dial 011 plus country code plus number.

Taxi cabs in the US are yellow.

Directory inquiries: Dial 411 for information assistance, which can provide telephone listings.

Operator: Dial "0" for assistance with local calls, 00 for international calls.

Time zone

Washington, Oregon and California are on Pacific Standard Time (PST), which is two hours earlier than Chicago, three hours earlier than New York and eight hours earlier than Greenwich Mean Time. During Daylight Savings time, which occurs from the second Sunday of March to the first Sunday of November, the clocks are rolled forward one hour and PST becomes only seven hours earlier than GMT.

Tipping

Just as in other parts of the country, service personnel on the West Coast rely on tips for a large part of their income. In most cases, 18–20 percent is the going rate for waiters and bartenders and 10–15 percent for taxi drivers. The accepted rate for baggage handlers at airports and hotels is around $1 per bag. The rule of thumb is to leave a minimum tip of one or two dollars per night stayed in the room for housekeeping staff. A doorman expects to be tipped at least $1 for unloading your car or for other services.

Tourist Information

California

California Tourism
555 Capitol Mall Suite 1100, Sacramento, CA 95814

Tel: 1-916-444 4429
www.visitcalifornia.com

Los Angeles Official Visitor Center
6801 Hollywood Boulevard
Tel: 323-467 6412
www.discoverlosangeles.com

San Diego Visitor Information Center
996-B North Harbor Drive, San Diego
Tel: 619-737 2999
www.sandiego.org

San Francisco Visitor Information Center
900 Market Street, San Francisco
Tel: 415-391 2000
www.sftravel.com

Oregon

Travel Oregon
Tel: 1-800-547 7842
https://traveloregon.com

Portland
Tel: 503-427 1372
www.travelportland.com

Washington

State of Washington Tourism
Tel: 1-800-544 1800
www.stateofwatourism.com

Visit Seattle
701 Pike Street, Suite 800
Tel: 206-461 5840
https://visitseattle.org

Tour operators and travel agents

Architecture Tours LA

Tel: 323-464 7868
www.architecturetoursla.com

Various Los Angeles tours, including neighborhood tours of Downtown and Hollywood, and tours devoted to specific architects such as Frank Lloyd Wright and Frank Gehry.

Clipper Vacations

Tel: 206-443 2560
www.clippervacations.com
Day-trips aboard a high-speed catamaran from Seattle to the beautiful San Juan Islands, including a stop for lunch.

Cycle Portland Bike Tours

Tel: 844-739 2453
https://portlandbicycletours.com
Cycling tours of downtown Portland and the Willamette River; longer trips include stops at two city breweries.

FOOT!

Tel: 415-793 5378
www.foottours.com
Fun, informative, San Francisco walking tours with professional comedians, who share their love and city knowledge.

Hellgate Jetboat Excursions

Tel: 541-479 7204
https://hellgate.com
Jet-boat tours of Hellgate Canyon on Oregon's Rogue River, departing from Grants Pass. Choose between a gentle 1-hour ride or a 5-hour wild water extravaganza.

Old Town Trolley Tours

Tel: 1-866-754 0966
www.trolleytours.com
Vibrant green-and-orange trolleys, driven by spirited conductors,

Downtown San Diego.

take visitors to San Diego's most popular sites, including Old Town, the San Diego Harbor Seaport Village, Petco Park, the Gaslamp Quarter, and Balboa Park.

San Francisco City Guides

Tel: 415-375 0468
www.sfcityguides.org
Eighty free architectural and history tours by trained volunteers, offered year-round. Tours cover topics from the murals of the missions to the mansions of Pacific Heights, and everything in between.

Spinreel Dune Buggy and ATV Rental

Tel: 541-759 3313
www.ridetheoregondunes.com
ATV and dune-buggy tours on the dramatic Oregon dunes, south of Florence.

Starline Tours

Tel: 323-463 3333
www.starlinetours.com
An assortment of LA sightseeing tours, from movie stars' homes to the delights of Disneyland.

Underground Tours

Tel: 206-682 4646
www.undergroundtour.com
Exciting 75-minute tours of the secret 19th-century streets that burrow beneath Seattle's Pioneer Square.

Victorian Home Walk

Tel: 415-252 9485
www.victorianhomewalk.com
Learn about San Francisco architecture and history from longtime residents, who go where the tour buses can't.

Warner Bros. Studios V.I.P. Tour

Tel: 1-818-977 8687
www.wbstudiotour.com
For two colorful hours, small groups of movie lovers can ride through this famous Burbank lot, visiting such classic sets as the Walton family home and Errol Flynn's Sherwood Forest as well as sound stages and post-production labs.

Wok Wiz Walking

Tel: 415-795 9303
www.wokwiz.com
An insider's view of the history, culture, and folklore of SF's Chinatown, the largest Chinatown outside of China. The daily tour can

include a seven-course dim-sum lunch. Reservations required.

U

Useful addresses

Each of the states covered in this book operates Welcome Centers in major cities, and at entry and exit points, to assist visitors and provide maps, brochures, and on-the-spot advice. For more information, go to: www.visitcalifornia.com, www.traveloregon.com, and www.stateofwa-tourism.com.

V

Visas and passports

Citizens of 35 countries – including the UK, Ireland, Australia, New Zealand and most Western European countries – are allowed to vacation in the United States for up to ninety days without visas. Instead, under the Visa Waiver Program, you must apply for ESTA (Electronic System for Travel Authorization) approval before you leave home. This is easily done, via the ESTA website (https://esta.cbp.dhs.gov), but you may have to wait for as long as 72hr before you receive your authorization number. ESTA authorization costs $14, and is valid for up to two years, unless your passport expires first. If you come from a country that's not covered by the Visa Waiver Program – check on https://travel.state.gov – contact your local US embassy or consulate to obtain a visa.

If a visitor loses their visa while in the country, a new one may be obtained from the embassy of the visitor's home country. Extensions are granted by various service centers of the Bureau of Citizenship and Immigration Services (tel: 1-800 375 5283; www.uscis.gov).

W

Weights and measures

The US uses the imperial system for measurement, Fahrenheit for temperature, and mile for distance.

FURTHER READING

GENERAL

Hollywood Babylon by Kenneth Anger. The original and still the best, this legendary and utterly scurrilous 1981 chronicle of Hollywood's greatest and goriest scandals has never been surpassed, despite repeated follow-up volumes.

The Times We Had: Life with William Randolph Hearst by Marion Davies. The mistress of one of America's richest men, Davies chronicles the glittering life she led at Hearst Castle and in Los Angeles.

The Kid Stays in the Picture by Robert Evans. A gripping insider's view of how Hollywood worked once the studio system came to an end, written with verve by a major LA player, the former head of Paramount.

The Los Angeles Watts Towers by Bud Goldstone and Arloa Paquin Goldstone. How Simon Rodia's creation came into being, plus the history of the Watts neighborhood.

Original Journals of the Lewis and Clark Expedition, 1804–1806 by Meriwether Lewis and William Clark. The first inland explorers of the Pacific Northwest filled eight volumes with notes on its flora, fauna and native inhabitants; abridged versions are available.

The California Gold Rush and the Coming of the Civil War by Leonard L. Richards. An award-winning historian reveals how the Gold Rush in California spurred contention between Northern industrialists and slave-owning Southerners.

The Mayor of Castro Street: The Life and Times of Harvey Milk by Randy Shilts. Quintessential biography of the first openly gay man elected to office in America, from his triumphant election and ground-breaking championing of gay rights, to his tragic assassination and the subsequent rioting upon the sentence of his killer.

My California: Journeys by Great Writers by Donna Ware (ed.). Several dozen great writers – including Pico Iyer, Michael Chabon, and Thomas Steinbeck – share stories to benefit the California Arts Council.

A Very Good Year: The Journey of a California Wine from Vine to Table by Mike Weiss. Award-winning journalist spent nearly two years with a Sonoma County winemaker to vividly chronicle all that goes into the process of winemaking.

FICTION

The Big Sleep by Raymond Chandler. Chandler's tales of hard-bitten private eye Philip Marlowe, and the classic movies that brought them to life, arguably did more than anything else to shape the city of LA in the popular imagination.

Snow Falling on Cedars by David Guterson. A compelling mystery novel, focussing on racial tensions in the postwar Pacific Northwest. Guterson's East of the Mountains is also recommended.

Tales of the City by Armistead Maupin. Originally serialized in the San Francisco Chronicle, Maupin's novel and its many sequels stitch together the lives of residents of the fictitious Barbary Lane, with delightful candor.

City Lights Bookstore, San Francisco.

East of Eden by John Steinbeck. A magnificent family saga, resonant with Biblical echoes, set in the Salinas Valley of a century ago.
The Day of the Locust by Nathanael West. The brooding tale of an ambitious artist on the fringes of 1930s Hollywood, West's novel lays bare the seamy underbelly of the movie industry.

GEOGRAPHY AND NATURAL HISTORY

California Wildlife Viewing Guide by Jeanne L. Clarke. Explores 150 of the state's top sites for wildlife viewing, including maps, access information, and nearly 100 color photos.
The Eternal Frontier by Tim Flannery. Oriented towards ecology as well as history, this fascinating study details the myriad ways in which the story of life in North America has been determined by the physical make-up of the continent.
Ancient Places: People and Landscape in the Emerging Northwest by Jack Nisbet. A fascinating overview of the geological and human history of Washington, Oregon and Idaho, by an eminent historian whose Sources of the River traced the journeys of pioneer fur trader David Thompson.
Birds of the Pacific Northwest by John Shewey and Tim Blount. Hundreds of beautiful photographs

of the distinctive birds of the Northwest make this compendium a delight.

GUIDES AND MANUALS

Movie Star Homes: The Famous to the Forgotten by Judy Artunian. Nearly 400 entries on homes of celebrities, from Gloria Swanson to Buster Keaton.
Stairway Walks in San Francisco by Adah Bakalinsky. A delightful guide to 27 urban hikes up and down some of the city's 350 stairways.
A Guide to Architecture in Los Angeles and Southern California by David Gebhard and Robert Winter. Considered a must-have guide to Los Angeles architecture by scholars and enthusiasts alike.
Day Hiker's Guide to California State Parks by John McKinney. Over 150 day hikes in California, from Lake Tahoe to Anza-Borrego.
Los Angeles A–Z: An Encyclopedia of City & Country by Leonard Pitt and Dale Pitt. A one-volume encyclopedia packed with information on everything from native trees and who the Black Dahlia was to Engine House No. 18 and O.J. Simpson.
Exploring the Oregon Coast Trail by Connie Soper. This enticing guide details 40 consecutive day hikes along Oregon's compelling shoreline; it may keep you coming back for years ahead.

☉ Send us your thoughts

We do our best to ensure the information in our books is as accurate and up-to-date as possible. The books are updated on a regular basis using destination experts, who painstakingly add, amend and correct as required. However, some details (such as opening times or travel pass costs) are particularly liable to change, and we are ultimately reliant on our readers to put us in the picture.

We welcome your feedback, especially your experience of using the book "on the road", and if you came across a great new attraction we missed.

We will acknowledge all contributions and offer an Insight Guide to the best messages received.

Please write to us at:
**Insight Guides
PO Box 7910
London SE1 1WE**

Or email us at:
hello@insightguides.com

Back Roads to the California Coast: Scenic Byways and Highways to the Edge of the Golden State by Earl Thollander and Herb McGrew. A guide for meandering through the state on 15 scenic back-road drives.

CREDITS

PHOTO CREDITS

iStockphoto 298T
Shutterstock 1, 4, 6ML, 6MR, 6BL,
6MR, 7TR, 7ML, 7MR, 7ML, 7BR, 7TL,
8, 9, 10BL, 10TR, 10TL, 11L, 11R,
12/13, 14/15, 16/17, 18, 19T, 19B, 20,
21, 22, 23, 24/25, 26T, 26B, 27, 28, 29,
30, 31, 32, 33, 34, 35, 36/37T, 36BR,
36BL, 37ML, 37BR, 37BL, 37TR, 38,
39, 40, 41, 42, 43, 44, 45, 46, 47, 48,
49, 50, 51, 52, 53, 54, 55, 56, 57, 58,
59, 60, 61, 62, 63, 64, 65, 66L, 66R,
67, 68, 69, 70, 71, 72R, 72L, 73, 74,
75, 76, 77, 78, 79, 80R, 80L, 81R, 81L,

82, 83, 84/85, 86/87, 88/89, 90, 91T,
91B, 94, 95, 97, 98, 99, 100, 101, 102,
103, 104, 106, 107, 108, 109, 110, 111,
113, 114, 115, 117, 118, 119, 120, 122,
123, 124, 125, 127, 128, 129, 130, 131,
132, 133, 134, 135, 136, 137, 138, 139,
140, 141T, 141B, 142, 143, 145, 146,
147, 148, 149, 152, 153, 154, 155, 156,
157, 158, 159, 160, 161, 162, 163, 165,
166, 167, 168, 169, 170, 171, 172, 173,
174, 175, 176, 177, 178, 179, 180,
181T, 181B, 182, 183, 184, 185, 187,
188, 189, 190, 191, 192, 193, 194, 195,

198, 199, 200, 201, 204, 205, 206, 207,
208, 209, 210, 211, 212, 213, 214, 215,
216, 217, 219, 221, 222, 223, 224, 225,
226, 227, 228, 229, 230, 231, 233, 234,
235, 236, 237, 238, 239T, 239B, 240,
241, 242, 243, 244, 245, 246, 247,
248/249T, 248BR, 248BL, 249ML,
249BR, 249BL, 249TR, 252, 253, 254,
255, 256, 257, 258, 259, 260, 261, 264,
265, 266, 267, 268, 269, 271, 272, 273,
274, 275, 277, 278, 279, 280, 281, 282,
284, 285, 286, 287, 288/289, 290, 291,
294, 296, 297, 298B

COVER CREDITS

Front cover: Bixby Bridge on the Pacific Coast Highway *Shutterstock*
Back cover: Rain forest in Olympic NP *Shutterstock*

Front flap: (from top) Trolley in San Francisco *Shutterstock*; Lake Crescent, Washington *Shutterstock*; Vineyard near Santa Barbara, California.

Shutterstock; San Juan Capistrano Mission *Shutterstock*
Back flap: Mount Rainier National Park *Shutterstock*

INSIGHT GUIDE CREDITS

Distribution
UK, Ireland and Europe
Apa Publications (UK) Ltd;
sales@insightguides.com
United States and Canada
Ingram Publisher Services;
ips@ingramcontent.com
Australia and New Zealand
Booktopia;
retailer@booktopia.com.au
Worldwide
Apa Publications (UK) Ltd;
sales@insightguides.com
Special Sales, Content Licensing and CoPublishing
Insight Guides can be purchased in bulk quantities at discounted prices. We can create special editions, personalised jackets and corporate imprints tailored to your needs. sales@insightguides.com www.insightguides.biz

Printed in China

All Rights Reserved
© 2023 Apa Digital AG
License edition © Apa Publications Ltd UK

First edition, 2023

Every effort has been made to provide accurate information in this publication, but changes are inevitable. The publisher cannot be responsible for any resulting loss, inconvenience or injury. We would appreciate it if readers would call our attention to any errors or outdated information. We also welcome your suggestions; please contact us at: hello@insightguides.com

www.insightguides.com

Editor: Kate Drynan
Author: Greg Ward
Picture Editor: Piotr Kala
Cartography: original cartography Carte
Layout: Greg Madejak
Picture Manager: Tom Smyth
Head of DTP and Pre-Press: Katie Bennett
Head of Publishing: Kate Drynan

Legend

City maps

	Freeway/Highway/Motorway
	Divided Highway
	Main Roads
	Minor Roads
	Pedestrian Roads
	Steps
	Footpath
	Railway
	Funicular Railway
	Cable Car
	Tunnel
	City Wall
	Important Building
	Built Up Area
	Other Land
	Transport Hub
	Park
	Pedestrian Area
	Bus Station
	Tourist Information
	Main Post Office
	Cathedral/Church
	Mosque
	Synagogue
	Statue/Monument
	Beach
	Airport

Regional maps

	Freeway/Highway/Motorway (with junction)
	Freeway/Highway/Motorway (under construction)
	Divided Highway
	Main Road
	Secondary Road
	Minor Road
	Track
	Footpath
	International Boundary
	State/Province Boundary
	National Park/Reserve
	Marine Park
	Ferry Route
	Marshland/Swamp
	Glacier / Salt Lake
	Airport/Airfield
	Ancient Site
	Border Control
	Cable Car
	Castle/Castle Ruins
	Cave
	Chateau/Stately Home
	Church/Church Ruins
	Crater
	Lighthouse
	Mountain Peak
	Place of Interest
	Viewpoint

CONTRIBUTORS

This first edition of *Insight Guide West Coast USA* was commissioned and edited by Kate Drynan.

This book contains excerpts from *Insight Guides California*, written by Lisa Dion and building on previous work by Barbara Rockwell, a writer, editor, and lifelong California resident. It also contains excerpts from *Insight Guide The Pacific Northwest*, 2006, updated by Pat Kramer.

ABOUT INSIGHT GUIDES

Insight Guides have more than 45 years' experience of publishing high-quality, visual travel guides. We produce 400 full-colour titles, in both print and digital form, covering more than 200 destinations across the globe, in a variety of formats to meet your different needs.

Insight Guides are written by local authors, whose expertise is evident in the extensive historical and cultural background features. Each destination is carefully researched by regional experts to ensure our guides provide the very latest information. All the reviews in **Insight Guides** are independent; we strive to maintain an impartial view. Our reviews are carefully selected to guide you to the best places to eat, go out and shop, so you can be confident that when we say a place is special, we really mean it.

INDEX

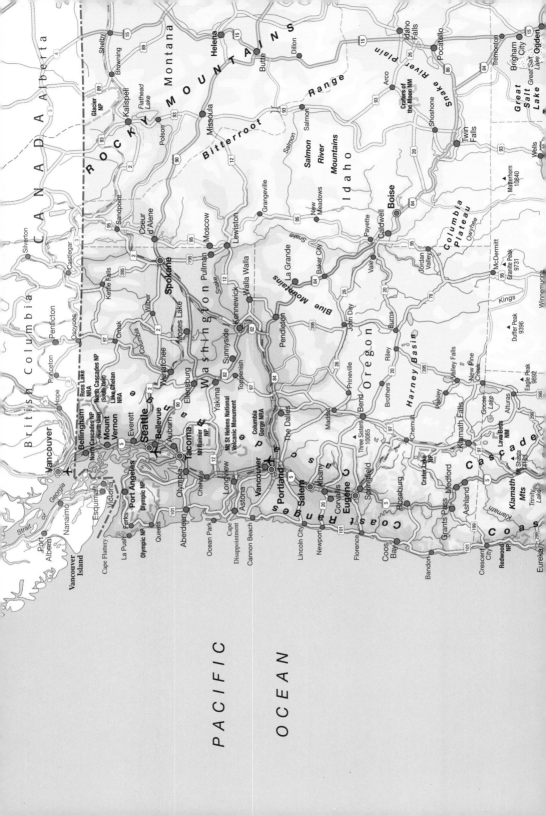